International Human Right to Conscientious Objection to Military Service and Individual Duties to Disobey Manifestly Illegal Orders

Hitomi Takemura

International Human Right to Conscientious Objection to Military Service and Individual Duties to Disobey Manifestly Illegal Orders

Springer

Dr. Hitomi Takemura
hitomi@mercury.ne.jp

ISBN 978-3-540-70526-0 e-ISBN 978-3-540-70527-7

Library of Congress Control Number: 2008935625

Cover design: WMX Design GmbH, Heidelberg, Germany

Printed on acid-free paper

9 8 7 6 5 4 3 2 1

springer.com

Preface

The task of this study lies in clarifying the efforts of contemporary public international law, across several categories, in relation to the rights and duties of individuals to the international community. Individual criminal accountability is an interesting development of the international community, challenging a traditional framework of public international law. At the same time, the argument whether individuals may stand up and take action against their own country on the basis of international obligations and international human rights is also a stimulating topic for public international law. It necessitates interdisciplinary research within public international law.

Therefore this study will tackle this ambitious task, though not exhaustively. Both international criminal justice and the right to conscientious objection in international human rights law are developing notions. Aspirations to create a world of peace and stability may contribute to the further development of these two notions. The importance given to the individual within the international community is at the heart of this study. Individuals should not sit on the sidelines, shielded by their States; instead, they need to take international law seriously in the twenty-first century, when, like it or not, the fearfully ambiguous word 'globalisation' is the word for our times (Annan 2000, pp. 9–17). The right to conscientious objection under international law may sometimes serve as a means of advancing peace and disarmament. In this connection, the duty of individuals to contribute to international peace and security will be discussed by means of examining international criminal law, specifically the issue of the defence of superior orders.

The rising number of conscientious objectors may be considered domestically as either a problematic or an illuminating phenomenon by many societies. This study aims to provide views to support the latter argument. In doing so, the issues are studied through the lens of public international law, especially international human rights law and international criminal law. Studies of international human rights law on the issue of conscientious objection and international criminal law on the issue of the defence of superior orders have guided this study in its 'rights and duties' approach.

It can be logically claimed that if individuals have the duty to disobey manifestly illegal orders under international criminal law, then they do not need to claim their rights to disobey manifestly illegal orders under public international law. However, the right and duty to disobey manifestly illegal orders under public international law may not necessarily be a case of 'either-or', as the rights and duties of individuals under public international law are often non-self-executing in the national dimension. Therefore the right and the duty of individuals to disobey manifestly illegal orders should supplement each other to strengthen their normativeness.

In order to clarify the rights and the duties of individuals, the relationship between the defence of superior orders and the right to conscientious objection is discussed in Chap. 1, followed by a brief background of the phenomenon of conscientious objection. Chapters 2–4 deal with the aspect of the right to disobey manifestly unlawful orders, though the argument is not confined to selective conscientious objectors, who only object to participating in unlawful wars and/or the use of weapons. Rather, Chaps. 2–4 provide a general view of the right to conscientious objection in international law, because its status under international law is by no means clear even today. Chapter 5 looks at conscientious objectors as asylum seekers from the viewpoint of international refugee law. As opposed to the rights of individuals, Chap. 6 focuses on the duty of individuals to disobey manifestly illegal orders. The restrictions on the defence of superior orders and several other humanitarian norms imposed on individuals are studied in view of the right to conscientious objection, discussed in Chaps. 2–4.

Japan, 2008 *Hitomi Takemura*

References

Annan KA (2000) Millennium Report: We the Peoples: The Role of the United Nations in the 21st Century. United Nations, New York

Acknowledgments

Over the years, I have been assisted by a number of people in accomplishing my doctoral study abroad.

First and foremost, I thank my supervisor Professor William A. Schabas and the Yoshida Scholarship Foundation for their invaluable support. Professor Schabas always shares his enthusiasm for studies in international criminal law with students. His wealth of knowledge and sophistication have inspired my study. The Yoshida Scholarship Foundation has provided me with generous assistance throughout my studies in Galway, Ireland. Without their financial and emotional support, my study would never have been achieved.

I thank my thesis examiners, Dr. Vinodh Jaichand and Professor Kevin Boyle of Essex University, for their comments and supports. The Irish Centre for Human Rights of National University of Ireland, Galway, provided students with an outstanding environment surrounded by friendly staff and colleagues. I thank all the Centre's staff and colleagues who shared academic interests in international criminal law and human rights.

I thank my supervisors in Japan, Professor Tetsuo Sato of Hitotsubashi University and Professor Sonoko Nishitateno of Tokyo University of Foreign Studies. Their encouragement has kept me motivated and has guided me towards academics.

Many people have provided English language editing assistance from time to time. Roisin Burke and Jennifer Schuetze-Reymann were always of great help.

My life in Galway would hardly have been so comfortable and joyful without such a nice flatmate, Christina Collins and her friend John Maher. My thanks especially go to friends who visited me in Galway from abroad and shared Guinness to cheer me up. Andleeb Chaudhry has been a rare friend. I sincerely thank everyone I encountered in Galway from the bottom of my heart.

Last but not least, I thank my parents, Nobushige and Masa Takemura for their love and kindness. My sister, Kanae, and my now-deceased grandmothers, Kazu Takemura and Tsune Iwano, have offered mental sustenance.

Contents

Chapter 1
Introduction

Abstract This chapter raises the question of how the defence of superior orders in international criminal law and the right to conscientious objection in international human rights law interact. Both legal norms relate to the duty to disobey manifestly illegal orders under international law. The right to conscientious objection includes selective conscientious objection to taking part in a certain armed conflict, with selective conscientious objectors and soldiers sometimes basing their rights to conscientious objection on the duty to disobey manifestly illegal orders under international law. In order to develop this issue, this chapter provides a description of what the notions of conscientious objection and conscientious objector are.

> All human beings are born free and equal in dignity and rights. They are endowed with reason and conscience and should act towards one another in a spirit of brotherhood.
>
> Article 1 of the Universal Declaration of Human Rights

1.1 Right to Conscientious Objection and Duty to Disobey

The study deals with the relationships between the notion of conscientious objection and the defence of superior orders under international law. A trend of international criminal prosecution shows that on the one hand international criminal law proscribes or restricts the defence of superior orders, and on the other hand the doctrine of superior responsibility is expanding and fully utilized. Consequently, the simple and traditional correlation that superior responsibility is the legal and logical concomitant to the defence to superior orders no longer exists for the sake of international criminal justice. The duty to disobey illegal orders is derived from the restrictions on the defence of superior orders, and conscientious objection to military service. Can the former as a duty to disobey manifestly illegal orders under international law become a reasonable ground for the latter as a right to disobey manifestly illegal orders under international law? Despite the fact that the right to conscientious objection has been constantly at issue in the domestic sphere in times of peace, the existence and scope of the right to conscientious objection to military

H. Takemura, *International Human Right to Conscientious Objection to Military Service and Individual Duties to Disobey Manifestly Illegal Orders.*

service as an international human rights remain unclear by any standard. The scope of the right to conscientious objection to military service in international legal system should be clarified for highlighting the relationship between the duty and the right to disobey manifestly illegal orders in international law.

'Conscientious objection' does not necessarily occur in connection with war (Sibley and Jacob 1952, p. 1). There are, for example, conscientious objectors among doctors, nurses and pharmacists who refuse to provide assistance with birth control (McGarry 2007, p. 9).[1] Historically the term 'conscientious objector' came from a phenomenon in the 1890s when it was applied briefly to those who opposed compulsory vaccination (Moskos and Chambers 1993, p. 3, 11). Mindful of this fact, this study will concern itself only with conscientious objection to military service.

The issue of conscientious objection has been the subject of discussion in both times of war and peace. Despite the fact that the right to conscientious objection has been constantly at issue in the domestic sphere in times of peace, the existence and scope of the right to conscientious objection in international law is still neither clear nor well-known. Arguably, recognition of certain forms of conscientious objection predates the various human rights instruments (Lubell 2002, p. 407, 409). Another assertion is that there is no right in international law to avoid military service because of one's conscientious objections, whether based on one's religious, ethical or political beliefs (Happold 2005, p. 29).

In some countries within the European Union – and Greece was a clear example – people are sent to prison because they refuse military service, particularly Jehovah's Witnesses, who object to military service everywhere in the world (Boyle 1999, p. 389). Conscientious objectors may sometimes be characterised as 'prisoners of conscience' by Amnesty International (Boyle 1999, p. 389). In addition to the fear of imprisonment and discriminatory treatment, there is also the problem that in some countries the alternative public service offered to conscientious objectors is punitive in intent, for example, where such civilian service is longer than the term of military service (Boyle 1999, p. 390).

Although it is argued that conscientious objection can potentially touch upon an unlimited spectrum of subjects, because there are unlimited possibilities where an individual may find a provision of the law going against the deepest dictates of his or her conscience (Decker and Fresa 2001, pp. 379, 380), here the argument mainly focuses on combatants, draftees or conscripts who refuse to participate in any kind of armed conflict or a particular type of armed conflict.

'Conscientious' objection is most likely to be deduced from an internal conviction of an ethical nature which may be inspired by religious or humanitarian ideals. Yet this conviction may also be inspired by the ethics of the community to which an individual belongs. Today, this notion of community and the environment surrounding individuals is not limited to the domestic or local community but also extends

[1] In October 2007, the Pope urges pharmacists to reject the abortion pill in a convention of Roman Catholic Pharmacists: "I invite your federation to consider conscientious objection which is a right that must be recognised for your profession so you can avoid collaborating, directly or indirectly, in the supply of products which have clearly immoral aims, for example abortion or euthanacia". *See e.g.*, P. McGarry (2007, p. 9).

to the international community. The ethics of international community have been greatly influenced by the rise of human rights in the twentieth century. Among others, the United Nations promoted the protection of human rights and the building of an international community. These achievements of the United Nations could influence the building of an individual's internal conviction.

Such a conviction may be formed by the educational efforts of the United Nations to protect human rights. Conscientious objection is sometimes invoked in the context of the so-called Nuremberg Principles. Resolution 95(I) of the United Nations General Assembly, unanimously adopted on 11 December 1946, affirms 'the principles of international law recognised by the Charter of the Nuremberg Tribunal and the judgment of the Tribunal.'[2] The Nuremberg Principles were formulated by the International Law Commission pursuant to United Nations General Assembly Resolution 177(II), paragraph (a).[3] Principle I of the Nuremberg Principles states: 'Any person who commits an act which constitutes a crime under international law is responsible therefore and liable to punishment.'[4]

The notion of individual criminal responsibility was firmly established in international law in the twentieth century, especially since the end of World War II and the Cold War. Individual criminal responsibilities in the international dimension thus emerged as the result of numerous grave infringements of human rights. The international community has regarded the protection of human rights and individual criminal responsibility as two sides of the same coin. By the same token, the humanisation of armed conflict has been supported by the international community. Human rights should be promoted in times of peace and war. The International Court of Justice in the Advisory Opinion on Legality of the Threat or Use of Nuclear Weapons observes that 'the protection of the International Covenant of Civil and Political Rights does not cease in time of war, except by operation of article 4 of the Covenant.'[5] In the recent 'Advisory Opinion on Legal Consequence of the Construction of a Wall in the Occupied Territory' of July 2004, the International Court of Justice again made it clear that the protection offered by human rights conventions does not cease in the event of armed conflict.[6]

Article 4(2) of the International Covenant on Civil and Political Rights enumerates several human rights which cannot be derogated even in times of public emergency, including a state of armed conflict. Freedom of thought, conscience and religion under article 18 of the International Covenant on Civil and Political Rights are accordingly one of the non-derogable rights in the event of armed conflict. Yet

[2] UNGA Res 95(1) 'Affirmation of the Principles of International Law Recognized by the Charter of the Nuremberg Trial' (1946) UN Doc A/64/Add.1, 188.

[3] UNGA Res 177(II)(a) (21 November 1947). UN GAOR, 2nd Session, Supp. 12, UN Doc A/1316, 11–14; Report of the International Law Commission to the General Assembly (1950) 2 Year Book of International Law Commission 374–378, UN Doc A/CN.4/SER.A/1950.

[4] UNGA Res 177(II)(a); UN Doc A/CN.4/SER.A/1950.

[5] *Legality of the Threat or Use of Nuclear Weapons* (Advisory Opinion) [1996] ICJ Rep 226 (8 July 1996) 240.

[6] *Legal Consequences of the Construction of a Wall in the Occupied Palestinian Territory* (Advisory Opinion) [2004] ICJ Rep, 136 (9 July 2004) 178 [106].

the General Comment on issues relating to reservations made upon ratification or the accession to the Covenant or the Optional Protocols explains that the reason why freedom of thought, conscience and religion is made non-derogable is because its suspension is irrelevant to the legitimate control of a state of national emergency and because derogation may indeed be impossible.[7]

The promotion of international human rights in both peacetime and wartime may impact on the formation of the individual's conviction. It also should be borne in mind that international human rights law, international humanitarian law and international criminal law promote the notion of duties of individuals in the international community.

Principle 4 of the Nuremburg Principles rejects the defence of superior orders: 'The fact that a person acted pursuant to order of his government or of a superior does not relieve him from responsibility under international law, provided a moral choice was in fact possible to him.'[8] Conscientious objection and the rejection of the defence of superior orders appear to be similar notions, to some extent. First, both normally relate to the soldier of lower rank. Secondly, both include a judgement of illegality of conflict or illegality of means of war. Therefore one may conclude that if there is a duty to disobey illegal orders under international criminal law, then one can invoke the right to disobey illegal orders, based on international law.

Before seeking to clarify the relationship between these two concepts, the notion of conscientious objection needs to be clarified. Firstly, the history of the system of conscientious objection as well as conscription will be examined briefly in Chap. 2. Subsequently a legal analysis of the issue will be made. The main topic of Chap. 2 will be the right to conscientious objection in international human rights law. The question that will be examined is this: What is the status of conscientious objection under international law – is it a human right under international law?

1.2 Road to Peace: Conscientious Objection as a Means of Achieving Peace

> CREON: And did you dare to disobey the law?
>
> ANTIGONE: Yes, it was not Zeus that made the proclamation; nor did Justice, which lives with those below, enact such laws as that, for mankind. I did not believe your proclamation had such power to enable one who will someday die to override God's ordinances, unwritten and secure. *They* are not of today and yesterday; they live forever; none knows when first they were. These are the laws whose penalties I would not incur from the gods, through fear of any man's temper.
>
> Sophocles, *Antigone* (441 BC) (Grene 1994, pp. 155–156)

---

[7] Human Rights Committee, General Comment No. 24, Issues relating to Reservations Made upon Ratification or Accession to the Covenant or the Optional Protocols thereto, or in relation to Declarations under Article 41 of the Covenant, CCPR/C/21/Rev.1/Add.6, 52nd Session, (4 November 1994) [10].

[8] UNGAOR, 5th Session, Supp. 12 (1950) UN Doc A/1316.

Conscientious objection is an age-old issue (Sibley and Jacob 1952, p. 1). If one looks at the issue of disobedience to law in general, one may trace it back to the Ancient Greeks. Sophocles described Antigone as an objector to the laws of the State (see Kellog 1919, p. 3), having illegally buried her brother, and was therefore sentenced to death.

In history, certain religious groups have been exempted from military service since the sixteenth century (Kellog 1919, p. 4). In this way, conscientious objection to military service had already existed in various forms among the Anabaptists and their continental successors, starting in the sixteenth century (Moskos and Chambers 1993, p. 3, 10). For instance, the Hutterian Brethren refused to pay war taxes or make weapons of war (Moskos and Chambers 1993, p. 3, 10). In the Netherlands, William of Orange granted the Mennonites formal exemption from military duties in exchange for payment or commutation (Moskos and Chambers 1993, p. 3, 10).

Modern conscientious objection is said to have first appeared in the United States of America (Chambers 1993, p. 23, 23). The recorded history of the conscientious objector to military conscription in the United States dates back as far as the seventeenth century.[9] Some of the early settlers rejected violence in resolving disputes and refused to cooperate with the local militia system (Kohn 1986, p. 11). Their intent was not to stop war through collective action or public civil disobedience; rather, their pacifism was an example and a personal religious statement for peace (Kohn 1986, p. 12). For example, the English colonies were settled by pacifist Protestants in the second half of the seventeenth century and they were prohibited from participating in any violence against other human beings by religious faith (Chambers 1993, p. 23, 25). In the seventeenth century other pacifist religious groups came to America, such as the Quakers, the Mennonites, the Amish and the Baptist Brethren or Dunkers (Chambers 1993, p. 23, 25). Colonial legislatures usually exempted the Quakers, Mennonites and Brethren (Chambers 1993, p. 26). This tolerance was only possible after colonial legislatures and military officers came to know that many of these religious objectors would rather suffer and die than take up arms and kill other humans (Chambers 1993, p. 26).

Conscientious objection to military service in the modern world is intimately related to the phenomenon of modern military conscription (Satow 1992, p. 113, 114 and Sibley and Jacob 1952, p. 2). In other words, conscientious objection is as old as the history of conscription. Historically speaking, on almost all occasions when governments have intensified forced recruitment, it has led to protest (Ajangiz 2002, p. 307, 315). The history of conscientious objection more or less reflects the rise and fall of military conscription. The emergence of national armies and conscription is connected with the French Revolution, which eventually introduced the notion of 'nation' to the forefront of politics. The French army continued to be recruited on a voluntary basis until 1798 (Barker 1944, p. 44). The French Directory passed the Law of Conscription (*la loi Jourdan*) and introduced conscription for the first time in Europe in 1798 (Barker 1944, pp. 44–45). The principle of conscription meant

[9] Kohn (1986, p. 6). The first recorded example of pacifist resistance to military conscription in America was in the province of Maryland in 1658 when Richard Keene was fined for refusing to be trained as a soldier.

that the regular army should normally be composed of conscripts and all 'unmarried' Frenchmen between the ages of 18 and 25, who were henceforth made liable to service (Barker 1944, p. 45). An annual review of the law decided how many servicemen were required in each year (Barker 1944, p. 45). As soon as the conscription system was introduced in Europe, alternative systems were made available by various governments.

Although the conscription law was intensely unpopular with a poor result in the first year,[10] Napoleon's abilities made it successful for a while. After the Restoration the law of conscription was abolished, but it was reintroduced by the Orléans Monarchy in its movement to adopt the principles of the Revolution (see Note 10). An alternative system of conscription was introduced by the law of 1832, in which a conscript was allowed to send a relative or a paid substitute in his place (see Note 10). A more ingenious system was soon introduced by Napoleon III in 1855 which allowed the conscript who did not wish to serve, instead of sending a paid substitute to pay a sum directly into the *Caisse de la dotation de l'armée*; the funds thus secured enabled the government to choose substitutes freely (Barker 1944, p. 46). Although there had been some forms of forced military service in existence before the eighteenth century, nothing was comparable to the French system (Sibley and Jacob 1952, p. 2). In the nineteenth century, Continental European countries followed French conscription policy and the United States and the United Kingdom adopted it during the twentieth century (Sibley and Jacob 1952, p. 2).

During the two World Wars, the law in relation to conscientious objection developed greatly in the United Kingdom.[11] There were numerous conscientious objectors during the two World Wars. It is estimated that there were approximately 16,000 objectors of various types in the United Kingdom during World War I.[12] The tribunals in charge of determining the cases of conscientious objection denied about 6,000 claims (Sibley and Jacob 1952, p. 3). Some 900 of them were absolutist objectors. Their stance was total opposition to any military service and they are not prepared to accept alternative civilian employment, they served prison sentences, 10 of them dying in prison (see Sibley and Jacob 1952, p. 3). In the United Kingdom conscientious objection was triggered by the older traditions of religious pacifism as well as a broad range of political, social, cultural and economic reasons (Harries-Jenkins 1993, p. 67).

After seeing the plight of conscientious objectors during World War I, popular opinion preferred more liberal provisions for them when the United Kingdom established conscription in 1939 (Sibley and Jacob 1952, p. 4). The National Service Act of 1939 established a more impartial registration system for conscientious objectors (Sibley and Jacob 1952, p. 4). Under the Act independent civilian tribunals

---

[10] Barker (1944, p. 45), '[O]f the 200,000 men required, in the first year of its application, the Directory only succeeded, after months of pressure, in actually raising less than 40,000'.

[11] Sibley and Jacob (1952, p. 2). "On the whole, Great Britain made [more] serious efforts to establish legal provision for conscientious objectors than any other state in the world".

[12] Sibley and Jacob (1952, pp. 2–3). "Of these, 5000 accepted alternative civilian service, 1,200 worked in the Friend's Ambulance Unit Overseas, 3,400 entered noncombatant work in the army and navy".

ruled on the claims of those seeking status as objectors (Sibley and Jacob 1952, p. 3). The tribunals operated in fifteen areas all over the country and were composed of a county court judge, a trade union representative, an academic and two others (Harries-Jenkins 1993, p. 67, 69). Since objection could be for any reason, the United Kingdom provided for non-combatant, alternative civilian service, and also for absolutist objection (Sibley and Jacob 1952, p. 4). This led to approximately four times as many objectors as in World War I (Sibley and Jacob 1952, p. 5).

The review procedures were also fruitful. From 18 December 1941, the legislation provided a procedure whereby those sentenced to prison for refusing medical examination could have their cases reviewed (Sibley and Jacob 1952, pp. 4–5). 'Even if one had not originally registered as an objector, there was provision for an advisory tribunal that had the power to review the cases of any persons who had committed military offences on allegedly conscientious grounds' (Sibley and Jacob 1952, p. 5).

The laws and regulations developed for conscientious objectors in the United Kingdom were 'the most elaborate and far-reaching (in terms of their concern and sensitivity for the individual conscience) in the world' (Sibley and Jacob 1952, p. 5). The reason for the liberal treatment of conscientious objectors during World War II was due to both improved public understanding of the position of the objector and administrative authorities who were better selected than during World War I (Sibley and Jacob 1952, pp. 6–7). 'There was nothing comparable in the United States' during World War II (Sibley and Jacob 1952, p. 7).

In the United States, there was no modern type of conscription until the Civil War (Sibley and Jacob 1952, p. 10). Since the law in the North permitted the hiring of substitutes, objectors may have taken advantage of it, while the Southern members of pacifist sects could secure exemption on the payment of five hundred dollars (Sibley and Jacob 1952, p. 10). During World War I, a conscription law was passed on 18 May 1917 (Sibley and Jacob 1952, p. 11). There was a limited possibility for conscientious objection. Section 4 granted a status of conscientious objector based on organisational membership rather than individual belief:

> Nothing in this act contained shall be construed to require or compel any person to serve in any of the forces herein provided for who is found to be a member of any well recognised religious sect or organization at present organized and existing and whose existing creed or principles forbid its members to participate in war in any form and whose religious convictions are against war or participation therein in accordance with the creed or principles of said religious organizations, but no persons so exempted shall be exempted in any capacity that the President shall declare to be noncombatant (Sibley and Jacob 1952, p. 10 and Chambers 1993, pp. 32–33).

What the brief history of evidences is that the issue of conscientious objection persists and resurfaces (see Kellog 1919, p. 4). The long history of conscientious objection also shows us the necessity of approaching this issue from not only a legal perspective but also from several other perspectives, such as disarmament, military and peace studies and possibly development studies.

1.3 Crisis of Conscription: Decline of the Authority of States

Even though compulsory military service has not been prohibited by international law, it has played an important role in disarmament. Those efforts must have been connected to the gradual waning of conscription. The trend to move away from conscription towards volunteer, professional armed forces in recent years was observed by the Office of High Commissioner for Human Rights in February 2006.[13] This trend is especially prominent in Europe (see Ajangiz 2002, p. 307). For example, Bosnia and Herzegovina abolished conscription on 1 January 2007.[14] Romania also ended conscription on 1 January 2007 (see Note 14), following its accession to the North Atlantic Treaty Organisation (NATO) in 2004. The 2006 Report of the Office of the High Commissioner for Human Rights contains the list of States which have ended or suspended compulsory military service in the recent past: Argentina (1994), Belgium (1995), the Czech Republic (2004), France (2001), Hungary (2004), Italy (2004), Jordan (1992), Kuwait (2001), the Netherlands (1996), Peru (1999), Portugal (2004), Slovakia (2004), Spain (2001), Slovenia (2003) (see Note 14). Australia's armed forces are voluntary, except that conscription can be introduced during wartime.[15] With the advent of the Gulf War in 1990, in Australia, selective conscientious objection was accommodated in the Defence Legislation Amendment Act 1992 (Cwlth), but it was not made available to volunteers (Gulam and O'Connor 2006, p. 68, 71). In Canada, the current National Defence Act does not recognise conscientious objection or conscription (Gulam and O'Connor 2006, p. 68, 71). While Israel maintains conscription for both men and women, recent figures show that about 25 per cent of eligible male draftees do not serve, more than double the number in 1980 (Heller 2007).

The leniency in taking conscription is also reported. A progressive reduction in the number of conscripts being recruited is observed in Kazakhstan in 2000.[16] In Greece there has been a reduction in the length of alternative service since 2004 (see Note 16). Armenia and the Russian Federation have recently adopted bills regarding the procedure for alternative service in 2003 and 2002 respectively (see Note 16). Belarus proposed such a bill in 2005 (see Note 16).

Behind the movement toward ending military conscription, there is a crisis of conscription (Ajangiz 2002, p. 308). Globalisation and the end of the Cold War cast doubt on the notions of the Nation-State and eventually national security. As the authority of a State declines, the capacity of States to inspire people to kill and the ability to wage traditional warfare are decreasing (Mjøset and S. Van Holde 2002, p. 94). The geostrategic scenario backed with the existence of mass armed forces and territorial defence has been called into question (Ajangiz 2002, p. 308). Social

[13] UNHCR, Civil and Political Rights including the Question of Conscientious Objection to Military Service – Analytical Report of the Office of the High Commissioner for Human Rights on Best Practices in relation to Conscientious Objection to Military Service (27 February 2006) UN Doc E/CN.4/2006/51 [8].

[14] UN Doc E/CN.4/2006/51, 5 [8].

[15] UN Doc E/CN.4/2006/51, 5 [9].

[16] UN Doc E/CN.4/2006/51, 5 [10].

reasons can also explain 'the sharp increase in the figures for conscientious objection' in Europe (Ajangiz 2002, p. 308). The rise in conscientious objectors in Italy, Spain and Germany is a sign that when the alternative to military service becomes less disproportionate, conscripts choose not to join the armed forces (Ajangiz 2002, p. 308). Ajangiz claims that the true cause of the reduction in the number of military personnel in Germany and Italy is conscientious objection (Ajangiz 2002, p. 314). In the case of Spain, national policy during the 1990s aimed to establish a force of 180,000 military personnel, first with conscription and then without it (Ajangiz 2002, p. 315). However, society showed some resistance toward this policy with high figures of conscientious objection and reluctance to be recruited on a contract basis (Ajangiz 2002, p. 315). Eventually the target for the armed forces was reduced to 130,000 (Ajangiz 2002, p. 315). This reluctance now extends beyond Europe and is almost global in scale (Ajangiz 2002, p. 308). The other rationales behind the crisis of conscription especially since the end of the Cold War are explained as being due to the decline of the mass army; the nuclearisation of defence; military intervention in other countries; the change of values and priorities in postmodern societies and the crisis in the social legitimacy of military service (Ajangiz 2002, p. 309). The trend for a reduction in the number of military personnel is also explained by various factors, such as international disarmament decisions, national decisions regarding the readjustment of strength and the abolition or change in the length of compulsory military service (Ajangiz 2002, p. 313).

The 1990s saw a high number of conscientious objectors in Europe and discussion about conscription re-entered the political agenda (Ajangiz 2002, p. 318). Yet the rise in the number of conscientious objectors is not necessarily chronologically identical in all European countries. Countries such as France, Belgium and Portugal have not had high figures of conscientious objection, though they saw a slight increase in the number after the Cold War era (Ajangiz 2002, p. 319). Denmark and Norway today have fewer objectors than 30 ago (Ajangiz 2002, p. 319).

1.4 Volunteer Soldiers and Conscientious Objection

It may be generally felt that the question of the recognition and the appropriate scope of conscientious objection primarily arises in countries with conscription (Lippman 1990/1991, p. 31, 36). Theoretically there may be an inference that '[b]y enlisting in the armed forces the adult volunteer soldier must be taken to have consented to certain aspects of military life. He has accepted that the military discipline system will apply to him' (Rowe 2006, p. 9). Therefore there may be a strong presumption that it is illogical for volunteer soldiers to claim conscientious objector status. However, the issue of conscientious objection arises not only for conscripted soldiers but for volunteer soldiers as well. The ability of professional or voluntary soldiers to declare their conscientious objection is limited (Bailliet 2006, p. 337, 344). It is unlikely that volunteer soldiers would be given, prior to their enlisting, a list of activities they will be required to perform as a soldier or the conditions under which they will live (Rowe 2006, p. 9). The application of the right to conscientious objection to persons who voluntarily serve in the armed forces is based on the view that an individual's deeply held convictions can evolve and that individuals voluntarily serving in armed forces may over time develop a conscientious objection to bearing arms.[17] Some States, including Germany, the Netherlands, the United Kingdom and the United States, have recognised that those persons who voluntarily serve in the armed forces may apply for conscientious objector status (see Note 17).

The right of conscientious objection for professional soldiers is associated with the issue of the time limits for applying for conscientious objector status (see Note 17). A strict time limit for making application for conscientious objector status prior to induction into the armed forces would preclude conscientious objector status for virtually all persons serving as volunteers in professional armed forces (see Note 17). Therefore in principle no time limits should be applicable for formulating a request for conscientious objector status.[18] Resolutions by the United Nations Commission on Human Rights and the Council of Europe adhere to this position. Resolution 1998/77 of the Commission on Human Rights stipulates that 'persons performing military service may develop conscientious objection'. Council of Europe Recommendation 1518 (2001) invites member States to introduce legislation recognising 'the right to be registered as a conscientious objector at any time before, during or after conscription, or performance of military service'.

1.5 Absolute Conscientious Objection and Selective Conscientious Objection

'Conscientious objector' in general stands for people who refuse to participate in the military or military service based on their internal conviction of what is right or wrong (Bailliet 2006, p. 342). They may be categorised into two groups, namely, absolute conscientious objectors and selective conscientious objectors.

These are two categories for distinguishing grounds of conscientious objector status. Absolute conscientious objectors are opposed to participation in war in any form because of their personal convictions. Selective, or partial, conscientious objectors are opposed to participation in a specific armed conflict, which is normally reflected as 'unjust' in the eyes of objectors (Bailliet 2006, p. 342).

In reality, this distinction between absolute conscientious objectors and selective conscientious objectors is decisive in granting conscientious objector status in numerous countries, notably the United States and Israel (Gulam and O'Connor 2006, pp. 70–71). In Israel, selective and politically motivated conscientious objection has become a phenomenon particularly since the Lebanon War of 1982 when about 165 reserve soldiers disobeyed the command to serve in the Lebanese zone (Linn 1996, p. 9 and Gans 2002, p. 19, 20). In Israel refusing soldiers are often

[17] UN Doc E/CN.4/2006/51, 9 [26].

[18] UN Doc E/CN.4/2006/51, 8 [25].

called "Refusers" (*sarvanim* in Hebrew). The term emphasises the obligation they were not fulfilling without any reference to possible moral concerns they might have held. Two years after the withdrawal from Lebanon the number of reservists rose again and 186 cases were reported up to September 1993 due to the reluctance to perform military service to suppress the *Intifada* (uprising) in the territories occupied by Israel (Linn 1996, p. 11). Thus the phenomenon of selective conscientious objector has been prominent in Israel.

However, the Supreme Court found that under the circumstances of the current situation in Israel, it saw no reason to intervene in the decision of the Minister of Defence not to grant exemptions for selective conscientious objectors.[19] Section 26 of the Defence Service Law of 1986 governs the issue of exemptions from military service. According to this provision;

> The Minister of Defence may, by order, if he sees fit to do so for reasons connected with the size of the regular forces or reserve forces in the Israeli Defence Forces or for reasons connected with the requirements of education, security, settlement or the national economy or for family or other reasons
>
> (1) exempt a person of military age from the duty of regular service or reduce the period of his service;
> (2) exempt a person of military age from the duty of reserve service for a specific period or absolutely.[20]

Here the interpretation of the 'other reasons' is debatable. While the Court recognises that every person in Israel is entitled to freedom of conscience,[21] it found that all agree that, when security needs are extreme, not even pacifists should be exempted.[22] In denying requests of selective conscientious objection, the Court gave reasons including problems concerning discriminative treatment, the difficulty to distinguish conscientious objection in good faith from that in bad faith and the danger of loosening the ties which hold people together as a nation.[23]

Israel and the United States are obvious countries which recognise absolute conscientious objections but not selective conscientious objection.[24] The United Kingdom and France also appear to take a similar position.[25] Although Germany

---

[19] *Zonshein v Judge Advocate General* (2002) reprinted in 'The Supreme Court Sitting as the High Court of Justice' (23 November 2002) 36 Isr. L. Rev. 1, 2.

[20] *Zonshein v Judge Advocate General* (2002) reprinted in 'The Supreme Court Sitting as the High Court of Justice' (23 November 2002) 36 Isr. L. Rev. [7]–[8].

[21] *Zonshein v Judge Advocate General* (2002) reprinted in 'The Supreme Court Sitting as the High Court of Justice' (23 November 2002) 36 Isr. L. Rev. [9].

[22] *Zonshein v Judge Advocate General* (2002) reprinted in 'The Supreme Court Sitting as the High Court of Justice' (23 November 2002) 36 Isr. L. Rev. [11].

[23] *Zonshein v Judge Advocate General* (2002) reprinted in 'The Supreme Court Sitting as the High Court of Justice' (23 November 2002) 36 Isr. L. Rev. [16].

[24] *Zonshein v Judge Advocate General* (2002) reprinted in 'The Supreme Court Sitting as the High Court of Justice' (23 November 2002) 36 Isr. L. Rev. [13].

[25] *Zonshein v Judge Advocate General* (2002) reprinted in 'The Supreme Court Sitting as the High Court of Justice' (23 November 2002) 36 Isr. L. Rev. 13. *See also* Gulam and O'Connor (2006, p. 7).

was regarded as taking the same stance (see Note 25), a recent decision by the German Administrative Court supports selective conscientious objection (Baudisch 2006, p. 911ff). Those countries recognising selective conscientious objection are the Netherlands and Australia,[26] though the latter's selective conscientious objection is available only for conscripts (Gulam and O'Connor 2006, p. 68, 71).

1.6 Conscientious Objection and Civil Disobedience

Along with the distinction between absolute conscientious objectors and selective conscientious objectors, a connected phenomenon to be noted is that of civil disobedience. Once a controversial armed conflict arises, not only the issue of conscientious objection but the issue of civil disobedience will arise. In other words, situations which induce conscientious objection and civil disobedience are alike and both phenomena often tend to take place simultaneously.

1.6.1 General Distinction

Conscientious objection and civil disobedience look similar, but they can be differentiated. Their primary purposes are said to be contrasting. The primary purpose of conscientious objection is not public education but private exemption, not political change but 'personal hand-washing' (Bedau 1991, p. 7). Conscientious objectors violate the law primarily in order to avoid conduct condemned by personal conscience even though required by public law, so that setting an example for others or forcing them to re-evaluate their support for the law is a secondary consideration (Bedau 1991, p. 7).

Civil disobedience may also be known as civil resistance. For example, the American peace activists in the 1970s and 1980s preferred calling their activities civil resistance rather than civil disobedience (Lippman 1990, p. 5, 7).

At one with the case of conscientious objection, civil disobedience also sometimes invokes international law and the Nuremberg Principles as justification. Throughout the history of America, civil disobedience has been an important phenomenon (Lippman 1990, p. 5, 7). As an example of one of the most famous conscientious objectors, Muhammed Ali should be mentioned. He was a professional boxer and one of the greatest world heavy weight champions who struggled with the American government as a Muslim and conscientious objector to the Vietnam War.[27]

---

[26] *Zonshein v Judge Advocate General* (2002) reprinted in 'The Supreme Court Sitting as the High Court of Justice' (23 November 2002) 36 Isr L Rev 1 [13].

[27] *See* Supreme Court of the United States *Cassius Marsellus Clay, Jr. also known as Muhammad Ali v. United States*, No. 783 (28 June 1971). 403 U.S. 698, 91 S. Ct. 2068, 29 L. Ed. 2d 810.

Despite the fact that ideas of civil disobedience and conscientious objection are distinguishable, the situation in which the two arise might almost always occur at the same time, namely, when a controversial armed conflict arises. Therefore it is 'not completely clear' how the distinction between conscientious objection and civil disobedience is to be understood (Enoch 2002, p. 227, 228). Nonetheless, the interests of this thesis mainly concern military conscientious objection in relation to international law.

1.6.2 Legal Philosophers' View

Legal philosophers tend to be keen on distinguishing between civil disobedience and conscientious objection. Raz finds that while civil disobedience is a political act, an attempt by the agent to change public policies, conscientious objection is a private act, designed to protect the agent from interference by public authority (Raz 1979, p. 276). Rawls defines civil disobedience as a public, non-violent, conscientious yet political act contrary to law, usually done with the aim of bringing about a change in the law or policies of the government (Rawls 1999, p. 320 and Bedau 1961, pp. 653–661). Conscientious objection or 'conscientious refusal' is defined more broadly, insofar as it is not necessarily based on political principles, and may be founded on religious or other principles (Rawls 1999, p. 324).

1.6.3 Objections to Conscientious Objection

It may be useful to look at general issues surrounding conscientious objection before viewing the whole development of the right to conscientious objection in international human rights law. Issues of conscientious objection and civil disobedience have been considered by legal philosophers.

Dworkin points out that many people believe that conscientious objection is the same as lawlessness since dissenters are 'anarchists who must be punished before their corruption spreads' (Dworkin 1977, p. 206). In a similar but more sophisticated vein, many lawyers recognise that 'disobedience may be *morally* justified, but they insist that it cannot be *legally* justified, and they think that it follows from this truism that the law must be enforced' (Dworkin 1977, p. 206). In replying to this statement Dworkin notes that: 'Society "cannot endure" if it tolerates all disobedience; it does not follow, however, nor is there evidence, that it will collapse if it tolerates some' (Dworkin 1977, p. 206). A prosecutor has discretion whether to enforce criminal laws in the United States and many other countries. Hence citizens of these societies expect prosecutors to have good reasons for exercising this discretion. Then there are also at least *prima facie* some good reasons for not prosecuting those who disobey the draft laws out of conscience (Dworkin 1977, p. 206).

There are five general arguments against the right to conscientious objection to military service. First, a state of emergency is alleged to be incompatible with the right to conscientious objection (de Long 2000, p. 176). A state of emergency allows States to have all possible manpower at their disposal in times of emergency. The second argument, relating to the first one, is about national security (de Long 2000, p. 176). It is argued that a State should be entitled to require the service of all its population in order to ensure the defence of its territory. The third argument relates to the sublimity of a duty to serve in the military (de Long 2000, p. 176). It is believed that people tend to find sublimity and heroism in military service. The fourth argument is concerned with the difficulties of distinguishing genuine conscientious objectors among *mala fide* conscientious objectors (de Long 2000, p. 176). The fifth argument relates to the interpretation of various international human rights instruments. While several treaties prohibit slavery, servitude and forced or compulsory labour, compulsory military service is excluded from the definition of those terms (Happold 2005, pp. 29–30). As we will see on this issue below, those provisions can be found in article 4(3) of the European Convention on Human Rights, article 8(3) of the International Covenant on Civil and Political Rights and article 6(3) of the American Convention on Human Rights. By the same token, punishment for refusal to undertake military service is not generally considered to be persecution for the purposes of the Refugee Convention and cannot found a claim for asylum.[28]

Some further arguments concern more specific circumstances. For instance, there are arguments mainly from Eastern European States that conscientious objection is not a real solution to the tensions in the world (de Long 2000, p. 180). Another argument is related to discrimination against poorer States:

> If the armies of States were going to be undermined by the recognition of conscientious objection, the rich countries could always hire mercenaries, but poorer countries had to rely solely on conscription. Furthermore, the rich countries could also use modern technology, such as nuclear weapons which could easily replace parts of the personnel (de Long 2000, p. 180).

This study will show these arguments are wide of the mark, especially regarding the right to conscientious objection for conscripts, soldiers and draftees facing the possibility of involvement in an internationally condemned conflict. It goes without saying that the gap between rich and poor should have nothing to do with the universality of human rights. Moreover, it should be kept in mind that the right to conscientious objection should be for individuals rather than for States' interests.

1.7 Concluding Remarks

Despite the trend of abolishing the system of conscription in many countries, the issue of conscientious objection has never waned. While the issue of conscientious objection touches upon national security, which has long been a traditionally

[28] Happold (2005, p. 30). Happold mentioned some exceptions: if the penalties for draft evasion are excessive or disproportionate; if conscription is administered in a discriminatory manner; or if conscription would result in having to participate in illegal activities. See Note 3.

sacrosanct area for States, the international community shares more and more interests and values. This reciprocal interplay between the promotion of human rights in international human rights law and individual criminal responsibility in international criminal law advances the movement breaking down the barriers of sovereignty.

Coupled with the recognition of the status of the individual as a bearer of legal rights and duties, the duties of the individual to the international community, as perceived since World War II, have been gradually recognised on a global scale. Therefore '[a]mong the first duties of the individual should be the duty to use his strength to maintain international peace and security.'[29] The right to conscientious objection to military service in international law may be the other side of the coin. Even if one identifies owing a duty to international peace and security at the individual level, the enforcement system of such duties is another issue. Here if the right to conscientious objection to military service is supported by the international community, especially in a situation threatening international peace and security, the individual's rights and duties in international law may well come into play.

Conscientious objectors face difficulties between the demands or duties of promoting national security and their inner conscience. This study devotes special attention to conscientious objectors who face a dilemma between their assignments of promoting national security, or international missions, and their consciences which may be influenced by the imperatives of international criminal law and the spirit of international humanitarian law. The phenomenon of conscientious objection should be one of the topics which require the commitment of the international community. Thus the next chapter will examine the status of the right to conscientious objection in international law.

References

Journal Article

Bedau HA (1961) On civil disobedience. J Philosophy, 58(21):653–661

Bailliet CM (2006) Assessing *jus ad bellum* and *jus in bello* within the refugee status determination process: contemplations on conscientious objectors seeking asylum. Georget Immgr Law J 20:337–384

Baudisch I (2006) German Federal Administrative Court Decision on a Soldier's Right to Refuse to Obey Military Orders for Conscientious Reasons. Am J Int Law 100:911–917

Decker DC, Fresa L (2001) The status of conscientious objection under article 4 of the European convention on human rights. New York University. J Int Law Polit 33:379–418

[29] UN Sub-Commission on Prevention of Discrimination and Protection of Minorities, 'Report by *Special Rapporteur* Erica-Irene A. Daes: The Individual's Duties to the Community and the Limitations on Human Rights and Freedoms under Article 29 of the Universal Declaration of Human Rights: A Contribution to the Freedom of the Individual under Law' (1983) UN Doc E/CN.4/Sub.2/432/Rev.2 [Daes Report] 53 [234].

Enoch D (2002) Some arguments against conscientious objection and civil disobedience refuted. Isr Law Rev 36(2):227–253
Gulam H, O'Connor M (2006) Selective conscientious objection: The court martial of flight lieutenant Malcolm Kendall-Smith. RAF ADF Health J 7:68–72
Lippman M (1990) Civil resistance: The dictates of conscience and international law versus the American judiciary. Fla J Int Law 6:5–62
Lippman M (1990/1991) The recognition of conscientious objection to military service as an international human right. Calif West Int Law J 21:31–66
Lubell N (2002) Selective conscientious objection in international law: Refusing to participate in a specific armed conflict. Neth Q Hum Right 20(4):407–422
Satow MS (1992) Conscientious objectors: Their status, the law and its development. George Mason Univ Civ Rights Law J 3:113–139

Book

Barker E (1944) The development of public services in Western Europe 1660–1930. Oxford University Press, London
Bedau HA (1991) Civil disobedience in focus. Routledge, London
De Jong CD (2000) The freedom of thought, conscience and religion or belief in the United Nations (1946–1992). Intersentia, Antwerpen
Dworkin R (1977) Taking rights seriously. Duckworth, London
Grene D (tr) (1994) The theban plays: Oedipus the king; Oedipus at colonus; Antigone. David Campbell Publishers, London
Happold M (2005) Child soldiers in international law. Manchester University Press, Manchester
Heller A (2007) Israel leaders warn the Jewish State is losing touch with its most admired institution. Associated Press, New York, p. 1
Kellog WG (1919) The conscientious objector. Boni and Liveright, New York
Kohn SM (1986) Jailed for peace. Praeger, New York
Linn R (1996) Conscience at war: The Israeli soldier as a moral critic. State University of New York Press, Albany
Rawls J (1999) A theory of justice, Revised edn. Oxford University Press, New York
Raz J (1979) The authority of law: Essays on law and morality. Clarendon Press, Oxford
Rowe P (2006) The impact of human rights law on armed forces. Cambridge University Press, Cambridge, Cambridge
Sibley MQ, Jacob PE (1952) Conscription of conscience: The American State and the conscientious objector, 1940–1947. Cornell University Press, New York

Book Chapter

Ajangiz R (2002) The European farewell to conscription? In Mjøset L, van Holde S (eds) The comparative study of conscription in the armed forces, comparative social research. JAI, Amsterdam, pp. 307–333
Boyle K (1999) Freedom of thought, freedom of conscience, freedom of religion and freedom of belief as internationally protected rights: What is agreed and what is not agreed. In Cotran E, Sherif AO (eds) Democracy, the rule of law and Islam. Kluwer Law International, Boston, pp. 373–392

Chambers JW II (1993) Conscientious objectors and the American State from colonial times to the present. In Moskos CC, Chambers JW II (eds) The new conscientious objection: From sacred to secular resistance. Oxford University Press, New York, pp. 23–46

Harries-Jenkins G (1993) Britain: From individual conscience to social movement. In Moskos CC, Chambers JW II (eds) The new conscientious objection: from sacred to secular resistance. Oxford University Press, New York, pp. 67–79

Mjøset L, Van Holde S (2002) Killing for the state, dying for the nation: An introductory essay on the life cycle of conscription into Europe's armed forces. In Mjøset L, van Holde S (eds) The comparative study of conscription in the armed forces, comparative social research. JAI, Amsterdam, pp. 3–94

Moskos CC, Chambers JW II (1993) The secularization of conscience. In Moskos CC, Chambers JW II (eds) The new conscientious objection: from sacred to secular resistance. Oxford University Press, New York, pp. 3–20

Chapter 2
Right to Conscientious Objection in the United Nations Human Rights Law

Abstract Chapter 2 traces the history of conscientious objection from the perspective of United Nations human rights law. Since its establishment the United Nations has consistently focused on the issue of conscientious objection. The change in attitudes toward 'conscientious objection to military service' and 'conscription' by the international community following the Cold War has been mirrored by the progressive interpretation of international human rights law by the Human Rights Committee. A major stumbling block to reading Article 18 of the International Covenant on Civil and Political Rights as basis for a right to conscientious objection is the language on conscientious objection in Article 8 of the Covenant. This construction prevented the recognition of the right to conscientious objection at international level for many years. However, following the General Comment to Article 18 of the Covenant the interpretation traditionally adopted by the Human Rights Committee has shifted significantly.

> The right to freedom of thought, conscience and religion is probably the most precious of all human rights, and the imperative need today is to make it a reality for every single individual regardless of the religion or belief that he professes, regardless of his status, and regardless of his conduction in life. The desire to enjoy this right has already proved itself to be one of the most potent and contagious political forces the world has ever known. But its full realization can come about only when the oppressive action by which it has been restricted in many parts of world is brought to light, studied, understood and curtailed through cooperative politics; and when methods and means appropriate for the enlargement of this vital freedom are put into effect on the international as well as on the national plane.
>
> Arcot Krishnaswami
>
> *Special Rapporteur* of the United Nations Sub-Commission on Prevention of Discrimination and Protection of Minorities.[1]

---

[1] UN Sub-Commission on Prevention of Discrimination and Protection of Minorities, 'Report of the *Special Rapporteur* Arcot Krishnaswami, Study of Discrimination in the Matter of Religious Rights and Practices' (14 October 1959) UN Doc E/CN.4/Sub.2/200/Rev.1, vii.

H. Takemura, *International Human Right to Conscientious Objection to Military Service and Individual Duties to Disobey Manifestly Illegal Orders*.

2.1 United Nations Human Rights Norms

The first and foremost legal basis of the right to conscientious objection to military service undoubtedly must be the right to freedom of thought, conscience and religion. The word 'conscientious' objection itself implies the relationship between two concepts. It is guaranteed by article 18 of the Universal Declaration of Human Rights (1948) and article 18 of the International Covenant on Civil and Political Rights (1966). At the regional level, it has also appeared in article 9 of the European Convention for the Protection of Human Rights and Fundamental Freedoms (1950) as well as article 12 of the American Convention on Human Rights (1969). Africa has the African (Banjul) Charter on Human and People's Rights, adopted 27 June 1981, which protects freedom of conscience, and the profession and free practice of religion, which will never be subject to law and order, under article 8.[2] Unlike article 18(1) of the International Covenant on Civil and Political Rights, article 8 of the African Charter does not expressly recognise freedom of thought (Ouguergouz 2003, p. 156). Nonetheless, this may not make this article less effective in providing a legal basis for the right to conscientious objection to military service as long as article 8 embraces freedom of conscience which alone may provide sufficient basis for the right to conscientious objection.

The non-discriminatory guarantee and application of freedom of conscience is required according to article 5 of the International Convention on the Elimination of All Forms of Racial Discrimination (see Epstein 2002, p. 305, 306). The non-discriminatory guarantee of freedom of conscience is again recognised by article 5 of the Teheran Proclamation of the International Conference on Human Rights held in 1968.[3]

Although it is true that this right consists of freedom of thought, conscience and religion, freedom of thought on its own may not be of much relevance here as far as the right to conscientious objection to military service is concerned. In practice, freedom of thought on its own, separated from freedom of conscience, is rarely likely to be resorted to by an individual. While freedom of conscience can be regarded as a particular instance of freedom of thought, both may be distinguishable from each other (Epstein 2002, p. 306). Freedom of thought includes research and political activities which are sometimes aimed at influencing a society rather than self-satisfaction (Epstein 2002, p. 306). By contrast, the activities legally based on freedom of conscience often relate more to one's own conviction and exemption of oneself from what one does not value. Freedom of thought may have some relevance to civil disobedience since it is designed to change a society, law or public policy and is not of a personal 'hand-washing' character. Therefore the right to freedom of thought itself is not considered in this Chapter.

As described below, a major stumbling block to reading article 18 of the International Covenant on Civil and Political Rights as basis for a right to conscientious

---

[2] African Charter on Human and People's Rights, adopted 27 June 1981, OAU Doc CAB/LEG/67/3 rev.5, 21 I.L.M. 58 (1982) entered into force 21 October 1986.

[3] Proclamation of Teheran, Final Act of the International Conference on Human Rights, Teheran, 22 April to 13 May 1968, UN Doc A/CONF. 32/41, 3.

objection is the language on conscientious objection in article 8 of the Covenant which has dogged the understanding of article 18. This construction had prevented the recognition of conscientious objection system at international level for a long time.

2.1.1 Activities Before 1970

The United Nations Sub-Commission on the Promotion and Protection of Human Rights (formerly Sub-Commission on Prevention of Discrimination and Protection of Minorities, which was established under the authority of the Economic and Social Council in 1947) had actively studied the general issue of conscientious objection and the right to conscientious objection since the 1970s. It had also been 'very active to strengthen the role of youth in the promotion and protection of human rights, including the question of conscientious objection to military service' (Angel 1995, p. 24). After a long debate over the shortcomings of the Sub-Commission, its mandate was terminated by the Human Rights Council as of June 2007. The Sub-Commission will be replaced by the Human Rights Council Advisory Committee.[4]

Although the activities of the Sub-Commission became prominent in the 1970s, based on the work of its *Special Rapporteur* on the question of discrimination in the matter of religious rights and practices, it had already affirmed the right to conscientious objection to military service in the context of freedom and non-discrimination in the matter of religious rights and practices.[5] Entrusted with the task of preparing a study on discrimination in the matter of religious rights and practices, in 1959 the Sub-Commission's *Special Rapporteur*, Arcot Kishnaswami, presented a report titled 'Study of Discrimination in the Matter of Religious Rights and Practices'.[6]

The report concludes that: 'There is no uniform solution to the problem of conscientious objection to military service based on the ground that such service is contrary to the prescription of a religion or belief', as the solution 'varies considerably from country to country, and even in various parts of the same country, according to circumstances and the state of public opinion'.[7] The report especially notes the delicate aspect of national sovereignty concerning conscientious objection: '[n]ormally recognition of the claim of conscientious objection to full or partial exemption from military service is left to the discretion of the State' (see Note 7). In order to support this position, the report refers to article 8 of the draft Covenant on Civil and Political Rights which dealt with forced or compulsory labour and

---

4 UN Doc. A/RES/60/251 (30 April 2006) [1]. The General Assembly decided to establish the Human Rights Council which replaces the Commission on Human Rights. *See also* 'United Nations Human Rights Council Institution Building President's text' (17 June 2007) 8ff.

5 UN Doc E/CN.4/2002/WP.2, Report of the High Commissioner submitted pursuant to the Commission Resolution 2000/34 [10].

6 UN Doc E/CN.4/Sub.2/200/Rev.1.

7 UN Doc E/CN.4/Sub.2/200/Rev.43.

which specifically laid down that this term shall not include: 'any service of a military character and, in countries where conscientious objection is recognised, any national service required by law of conscientious objectors' (see Note 7). Nevertheless, the word 'normally' in the wording of the report implies that there must be a situation in which the international concern for recognition of the right to conscientious objection overrides the interests arising from the national sovereignty of a State. Moreover, the report recognises the difficulties by stating that: 'It must be realized that even though the right to conscientious objection is recognised by the law, impediments may be placed in the way of conscientious objection by the public particularly in regard to their access to employment and to social life' (see Note 7). Notwithstanding this generous understanding of the issue of conscientious objection, at the end of the section dealing with conscientious objection the report includes the warning that, whether an individual is reluctant to perform any services remotely connected with a military effort, or is willing to perform alternative compensatory national service, 'the population of the country as a whole may feel that any exemption (from military service) creates a privilege entailing discriminatory treatment of others',[8] so that 'where the principle of conscientious objection to military service is recognised, exemption should be granted to genuine objectors in a manner ensuring that no adverse distinction based upon religion or belief may result' (see Note 8). The programme for action proposed in this report states: 'In a country where the principle of conscientious objection is recognised, exemptions should be granted to genuine objectors in a manner ensuring that no adverse distinction based upon religion or belief may result' (Rule 13).[9]

The impact of adverse discrimination caused by exemptions of conscientious objectors from military service was not completely clarified by this report, though this is the report of the study on *discrimination* in the matter of religious rights and practices. The recognition of conscientious objection to military service requires a system for ensuring the right to freedom of thought, conscience and religion, and the need of such a mechanism is to eliminate any inconvenience and discrimination for the sake of those who find their government's policy or the duty to military service opposed to their beliefs or conscience. Hence the necessity to recognise conscientious objection should be weighed against potentially adverse discriminatory effects, as the latter may be a minor side-effect in order to achieve a greater objective.

2.1.2 *Travaux Préparatoires of the International Covenant on Civil and Political Rights*

The Universal Declaration on Human Rights of 1948 is a basic catalogue of human rights and does not directly contain and raise the issue of a right to conscientious objection. A limited substantive discussion on the subject of conscientious objection

[8] UN Doc E/CN.4/Sub.2/200/Rev.44.

[9] UN Doc E/CN.4/Sub.2/200/Rev.65.

to military service can be found in the course of drafting the International Covenant on Civil and Political Rights of 1966. The United Nations Commission on Human Rights was first charged with the task of translating the content of the Universal Declaration of Human Rights. Then the further drafting of covenants was referred to the General Assembly's Third Committee. The International Covenant on Civil and Political Rights and the International Covenant on Economic, Social and Cultural Rights were simultaneously and unanimously adopted by the United Nations General Assembly on 16 December 1966.[10]

The discussion of conscientious objection can be found in the *travaux préparatoires* of article 8, dealing with slavery, instead of those of article 18, which concerns freedom of conscience. This is due to the fact that the only article of the International Covenant of Civil and Political Rights that refers to 'conscientious objection/conscientious objectors' is article 8(3)(c)(ii):

> 3. (c) (ii) Any service of a military character and, in countries where conscientious objection is recognized, any national service required by law of conscientious objectors;

The fact that this is the only article directly referring to conscientious objection has made the Human Rights Committee, established under article 28 of the International Covenant of Civil and Political Rights, construe this provision as providing discretion for States to recognise conscientious objection. The *travaux préparatoires* of this article indeed show that this line of argument is in favour of discretion of States. Nevertheless, it should be noted that there was an argument that at least the idea of conscientious objection should be mentioned since it was 'the beginning of a growing movement'[11] of State practices.

The starting point in the drafting of article 8(3)(c)(ii) was a paragraph prepared by the Drafting Committee:

> 3. For the purposes of the article, the term 'forced or compulsory labour' shall not include:
> (a) Any service of a purely military character, or service in the case of conscientious objectors, enacted in virtue of compulsory military service laws, provided that the service of conscientious objectors be compensated with maintenance and pay not inferior to what a soldier of the lowest rank receives.[12]

At the Fifth Session of the Commission on Human Rights, the United States of America proposed a simpler paragraph: 'The term "forced or compulsory labour" shall not include: (a) Services pursuant to compulsory military service laws'.[13] However it was not voted upon (Bossuyt 1987, p. 177). Following this United States proposal, the United Kingdom proposed a similar paragraph, stating that 'For the purposes of this article the term "forced or compulsory labour" shall not

[10] International Covenant on Economic, Social and Cultural Rights, G.A. res. 2200A (XXI), 21 U.N.GAOR Supp. (No. 16) at 49, U.N. Doc. A/6316 (1966), 993 U.N.T.S. 3, entered into force Jan. 3, 1976.

[11] UN Commission of Human Rights, 5th Session, Summary Record of the Hundred and Fourth Meeting, held at Lake Success, New York, on Friday 27 May 1949 (31 May 1949) UN Doc E/CN.4/SR. 104, 7.

[12] UN Commission on Human Rights, Report of the 3rd Session (28 June 1948) UN Doc E/800.

[13] UN Commission on Human Rights, 5th Session (18 May 1949) UN Doc E/CN.4/170/Add.3.

include: (a) any service of a purely military character or in the case of conscientious objectors exacted in virtue of compulsory military service laws'.[14] It was withdrawn in favour of the revised version (Bossuyt 1987, p. 177). The revised proposal took out the term 'purely' in front of 'military character'.

The first part of the proposal by the Drafting Committee stating that 'any service of a military character or', was adopted by 14 votes to none, with 2 abstentions.[15] The Chilean delegate requested a roll-call vote on the next part, reading 'or, in the case of conscientious objectors', because of the grave responsibility involved in the case of those countries which did not recognise that concept (see Note 15). It was adopted by 7 votes to 4, with 5 abstentions. Accordingly, Belgium, Denmark, Egypt, France, India, the United Kingdom and the United States of America voted in favour of it. Chile, Guatemala, Iran and Uruguay voted against it. China, Philippines, Ukrainian Soviet Socialist Republic, the USSR (Union of Soviet Socialist Republics) and Yugoslavia abstained (see Note 15).

The third paragraph of the proposal by the Drafting Committee that: '[...] exacted in virtue of laws requiring compulsory national service' was adopted by 10 votes to none, with 6 abstentions (see Note 15). Eventually, sub-paragraph (b) of the Drafting Committee as a whole was adopted by 7 votes to 1, with 8 abstentions (see Note 15).

Considering the fact that the concept of conscientious objection was not recognised in many countries, the phrase 'in countries where conscientious objection is recognized' was inserted by the French proposal.[16] This French proposal was adopted by 8 votes to 2, with 6 abstentions.[17] Delegates from Chile, Iran and Egypt stated that such an amendment was essential since numerous countries did not recognise this concept (see Note 16). Iran would even have preferred that the question of conscientious objectors had been omitted from the Covenant (see Note 16).

Before voting on the French proposal, the Chairman, and representative of the United States, Mrs. Roosevelt, spoke in favour of the inclusion of the concept of conscientious objection, arguing that:

> Modern means of transportation and travel would spread concepts and traditions which, in the past, had been held by only a limited number of countries. Immigration and other factors contributed to the dissemination of ideas and the possibility of rapid development in that field would have to be taken into consideration in the drawing up of the Covenant.[18]

The delegate of Lebanon supported the Chairman's argument:

> The Commission should take into consideration the fact that the concept of the conscientious objector was not a dying tradition but the beginning of a growing movement. The idea should be included in the text although there were States which did not recognize it, just as the Covenant referred to slavery although it no longer existed (see Note 19).

---

[14] UN Commission on Human Rights, 5th Session (19 May 1949) UN Doc ECN.4/202.

[15] UN Doc E/CN.4/SR.104, 9.

[16] UN Doc E/CN.4/SR.104, 6.

[17] UN Doc E/CN.4/SR.104, 8.

[18] UN Doc E/CN.4/SR.104, 7.

The adopted proposal of the French, with the wording 'in countries where conscientious objection is recognized', 'made it clear that it was applicable only to those countries which already recognized that principle' according to the Lebanese delegate (see Note 18). Therefore, 'the misgivings expressed by some delegations that the proposed text might imply the inclusion of the concept of the conscientious objector in their national legislations was unfounded' (see Note 18).

The French delegate subsequently suggested the following amendment in the Sixth Session of the Commission on Human Rights:

> Any service of a military character or exacted in virtue of laws requiring compulsory national service, including services required to be done by conscientious objectors, in countries where they are recognized.[19]

Subsequently, the French and the British delegates proposed to substitute the following text:

> Any service exacted by virtue of laws requiring military service, including any service required of conscientious objectors in countries where they are recognized.[20]

The delegate of Australia suggested that the word 'service' should be inserted after 'recognized'.[21] While the Australian proposal was adopted, the Chairman recalled that the representative of France had requested that the vote on sub-paragraph (b) should be postponed.[22] She therefore proposed that the vote on the article as a whole should be postponed to a later stage (see Note 22).

Hence this sub-paragraph was the last paragraph which remained to be settled amongst other parts of article 8.[23] As the French and the British joint amendment was withdrawn, the original draft text as amended by Australia was voted on.[24] The draft text was adopted by 11 votes to none with 2 abstentions.[25] These changes had been made by 1950.

France tried to modify the text later, in 1952, proposing replacement of the text of this subparagraph as follows, though it was withdrawn in favour of the revised version (see Bossuyt 1987, p. 179):

> Any service of a military character, or, in the case of conscientious objectors in countries where conscientious objection is taken into consideration, any other national service instituted by law in place of compulsory military service.[26]

---

[19] UN Commission on Human Rights, 6th Session, Compilation of the Comments on the Draft International Covenant on Human Rights and the Proposed Additional Articles (22 March 1950) UN Doc E/CN.4/365, 29.

[20] UN Commission on Human Rights, 6th Session (31 March 1950) UN Doc E/CN.4/391, 1.

[21] UN Commission on Human Rights, 8th Session (17 April 1950) UN Doc E/CN.4/149, 3 [1].

[22] UN Doc E/CN.4/149 3 [3].

[23] UN Commission on Human Rights, 6th Session (21 April 1950) UN Doc E/CN.4/SR.154, 3 [4].

[24] UN Commission on Human Rights, 6th Session (21 April 1950) UN Doc E/CN.4/SR.154, 3 [4]–[6].

[25] UN Commission on Human Rights, 6th Session (21 April 1950) UN Doc E/CN.4/SR.154, 3 [8].

[26] UN Commission on Human Rights, 8th Session, Agenda Item 4, Original French (19 May 1952) UN Doc E/CN.4/L.158.

The French delegate proposed the revised amendment, which reads as follows:

> Any service of a military character and, in countries where conscientious objection is recognized, any national service required by law of conscientious objection.[27]

This amendment was intended to avoid any discussion of service of a military character.[28] Although the United Kingdom understood perfectly the French representative's objection to paragraph 3(c)(ii), the delegate of the United Kingdom wondered whether the legal scope of the expression 'in virtue of laws requiring compulsory national service or compulsory military service' of the draft would not be sufficiently wide in France to allow for the idea of conscientious objection.[29] The United Kingdom felt that: 'the idea of compulsory military service was included in that of compulsory national service' (see Note 29). In addition, the United Kingdom suggested that: 'the French delegation's amendment to paragraph 3(c)(ii) was not satisfactory because it might imply that a special law providing for special work for conscientious objectors would have to be adopted'.[30] Eventually the French amendment to paragraph 3(c)(ii) was adopted by 11 votes to 3, with 4 abstentions.[31]

It is remarkable that, at the time of drafting article 8 of the International Covenant on Civil and Political Rights, there was a proposal with regard to decent treatment of conscientious objectors. The Lebanese amendment to insert the words, 'provided that the services of conscientious objectors be carried out in conditions equal to those accorded to all other citizens subjected thereto' was put to the vote. It was rejected by 3 votes to 1, with 12 abstentions (see Note 17). As their amendment had been rejected, the Lebanese delegation proposed the insertion of the sentence used in the Drafting Committee's text (see Note 17). Accordingly, the Lebanese proposal to insert the following sentence, 'provided that the service of conscientious objectors be compensated with maintenance and pay not inferior to that a soldier of the lowest rank receives', was rejected by 5 votes to one with 10 abstentions (see Note 15), even though the Lebanese delegate had made it clear that the text proposed by the Drafting Committee was not designed to require nations to accept principles of conscientious objection, but rather to protect conscientious objectors in those countries where the principle was supposedly recognised (see Note 15).

Those who supported the proposals pointed out that in certain countries where conscientious objectors were released from military obligations, they were subjected

---

[27] UN Doc E/CN.4/L.158/Rev.1.

[28] UN Commission on Human Rights, 8th Session, Summary Record of the Three Hundred and Thirteenth Meeting (10 June 1952) UN Doc E/CN.4/SR.313, 9.

[29] UN Commission on Human Rights, 8th Session, Summary Record of the Three Hundred and Thirteenth Meeting (10 June 1952) UN Doc E/CN.4/SR.313, 10.

[30] UN Commission on Human Rights, 8th Session, Summary Record of the Three Hundred and Thirteenth Meeting (10 June 1952) UN Doc E/CN.4/SR.313, 11.

[31] UN Commission on Human Rights, 8th Session, Summary Record of the Three Hundred and Thirteenth Meeting (10 June 1952) UN Doc E/CN.4/SR.313, 12.

to treatment inconsistent with human dignity, so that it was essential to provide some minimum safeguards (see Bossuyt 1987, p. 178). In the Lebanese delegate's view:

> Although he was not in sympathy, with the views of conscientious objectors, he had been impressed by their experiences. In certain countries where conscientious objectors were permitted release from military obligations, they were treated in a manner inconsistent with human dignity. They were set to compulsory labour, were paid little or nothing, and in many cases their health or sanity broke down. If the system of conscientious objection were permitted at all, the countries permitting it must honestly accept their responsibility to grant the objectors human treatment. [...] It would be more advisable, however, to adopt the original text, with its vital stipulation that conscientious objectors should receive maintenance and pay not inferior to that of the lowest rank of soldier. Such a stipulation provided at least a minimum safeguard.[32]

Some of the delegates appreciated the remarks by the Lebanese delegate. The Australian delegate fully appreciated the position of the Lebanese representative in regard to conscientious objectors and he held he would support any suitable text that would ensure decent treatment of conscientious objectors (see Note 32). The United States' delegate, the Chairman, 'could not but agree that the provision in the original text which guaranteed them a minimum living wage was of the utmost importance. If the rights of conscientious objectors were to be respected, a living wage had to be assured first of all; other aspects of the problem might be taken are of by a gradual development in various countries' (see Note 32).

The other delegates, who opposed the proposals, argued that it was inappropriate to go into details concerning the treatment of conscientious objectors.[33] For example, for the delegate of the USSR, 'the Drafting Committee's text went too far in laying down exactly what the pay of conscientious objector should be'.[34] The Chilean delegate described it as 'dangerous' (see Note 34). The delegate of Denmark held that the question of pay was only one of many points on which they should be protected; for example, there was the matter of hours of work or length of service. Since the problem was such a complicated one the covenant should not stress only one aspect of it (see Note 36).

For the French delegate, a reference to the treatment of conscientious objectors might have an impact upon many States without such a system. The French delegate:

> did not think it necessary to include in the article the provision with respect to remuneration of conscientious objectors which appeared in the original draft [of the Drafting Committee]; it might make an unfortunate impression on a number of States which did not recognize the right of the individual to refuse to fight for his country.[35]

There was the embarrassment of a country not recognising the system of conscientious objection in the midst of heated debate of how the Covenant dealt with it. The Belgian delegate showed his regret 'that his country, which considered a conscientious objector to be guilty of a serious violation of the law, followed a less

[32] UN Doc E/CN.4/SR.94, 10.

[33] The statement of the delegate of the United Kingdom, UN Doc E/CN.4/SR.104, 5.

[34] UN Doc E/CN.4/SR.104, 5.

[35] UN Doc E/CN.4/SR.94, 12.

liberal policy in that regard than the United Kingdom'.[36] According to the Belgian delegate, '[t]he Commission's major concern should be to ensure legal recognition of the position of the conscientious objector and of his right to fulfil his duty to his country in some way or other than by military service, without fear of punishment' (see Note 36).

The substantive discussion on article 8 was mainly carried out before the Commission on Human Rights. The original text submitted by the Commission on Human Rights was adopted by the Third Committee with only a minor change (United Nations Yearbook 1958, p. 205). The change was essentially nothing to do with the issue of conscientious objection to military service. The only sub-paragraph within paragraph 3 that was amended by the Third Committee is paragraph 3(c)(i) in accordance with the proposed amendment by the Netherlands.[37] The other point of draft article 8 discussed to some extent by the Third Committee was whether a reference should be made in article 8 to the existing international convention on slavery and on forced labour, i.e., the Supplementary Convention on the Abolition of Slavery and the Slave Trade and Institutions and Practices Similar to Slavery of 1956 and the Abolition of Forced Labour of 1957.[38] While the amendment was not put to the vote, the Committee adopted, by 30 votes to 26, with 16 abstentions, a proposal by Bulgaria that action on the amendment should be postponed until part II of the Draft Covenant was considered.[39]

At the request of the Philippines, paragraph 3(c)(ii) was voted on by parts.[40] A separate vote was preferred by the Philippines since its delegate wished to abstain in the vote on that section as conscientious objection did not exist in the Philippines.[41] The words 'any service of a military character' were adopted by 68 votes to none, with 1 abstention (see Note 41). The remaining words were adopted by 61 votes to nine, with 11 abstentions (see Note 41). Some delegates were displeased at the phrase regarding conscientious objection since their countries were not familiar with the concept.[42]

Then article 8 as a whole was put to a roll-call vote.[43] The article was adopted by 70 votes to none, with 3 abstentions.[44] Even though there was almost unanimity

---

[36] UN Doc E/CN.4/SR.94, 8.

[37] UN Doc. A/4045 (9 December 1958) [26] and [30]; A/C.3/L.682 and A/C.3/SR.860 [36].

[38] UN Doc. A/4045 [29].

[39] UN Doc. A/4045 [30(b)], *see also* UN Doc. A/C.3/SR.860 [37].

[40] UN Doc. A/4045 [30(c)], *see also* A/C.3/SR.860 [39].

[41] A/C.3/861 [2].

[42] The delegate for Israel said that he had voted for the article as a whole although he had abstained on the phrase regarding conscientious objection, because of doubt that that concept, as formulated in paragraph 3(c)(ii), existed in Israel's legislation. A/C.3/860 [47]. The Cambodian delegate also claimed that he had abstained on the second part of paragraph 3(c)(ii) because conscientious objection was unknown in Cambodia, there being no compulsory military service. A/C.3/SR.861 [5].

[43] UN Doc. A/4045 [30 (d)].

[44] UN Doc. A/4045 [30 (d)]; UN Doc. A/C.3/SR.860 [40]. Iraq, Lebanon, and the Union of South Africa abstained, though Iraq seemingly abstained in error. The delegate said that she had been

on the votes for the paragraph and the article and this fact would imply international recognition for the system of conscientious objection to military service, there appears to have been no consensus on the issue of conscientious objection as an international human right among drafters of the *travaux préparatoires* of article 8 of the Covenant. Questions remain regarding the relationship between article 8(3)(c)(ii) and article 18, which concerns freedom of thought, conscience and religion.

In the course of the drafting of article 8, only the Philippine delegate expressed the view that: 'the provision concerning conscientious objectors might be taken up in connection with [draft] article 16 [draft article 16 became article 18 in the final version], which dealt with the freedom of thought, conscience and religion'.[45] No other delegates followed up this remark. Therefore it can be concluded that drafters had not discussed the relationship between article 8(3)(c)(ii) and article 18.

2.1.3 NGO Initiatives from the Late 60s

The active involvement of the Commission on Human Rights on this issue was supported by studies by NGOs in the late 1960s. In 1967, five NGOs, the International Peace Bureau, Amnesty International, Friends World Committee for Consultation, War Resisters International and Service Civil International, began a study on conscientious objection.[46] These initiatives in the United Nations must have been the result of the European activities on this issue, since the first formal attempts to establish an international right to conscientious objection occurred at the European regional level (Lippman 1990/1991, p. 46, 48).

The Vietnam War in the 1960s and 1970s had motivated NGOs to act on behalf of conscientious objectors to military service. In the United States, one of the founders of Pax Christi USA established a 'Rights of Conscience' campaign during the Vietnam War.[47] The end of the Vietnam War also gave American NGOs incentives to act for preventing future wars. A series of actions taken by the founder of Pax Christi USA included obtaining NGO status for Pax Christi International and establishing an experienced team of representatives at the UN in New York in the late 1980s.

---

under misapprehensions when the vote had been taken on article 8 as a whole. She abstained in error, and declared that she was in favour of the original text. A/C.3/SR.861 [6].

[45] UN Doc E/CN.4/SR.142, 8 [30].

[46] International Peace Bureau, 'The Role of Youth in the Promotion and Protection of Human Rights, Including the Question of Conscientious Objection to Military Service: Written Statement Submitted by the International Peace Bureau, a non-governmental organization on the Roster' (8 March 1971) UN Doc E/CN.4/1989/71, 2.

[47] Pax Christi UK website, <http://www.paxchristi.org.uk/JustPeace/jp222.HTM> accessed 20 October 2007.

2.1.4 Discussion Before the Third Committee of the General Assembly in 1970

On 18 September 1970, the General Assembly allocated to the Third Committee agenda item 55 titled 'Youth, its education in the respect for human rights and fundamental freedoms, its problems and needs, and its participation in national development: report of the Secretary-General'.[48] The Third Committee considered the item at its Twenty-fifth Session. During this Session, the General Assembly discussed the results of the World Youth Assembly and the Seminar on the Role of Youth in the Promotion and Protection of Human Rights and consequently adopted Resolution 2633 (XXV).

While discussing the agenda, the delegate of Saudi Arabia to the Third Committee referred to the problem of the conscription of young people for service in the armed forces of their countries and of the conscientious objection of many of them to taking part in murderous wars.[49] The same representative demanded that the United Nations take action in the form of suggesting to governments that they should recruit only volunteers for their armed forces (see Note 49).

The Saudi Arabian delegate, Baroody, explained the contents of the draft:

> Armies should be made up of volunteers and... young people should on no account be coerced into joining the armed forces, not even to defend their country from aggression, since nobody should be forced to be involved in the act of killing. Unquestionably, it was adults between the ages of 25 and 50 who unleashed wars. For that very reason, it was they who should join the armed forces in order to give the youth of the world the opportunity to attain its full development. There were of course many young people who considered it a sacred duty to participate actively in the defence and protection of their country and they should certainly not be denied the opportunity of doing so. On the other hand, they should not be compelled to take part in acts of slaughter or aggression.[50]

Thus the delegate of Saudi Arabia submitted a draft resolution to the Third Committee.[51] The interests of the Saudi Arabians in a system of conscientious objection seem to have been so profound that the delegate proposed the following as operative paragraph 1 of the original draft:

1. Calls upon Member States:
   (a) To refrain from coercing any youth to join the armed forces of his country if such youth conscientiously objects to being involved in the act of

---

[48] UNGA, 'Youth, Its Education in the respect for Human Rights and Fundamental Freedoms, Its Problems and Needs, and Its Participation in National Development, Report of the Third Committee', Rapporteur: Mrs. E. Gunawardana (Belgium) (6 November 1970) UN Doc A/8149 [1].

[49] UN Doc A/8149 [18].

[50] UN Doc A/CN.3/SR.1749 (5 October 1970) 75 [39].

[51] UN Doc A/C.3/L.1766 (28 September 1970) Youth, Its Education in the Respect for Human Rights and Fundamental Freedoms, Its Problems and Needs, and Its Participation in National Development, Saudi Arabia: Draft Resolution.

killing regardless of whether the armed forces are engaged to repel foreign aggression or protect economic interests abroad;

(b) Only to enlist in the armed forces those youths who volunteer strictly to defend their country from flagrant aggression (see Note 51);

However, such strong wording of the draft generated resentment from not a few countries, even though Saudi Arabia introduced a revised text whose paragraph 1(a) was worded differently from the previous draft resolution at the 1752nd Meeting:

1. *Suggests* to Member States:

   (a) Not to conscript arbitrarily any youth to join the armed forces of his country if such youth conscientiously objects to being involved in war;[52]

A further revised version was introduced at the 1754th Meeting:[53]

1. *Suggests* to Member States:

   (a) Not to punish any youth who refuses to join the armed forces of his country if such youth conscientiously objects to being involved in war and to take into consideration his deep convictions;[54]

Some representatives, while praising the generosity which had promoted the proposal, pointed out the constitutional and practical difficulties with regard to the issue (see Note 49). Some also pointed out that defensive wars and wars of national liberation should be distinguished from aggressive wars of occupation and domination (see Note 49).

Later Saudi Arabia decided not to keep the text it had submitted in the form of a draft resolution after two revisions of the draft.[55] Rather, the delegate of Saudi Arabia submitted the text in the form of a document and mentioned it in a draft resolution.[56] At last the delegate of Saudi Arabia revealed that it would suffice if the document was mentioned in the Committee's report and, through the Economic and Social Council, referred to the Commission on Human Rights.[57] The Committee, therefore, made a reference to Saudi Arabia's document in its recommendation. The interests of Saudi Arabia in the question may be explained by its strong will for playing significant role in the Middle East peace process at the earlier time of King Faisal's reign (see Sullivan 1970, p. 431, 451).

52 UN Doc A/C.3/L.1766/Rev.1 (6 October 1970).

53 UN Doc A/8149 [18].
UN Doc A/8149 [20]-[21].

54 UN Doc A/C.3/L.1766/Rev.2 (9 October 1970).

55 UN Doc A/8149 [22].

56 UN Doc A/8149, 9 [22]. *See also* A/C.3/L.1791.

57 UN Doc A/8149, 11 [25].

Another draft resolution was submitted by 24 States.[58] This original draft resolution does not mention the issue of conscientious objection itself. However, it touches on opposition to the military when the Byelorussian Soviet Socialist Republic later submitted an amendment to insert the following paragraph to the draft resolution: 'Considers it important that young people of all countries of the world should resolutely oppose military and other action designed to suppress liberation movements of peoples still under colonial or racist domination, and should support those peoples in every way possible in their efforts to attain independence in accordance with the inalienable right of self-determination'.[59] It was later orally amended by the sponsors.[60]

This proposed paragraph was adopted by roll-call vote at the request of the representatives of Iraq and Yugoslavia.[61] The vote clearly showed the effects of the Cold War, with the Eastern bloc and African countries voting for this paragraph, and the Western countries opposing it.

The countries voting in favour were in fact in the minority.[62] Paragraph 10 of the adopted Resolution 2,633 states:

> Considers it important that young people of all countries of the world should resolutely oppose military and other action designed to suppress the liberation movements of peoples still under colonial, racist, or alien domination and under military occupation, and should support those peoples in every way possible in conformity with the principles of the Charter of the United Nations and the legitimacy of the struggle of the peoples for their freedom and independence, in their efforts to attain independence in accordance with the inalienable right of self-determination.[63]

---

[58] Afghanistan, Algeria, Ceylon, Chile, Cyprus, Ethiopia, Guyana, India, Kenya, Kuwait, Libya, Nigeria, Pakistan, People's Republic of the Congo, Uganda, United Arab Republic, Upper Volta, Yugoslavia and Zambia. 'Youth, Its Education in the Respect for Human Rights and Fundamental Freedoms, Its Problems and Needs, and Its Participation in National Development', UN Doc. A/C.3/L.1767 (6 October 1970). UN Doc A/8149, 11 [26].

[59] UN Doc A/8149, 14 [27].

[60] UN Doc A/C.3/L.1775; *cf.* UN Doc A/8149, 28 [33].

[61] UN Doc A/8149, 37 [61].

[62] The amendment was adopted by 51 votes to 15, with 38 abstentions. UN Doc A/8149, 37-38 [61]: In favour: Afghanistan, Algeria, Bolivia, Bulgaria, Burundi, Byelorussian Soviet Socialist Republic, Cambodia, Cameroon, Central African Republic, Ceylon, Chad, Cuba, Cyprus, Czechoslovakia, Ghana, Guinea, Guyana, Hungary, India, Iran, Iraq, Jordan, Kenya, Kuwait, Lebanon, Libya, Mali, Mongolia, Morocco, Nepal, Nigeria, Pakistan, People's Republic of the Congo, Peru, Poland, Romania, Saudi Arabia, Senegal, Sierra Leone, Somalia, Syria, Tunisia, Turkey, Uganda, Ukrainian Soviet Socialist Republic, Union of Soviet Socialist Republics, United Arab Republic, United Republic of Tanzania, Yemen, Yugoslavia, Zambia. Against: Australia, Belgium, Canada, Denmark, Finland, France, Israel, Italy, Netherlands, New Zealand, Norway, Portugal, Sweden, United Kingdom of Great Britain and Northern Ireland, United States of America. Abstaining: Argentina, Austria, Barbados, Brazil, Burma, Chile, China, Colombia, Costa Rica, El Salvador, Ethiopia, Gabon, Greece, Guatemala, Honduras, Indonesia, Ireland, Ivory Coast, Jamaica, Japan, Lesotho, Liberia, Luxembourg, Madagascar, Malawi, Malaysia, Mexico, Nicaragua, Niger, Philippines, Rwanda, Spain, Swaziland, Togo, Trinidad and Tobago, Upper Volta, Uruguay, Venezuela.

[63] UNGA Res 2633 (XXV), 'Youth, its education in the respect for human rights and fundamental freedoms, its problems and needs, and its participation in national development (A/8149, A/L.609/Rev.1, A/L.610, A/L.611)' (11 November 1970).

This paragraph may be evaluated as a 'direct appeal to object to certain military services' (De Jong 2000, p. 173). Operative paragraph 10 was adopted by 92 votes to none, with 11 abstentions, on 14 October 1970.[64]

Considering the successful outcome of the draft resolution by Eastern European and African countries, and the altogether failed attempt of the other draft resolution by Saudi Arabia, the cause of conscientious objection has been a focal point. Certainly the tide of the national liberation movements of the 1970s might have influenced the outcomes of the draft resolutions. While the Saudi Arabian draft was ready to accept any claim of conscientious objection from youth, irrespective of the nature of the conflict to which the conscientious objector objected, the adopted successful paragraph only supports conscientious objections of youth as long as they object to military service which suppresses liberation movements.

2.1.5 Resolution 11 B (XXVII) of 1971 by the Commission on Human Rights

The issue of conscientious objection has been on the agenda of the United Nations Commission on Human Rights since 1971 (Alfredsson and Eide 1999, p. 388). The United Nations Commission on Human Rights was undoubtedly another driving force behind the recognition of the right to conscientious objection in the context of international human rights law. The prolonged debate at the Commission reveals the tension between the most delicate issue for States – national security and the liberty of each individual's inner thoughts.

The 1970s saw the germination of the movement to recognise conscientious objection as a human right before the Commission on Human Rights. The World Youth Assembly, which was assembled in support of the United Nations, recommended that conscientious objection should be treated as a human right and that the subject would be on the agenda of the twenty-seventh session of 1971 of the United Nations Commission on Human Rights.[65] Meanwhile, an organisation of conscientious objectors, War Resisters International, collected 40,000 signatures from 27 countries in 1970 to call upon the Commission on Human Rights to recognise conscientious objection as a human right, and Pax Romana, an international association of Roman Catholic professionals and intellectuals, brought this petition to the attention of the Commission in 1970 in a statement on conscientious objection.[66]

64 *Official Records of the General Assembly 25th Session, Third Committee, Social, Humanitarian and Cultural Questions, summary records of meetings, 15 September–11 December 1970* (United Nations, New York 1974) 129.

65 UN Doc 56/WAY/P/10, cited in Schaffer and Weissbrodt (1972). *See also* van Bueren (1995, p. 153).

66 Pax Romana, 'Study of the Question of the Education of Youth All Over the World for Development of the Personality and the Strengthening of Its Respect for the Rights of Man and Fundamental Freedoms: Statement by Pax Romana, a non-governmental organization in consultative status, category II' (17 March 1970) UN Doc E/CN.4/NGO/153.

What does the term 'youth' stand for? When the United Nations refers to 'youth', it refers to persons between the ages of 15 and 24 years.[67] Aside from youth, more broadly even 'children', who are defined under article 1 of the United Nations Convention on the Rights of the Child as persons up to the age of 18, are vulnerable to recruitment by armies.[68] Oppression, militarisation, ideology and living in certain social situation are factors likely to predispose children to become involved in armed conflicts (Wessells 2002, p. 249). As seen in the case of Sierra Leone, abject poverty results in frustration and hopelessness (Wessells 2002, p. 249). Under these severe circumstances, joining a military group may provide a channel for meeting basic needs (Wessells 2002, p. 249).

The issue of conscientious objection before the United Nations Commission on Human Rights emerged as a human right of youth. Conscientious objection is described as a human right particularly applicable to youth because normally only young people are called upon to do military service (Schaffer and Weissbrodt 1972, p. 35). Eligibility for military service is usually set at an age between 16 and 18 (Schaffer and Weissbrodt 1972, p. 35). Hence the duty to perform military service may arise before conscripts have attained the legal right to vote or take part in the decisions that affect their own lives (Schaffer and Weissbrodt 1972, p. 35). Therefore the right to conscientious objection is effectively promoted and protected as a right of children and of youth.[69] The awareness among the Member States of the United Nations of prohibition of the use of child soldiers had already grown since the 1960s against the backdrop of the increasing use of children in armed conflicts especially in Indochina (Mann 1987, p. 32). In the course of drafting the Convention on the Rights of the Child, the terminal point of the concept of child became a moot point.[70] Columbia described the minimum age of 15 years for taking part in armed conflicts, set forth in article 38 of the Convention on the Rights of the Child, as the outcome of serious negotiations which reflect various legal, political and culturals

[67] UN Doc A/40/256 (6 May 1985) [19]; UN Doc A/RES/50/81 (4 December 1995) [9].

[68] Article 1 of the Convention on the Rights of the Child stipulates that: 'For the purposes of the present Convention, a child means every human being below the age of 18 years unless under the law applicable to the child, majority is attained earlier', Convention on the Rights of the Child (adopted 20 November 1989, entered into force 2 September 1990) UNGA Res 44/25, 44 UN GAOR, Supp. (No. 49), UN Doc A/44/49, 166, reprinted in (1989) 28 ILM 1448, with 191 States parties.

[69] With regard to the special position of children in an armed conflict, article 77(2) of the Additional Protocol I to the Geneva Conventions of 12 August 1949 stipulates that: 'The parties to the conflict shall take all feasible measures in order that children who have not attained the age of 15 years do not take a direct part in hostilities and, in particular, they shall refrain from recruiting them into their armed forces. In recruiting among those persons who have attained the age of 15 years but who have not attained the age of eighteen years the parties to the conflict shall endeavour to give priority to those who are oldest'. *See also* article 4(3)(c) of the Additional Protocol II; article 38 of the Convention on the Right of the Child, adopted and opened for signature, ratification and accession by UNGA Res 44/25 (20 November 1989) UN Doc A/44/49.

[70] UN Doc E/CN.4/L.1542 (10 March 1980) [28]–[36].

systems in the world.[71] Thus Columbia made the reservation upon ratification that for the purpose of article 38(2) and 38(3) of the Convention, the age referred to in said paragraphs shall be understood to be 18 years (see Note 71). The same reservation was made by Uruguay upon its ratification.[72] Similarly Argentina made a declaration upon signature that child means every human being from the moment of conception up to the age of 18.[73] Germany also expressed regret at the 15 year old age limit of article 38.[74] Germany and Austria declared that they would not make any use of the possibility afforded by the Convention of fixing the age limit at 15 years.[75] The Netherlands put a similar declaration on article 38 to raise the minimum age for recruitment.[76]

The question of the system of conscientious objection to military service was incorporated in the agenda item: 'Study of the Question of the Education of Youth all over the World for the Development of its Personality and Strengthening of its Respect for the Rights of Man and Fundamental Freedoms', for the United Nations' Twenty-seventh Session in 1971.[77] The discussion at this session shows that:

> There was general agreement as to the duty of the individual citizen to contribute to his country's response to treaty obligations arising, for example, under the United Nations Charter or other treaties of collective or mutual defence against aggression. Differences of opinion, however, arose concerning the possibility of permitting exceptions to bearing arms for active military service on grounds of conscientious objection, religious belief or moral conviction.[78]

At the 1128th Meeting, on 19 March 1971, a draft resolution concerning conscientious objection was submitted by Austria, Chile, the Netherlands, New Zealand and Uruguay.[79] The draft resolution noted the increasing interest among young people in the question of conscientious objection to military service; considered it to be of importance that the domestic laws of all countries should provide for the recognition and just treatment of conscientious objectors to military service; and finally requested the Secretary-General to submit a report on this matter to the Commission (see Note 79). The basic idea of the draft was explained by the delegate of the Netherlands, van Boven, as the right of every individual to refuse to perform

---

[71] Columbia's reservation upon signature, available at <http://www.unhchr.ch/html/menu3/b/treaty15_asp.htm> accessed 17 October 2007. For the study of reservations to the Convention on the Rights of the Child, *see* Lebranc (1996, p. 357 (especially 365)).

[72] Uruguay, reservation, *see* Lebranc (1996, p. 357 (especially 365)).

[73] Argentina, declaration, *see* Lebranc (1996, p. 357 (especially 365)).

[74] Germany, declaration upon ratification, *see* Lebranc (1996, p. 357 (especially 365)).

[75] Germany, declaration upon ratification; Austria, declaration upon ratification, *see* Lebranc (1996, p. 357 (especially 365)).

[76] The Netherlands, declaration upon ratification, see <http://www2.ohchr.org/english/bodies/ratification/11.htm> accessed 30 October 2008.

[77] Hammer (2001, p. 197); *see* UN Commission on Human Rights, Report on the 27th Session (22 February–26 March 1971) ESCOR, Supp. 4, (1971) UN Doc E/4949, E/CN.4/1068, 48 [202].

[78] UN Doc E/4949, E/CN.4/1068, 48 [202].

[79] UN Doc E/4949, E/CN.4/1068, 49 [209].

military service on the grounds of conscience.[80] It raises the issue of the security of States and the relationship between the State and the individual (see Note 80).

The reaction to the draft resolution was that the question concerned the interests of young people in certain countries rather than all countries.[81] Therefore the sponsors accepted an oral amendment by India and modified the draft to indicate the desirability of having more information before proceeding to further study of the question (see Note 81).

The representatives sympathetic to recognition of conscientious objections stressed the importance of collecting the information of State practices at an international level without necessarily prejudging the issue. The delegate of the United Kingdom, Sir Keith Unwin, was aware of the emerging trend towards recognition of the right to conscientious objection: 'A number of countries, however, were beginning to recognise the right to conscientious objection and to agree that those who refused to bear arms could serve the community in another way'.[82] However, the following idea proposed by Sir Keith must be a unique one:

> Perhaps it might be possible to organize some kind of service under civilian control which would give conscientious objectors an opportunity to serve mankind under the auspices of the United Nations. By adopting a Resolution on the recognition of that right, the Commission would demonstrate that it did not confine itself to condemning war but that it was also capable of taking a positive decision in support of freedom of conscience and of the ideals of many young people who wanted to serve humanity and not war.[83]

Representatives whose countries support mandatory military service in all just wars claimed that no exceptions could be made to what was a duty to one's country and society.[84] They preferred to have discretion for their own national authorities on the entire question of conscientious objection to military service rather than being subject to international regulation.[85] However, these representatives at least noted that individuals could be expected to object on grounds of conscience to wars unjustly undertaken by their governments, such as wars of aggression and colonialist oppression.[86] This sort of conditional conscientious objection in the representatives' minds would have been recognised as mere illusion if they had regarded the question of conscientious objection as an internal matter essentially within domestic concerns. In that case, it is hard to imagine that a government would recognise objection on the ground of unjust war undertaken by the government itself.

80 UN Doc E/CN.4/SR.1132, at 80.

81 UN Doc E/4949, E/CN.4/1068, 49 [210].

82 UN Doc E/CN.4/SR.1125 at 14.

83 UN Doc E/CN/4/SR.1125, 15.

84 For example, *see* the comment of the delegate of the USSR, UN Doc E/CN.4/SR. 1129 at 53; the comment of the delegate of the United Arab Republic, UN Doc E/CN.4/SR. 1129, 58; UN Doc E/4949, E/CN.4/1068, 48 [204].

85 UN Doc E/CN.4/SR.1129, 58-59 (the United Arab Republic); UN Doc E/4949, E/CN.4/1068, 48 [204].

86 UN Doc E/4949, E/CN.4/1068, 48 [204].

The counter-argument for objection to the notion of conscientious objection in favour of the right to self-defence was presented by the delegate of the United Kingdom:

> The right of self-defence was of course universally recognised, but the United Nations was an organization created in the interests of peace, and young people who objected to compulsory military service on conscientious grounds were taking those ideas a step further. Those who held such ideas were sometimes ready to risk their lives in order not to kill; that often showed a higher courage than in reacting to violence with violence.[87]

Strong objections to conscientious objection were raised by some countries. From the perspective of one of the Muslim countries, the delegate of Iraq said that: 'Holy War is a sacred duty for every Moslem and to renounce it would be to renounce one of the bases of the Islamic religion'.[88] The representative of the Ukrainian Soviet Socialist Republic severely criticised a Draft resolution to support the idea of conscientious objection: 'To ask the Commission to adopt a Resolution in support of conscientious objection would be almost like forcing the tradesmen's entrance in a house whose main door was wide open'.[89]

To the objection from the USSR[90] that the issue of conscientious objection is contrary to its Constitution, the delegate of the Netherlands responded that: 'It did not seem to be contrary to the Marxist-Leninist doctrine, however, since a decree signed by Lenin in 1920 had provided for the exemption of certain persons from military service'.[91]

Other representatives observed a difference between the bigger and the smaller States. The argument was that the question of conscientious objection was of less immediate interest to countries with large manpower reserves than to small countries, and that geographically vulnerable countries or newly independent countries could be expected to have varying approaches to the question of universal national service and to the complementary question of compulsory military service.[92] The delegate of the Ukrainian Soviet Socialist Republic argued: 'It was perhaps in the interests of the wealthy countries that the Draft resolution on conscientious objection should be adopted, since these countries could always recruit mercenaries; they had long experience of that practice. The poor countries could not pay their soldiers'.[93]

Another controversy concerned the question whether the right to life relates to the issue of conscientious objection. As regards the reference to the right to life, Egypt (The United Arab Republic) observed that 'it was impossible to link the principle of conscientious objection with the notion of the right to life, which might raise serious problems connected with war of aggression, disarmament, and even the progress of

[87] UN Doc E/CN.4/SR.1129, 61–62.

[88] UN Doc E/CN.4/SR.1129, 55.

[89] UN Doc E/CN.4/SR.1125, 16.

[90] UN Doc E/CN.4/SR.1129, 53.

[91] UN Doc E/CN.4/SR.1131, 80.

[92] UN Doc E/4949, E/CN.4/1068, 48 [205].

[93] UN Doc E/CN.4/SR.1131, at 79. UN Doc E/4949, E/CN.4/1068, 48 [205].

the developing countries'.[94] The Netherlands defended the Draft resolution and its reference to the right to life, 'since article 3 of the Universal Declaration of Human Rights, which mentioned that right, did not refer solely to the right of a person to his own life but also to the right of others to life. That was why that right implied the right not to take the life of others'.[95] Eventually reference to the right to life, that is, article 3 of the Universal Declaration of Human Rights, was made in the adopted Resolution. Preambular paragraph 2 mentions that: 'Recalling articles 3 and 18 of the Universal Declaration of Human Rights, enunciating the right to life, liberty and the security of person and the right to freedom of thought, conscience and religion'.[96]

In the end, at the 1131st Meeting, the Draft resolution, as amended, was adopted by 18 votes to 3, with 7 abstentions.[97] The delegation of Iraq explained its vote against the draft resolution as follows: 'Despite its moderate wording the draft resolution dealt with a substantial question and was in conflict with constitutional and moral principles of vital importance' (see Note 97). The delegation of the USSR voted against the draft. For the Soviet delegate, 'In cases where Governments were engaged in aggressive or colonial wars, a refusal to undertake military service was entirely justified', but the idea of conscientious objection was contrary to the Constitution of the USSR and legislation for exemption from military service falls within 'the domestic competence of States'.[98] The Ukrainian Soviet Socialist Republic explained its abstention vote by stating that: 'The resolution [...] applied only to certain States which were waging wars condemned by the conscience of mankind; it did not in any way concern his country' (see Note 97).

2.1.6 *The Secretary-General's Activities Following Resolution 11 B (XXVII) of 1971*

In Resolution 11 B (XXVII) of 19 March 1971,[99] the Commission requested the Secretary-General of the United Nations to prepare a report on the matter of conscientious objection and to seek from Member States 'up-to-date information on national legislation and other measures and practices relating to conscientious objection and alternative service'.

---

94 UN Doc E/CN.4/SR.1129, 58.

95 UN Doc E/CN.4/SR.1131, 81.

96 UN Doc E/4949, E/CN.4/1068, 88.

97 UN Doc E/CN.4/SR.1131, 90.

98 UN Commission on Human Rights, Summary Record of the 1132nd Meeting, held on Tuesday, 23 March 1972, at 10.20 am, UN Doc E/CN.4/SR.1132, 93.

99 At its 1131st Meeting, on 22 March 1971, the Commission adopted the Draft Resolution (E/CN.4/L.1176) as orally amended, by 18 voters to 3, with 7 abstentions. UN Doc E/4949, E/CN.4/1068.49 [211].

Following this Resolution, the Secretary-General sent a letter to the permanent representative of each of the Member States of the United Nations requesting any pertinent information especially for the purpose of responding to questions such as:

> Whether there is any national legislation, other measure or practice relating to conscientious objection to military service and alternative service; the grounds upon which conscientious objection to military service may be claimed; the authorities competent to determine exemptions from military service on grounds of conscientious objection, and the procedures applicable to conscientious objectors; the forms of alternative service required or permitted, and the conditions of such alternative service in relation to military service; and whether national legislation or other measures and practices relating to these matters apply equally in peacetime and emergency situations (Schaffer and Weissbrodt 1972, p. 33).

The Secretary-General prepared a report on 'Role of the Youth in the Promotion and Protection of Human Rights: The Question of Conscientious Objection to Military Service' accordingly in 1972.[100] This report is nothing more than a compilation of national legislation on conscientious objection and was not supposed to serve for addressing the issue of conscientious objection to military service as a human right (Engram 1982, p. 359, 363). Although consideration of the question was repeatedly postponed (Angel 1995, p. 26), the Commission on Human Rights mentioned the report on the question of conscientious objection to military service prepared by the Secretary-General in its Resolution 1 A (XXXII) of 11 February 1976 by stating that: '[n]oting the report on the question of conscientious objection to military service prepared by the Secretary-General pursuant to its Resolution 11 B (XXVII) (E/CN.4/1118 and Corr. 1 and Add. 1–3)'.[101] Not much progress had been made in the Commission on Human Rights after this resolution in the late 70s. The topic of conscientious objection to military service was regularly postponed. On 11 March 1977, the Commission on Human Rights postponed until 1978 consideration of the issue of conscientious objection to military service as an item on the role of youth in the promotion and protection of human rights (Yearbook of the United Nations 1977, Sales No. E.71.I.1, pp. 732–733). On 14 March 1979, the Commission on Human Rights again postponed until 1980 consideration of its agenda item on the role of youth in the promotion and protection of human rights, including the question of conscientious objection to military service (Yearbook of the United Nations 1979, Sales No. E.82.I.1, p. 864, 983). Nonetheless a significant resolution concerning the right to conscientious objection was adopted by the General Assembly in 1978.

---

[100] UN Doc E/CN.4/1118 (15 December 1972) and Corr. 2 (22 March 1974). *See also* UN Doc E/CN.4/1118/Add. 1(5 March 1973), where the Secretary-General added the communication dated 20 January 1973 from the permanent representative of New Zealand to the UN Office at Geneva, noting that: 'Legislation relating to compulsory military training in New Zealand is under review'; Add. 2 (21 March 1973), adding the fact that Australia abolished the former law and there will be no further call-ups in the country; Add. 3 (12 March 1973), adding the reply from India as of 27 June 1973 that there is no compulsory military service in India, and therefore, the question of furnishing any report on the subject does not arise.

[101] UN ESC Res 1A (XXXII), Commission on Human Rights Report on the 32nd Session (2 February–5 March 1976) 60 UN ESCOR Supp. (No. 3) at 52, UN Doc E/5768; E/CN.4/1213 (1976).

2.1.7 General Assembly Resolution 33/165 of 1978

The General Assembly as one of the principal organs of the United Nations is charged with realising human rights and fundamental freedoms. It has provided significant legal grounds for the crystalisation of the right to conscientious objection to military service. This practice of the General Assembly relates to international condemnation for the *apartheid* regime in South Africa.

The international criticism of *apartheid* resulted in its criminalisation. The General Assembly adopted the International Convention on the Suppression and Punishment of the Crime of Apartheid on 30 November 1973.[102] The Apartheid Convention, like the Nuremberg Charter, imposes individual responsibility in a broad manner (Sunga 1992, p. 77). The Draft Code of Offences against the Peace and Security of Mankind also enumerates the act of *apartheid* as a crime. Thus it is said that there is not only a right but a duty under international law to refuse to participate in the crime of *apartheid* (Major 1992, p. 349, 367). Such perception is further strengthened by Resolution 33/165 of the General Assembly.

In 1978, the United Nations General Assembly recognised 'the right of all persons to refuse service in military or police forces which are used to enforce apartheid'.[103] The Resolution is not so much about the right to conscientious objection *per se*, but more about the recognition and encouragement of asylum status, safe transit and protection similar to that for refugees for persons compelled to leave their country of nationality solely because of conscientious objection to assisting in the enforcement of *apartheid*. Despite not really being a recognition of the right to conscientious objection and the demands of national sovereignty with regard to military issues, the Resolution can be interpreted as acknowledging that there are certain types of conflicts in which international law recognises the right of individual to refuse to participate (Lippman 1990/1991, p. 49). At least it is safe to say that a general right of conscientious objection to military service 'had in part been recognised with respect to situations, where the fulfilling of military service would help regimes involved in certain types of gross and consistent violations of human rights' (De Jong 2000, p. 173). In fact, Resolution 33/165 is also recognised as the acceptance of the notion of selective conscientious objection by the United Nations (Major 1992, pp. 354–355).

Interestingly, the preambular paragraph of the Resolution reveals that: '*Conscious* that the Proclamation of Teheran, the Lagos Declaration for Action against Apartheid and other United Nations declarations, conventions and Resolutions have condemned apartheid as a crime against the conscience and dignity of mankind'.[104] It is true that apartheid as a crime against humanity has been described as 'a crime against the conscience and dignity of mankind'.

The wordings 'a crime against the conscience and dignity of mankind' appear in the many Resolutions and declarations concerning *apartheid* (see Jorgensen 2000,

---

[102] GA Res 3068 (XXVIII), 1015 UNTS 244 reprinted in 13 ILM 50 (1974).

[103] UNGA Res 33/165, 33 UN GAOR Supp. (No. 45) (1978) at 154, UN Doc A/33/45 [1].

[104] UN Doc GA/33/165 (20 December 1978) preamble.

p. 119). For example, in 1970 the General Assembly announced: 'We strongly condemn the civil policy of apartheid, which is a crime against the conscience and dignity of mankind and, like Nazism, is contrary to the principles of the Charter'.[105] This was later affirmed in the Lagos Declaration for Action against Apartheid of 1977.[106] Its paragraph 5 recognises that: 'Apartheid, the policy of institutionalized racist domination and exploitation, imposed by a minority regime in South Africa, is a flagrant violation of the Charter of the United Nations and the Universal Declaration of Human Rights. It rests on the dispossession, plunder, exploitation and social deprivation of the African people since 1652 by colonial settlers and their descendants. It is a crime against the conscience and dignity of mankind... '. In the 1989 Declaration on Apartheid and its Destructive Consequences in South Africa, the General Assembly spelled out that:

> apartheid, characterized as a crime against the conscience and dignity of mankind, is responsible for the death of countless numbers of people in South Africa, has sought to dehumanize entire peoples and has imposed a brutal war on the region of Southern Africa, which has resulted in untold loss of life, destruction of property and massive displacement of innocent men, women and children and which is a scourge and affront to humanity that must be fought and eradicated in its totality.[107]

The call for assisting conscientious objectors against the South African *apartheid* regime was invoked again by the General Assembly in Resolution 3972A, adopted on 13 December 1984.[108] The Resolution has an operative paragraph inviting all governments and organisations to assist conscientious objectors who had refused to serve in the military or police force of the *apartheid* regime, and were genuinely compelled to leave South Africa.

> 22. *Strongly supports* the movement against conscription into the armed forces of the racist régime of South Africa;
>
> 23. *Invites* all Governments and organizations to assist, in consultation with the liberation movements, persons genuinely compelled to leave South Africa because of their objection on the grounds of conscience to serving in the military or police force of the *apartheid* régime.

After the adoption of this Resolution, the General Assembly, in resolution 35/206B of 16 December 1980, appealed to the youth of South Africa to refrain from enlisting in the South African armed forces and invited all governments and organisations to assist persons compelled to leave South Africa because of their

---

105 UNGA Resolution 2627(XXV) Declaration on the Occasion of the Twenty-Fifth Anniversary of the UN, 24 October 1970.

106 22–26 August 1977, S/12426, 28 October 1977, in the United Nations, *The United Nations and Apartheid 1948–1994*, vol. I, Document 87, 344; endorsed by GA Resolution 32/105B, 14 December 1977.

107 UNGA Res S-16/1, 14 December 1989, in *The United Nations and Apartheid 1948–1994*, Document 135, 419.

108 UNGA Res 39/72A, General Assembly, 99th Plenary Meeting, (13 December 1984) [22]–[23], in UN Doc A/39/51, 42.

objection, on grounds of conscience, to serving in its military or police force.[109] The Commission on Human Rights condemned South Africa for 'the imposition of military conscription on all Namibian males between 17 and 55 years of age into the occupying colonial army'.[110] This is very important because the international community did not remain silent on the recruitment of adults for the purpose of advancing a situation contrary to international law despite there not existing a prohibition of the system of conscription under international law.

2.1.8 Report on Conscientious Objection Prepared by the Sub-Commission of 1984

Although the discussion of the right to conscientious objection at the United Nations level had become stagnant in the late 1970, the General Assembly decided to designate 1985 as international youth year by Resolution 34/151 in December 1979.[111] In 1980, the Commission sought information from Member States on national legislation relating to conscientious objection to military service in connexion with its examination of the role of youth in the promotion and protection of human rights.[112]

At its Thirty-sixth Session, the Commission on Human Rights requested the Secretary-General to seek from Member States up-to-date information on national legislation and practices relating to conscientious objection to military service and alternative service in Resolution 38 (XXXVI) of 12 March 1980.[113] Through Resolution 40 (XXXVI) of 1981, the Commission welcomed the replies of Member States to the Secretary-General's requests for information, and requested the Sub-Commission on Prevention of Discrimination and Protection of Minorities to study the question of conscientious objection to military service.[114] In accordance with this Resolution, in 1981 the Secretary-General prepared a report on the role of youth in the promotion and protection of human rights, including the

---

[109] UN Doc A/RES/35/206 B [5] and [6], as proposed by 60 powers, A/35/L.14 and Add. 1, adopted by Assembly on 16 December 1980, meeting 98, by recorded vote of 127 to 4, with 13 abstentions. Against: France, Federal Republic of Germany, United Kingdom, United States. Abstaining: Belgium, Canada, Dominican Republic, Greece, Italy, Japan, Luxembourg, Malawi, Netherlands, New Zealand, Portugal Spain, Uruguay.

[110] UN Commission on Human Rights, Res. 1985/7 in UN Doc E/1985/22, 30 [4(e)]. *See* de Jong (2000, p. 174).

[111] UN Doc A/34/151, International Youth Year: Participation, Development, Peace (17 December 1979).

[112] Yearbook of the United Nations 1980, vol. 34 (Department of Public Information, United Nations, New York) Sales No. E.83.I.1.850.

[113] UN ESC Res 38 (XXXVI), 36 UN ESCOR Supp. (No. 3) (1980) at 198, UN Doc E/1980/13; E/CN.4/1408.

[114] UN ESC Res 40 (XXXVII), 37 UN ESCOR Supp. (No. 5) (1981) at 243, UN Doc E/1981/25; UN Doc E/CN.4/1475.

question of conscientious objection to military service.[115] Although the replies of the governments of the States which reported that no compulsory military service existed in their countries were not reproduced in the report prepared by the Secretary-General, the replies of the United Kingdom and the United States were included to show certain information on conscientious objection to service when it occurred after voluntary enlistment.[116]

At its Thirty-fourth Session, in 1981, the Sub-Commission on Prevention of Discrimination and Protection of Minorities requested Asbjørn Eide and Charna L. C. Mubanga-Chipoya to make an analysis of the various dimensions of the question and its interrelationship with the promotion and protection of human rights. The final version of their report[117] on the subject, presented to the Sub-Commission at its Thirty-sixth Session, includes an analysis of the information received from all sources on such matters as the grounds recognised as valid reasons for conscientious objection; procedures for obtaining conscientious objection status, the question of alternative service; the status and experience of conscientious objection in countries which permit it only on limited grounds; and the question of asylum for persons who have fled their country because of their objection to military service. The report also includes a set of recommendations for bringing national law and practice into conformity with international standards. On 24 May 1984, the Economic and Social Council decided to give the widest possible distribution to the report prepared by Eide and Mubanga-Chipoya (see Note 117). The definition used in this report is broader than the definitions adopted later by the Commission on Human Rights. It contains most notably standards of international law as one of the sources of forming one's genuine ethical convictions. This report resulted in Resolution 1987/46 of the Commission on Human Rights on 10 March 1987, in which the Commission recognised that conscientious objection to military service derives from principles and reasons arising from religious, ethical, moral and similar values.

The report prepared by Eide and Mubanga-Chipoya enumerates seven standards of international law, which are derived from international law, for the purpose of possible grounds of conscientious objection to military service: (1) right to freedom of thought, conscience and religion; (2) right to life; (3) *jus contra bellum*; (4) *jus in bello*; (5) genocide; (6) right to self-determination; and (7) violation of human rights by armed force (Eide and Mubanga-Chipoya 1985, pp. 4–7). Among these grounds, the right to self-determination and the right to life may appear controversial to be named as the relevant international standards which circumscribe the right to use certain means and methods in warfare and thereby influence the conscience of individuals. It is particularly contentious how the right to self-determination of people has something to do with the right to conscientious objection of individuals.

---

[115] The replies from governments received in response to that resolution before 31 January 1981 were considered at the 37th Session and are contained in UN Doc E/CN.4/1419 (20 November 1980), and Add.1–5, and the replies received after 13 March 1981 and the additional replies are contained in E/CN.4/1509 (31 August 1981).

[116] UN Doc E/CN.4/1419 (1980) 2 [3].

[117] UN Doc E/CN.4/Sub.2/1983/30.

The logic behind listing the right to self-determination as the ground of the right to conscientious objection to military service must be related to the legality of the use of force. The report by Eide and Mubanga-Chipoya describes that: 'An individual, whose conscience with regard to the taking of the life of others is informed by the normative efforts of the international community, might be considered to be entitled to refuse to participate in action contrary to the above [self-determination] principle (Eide and Mubanga-Chipoya 1985, p. 6[52]).' Moreover, such an objection to participation in armed repression of self-determination will no doubt be particularly strong in the case of individuals who belong to a people whose self-determination is denied (Eide and Mubanga-Chipoya 1985, p. 6[52]). The resistance of the young people of Namibia and South Africa to military service in the South African-controlled armed forces provides an example of such a case. A few examples of the right to self-determination of people supported by the international community may exemplify instances where individuals are able to see a clear-cut *jus ad bellum* violation on the one hand and justified use of force on the other hand under international law. Although the right to self-determination and the right to conscientious objection to military service are two different rights, it is understandable that the two rights may be invoked by individuals and supported by the international community at the same time.

The following remarks provided by the Eide and Mubanga-Chipoya report support the idea of associating the right to determination with the right to conscientious objection:

> the principle of self-determination can be invoked by an objector to argue that he must refuse to participate in any action that tends or would tend to deprive people of their right to self-determination (Major 1992, p. 368).

It may be summarised that the individual basing his conscientious objection to military service on the right to self-determination belong to the people whose self-determination is at stake.

Another controversial point with regard to this report is whether there is a need or a possibility to resort to the right to life as a basis of the right to conscientious objection to military service? In other words, '[i]s there a need for the right to refuse to kill to be explicitly recognised in the international standards on conscience?' (Boyle 1999, p. 373, 389).

The right to conscientious objection on the basis of the right to life of others would most likely be invoked by absolute conscientious objectors instead of selective conscientious objectors. The right to life of others may also be concerned with the notion of pacifism. The provisions of the right to life in international and regional human rights instruments,

> [...] do not ensure an absolute protection for the life of the individual. The essence is that no one shall be arbitrarily deprived of his life. This means that there may be, in national and international law, a legitimate basis for taking the life of others when this is not arbitrary. Specific norms to this effect have been developed in all societies. To deprive a person of his life is everywhere considered as something that can be justified only under extreme circumstances and for reasons clearly defined in advance. This principle forms part of the conscience of every moral person, and it therefore reinforces the conviction that one shall

not participate in the taking of life of others unless there exists an extreme situation that is clearly justified' (Eide and Mubanga-Chipoya 1985, p. 5)

Since article 6 of the International Covenant on Civil and Political Rights deals with the deprivation of life, the suggestion was made to include the wording used in that article in the paragraph dealing with conscientious objection in General Comment No. 22 of article 18 of the International Covenant on Civil and Political Rights when it was drafted by the Human Rights Committee. However, such a proposal was rejected by the principal drafter of the paragraph because the right to conscientious objection was formulated on the basis not of article 6 but article 18.[118]

Still, the right to life of both others and oneself may be regarded as one of the legal bases of the right to conscientious objection to military service in accordance with the practices of the Commission on Human Rights. The Resolutions by the United Nations Commission concerning 'Conscientious Objection to Military Service' always advocate the right to life, which is recognised in the Universal Declaration of Human Rights and the International Covenant on Civil and Political Rights, in preambular paragraphs.[119]

The relevance of the right to life is recognised in the context of the right to asylum of conscientious objectors in the Handbook of the United Nations High Commissioner for Refugees. This Handbook suggests that a conscientious objector who has fled his or her country and claimed asylum should automatically be recognised as a refugee if it can be shown that he or she has a well-founded fear of persecution which may include serious human rights violation and the violation of the right to life of the person concerned (UNHCR 1979, pp. 51–53, 156).

2.1.9 Draft Resolution of 1985 by the Commission on Human Rights

In International Youth Year of 1985, the Netherlands submitted a Resolution to the United Nations Commission on Human Rights in order to promote conscientious objection as a human right. The subject of conscientious objection was discussed under an agenda item entitled: 'The Role of Youth in the Promotion and Protection of Human Rights, including the Question of Conscientious Objection to Military Service'. Nonetheless, the Spanish delegate pointed out that conscientious objection also affected society in general.[120] On 27 February 1985, Austria, Costa Rica, the Netherlands and Spain submitted a draft resolution titled, 'Conscientious objection to military service'.[121] Later, the consideration of the draft resolution

---

[118] Mr. Dimitrijevic, CCPR/C/SR.1237, 6 [33].

[119] *See* UN Commission of Conscientious Objection to Military Service, Resolutions 1989/59, 1993/84; 1995/83; 1998/77; 2000/34, 2002/45.

[120] UN Doc E/CN.4/1985/SR.27 (1985) [2].

[121] UN Doc E/CN.4/1985/L.33; UN Commission on Human Rights, Report on the 41st Session (4 February–15 March 1985) Supplement No. 2, United Nations, New York (1985), UN Doc E/1985/22; E/CN.4/1985/66 [390].

was deferred at the request of the representative of the Netherlands at the 51st Meeting.[122]

On 13 March 1985, the Netherlands introduced a revised draft with the delegates from Austria, Costa Rica, France, Spain and the United Kingdom at the 55th Meeting.[123] The Netherlands' delegate, Kooijmans, stressed that: 'the draft resolution constituted a very modest measure'.[124]

At the same meeting which saw the introduction of the revised draft sponsored by the Netherlands and others, the representative of Bulgaria introduced amendments to draft resolution E/CN.4/1985/L.33, contained in document E/CN.4/1985/L.60, which was sponsored by Bulgaria and the German Democratic Republic.[125] Only a few minor amendments suggested by the former proposal were taken into consideration by the latter.

The reason the proposal of Bulgaria and Germany (E/CN.4/1985/L.60) was not accepted fully must have been that the wording of the Bulgarian and East German draft was softer than the original draft proposal by the Netherlands and others overall and appeared to allow authorities of States a more modest approach than the draft sponsored by the Netherlands.[126] Indeed, the representative of the Netherlands had endeavoured to facilitate an agreement by proposing to accept more of the amendments into the draft resolution (E/CN.4/1985/L.33/Rev.1), but it had unfortunately proved impossible to arrive at a compromise text.[127]

The amended draft of the Netherlands and others (E/CN.4/1985/L.33/Rev.1) made 'a considerable concession' by deleting the words 'the right to' from operative paragraph 1.[128] The original draft resolution of 1985 (E/CN.4/1985/L.33) reads as follows: '*Considers* that the right to conscientious objection to military service is a legitimate exercise of the right to freedom of thought, conscience and religion recognised by the Universal Declaration of Human Rights and the International Covenant on Civil and Political Rights'.[129] However, operative paragraph 1 of the amendment proposed by Bulgaria and Germany (E/CN.4/1985/L.66) was shorter and 'would have deprived the text of its meaning'[130]: '*Considers* that conscientious objection to military service, when exercised in accordance with national legislation, can be considered as an expression of the right to freedom of thought, conscience and religion'.[131] Therefore the amended draft by the Netherlands and others (E/CN.4/1985/L.33/Rev.1) retained the words of the original proposal (E/CN.4/1985/L.33) except deleting 'the right to'.

---

122 UN Doc E/1985/22; E/CN.4/1985/66 [391].

123 UN Doc E/CN.4/1985/L.33/Rev.1 (11 March 1985).

124 UN Doc E/CN.4/1985/SR.55 (20 March 1985) [23] and [29].

125 UN Doc E/1985/22; E/CN.4/1985/66 [392].

126 UN Doc E/CN.4/1985/L.33/Rev.1.

127 UN Doc E/CN.4/1985/SR.55 (Kooijmans, the Netherlands) (20 March 1985) [27].

128 UN Doc E/CN.4/1985/SR.55 (Kooijmans, the Netherlands) (20 March 1985) [28].

129 UN Doc E/CN.4/1985/L.33 (27 February 1985) [1].

130 UN Doc E/CN.4/1985/SR.55 (20 March 1985) [28].

131 UN Doc E/CN.4/1985/L.60 (7 March 1985) [7].

Nonetheless, the amendment of Bulgaria and the German Democratic Republic suggested an interesting additional preambular paragraph which related to international peace and an absolute abandonment of national military service: '*Convinced* that consistent and sincere efforts on the part of all States aimed at the threat of war, the preservation of international peace and at the development of international cooperation in accordance with the Charter of the United Nations, would ultimately result in the creation of conditions under which military service would become unnecessary'.[132]

The 1985 draft includes a strong message to enlighten the right to conscientious objection compared with the following Resolutions of the Commission on Human Rights. For example, the draft even requests States to recognise the right to be released from the obligation to perform military service along with the right to refuse to perform armed service.[133]

After it appeared that the Dutch proposal would be defeated if brought to a vote, it was withdrawn and placed on the Commission's agenda for 1987.[134] The representative of the Netherlands said that the sponsors concluded that it would not be possible to achieve a consensus and that it would be advisable to defer the remainder of the discussions on the subject to the Fourty-third Session, since it was taken up on a biennial basis.[135] Therefore the representative of the Netherlands moved, under rule 49 of the rules of procedure of the functional commissions of the Economic and Social Council, adjournment of debate on the item under discussion on 14 March 1985.[136] The representative of Senegal spoke in favour of the motion.[137] The United Republic of Tanzania held that governments must be allowed more time to give careful study to the subject matter of the draft resolution, which was E/CN.4/1985/L.33/Rev.1 sponsored by the Netherlands and others, in order to be able to formulate appropriate policies. The motion was adopted without a vote (see Note 138). The question of conscientious objection to military service in draft resolution E/CN.4/1985/L.33/Rev.1 would therefore be taken up at the Fourty-third Session of the Commission, as the representative of the Netherlands had proposed.[138]

The debates during the drafting of the Resolution of 1985 reveal the lack of consensus among States even within Western countries at this stage. In spite of the unsuccessful outcome of the draft resolution of 1985, the debate by the Commission during 1985 constituted the first substantive discussion of conscientious objection to military service in many years and offered an insight into the attitudes of various delegations of the Commission (see Weissbrodt 1988, p. 53, 55). In addition,

---

[132] UN Doc E/CN.4/1985/L.60 [3].

[133] UN Doc E/CN.4/1985/L.33/Rev.1 [3].

[134] UN Doc E/1985/22; E/CN.4/1985/66 [391]; *see* Weissbrodt (1988, p. 53, 55).

[135] UN Doc E/CN.4/1985/SR.57 (21 March 1985) [125].

[136] UN Doc E/1985/22; E/CN.4/1985/66 [399].

[137] UN Doc E/1985/SR.57, [126]: 'Mr. Sene (Senegal) endorsed the position of the sponsors of the draft'.

[138] UN Doc E/1985/SR.57, [128].

the contents of the draft resolution of 1985 were more or less carried over to the coming resolution of the Commission, as described below (see Sect. 2.1.10). The outcome of the debate of the draft resolution of 1985 was regrettable. Nonetheless, the debate itself became an important cornerstone of the right to conscientious objection in international human rights law. In Resolution 1985/13 of the Commission on Human Rights, on 11 March 1985, the Sub-Commission was requested to pay due attention to the role of youth in the field of human rights, particularly in achieving the objectives of the International Youth Year.[139] Following the Commission's Resolution 1985/13, the Sub-Commission, in its Resolution 1985/12, requested Dumitru Mazilu, as *Special Rapporteur*, to prepare a report on human rights and youth analysing the efforts and measures for securing the implementation and enjoyment by young people of human rights. Four years later, in 1992, the final report was submitted by Mazilu and during these 4 years some developments with regard to Resolutions by the Commission can be seen to have taken place.

2.1.10 Resolution 1987/46 by the Commission on Human Rights

The Commission on Human Rights finally adopted a Resolution recommending that States with a system of compulsory military service consider introducing various forms of alternative service in 1987.[140] It is unclear which government was willing to take an initiative for the proposal of the 1987 Resolution on conscientious objection, since the Netherlands was no longer a member of the Commission on Human Rights (Weissbrodt 1988, p. 55). At least the following fact is clear. One of the then members of the Commission, Austria, had been a supporter of this issue for years and agreed to work with the observer delegation of the Netherlands in drafting a new Resolution less ambitious than the 1985 proposal (Weissbrodt 1988, p. 55). The draft of the 1987 Resolution was first shown to delegates from France, Italy, Spain, the United Kingdom and Costa Rica (Weissbrodt 1988, p. 55). These delegates agreed to co-sponsor the Resolution (Weissbrodt 1988, p. 55). The co-sponsors discovered that many delegations were unfamiliar with the concept of conscientious objection to military service and needed to be reassured that recognition of conscientious objection would not imply the abolition of compulsory military service (Weissbrodt 1988, pp. 55–56).

The 1987 Resolution adheres fundamentally to the 1985 draft in terms of its contents. However, in order to gain wider support, the 1987 Resolution was less ambitious than the 1985 draft resolution on the following three points. Firstly, whereas the preamble of the 1985 draft resolution recognises conscientious objection as 'a

[139] UN Doc. E/CN.4/Sub.2/1992/36, "Final report on human rights and youth, submitted by Mr. Dumtru Mazilu, Special Rapporteur" (18 June 1992) [1].

[140] UN Commission on Human Rights Res 1987/46, 'Conscientious Objection to Military Service', adopted at the 54th Meeting (10 March 1987) UN Doc E/CN.4/1987/L.73.

legitimate expression of the right to freedom of thought, conscience and religion', the preamble of the 1987 resolution fails to include such a phrase. Secondly, whereas the 1985 draft resolution considers that conscientious objection to military service is a legitimate exercise of the right to freedom of thought, conscience and religion recognised by the Universal Declaration of Human Rights and the International Covenant on Civil and Political Rights, the 1987 Resolution only '[a]ppeals to States' to do so.[141] Thirdly, the 1987 Resolution does not attempt to embrace conscientious objectors who assert their objection for the first time while already serving in armed forces (Weissbrodt 1988, p. 55). Despite all these compromises, the 1987 draft achieved a successful outcome and became a Resolution. The result of the vote was 26 in favour, 2 against, 14 abstaining.[142]

Resolution 1987/46 is the first Resolution by the Commission on Human Rights that firmly establishes the right of conscientious objection to military service as part of the right to freedom of thought, conscience and religion (De Jong 2000, p. 170). Moreover, the Resolution can be interpreted as more strongly worded than many of the draft resolutions submitted in the 1970s (De Jong 2000, p. 171). It was an important first clear message by the international community on this subject and became an essential tool for those who tried to claim conscientious objector status. It is now appraised by the United Nations High Commissioner for Human Rights as appealing to States to recognise that conscientious objection to military service should be considered a legitimate exercise of the right to freedom of thought, conscience and religion.[143]

The positive effect of the 1987 Resolution immediately appeared when the Sub-Commission on Prevention of Discrimination and Protection of Minorities adopted a Resolution on El Salvador in the same year.[144] In Resolution 1987/18, which was adopted by 11 votes to 2, with 6 abstentions, at the 35th Meeting on 2 September 1987,[145] the Sub-Commission '[s]tresses the importance of the recognition of

---

[141] *See* UN Doc E/CN.4/1985/L.33/Rev.1 (1985) [1]; Resolution 1987/46 (1987) [1].

[142] UN Doc E/CN.4/1987/SR.54/Add.1, 26 [115]. In favour: Argentina, Australia, Austria, Bangladesh, Belgium, Brazil, Columbia, Costa Rica, France, Gambia, Germany, Republic of Ireland, Italy, Japan, Liberia, Norway, Pakistan, Peru, Philippines, Rwanda, Senegal, Somalia, Sri Lanka, Togo, United Kingdom, United States. Against : Iraq, Mozambique. Abstaining: Algeria, Bulgaria, Byelorussian Soviet Socialist Republic, China, Congo, Cyprus, Ethiopia, German Democratic Republic, India, Mexico, Nicaragua, USSR, Venezuela, Yugoslavia.

[143] UN Commission on Human Rights, 'Civil and Political Rights Including the Question of Conscientious Objection to Military Service: Analytical report of the Office of the High Commissioner for Human Rights on best practices in relation to conscientious objection to military service' (27 February 2006) UN Doc E/CN.4/2006/51, 6 [14].

[144] *See* UN Sub-Commission on Prevention of Discrimination and Protection of Minorities, 'Report of the Sub-Commission on Prevention of Discrimination and Protection of Minorities on its 39th Session, Geneva, 10 August–4 September 1987: Rapporteur: Mr. Louis Joinet' (23 November 1987) UN Doc E/CN.4/1988/37 and E/CN.4/Sub.2/1987/42, pp. 29–30. *See also* de Jong (2000, p. 171).

[145] A Draft Resolution (E/CN.4/Sub.2/1987/L.37) for this resolution was submitted by the representatives of Cuba, the Netherlands, France, Zambia, Ghana, Yugoslavia and Ethiopia on 27 August 1987. Although a motion was introduced by Mr Whitaker (United Kingdom) to postpone the consideration of the draft resolution until the next session of the Sub-Commission, the motion

conscientious objection to military service as contained in Resolution 1987/46 of the Commission on Human Rights, in view of the massive recruitment policies of the Government of El Salvador'.[146]

2.1.11 Resolution 1989/59 by the Commission on Human Rights

On 8 March 1989, the Commission on Human Rights, for the first time, '*[r]ecognises* the right of everyone to have conscientious objections to military service as a legitimate exercise of the right of freedom of thought, conscience and religion as laid down in article 18 of the Universal Declaration of Human Rights as well as article 18 of the International Covenant on Civil and Political Rights'[147] (Resolution 1989/59).[148] Arguably, the subsequent recognition as opposed to the previous appeal strengthened the normative quality of this Resolution (Van Bueren 1995, p. 154). In Resolution 1989/59, the Commission also appealed to States to enact legislation aimed at exemption from military service on the basis of genuinely held conscientious objection.[149] This Resolution of 1989 has been praised for 'tak[ing] on board all the missing elements that were mentioned with regard to the 1987 Resolution' (De Jong 2000, p. 171). In addition, its fourth paragraph is noteworthy since it states that the nature of an alternative service should not be punitive. The rejection of punitive nature means that the length of alternative service ought not to be considerably longer than that of military service and also that the duration of this service should be comparable to that of military service (De Jong 2000, pp. 171–172).

Resolution 1989/59 was adopted without a vote, after the representative of Spain orally revised the last paragraph of the preamble of the draft resolution by deleting the words 'ethical, moral' between the words 'religious' and 'or similar motives'.[150] Accordingly, the motives of conscientious objection, which the Commission recognised at the time, had shrunk through this modification. Those were eventually only religious motives or 'similar motives'. This defect was slightly cured by the preamble of the next Resolution adopted by the Commission on Human Rights in 1993.

---

was rejected by 11 votes to 8, UN Doc E/CN.4/1988/37 and E/CN.4/Sub.2/1987/42, (23 November 1987) 84 [176] and [178].

[146] UN Sub-Commission on Prevention of Discrimination and Protection of Minorities Res 1987/18 [5]; *see* UN Doc E/CN.4/1988/37 and E/CN.4/Sub.2/1987/42, 30.

[147] UN Commission on Human Rights, Res 1989/59 [1].

[148] The resolution was sponsored by Austria, Canada, Costa Rica, France, Germany, Federal Republic of Hungary, the Netherlands, Spain and Sweden. Portugal and the United Kingdom subsequently joined the sponsors. UN Doc E/CN.4/1989/L.19/Add.15 (9 March 1989) [8].

[149] UN Doc E/CN.4/2006/51, 6 [14].

[150] UN Doc E/CN.4/1989/L.19/Add.15 (9 March 1989) [9].

2.1.12 Convention on the Rights of the Child of 1989

The initial standards prohibiting child recruitment were established by the 1977 Additional Protocols to the four Geneva Conventions of 1949[151] and by the Convention on the Rights of the Child of 1989,[152] which establishes 15 years as the minimum age for recruitment and participation in hostilities.[153] The African Charter on the Rights and Welfare of the Child, adopted on 11 July 1990 and entered into force on 29 November 1999, also prohibits the recruitment of children in article 22(2).[154]

The international community did put a great deal of effort into protecting the right of youth to conscientious objection to military service from the late 1970s to the 1980s. Youth is the generation moving from childhood to adulthood. If young people are the most likely targets of conscription, the right to conscientious objection as a right of the child may have to be examined. How is the right to conscientious objection as a right of the child promoted? The United Nations Convention on the Rights of the Child was unanimously adopted by the General Assembly as Resolution 44/25 on 20 November 1989 and entered into force on 2 September 1990, in accordance with article 49.

The Polish government, in early 1978, recommended that the United Nations Commission on Human Rights adopt a convention on the rights of the child.[155] Poland has often shown its special concern for children in international fora, recalling the past sufferings of its own younger generations. The drafting of the Convention on the Rights of the Child took place within the context of the United Nations, and in particular in a working group set up by the Commission on Human Rights at its Thirty-fifth Session held in 1979 (see Note 156). The drafting body was officially known as 'the open-ended Working Group on the Question of a Convention on the Rights of the Child' (see Note 156).

It took the 'open-ended Working Group' almost 9 years to finish its work, having completed the first reading of the Convention in March 1988 (see Note 156). Following a review of the draft text of the Convention within the United Nations Secretariat, it completed the second reading in December 1988, and this final text of

---

[151] Article 77(2) of Protocol Additional to the Geneva Convention, and Relating to the Protection of Victims of International Armed Conflicts (Additional Protocol I); Article 4(3) of Additional Protocol to the Geneva Conventions of 1949, and Relating to the Protection of Victims of Non-International Armed Conflicts (Protocol II).

[152] Article 38 of the Convention on the Rights of the Child, which came into force on 2 September 1998.

[153] *See* The United Nations Children's Fund (UNICEF), Guide to the Optional Protocol on the Involvement of Children in Armed Conflict, (December 2003) 7.

[154] African Charter on the Rights and Welfare of the Child, OAU Doc CAB/LEG/24.9/49 (1990), adopted 11 July 1990, came into force 29 November 1999.

[155] At the 1438th Meeting, the representative of Poland introduced Draft Resolution E/CN.4/L.1366/Rev.1, sponsored by Austria, Bulgaria, Columbia, Jordan, Poland, Senegal and the Syrian Arab Republic. Chapter XIX of the report of the Commission on Human Rights on its 34th Session, Official Records of the Economic and Social Council, 1978, Supplement No. 4, UN Doc E/1978/34 [306], Detrick (1992, p. 31).

the Convention was put forward to the Commission on Human Rights for discussion and approval (see Note 158). In turn, the Commission approved the Convention and sent the finalised text up to the United Nations Economic and Social Council (see Note 158). The Economic and Social Council discussed and approved the draft text and sent it to the General Assembly for its adoption (see Note 158).

The Declaration of the Rights of the Child promulgated by the General Assembly on 20 November 1959 exists as a predecessor of the United Nations Convention on the Rights of the Child. However, the contents of the former leaned heavily towards economic, social and cultural rights (see Note 158, p. 21). The *travaux préparatoires* of the United Nations Convention on the Rights of the Child also reveal no specific discussion of conscientious objection during the drafting of the Convention. The lack of discussion of the right to conscientious objection to military service may be due to differing limits on the concept of the child in various national legislations. The lack of debate on the right to conscientious objection left the issue of how to treat the claims of conscientious objectors over 15 years old, unsolved, especially because article 1 of the Convention on the Rights of the Child defines a child as anybody below the age of 18 years old. [156]

The Convention on the Rights of the Child proscribes any person under the age of 15 from taking a direct part in hostilities.[157] It also places a duty on States parties when recruiting those aged between 15 and 18 to endeavour to recruit the oldest first.[158] The acts of conscripting or enlisting children under the age of 15 years into armed forces or groups or using them to participate actively in hostilities constitute war crimes under article 8(2)(b)(xxvi) and (2)(e)(vii) of the Rome Statute of the International Criminal Court of 1998 and article 4(c) of the Statute of the Sierra Leone Special Tribunal as seen below.

Recent developments in relation to the definition of children should be noted for updating the standard of the age of conscription. The Optional Protocol to the Convention on the Rights of the Child on the Involvement of Children in Armed Conflicts was adopted and opened for signature, ratification and accession by General Assembly Resolution A/RES/54/263 (2000).[159] The Optional Protocol raises the standard that previously had been set at 15 years by international law (Vandewiele 2006, p. 30). The compulsory recruitment of 'persons who have not attained the age of 18 years' is now prohibited under article 2 of the Optional Protocol. Of course, for those States who have not ratified this protocol, the rule remains that of article 38 of the Convention on the Rights of Child, which prohibits recruitment into the armed forces only under the age of 15 (Brems 2006, p. 14). The issue of conscientious objection of children remains an issue for conscripts aged 15–18 years (Brems 2006, p. 14). The Optional Protocol entered into force on 12 February 2002, after receiving 10 ratifications. The Optional Protocol appears to prohibit a child's participation in armed forces only in the case of conscription, yet it should

[156] Article 1 of the Convention on the Rights of the Child, adopted and opened for signature, ratification and accession by GA Res 44/25 (20 November 1989).

[157] Art 38(2) of the Convention on the Rights of the Child.

[158] Art 38(3) of the Convention on the Rights of the Child.

[159] UN Doc A/RES/54/263 (25 May 2000).

be remembered that while young people may appear to choose military service, the choice may not be necessarily made voluntarily.[160] The Optional Protocol raises the minimum age to at least 16 years to be enlisted voluntarily by governments and includes special safeguards to ensure that the recruitment is not coercive.[161] Thus article 3(3)(a)–(d) of the Optional Protocol sets forth the requirements of proof of age and the consent of both the volunteer and the parents.

Recent developments of international criminal law also reveal great concerns over the involvement of children in armed conflicts. Conscripting or enlisting children under the age of 15 years into national or international armed conflict or using them to participate actively in hostilities is prohibited by articles 8(2)(b)(xxvi) and 8(2)(e)(vii) of the Statute of the International Criminal Court.[162] Article 4(c) of Statute of the Special Court for Sierra Leone, annexed to the 'Agreement between the United Nations and the Government of Sierra Leone on the Establishment for the Special Court for Sierra Leone', has the same provision prohibiting conscripting and enlisting children as article 8(2) of the Statute of the International Criminal Court.

There have been two international criminal proceedings of note concerning the use of child soldiers by the International Criminal Court and the Special Court for Sierra Leone. A decision on a preliminary motion challenging the legality of a charge, which also includes discussion of the crime of conscripting children, came from the Special Court for Sierra Leone in the case of *Prosecutor v Sam Hinga Norman*.[163] The Appeals Chamber held that the prohibition on conscripting child soldiers had already become customary international law when the Statute of the Special Court was drafted.[164] The second proceeding is before the International Criminal Court. When the Pre-Trial Chamber I issued a warrant of arrest for Thomas Lubanga Dyilo who was charged with conscripting child soldiers, it considered that any case arising from an investigation before the Court would meet the gravity threshold provided for in article 17(1)(d) including the social alarm caused to the international community by the relevant type of conduct.[165] The Prosecutor applied the warrant of arrest for war crimes of conscripting and enlisting children under 15, and using children under 15 to participate actively in hostilities punishable under either article 8(2)(b)(xxvi) or article 8(2)(e)(vii) of the Statute. The Pre-Trial Chamber I held that it was aware of the social alarm caused to the international community by the extent of the practice of enlisting and conscripting into armed groups

---

[160] UN Doc. A/51/306, Promotion and Protection of the Rights of Children: Impact of Armed Conflict on Children: Note by Secretary-General (26 August 1996) [38] 17.

[161] UNICEF Press Centre, Bellamy and Otunnu hail entry into force of Optional Protocol on Child Soldiers (12 February 2002).

[162] UN Doc A/CONF. 183/9 (17 July 1998). The Statute came into force on 1 July 2002.

[163] *Prosecutor v Sam Hinga Norman*, Decision on preliminary motion based on lack of jurisdiction (child recruitment) The Appeals Chamber, Case No. SCSL-2004-14-AR72(E) (31 May 2004).

[164] *Prosecutor v Sam Hinga Norman* [17].

[165] *Prosecutor v, Thomas Lubanga Dyilo*, Case No. ICC-01/04-01/06, 10 February 2006, Pre-Trial Chamber I, Decision on the Prosecutor's Application for a Warrant of Arrest, Artcile 58 [63].

children under the age of 15 and using them to participate actively in hostilities.[166] The Chamber confirmed that there were substantial grounds to believe that Lubanga was responsible for the conscription and enlistment of child soldiers and their active use in combat under the age of 15 years old into the *Forces Patriotiques pour la Libération du Congo* (FPLC).[167]

Security Council Resolutions have also demonstrated that the United Nations is actively involved in this issue of children in armed conflict. In Resolution 1261, the Security Council strongly condemned the abduction and recruitment of children in armed conflict.[168] In Resolution 1314, the Council urged Member States 'to sign and ratify the Optional Protocol to the Convention on the Rights of the Child on the Involvement of Children in Armed Conflict'.[169] Similar Resolutions have subsequently been passed by the Security Council.[170]

These efforts of rule-making for prohibiting the conscription of children will clearly be an important step for international peace and security. Although the Optional Protocol to the Convention on the Rights of the Child does not deal with the right to conscientious objection *per se*, the prohibition of the conscription of children will enhance 'their development and education in conditions of peace and security'.[171] Moreover, in the words of the Pre-Trial Chamber I of the International Criminal Court, 'social alarm' is caused to the international community by the extent of the practice of enlisting and conscripting into armed groups and using to participate actively in hostilities children under the age of 15.[172] Hence, even if international law tolerates the system of conscription, international law does not tolerate the conscription of children.

---

166 *Prosecutor v, Thomas Lubanga Dyilo*, Case No. ICC-01/04-01/06, 10 February 2006, Pre-Trial Chamber I, Decision on the Prosecutor's Application for a Warrant of Arrest, Artcile 58 [66].

167 *Le Procureur v Thomas Lubanga Dyilo*, Case No. ICC-01/04-01-06, 29 janvier 2007, la Chambre Préliminaire I, Décision sur la Confirmation des Charges: Version Publique avec Annex I [404].

168 UNSC Res 1261 (1999), adopted by the Security Council at its 4037th Meeting on 25 August 1999.

169 UNSC Res 1314 (2000), adopted by the Security Council at its 4185th Meeting on 11 August 2000.

170 UNSC Res 1379 (2001), adopted by the Security Council at its 4423th Meeting on 20 November 2001; '*Noting* the fact that the conscription or enlistment of children under the age of 15 into the national armed forces or using them to participate actively in hostilities is classified as a war crime by the Rome Statute of the International Criminal Court, which recently entered into force', UNSC Res 1460 (2003), adopted by the Security Council at its 4695th Meeting, on 30 January 2003; UNSC Res 1539 (2004), adopted by the Security Council at its 4948 Meeting on 22 April 2004; UNSC Res 16112 (2005), adopted by the Security Council at its 5235 Meeting on 26 July 2005.

171 Second preambular paragraph of the Optional Protocol to the Convention on the Involvement of Children in Armed Conflict, Adopted and opened for signature, ratification and accession by General Assembly Resolution A/RES/54/263 of 25 May 2000, entry into force 12 February 2002.

172 *Prosecutor v Thomas Lubanga Dyilo* 'Decision on the Prosecutor's Application for a Warrant of Arrest, Article 58' Pre-Trial Chamber I, Case No. ICC-01/04-01/06 (10 February 2006) 33 [66].

2.1.13 Report by Special Rapporteur of 1992

The Persian Gulf War in early had enhanced the political sensitivity of the topic of conscientious objection. The Gulf War overshadowed the forty-seventh Session of the Commission on Human Rights met from January to March 1991. The Commission only managed to adopt a resolution putting off consideration of the issue of conscientious objection until a later session.[173]

Between the Commission on Human Rights' Resolution 1989/59 and Resolution 1993/84, a report was issued by the *Special Rapporteur* on human rights and youth. On 18 June 1992, Mazilu submitted the final report on human rights and youth following the above Sub-Commission's Resolution 1985/12.[174] On the one hand, during the 4 years between 1989 and 1992, some countries, such as Hungary and Poland, had recognised the right of conscientious objection in their rules and regulations.[175] On the other hand, recommendations adopted in Commission on Human Rights' Resolution 1989/59 had not been applied, and conscientious objectors had been imprisoned or forced into military service in many countries.[176] This report clearly states that on the basis of Resolution 1989/59 of the Commission on Human Rights 'all States should take appropriate steps to recognise the right of conscientious objection to military service as a legitimate right.'[177] It also makes it clear that the claim for conscientious objector status 'is an exercise of the fundamental right to freedom of thought, conscience and religion' (see Note 178). Going one step further, following the fact that many people were compelled to participate in armed conflicts and killed contrary to their convictions, this report warns that: 'there is an urgent need to recognise the right of everyone to refuse to kill' (see Note 177). It also states: 'It is urgent for all States to respect the right to conscientious objection to military service. More than that, States should also recognise the right of individuals to be released from the armed forces on grounds of conscience'.[178]

2.1.14 Resolution 1993/84 by the Commission on Human Rights

On 10 March 1993, the Commission adopted Resolution 1993/84, by which the Commission referred to three Resolutions of the General Assembly concerned with youth rights, namely 34/51 of 1 December 1979, 2037 (XX) of 7 December 1965 and 2447 (XXIII) of 19 December 1968, and noted the important role of youth in the promotion of international peace and cooperation as well as of human

---

[173] Commission on Human Rights Res. 1991/65, 47 UN ESCOR Supp. (No. 2) 152; UN Doc E/CN.4/1991/91 (1991). *See* Parker and Weissbrodt (1991, p. 573, 579) .

[174] UN Doc E/CN.4/Sub.2/1992/36.

[175] UN Doc E/CN.4/Sub.2/1992/102.

[176] UN Doc E/CN.4/Sub.2/1992/103.

[177] UN Doc E/CN.4/Sub.2/1992/104.

[178] UN Doc E/CN.4/Sub.2/1992/107.

rights and fundamental freedoms (Angel 1995, p. 27). The draft was introduced by the representative of the Netherlands before the Commission's 67th Meeting (Angel 1995, p. 381). The draft resolution was co-sponsored by Austria, Costa Rica, Hungary, Portugal and the United Kingdom (Angel 1995, p. 381). Canada, the Russian Federation and the United States of America subsequently joined the sponsors (Angel 1995, p. 381). The Commission, in the Resolution's preamble, also noted the final report on human rights and youth submitted by Domitru Mazilu, the *Special Rapporteur* of the Sub-Commission (E/CN.4/Sub.2/1992/36), which draws attention to the continuing need for provision for conscientious objection to military service in many countries. Resolution 1993/84 reminds States with a system of compulsory military service, where such provision has not already been made, of its recommendation that they introduce for conscientious objectors various forms of alternative service which are compatible with the reasons for conscientious objection.[179] It emphasises that such forms of alternative service should be of a non-combatant or civilian character, in the public interest and not of a punitive nature.[180] Resolution 1993/84 includes ethical alongside religious motives as grounds for military conscientious objection, though the Resolution does not mention moral grounds.

2.1.15 General Comment by the Human Rights Committee of 1993

General Comment No. 22 [48] was adopted by the Human Rights Committee on 20 July 1993. Its drafting record shows that the Committee Members faced difficulties reaching a consensus on the issue of conscientious objection. The other side of the coin of this drafting history is that the completed General Comment is a careful consensus on this issue at the time of its drafting. Although general comments tend to be common denominators of the Committee's jurisprudence rather than embracing *lex lata*, paragraph 11 of General Comment No. 22 may be evaluated as progressive and has had a significant impact on the later jurisprudence of the Committee. Before dealing with the drafting history, the nature of the 'general comment' will be clarified below.

The functions of the Human Rights Committee under article 40(4) of the International Covenant on Civil and Political Rights could be divided into three specific parts: firstly, the study proper; secondly, the submission of reports by the Committee as a result of the study; thirdly, the adoption by the Committee of general comments.[181] The last function is optional whereas the first two are obligatory.[182] Accordingly, the adoption of general comments is a discretionary act.

---

179 UN Commission on Human Rights, Res 1993/84 [5].

180 UN Commission on Human Rights, Res 1993/84 [6].

181 *Report of the Human Rights Committee, General Assembly, Official Records, 35th Session, Supplement, No. 40*, UN Doc A/35/40 (United Nations, New York, 1980) 85 [376].

182 UN Doc A/35/40, 85 [376].

The purpose of the general comments is to combine an overall study of reports of States parties which might highlight matters of common interest to them.[183] The purpose of the general comments is to make this experience available for the benefit of all States parties in order to promote their further implementation of the Covenant; to draw their attention to insufficiencies disclosed by a large number of reports; to suggest improvements in the reporting procedure; and to promote and protect human rights.[184] The principles guiding the General Comments are enumerated as follows: (a) They should be addressed to the States parties in conformity with article 40, paragraph 4, of the Covenant; (b) they should promote co-operation between States parties in the implementation of the Covenant; (c) they should summarise the experience the Committee had gained in considering State reports; (d) they should draw the attention of States parties to matters relating to the improvement of the reporting procedure and the implementation of the Covenant; and (e) they should stimulate activities of States parties and international organisations in the promotion and protection of human rights.[185] The Committee further agreed that the general comments could be related to the following subjects: (a) the implementation of the obligation to submit reports under article 40 of the Covenant; (b) the implementation of the obligation to guarantee the rights set forth in the Covenant; (c) questions related to the application and the content of individual articles of the Covenant; and (d) suggestions concerning co-operation between States parties in applying and developing the provisions of the Covenant.[186]

The timing of drafting a General Comment for article 18 coincides exactly with the changing attitude of the Committee with regard to interpretation of article 18. By the time of drafting the General Comment, the Committee had considered the claims of individuals asserting violations of their Covenant rights in relation to their claims of conscientious objection to military service. In its earliest decision regarding a conscientious objector to military service, the Committee rejected the claim of violations of article 18 on the ground that article 18 could not be construed as implying the right to conscientious objection.[187] However in 1992 the Committee changed its attitude and it held that conscientious objection to military service and expenditures was protected by article 18 in *obiter*.[188] Therefore the jurisprudence of the Committee was inconsistent at the time.

---

[183] UN Doc A/35/40at 85, [379].

[184] *Report of the Human Rights Committee, General Assembly, Official Records: 36th Session, Supplement, No. 40* (UN Doc A/36/40) (United Nations, New York, 1981) 29 September 1981, Annex VII, 107.

[185] *Report of the Human Rights Committee, General Assembly Official Records: 39th Session, Supplement No. 40* (UN Doc A/39/40) (United Nations, New York, 1984) 106 [542].

[186] UN Doc A/39/40, 106–107 [542]. *Cf.* The method of the preparation of general comments can be found in *Report of the Human Rights Committee, General Assembly Official Records: 39th Session, Supplement No. 40* (UN Doc A/39/40) (United Nations, New York, 1984) [546]–[547].

[187] L.T.K. v. Finland, Comm. No. 185/1984, Report of the Human Rights Committee, U.N. GAOR, 14th Sess., Supp. No. 40 at 242, U.N. Doc. A/40/40 (1985).

[188] J.P. v. Canada, Comm. No. 446/1991, Report of the Human Rights Committee, U.N. GAOR, 47th Sess., Supp. No. 40, at 434, U.N. Doc. A/47/40 (1992).

The issue of conscientious objection was first dealt with in the course of drafting a General Comment by the Human Rights Committee at its Fourty-seventh Session on 12 May 1993. The Draft General Comment on article 18 of the Covenant contained the issue of conscientious objection in paragraph 11:

> The Committee is aware that the right to refuse to perform military service (conscientious objection) has been claimed by many individuals on the basis of their freedoms under article 18. In response to such claims, a growing number of State have in their laws exempted from compulsory military service citizens who genuinely held religious and other beliefs that forbid the carrying or use of weapons or the performance of military service and replaced it with alternative national service. The Covenant does not explicitly refer to a right of conscientious objection, but the Committee believes that it can be derived from article 18, inasmuch as the obligation to use lethal force may seriously conflict with the freedom of conscience and the right to manifest and express religious or other beliefs. When this right is recognised by law or practice, there shall be no differentiation among conscientious objectors on the basis of the nature of their particular beliefs as well as no discrimination against conscientious objectors because they have failed to perform military service. The Committee invites States parties to report on the conditions under which persons can be exempted from military service and on the nature of alternative national service.[189]

The first question raised was whether the issue of conscientious objection should be dealt with at all in the General Comment.[190] Higgins (United Kingdom) said: 'The Committee should definitely deal with conscientious objection, an issue that was the subject of numerous communications under the Optional Protocol and from non-governmental organizations'.[191] Pocar (Italy), Lallah (Mauritius) and El-Shafei (Egypt) agreed to retain the paragraph concerning conscientious objection.[192] Only Evatt (Australia) argued that the issue of conscientious objection should be dealt within a paragraph dealing with state religion.[193] Dimitrijević (Yugoslavia) agreed that the paragraph dealing with conscientious objection should be retained subject to perusal of the Committee's jurisprudence, but its jurisprudence had never touched on the right of conscientious objection *per se*.[194]

The draft paragraph was provisionally adopted with slight modification as follows:

> Many individuals have claimed the right to refuse to perform military service (conscientious objection) on the basis that such right derives from their freedoms under article 18. In response to such claims, a growing number of States have in their laws exempted from compulsory military service citizens who genuinely hold religious and other beliefs that forbid the performance of military service and replaced it with alternative national service. The Covenant does not explicitly refer to a right of conscientious objection, but the Committee believes that such a right can be derived from article 18, inasmuch as the obligation to use lethal force may seriously conflict with the freedom of conscience and the right to manifest

[189] UN Doc CCPR/C/48/CRP.2 (8 July 1993) 5 [11].

[190] United Nations Human Rights Committee, 47th Session, Summary Record of the First Part of the 1226th Meeting, held at headquarters, New York, on Monday, 5 April 1993 (12 May 1993) UN Doc CCPR/C/SR.1226, 6 [28].

[191] UN Doc CCPR/C/SR.1226 [42].

[192] UN Doc CCPR/C/SR.1226 [43]–[44].

[193] UN Doc CCPR/C/SR.1226 [46].

[194] UN Doc CCPR/C/SR.1226 [45].

and express religious or other beliefs. When this right is recognised by law or practice, there shall be no differentiation among conscientious objectors on the basis of the nature of their particular beliefs, likewise, there shall be no discrimination against conscientious objectors because they have failed to perform military service. The Committee invites States parties to report on the conditions under which persons can be exempted from military service on the basis of their rights under article 18 and on the nature of alternative national service.[195]

According to Dimitrijević (Yugoslavia), the third sentence of draft paragraph 11 was carefully drafted by the Working Group to make it clear that the Covenant did not refer explicitly to conscientious objection as a right although the phenomenon was mentioned under article 8.[196] The first sentence of the General Comment was suggested by Francis (Jamaica) but subjected to some criticisms.[197] Sadi (Jordan) and Ndiaye (Senegal) questioned the need for such a lengthy paragraph since it was not customary to explain the historical background to articles in the Covenant.[198] Evatt (Australia) also agreed to its deletion.[199] Other speakers, El-Shafei (Egypt) and Aguilar Urbina (Costa Rica), supported the first sentence, recognising the importance of the introduction to explain the content of the third sentence.[200] Herndl (Austria) said that the introduction was essential since it indicated that there was a growing trend to recognise conscientious objection.[201]

The reference to the right to life was also discussed in some detail with regard to the use of lethal force. Evatt (Australia) was of the view that if the paragraph referred to conscientious objection as a right, then by way of justification it should also state that the obligation to use lethal force might result in actual violations of the right to life or the right to liberty or security of other persons.[202] For Wennergren (Sweden), the central issue raised by the paragraph on conscientious objection was the right to life, so that he preferred to link the paragraph with the wording used in article 6.[203] El-Shafei (Egypt) saw no justification when dealing with the very specific issue of performance of military service under article 18 for attempting to create a link with the issue of deprivation of life under article 6.[204]

The term ‘lethal force’ was also debated. Sadi (Jordan) showed his preference for referring to ‘fire arms’ rather than to ‘lethal force’. Herndl (Austria) expressed a preference for the wording ‘the obligation to serve in armed forces and consequently to be under the obligation to use arms’, for even killing in self-defence involved the use of lethal force, which was not intended in that sentence.[205] Ndiaye (Sudan) suggested the wording ‘the bearing or use of weapon or performance

[195] UN Doc CCPR/C/48/CRP.2/Rev.1 (14 July 1993) 6 [11].
[196] UN Doc CCPR/C/SR.1237 [10].
[197] UN Doc CCPR/C/SR. 1237 [11].
[198] UN Doc CCPR/C/SR. 1237 [12] and [22].
[199] UN Doc CCPR/C/SR. 1237 [16].
[200] UN Doc CCPR/C/SR. 1237 [13] and [26].
[201] UN Doc CCPR/C/SR. 1237 [19].
[202] UN Doc CCPR/C/SR. 1237 [18].
[203] UN Doc CCPR/C/SR. 1237 [23]. *See also* [37] (Mr. Wennergren).
[204] UN Doc CCPR/C/SR. 1237 [28].
[205] UN Doc CCPR/C/SR. 1237 [20].

of military service' to render the text 'less clumsy'.[206] Mindful of the fact that the central issue raised by the paragraph on conscientious objection was the right to life, Wennergren (Sweden) suggested that the wording 'the obligation to use lethal force' should be replaced by an appropriate phrase based on article 6 of the right to life along the lines of 'the obligation to deprive other persons of their lives'.[207] Urbina (Costa Rica) recalled that the matter had been discussed at length by the Working Group, which had finally opted for the former term since it was not the use of arms that the persons in question objected to but rather any act of aggression that might lead to homicide.[208] With regard to Herndl's remarks, Urbina recalled that the Working Group had chosen that term with certain religious sects in mind such as the Mennonites, who forbade any contact with arms whatsoever, even in the case of self-defence.[209]

Lastly, the most controversial point of the draft of General Comment No. 22 in respect of the issue of conscientious objection was whether the Committee was to refer clearly to article 18 as the basis for a right of conscientious objection.[210] To put it another way, the question was whether the Committee wished to depart from its previous practice by saying that a right to conscientious objection could be derived from article 18.[211] There were arguments on both sides.[212] Therefore the condition of the use of lethal force was introduced as a middle course approach (see Note 112). It was therefore considered that: 'it would be incorrect to say that it recognised all forms of objection as legitimate. In the third sentence there was simply no better expression than "to use lethal force"'.[213]

In General Comment No. 22 on article 18 of the International Covenant on Civil and Political Rights, adopted on 30 July 1993, the Human Rights Committee eventually stated that it believed that a right to conscientious objection can be derived from article 18, 'in as much as the obligation to use lethal force may seriously conflict with the freedom of conscience and the right to manifest one's religion or belief'.[214] The Committee 'seems to limit the right to conscientious objection to a right to refuse to use lethal force, and does not add the conclusion that all States are required to exempt conscientious objectors from military service or the use of lethal force' (Brems 2006, p. 14).

The wording of the General Comment was the subject of critical comment by one of the Committee Members, Higgins (United Kingdom), at the time of drafting: 'The paragraph did not seem to provide clear guidelines for States parties on their

---

[206] UN Doc CCPR/C/SR. 1237 [22].

[207] UN Doc CCPR/C/SR. 1237 [23].

[208] UN Doc CCPR/C/SR. 1237 [15].

[209] UN Doc CCPR/C/SR. 1237 [26].

[210] UN Doc CCPR/C/SR. 1237 [38]

[211] UN Doc CCPR/C/SR. 1237 [45].

[212] UN Doc CCPR/C/SR.1247 (29 July 1993) 8 [45].

[213] UN Doc CCPR/C/SR.1247 (29 July 1993) 8 [51].

[214] United Nations Human Rights Committee, General Comment No. 22: The Right to Freedom of Thought, Conscience and Religion (article 18) (1993) UN Doc CCPR/C/21/Rev.1/Add.4, [11].

obligation to grant the right of conscientious objection under article 18, but merely indicated that it was possible to derive such a right from that article and invited States parties which did so to inform the Committee accordingly'.[215] Nonetheless, she did not stand in the way of a consensus on this paragraph. The issue of conscientious objection in article 18 may be evaluated as well-debated and as the minimum safeguard at the time of drafting it. Despite its weakness in respect of the duty of the States parties to recognise such a right, the adoption of General Comment No. 22 contributed to changing the future attitude of the Committee after its adoption.

2.1.16 Resolutions Following Resolution 1993/84 of the Commission on Human Rights

In December 1994, the Secretary-General prepared a report pursuant to Resolution 1993/84, by which the Commission on Human Rights requested the Secretary-General to report on the question of conscientious objection to military service.[216] Nineteen countries submitted information in reply to his request. Resolution 1993/84 was followed by the Commission's Resolutions 1995/83 of 8 March 1995,[217] 1998/77 of 22 April 1998,[218] 2000/34 of 20 April 2000,[219] 2002/45 of 23 April 2002[220] and 2004/35 of 2004.[221]

On 2 March 1995, the Netherlands submitted a draft resolution on the role of youth in the promotion and protection of human rights, including the question of conscientious objection to military service.[222] Afterwards, the representative of the Netherlands introduced a revised draft resolution,[223] sponsored by Austria, Canada, Germany, Hungary and the Netherlands. The Czech Republic, Costa Rica, Sweden, the United Kingdom and the United States subsequently joined the sponsors.[224]

Much progress was made compared to Resolution 1993/84. The first aspect of progress is the reference in the ninth preambular paragraph to General Comment

215 UN Doc CCPR/C/SR.1247, [74].

216 Report of the Secretary-General prepared pursuant to Commission Resolution 1993/84 (19 December 1994) UN Doc E/CN.4/1995/99.

217 UN Commission on Human Rights , UN Doc E/CN.4/ 1995/176, Chap. XXVI, adopted without a vote (8 March 1995).

218 UN Commission on Human Rights (1998) ESCOR Supp. (No. 3) UN Doc E/CN.4/Res/1998/77 at 253, adopted without a vote (22 April 1998).

219 UN Commission on Human Rights (2000) UN Doc E/CN.4/Res/2000/34, adopted without a vote.

220 UN ECOSOC Res 2002/45, E/CN.4/RES/2002/45, adopted on 23 April 2002 without a vote. E/2002/23 - E/CN.4/2002/200, see chap. XI.

221 UN ECOSOC Res 2002/45, E/CN. 4/RES/2002/45, chap. XI.- E/2004/23 – E/CN.4/2004/127.

222 UN Commission on Human Rights, 55th Session (2 March 1995) UN Doc E/CN.4/1995/L.82.

223 UN Doc E/CN.4/1995/L.82/Rev.1 (7 March 1995).

224 *See* UN Commission on Human Rights, report on the 55th Session (30 January–10 March 1995) ESCOR, 1995, Supp. 4 (1995) [921], UN Doc E/1995/23, E/CN.4/1995/176.

No. 22(48) of the Human Rights Committee on article 18 of the International Covenant on Civil and Political Rights.[225] General Comment No. 22(48) is of significance because thereby the Committee of Human Rights clearly recognised that the right to conscientious objection to perform military service can be derived from article 18. The second is that in the penultimate preambular paragraph, humanitarian motives were added to the list of those that formed the basis for conscientious objection.[226] The third is that in paragraph 2 the words 'compulsory military service', which had been used in previous Resolutions, were amended to read simply 'military service'.[227] This change is significant, because while it was recognised that persons who were performing their military service on a compulsory basis should not be excluded from the right to conscientious objection, it should be recognised that persons who served in the military on a voluntary basis had the same right (see Note 227). At paragraph 11, the decision was made to change the title of the agenda item, 'The role of youth in the promotion and protection of human rights, including the question of conscientious objection to military service', to a new one, 'The question of conscientious objection to military service'. This change corresponded to the sponsors' belief that 'the Resolution's focus had always been predominantly on conscientious objection rather than the role of youth in the promotion and protection of human rights'.[228] The fourth aspect of progress is a reference to article 14 of the Universal Declaration of Human Rights with regard to asylum, which is to serve as a basis for military conscientious objectors facing persecution.[229] The fifth is paragraph 4 which was newly added to urge States not to differentiate in their treatment of military conscientious objectors who maintain different forms of beliefs (see Note 229). The sixth aspect of progress is paragraph 7 where the drafters incorporated an emerging practice among some States that the military conscientious objector's claim is accepted as 'valid without inquiry' by those governments (see Note 229).

On 22 April 1998, the observer for Finland introduced a draft resolution,[230] sponsored by Austria, the Czech Republic, Denmark, Finland, Germany, Hungary, Ireland, the Netherlands, Norway, Portugal, Sweden and the United Kingdom.[231] The Commission on Human Rights adopted Resolution 1998/77, entitled 'Conscientious

[225] UN Commission on Human Rights, 51st Session, Summary Record of the 62nd Meeting (15 March 1995) UN Doc E/CN.4/1995/S.62, 4 [13].

[226] UN Commission on Human Rights, 51st Session, Summary Record of the 62nd Meeting (15 March 1995) UN Doc E/CN.4/1995/S.62, 4 [14].

[227] UN Commission on Human Rights, 51st Session, Summary Record of the 62nd Meeting (15 March 1995) UN Doc E/CN.4/1995/S.62, 4 [15].

[228] UN Commission on Human Rights, 51st Session, Summary Record of the 62nd Meeting (15 March 1995) UN Doc E/CN.4/1995/S.62, 4 [16].

[229] For the last preambular paragraph of Resolution 1995/83, *see* Hammer (2001, p. 201, fn 72).

[230] UN Commission on Human Rights, Report on the 54th Session (16 March–24 April 1998) ESCOR, 1998, Supp. No. 3 (1998) UN Doc E/1998/23, E/CN.4/1998/177253-255.

[231] Canada subsequently joined the sponsors. *See* UN Doc E/1998/23, E/CN.4/1998/177, UN Commission on Human Rights, Report on the 54th Session (16 March-24 April 1998) ESCOR, 1998, Supp. No. 3 (1998) 396 [631].

objection to military service' without a vote at its 58th Meeting.[232] The observer for Finland, introducing the draft resolution, said that: 'increasing weight was being attached to the issue of conscientious objection in the efforts of many States to revise and develop their national legislation. The text recognised the right of everyone to have conscientious objection to military service and reminded States with compulsory military service that they should provide for conscientious objectors various forms of alternative service which were not of a punitive nature'.[233] After voting, while joining the consensus on the draft, the delegation of the Republic of Korea emphasised the Korean government's basic position on the issue: '[t]he government of the Republic of Korea had always attached great importance to the right of freedom of conscience and religion but, at the same time, it recognised its sovereign right and solemn responsibility to defend its territory and maintain public order'.[234] The Korean delegation continued that: '[t]he draft resolution suggested an alternative service system, but it would be impractical and not even feasible for some countries in which the burden of military service was very great and the universality of the application of the law strongly upheld by the people'.[235]

At the 60th Meeting of the Commission on Human Rights, on 20 April 2000, the observer for Finland introduced a draft resolution,[236] sponsored by Bulgaria, Canada, the Czech Republic, Denmark, Finland, Germany, Hungary, Ireland, Norway, Portugal, Romania, Sweden and the United Kingdom.[237] Introducing the draft, the observer for Finland stressed that: 'the draft resolution did not deal with the right of States to maintain an army, nor did it undermine national values or breach the principle of equal application of law'.[238] The draft resolution was adopted without a vote. Resolution 2000/34 is a shorter Resolution, with only three preambular paragraphs and two operating paragraphs so that its objectives must be mainly to recall the contents of Resolution 1998/77 and to encourage States to comply with the Resolution's purpose. The same approach was again taken for a Resolution adopted before the Commission in 2002. At the 51st Meeting of the Commission, the representative of Croatia introduced a draft resolution[239] concerning conscientious objection to military service.[240] The draft resolution was

[232] Reprinted in, UN Commission on Human Rights, Report to the Economic and Social Council on the 44th Session of the Commission: Draft Report of the Commission (22 April 1998), UN Doc E/CN.4/1998/L.11/Add.6, 33–34.

[233] UN Commission on Human Rights 54th Session, Summary Record of the 58th Meeting (27 April 1998), UN Doc E/CN.4/1998/SR.58, 11 [54].

[234] UN Commission on Human Rights 54th Session, Summary Record of the 58th Meeting (27 April 1998), UN Doc E/CN.4/1998/SR.58, 12 [57].

[235] UN Commission on Human Rights 54th Session, Summary Record of the 58th Meeting (27 April 1998), UN Doc E/CN.4/1998/SR.58, 12 [59].

[236] UN Doc E/CN.4/2000/L/43.

[237] Austria, Azerbaijan and the Netherlands subsequently joined the sponsors.

[238] UN Commission on Human Rights, 56th Session, Summary Record of the 60th Meeting (3 May 2000), UN Doc E/CN.4/2000/SR.60, 9 [37].

[239] UN Doc E/CN.4/2002/L.62 (16 April 2002).

[240] *See*, UN Commission on Human Rights, Report on the 58th Session, 18 March–26 April 2002 (2002) UN Doc E/2002/23, E/CN.4/2002/200, 486 [391].

sponsored by Bulgaria, Canada, Croatia, the Czech Republic, Denmark Finland, Germany, Hungary, Ireland, the Netherlands, Poland, Romania, Slovenia and the United Kingdom (see Note 240). The draft resolution was adopted without a vote on 23 April 2002.[241]

The Office of the High Commissioner for Human Rights, in its Report of March 2002, clearly stated that it is possible to identify certain trends in the implementation of the right to conscientious objection at the national level.[242] Firstly, an alternative to military service is provided for by law in many States.[243] Secondly, in many countries the conscientious objector's case is examined at some kind of hearing to determine the validity of the claim, though Finland has no individual examination of applications (see Note 243). Thirdly, most NGOs make reference to the fact that a right to conscientious objection is considered by international human rights monitoring bodies as deriving from the fundamental right of freedom of religion and conscience.[244] However, Sudan and Singapore considered that 'resolution 2000/34 goes beyond what is prescribed in the international law and the applicable human rights instruments' (see Note 242).

In 2004, the representative of Croatia introduced a draft resolution[245] at the 44th Meeting of the Sixtieth Session of the Commission.[246] It was sponsored by Albania, Armenia, Australia, Austria, Bosnia and Herzegovina, Brazil, Bulgaria, Canada, Costa Rica, Croatia, Czech Republic, Denmark, Finland, France, Georgia, Germany, Hungary, Ireland, Italy, Netherlands, Norway, Poland, Portugal, Republic of Moldova, Romania, Russian Federation, San Marino, Serbia and Montenegro, Slovakia, Slovenia, Spain, Switzerland, The Former Yugoslav Republic of Macedonia, United Kingdom. Thus 34 sponsors promoted the draft resolution. Moreover, the Dominican Republic, Latvia, Nicaragua and Sweden subsequently joined the sponsors. The representative of Croatia, introducing the draft, stated that: 'It called upon States which had not yet done so to review their laws and practices in relation to conscientious objection to military service, taking account of the report [of the Office of High Commissioner for Human Rights]'.[247] The delegation of the United

---

[241] For the text as adopted, *see* UN Doc E/2002/23, E/CN.4/2002/200, 197–198.

[242] UN Commission on Human Rights, Civil and Political Rights, including the Question of Conscientious Objection to Military Service, Report of the High Commissioner submitted pursuant to Commission Resolution 2000/34 (14 March 2002), UN Doc E/CN.4/2002/WP.2, 2.

[243] UN Commission on Human Rights, Civil and Political Rights, including the Question of Conscientious Objection to Military Service, Report of the High Commissioner submitted pursuant to Commission Resolution 2000/34 (14 March 2002), UN Doc E/CN.4/2002/WP.2, 5.

[244] UN Commission on Human Rights, Civil and Political Rights, including the Question of Conscientious Objection to Military Service, Report of the High Commissioner submitted pursuant to Commission Resolution 2000/34 (14 March 2002), UN Doc E/CN.4/2002/WP.2, 6.

[245] UN Doc E/CN.4/2004/L.54 (14 April 2004).

[246] UN Commission on Human Rights, Report on the 60th Session, 15 March–23 April 2004, ESCOR Supp. No. 3 (2004) UN Doc E/2004/23, E/CN.4/2004/127, 411 [354].

[247] UN Commission on Human Rights, Summary Record of the 55th Meeting (9 December 2005), UN Doc E/CN.4/2004/SR.55, 10 [53].

States made a statement that the United States joined the consensus on the draft resolution:

> [. . .] because the United States fully supported the right of everyone to have personal objections to military service as one element of the exercise of freedom of thought, conscience and religion. In countries with military conscription, everyone should have that right in the context of a fair and impartial process established by law. But no one had an absolute right to be granted conscientious objector status, and unsuccessful applicants who refused to perform military service or other alternatives must be prepared to accept the consequences provided by law.[248]

For the delegate of the United States, 'the granting of amnesties and restitution for those who had refused to undertake military service on grounds of conscientious objection [should] be limited to civil war situations and their aftermath'.[249] The draft resolution was adopted without a vote.

The Commission on Human Rights adopted a broader view that the notion of conscientious objection goes beyond pacifism. This more lenient attitude toward conscientious objection might have been affected by the Human Rights Committee's General Comment No. 22 on article 18 of the International Covenant of Civil and Political Rights in 1993, by which the Human Rights Committee changed its early position and recognised that the right to conscientious objection can be derived from article 18.[250] Hence the right to military conscientious objection is regarded as a right emanating from the freedom of conscience, along with a number of other human rights, by the Commission on Human Rights. The Human Rights Committee stated that it believes that a right to conscientious objection can be derived from article 18, 'in as much as the obligation to use lethal force may seriously conflict with the freedom of conscience and the right to manifest one's religion or belief'.[251]

On the one hand the Commission on Human Rights seems to recognise the right to conscientious objection as a right emanating from the freedom of conscience (Hammar 2001, p. 201). On the other hand the Human Rights Committee seems to limit this right to a right to refuse to use lethal force, and hesitates to recommend that States exempt conscientious objectors from military service in general (Brems 2006, p. 14). The Commission on Human Rights had fostered a consensus on this issue since the 1970s and had passed not a few cumulative Resolutions on the issue of conscientious objection to military service. The Commission may have taken a broader and more comprehensive approach against this backdrop, while the Human Rights Committee had to reach a consensus on this issue in a much shorter period of time to draft the General Comment.

---

248 UN Doc E/CN.4/2004/SR.55, 10 [56].

249 UN Doc E/CN.4/2004/SR.55, 10 [57].

250 United Nations Human Rights Committee, General Comment No. 22: The Right to Freedom of Thought, Conscience and Religion (article 18) (1993) UN Doc CCPR/C/21/Rev.1/Add.4, (48) [11].

251 General Comment No. 22 (UN Doc CCPR/C/21/Rev.1/Add.4) (48) [11].

Paragraph 5 of Resolution 2004/35 on conscientious objection requests the Office of the High Commissioner for Human Rights to prepare an analytical report to provide supplementary information on best practices in relation to conscientious objection to military service, drawing on all appropriate sources, and to submit this report to the Commission at its Sixty-second Session under the same agenda item.[252]

2.1.17 Study of the Issue of the Administration of Justice Through Military Tribunals of 2005

This study by a working group of Sub-Commission on the Promotion and Protection of Human Rights on the issue of the administration of justice by military tribunals also addressed the issue of conscientious objection to military service. The report submitted on 2 June 2005 by the *Special Rapporteur* on the universal implementation of international human rights treaties, Professor Emmanuel Decaux, devoted a few pages to the issue of conscientious objection to military service.[253] Professor Decaux clearly acknowledged the legitimacy of exercising conscientious objection to military service under the United Nations legal system, stating that:

> The United Nations has recognized the existence of conscientious objection to military service as a legitimate exercise of the right to freedom of thought, conscience and religion, as laid down in the Universal Declaration of Human Rights and the International Covenant on Civil and Political Rights. The Human Rights Committee has very clearly linked conscientious objection to the principle of freedom of conscience enshrined in article 18 of the Covenant.[254]

He not only underscored a general recognition of the right to conscientious objection to military service but also the right of conscientious objection to military service for those who are in the service with reference to the Observations of the Human Rights Committee.[255] As for applications lodged in the course of military service, the report ensures military personnels that such an application should not be punished *ipso facto* as an act of insubordination or desertion, independently of any consideration of its substance, but should be examined in a fair manner.[256] The *Special Rapporteur* was concerned about conscientious objectors being tried by military

252 UN Doc E/CN.4/2004/L.11/Add.4, 30.

253 UN Doc E/CN.4/Sub.2/2005/9, Administration of Justice, Rules of Law and Democracy: Issue of the Administration of Justice through Military Tribunals, Report submitted by the *Special Rapporteur*, Emmanuel Decaux, original French (2 June 2005).

254 UN Doc E/CN.4/Sub.2/2005/9, 10 [18]: Referring to General Assembly Resolution 33/165 of 20 December 1978; Commission on Human Rights, Resolution 38 (XXXVI) of 1980, 1987/46 of 1987, 1989/59 of 1989, 1993/84 of 1993, 1995/83 of 1995 and 1998/77 of 1998; Human Rights Committee, General Comment no. 22 (1993); Committee's decision for communications no. 446/1991 (par. 4.2), 483/1991 (par. 4.2) and 402/1990).

255 UN Doc E/CN.4/Sub.2/2005/9, 9 [18]: Referring to Observations of the Human Rights Committee; France, 4 August 1997, CCPR/C/79/Add.80 [19]; Final Observation of the Human Rights Committee, Spain, 3 April 1996, CCPR/C/79/Add.1 [15].

256 UN Doc E/CN.4/Sub.2/2005/9, 9 [19].

tribunals. In his view conscientious objectors are civilians and so should be tried in civil courts, under the supervision of ordinary judges.[257]

2.2 Enforcement Mechanism

One of the excuses for the UN and the European international human rights enforcement mechanisms not to relates to the articles referring to conscientious objection system. The drafters of article 18 of the International Covenant on Civil and Political Rights did not choose to incorporate the right to military conscientious objection into the provision, though it was proposed by the Philippines.[258] While there is no provision regarding the right to conscientious objection itself in either the International Covenant on Civil and Political Rights or the European Convention on Human Rights, both the International Covenant on Civil and Political Rights and the European Convention on Human Rights refer to 'conscientious objection' in the articles specifically dealing with the prohibition of slavery and forced labour. Article 8(3)(c)(ii) and article 4(3)(b) remained an obstacle for both the Human Rights Committee and the European Commission and European Court of Human Rights, which is an enforcement body of the European Convention on Human Rights. Because both provisions contain the wordings 'in case of conscientious objectors in countries where they are recognised (article 4(3)(b) of the European Convention on Human Rights)' and 'in countries where conscientious objection is recognised (article 8(3)(c)(ii) of the International Covenant on Civil and Political Rights)',[259] these wordings led to the interpretation that these international and regional human rights instruments did not necessarily require State parties to recognise the right to conscientious objection to military service. Therefore it remained debatable whether these instruments guaranteed the right to conscientious objection to military service.

2.2.1 Individual Communication and Evolving Interpretation of the Covenant

The Human Rights Committee has addressed the issue of conscientious objection mainly in the context of individual communications by conscientious objectors (Nowak 2005, p. 421), while it is also true that a number of national reports mention the issue of conscientious objectors. A few early cases indicated that article

[257] UN Doc E/CN.4/Sub.2/2005/9, 9 [17].

[258] UN Doc E/CN.4/353/Add.3 and E/CN.4/SR.119.

[259] Cf. The Charter of the Fundamental Rights of the European Union does not enumerate the exceptional instances of forced or compulsory labour in its article 5. Nonetheless, in its article concerning freedom of thought, conscience and religion, article 10(2), it says conscientious objection is recognised 'in accordance with the national law governing the exercise of this right'. C/364/11 (18 December 2000).

18 does not guarantee a right of conscientious objection in a right to freedom from compulsory military service on the basis of one's conscientious objection to military force by the interpretation of the Committee. The Committee even avoided deciding whether article 18, paragraph 1, guaranteed a right of conscientious objection to military service.

In *Paavo Muhonen v Finland*, the Committee was of the opinion that: "the Question whether article 18, paragraph 1, guaranteed a right of conscientious objection to military service did not have to be determined by the Committee" since the decision handed by Finnish Military Service Examining Board had already provided the opinion on the issue of the compliance with article 18(1) of the Covenant.[260]

In *L.T.K v Finland*, the Human Rights Committee unequivocally found that the Covenant does not provide for the right to conscientious objection; neither article 18 nor article 19 of the Covenant can be construed as implying that right.[261]

> The Covenant does not provide for the right to conscientious objection; neither article 18 nor article 19 of the Covenant, especially taking into account paragraph 3 (c) (ii) of article 8, can be construed as implying that right.[262]

On this basis, the Committee declared claims based on conscientious objection to be inadmissible. In doing so, the Human Rights Committee put much weight on paragraph 3(c)(ii) of article 8 which excludes any military service and any national service required by law of conscientious objectors from the prohibition against forced or compulsory labour.

In the International Covenant on Civil and Political Rights, the lone article to mention 'conscientious objection' is article 8(3)(c)(ii). Article 8 deals with the prohibition of slavery, and its paragraph 3(c)(ii) excludes any service of military character and any national service required by law of conscientious objectors from the use of the term 'forced or compulsory labour'. However, this article has not been seen as inferring the right of conscientious objection (Nowak 1993, p. 154). On the contrary, the passage 'in countries where conscientious objection is recognized' was expressly adopted by the Human Rights Committee at the initiative of France, since the right of conscientious objection was recognised in only a few States (see Sect. 2.1.2. p. 52ff). The phrase has been interpreted by the Committee to indicate that States are free to decide whether they recognise conscientious objection (Alfredsson and Eide 1999, p. 389). It is not entirely clear whether the Human Rights Committee had thought the provision of safeguards for conscientious objection was inappropriate under this particular provision or the entire the International Covenant on Civil and Political Rights. From the earlier negative attitude of the Human Rights Committee towards the right of conscientious objection one can assume that it did not want to go into detail in an area where State practice is not consistent and it touches upon national security issues.

260 Human Rights Committee, *Paavo Muhonen v Finland*, Communication No. 89/1981, UN Doc CCPR/C/24/D/89/1981 (8 April 1985) [3].

261 *L.T.K. v. Finland*, Comm. No. 185/1984, Report of the Human Rights Committee, U.N. GAOR, 14th Sess., Supp. No. 40 at 242, U.N. Doc. A/40/40 (1985).

262 *L.T.K. v. Finland*, Comm. No. 185/1984, Report of the Human Rights Committee, U.N. GAOR, 14th Sess., Supp. No. 40 at 242, U.N. Doc. A/40/40 (1985) [5.2.].

In any case, this limited interpretation of article 8(3)(c) has been criticised. Firstly, the right which is protected and limited in article 8(3)(c) is not freedom of conscience but personal liberty (Eide and Mubanga-Chipoya 1985, p. 5 and Alfredsson and Eide 1999, p. 389). Secondly, the phrase can only be interpreted to indicate that all States where conscription exists are not under all circumstances obliged to recognise the right to object (Alfredsson and Eide 1999, p. 389).

After a large number of individual claims concerning the right to conscientious objection were made based upon article 18 of the Covenant, the Human Rights Committee began to support a wide range of reasons for conscientious objection and recognised article 18 as the legal basis of the right. In the *obiter dictum* of *J.P. v Canada*, the Committee for the first time stated that 'conscientious objection to military service and expenditures' was 'certainly' protected by article 18.[263] More clearly, the Human Rights Committee later in effect overruled the *L.T.K.* case in the General Comment of article 18, holding that a right to conscientious objection, which is not explicitly referred to by the Covenant, can be derived from article 18.[264] In this General Comment, the Committee observes that no differentiation should be made between conscientious objectors on the basis of their beliefs (see Note 264).

In 1999, the Human Rights Committee examined an individual complaint of a person whose application for recognition as a conscientious objector had been rejected because the type of (non-religious) objections he advanced did not fall within the criteria of Dutch law, which required 'an unsurmountable objection of conscience to military service...because of the use of violent means' (see Brems 2006, p. 15). The Human Rights Committee referred to the statement in its General Comment that the right to conscientious objection to military service can be derived from article 18 (Brems 2006, p. 15). Nonetheless, the Committee regarded Dutch legislation providing for exemptions for conscientious objectors as compatible with article 18 of the International Covenant on Civil and Political Rights, since the Committee found the national authority's finding reasonable that this case fell outside the scope of this provision and there was no interference with the applicant's freedom of conscience (Brems 2006, p. 15). Five Committee members appended their Individual (Dissenting) Opinion to this decision. For them, 'the State party has failed to provide justification for its decision to interfere with the author's right under article 18 of the Covenant in the form of denial of conscientious objector's status and imposing a term of imprisonment'.[265] Thus they promoted the principle stipulated by General Comment 22 that there should be no differentiation between conscientious objectors on the basis of the nature of their particular beliefs.

According to Brems, from this case several conclusions may be drawn with regard to the Human Rights Committee's interpretation of the freedom of conscience

---

[263] United Nations Human Rights Committee No. 446/1991, [4.2]; *see also* no. 483/1991 [4.2].

[264] General Comment 22 [11].

[265] United Nations Human Rights Committee, Communication No. 682/1996, *Paul Westerman v The Netherlands* (Views adopted on 3 November 1999, 67th Session), Individual Opinion (Dissenting) by Committee Members, P. Bhagwati, L. Henkin, C. Medina Quironga, F. Pocar and M. Scheinin, in A/55/40, United Nations Report of the Human Rights Committee vol. II, General Assembly Official Records, 55th Session, Supplement, No. 40, (A/55/40) 48.

in article 18 of the International Covenant on Civil and Political Rights. Firstly, the freedom of conscience is no longer seen as a purely private freedom, taking into account the fact that the Human Rights Committee has examined, through individual communications, whether the imposition of sanctions to enforce the performance of military duty constitutes an infringement of one's freedom of conscience (Brems 2006, pp. 15–16). Secondly, it is not clear at this stage whether the limits of the right to freedom of conscience are determined only by the type of convictions that fall within the scope of the freedom or whether in addition they are also determined by a balancing exercise with other interests (Brems 2006, p. 16).

The Human Rights Committee thus started changing its attitude toward the right to conscientious objection and criticising the excessive period of alternative service,[266] in comparison with military service, the lack of alternative assessment of applications other than under the control of the Ministry of Defence[267] and of any provision for conscientious objectors to military service. Instead of indicating the authorised conditions under which the right to conscientious objection is allowed, the Human Rights Committee invited States parties to report on the conditions of the right, the nature and the length of alternative national service.[268] The refusal to pay taxes on the grounds of conscientious objection has so far been recognised as 'outside the scope of protection' of article 18.[269]

The right to freedom of thought, conscience and religion of article 18 of the International Covenant on Civil and Political Rights is so fundamental that article 4(2) of the International Covenant on Civil and Political Rights states these freedoms cannot be derogated from, even at a time of public emergency. Furthermore, it is noted that article 18 did not occasion any reservations or declaration of interpretation (Nowak 2005, p. 310).

To date, the Human Rights Committee has called for no distinctions to be drawn between conscientious objectors on the basis of their beliefs. Therefore it would amount to discrimination if only certain, i.e., religion-based, objections were recognised (Boyle 1999, pp. 389–390).

2.2.2 *Yeo-Bum Yoon and Myung-Jin Choi V Republic of Korea*

The latest decision by the Committee concerning conscientious objectors relates to South Korean conscientious objectors. South Korea has witnessed a rapidly changing domestic status of the right to conscientious objection. South Korea maintains a compulsory conscription system which requires men aged over 20 to serve in the military for 2 years. To date, there is neither recognition of a conscientious objection

---

[266] Cyprus (1994) UN Doc CCPR/C/9/Add.39 [10]; *see also* Concluding Comments on Slovakia (1997) UN Doc CCPR/C/79/Add.79 [12].

[267] Greece (2005), UN Doc CCPR/CO/83/GRC [15].

[268] General Comment 22 [11].

[269] *J.P. v Canada* (446/91); *J.v.K. and C.M.G.c.K.-S. v The Netherlands* (483/91) and *K.V. and C.V. v Germany* (560/93).

system nor an alternative service to military service in South Korea. It is reported that every year about 700 conscientious objectors are punished, mostly with gaol terms, and at present there are about 450 young men imprisoned for this offence.[270] Another source reports that 12,324 conscientious objectors have been imprisoned for refusing mandatory military service over the past 66 years.[271] Half of the conscientious objectors among those figures suffered torture, such as standing still, binding hands or beating (see Note 271).

Recently, a new movement regarding conscientious objection emerged in South Korea. On 26 December 2005 the National Human Rights Commission officially recommended that the government recognise conscientious objector status.[272] The Commission recognises it within the protection of the freedom of conscience enshrined in the Constitution.[273] In addition to that, the Commission also suggested providing alternative service in lieu of conscription for the objectors (see Note 272).

This recommendation deviates from a Constitutional Court decision rendered in August 2004 that affirmed the current conscription law as constitutional, based on its principle that religious beliefs cannot come before national security (see Note 272). The Constitutional Court decision bolstered the Supreme Court's opinion that upheld the conviction of a 23-year-old Jehovah's Witness who refused to obey his draft order (see Note 272).

The Commission is an independent government organ under the South Korean President, established on 25 November 2001 in accordance with the National Human Rights Commission Act.[274] Since the recommendation of the Commission does not have any legally binding force, the government is not required to introduce immediate changes to the current conscription system (see Note 272). Nonetheless, this decision is of importance in that it was the first time that a State institution officially recognised the right to conscientious objection (see Note 272). Although in December 2005 the Defence Ministry expressed regret over the Commission's decision and stated that it would be unrealistic at this time to offer alternative civil service for regular military service without compromising military preparedness (see Note 272), in January 2006 the Korean Defence Ministry revealed that it plans to launch a pan-governmental committee to study alternative military services for conscientious objectors (see Note 270). It was estimated that the decision on whether to implement the conscientious objection system will be made after the committee finishes its analysis of a system offering alternate forms of service for objectors in 2006 (see Note 281).

---

270 'Defense Chief to Review Conscientious Objector Issue', *Hankook Iibo Korea Times* (7 January, 2006).

271 This is according to an association of family members of conscientious objectors to military service. The research was conducted from March to April 2006. This is the first report to calculate the number of conscientious objectors for a period, though it is not of an official character. *See* P Chung-a, 'Conscientious Military Objectors Surpass 12,000', *The Korea Times* (21 March 2007).

272 'Debate Rekindled over Military Objectors', *Hankook Iibo Korea Times* (28 December 2005).

273 *Asahi Shinbun* (28 December 2005) 7.

274 *See* http://www.humanrights.go.kr/eng/index.jsp (last visited, 19 January 2006).

Due to no system of conscientious objection in South Korea, two South Korean Jehovah's Witnesses filed communications to the Human Rights Committee to accuse South Korea of violation of article 18(1) of the Covenant. In complaints under the Optional Protocol Procedure to the International Covenant on Civil and Political Rights, in the case of *Yeo-Bum Yoon and Myung-Jin Choi v Republic of Korea*, the Human Rights Committee found that the imprisonment of two conscientious objectors to compulsory military service was a violation of article 18 paragraph 1 of the Covenant.[275] At the same time it found that the Republic of Korea had not demonstrated that in this case the restriction on the freedom of conscience and religion justifiable under article 18, paragraph 3, of the Covenant, was necessary.[276]

There were two dissenting opinions by members of the Committee in *Yeo-Bum Yoon and Myung-Jin Choi v Republic of Korea*.[277] The Argentine member, Hipólito Solari-Yrigoyen, argued that since Korea does not recognise the fundamental right to conscientious objection, the communication should have been considered solely under paragraph 1 of article 18, not paragraph 3.[278] According to this dissenting opinion, 'The mention of freedom to manifest one's religion or belief in article 18, paragraph 3, is a reference to the freedom to manifest that religion or belief in public, not to recognition of the right itself, which is protected by paragraph 1'.[279] Even though the communication was supposed not to deal with recognition of the objector's right itself, article 18, paragraph 3, of the International Covenant on Civil and Political Rights by no means implies that 'the existence of the right itself is a matter for the discretion of States parties' (see Note 279).

The majority's opinion makes it clear that the lone article touching upon the issue of conscientious objection, article 8, itself neither recognises nor excludes a right of conscientious objection (see Note 279). Yet the majority opinion appears silent on the issue whether recognition of the right to conscientious objection itself may be at the discretion of States parties. While the majority opinion 'concludes that the facts as found by the Committee reveal, in respect of each author violations by the Republic of Korea of article 18, paragraph 1, of the Covenant', the concrete violation recognised by the Committee seemed to be rather one of article 18, paragraph 3 of the Covenant as stated above.[280] The majority opinion of the Committee's argument

---

275 UN Doc CCPR/C/88/D/1321-1322/2004 (23 January 2007) Communication Nos. 1321/2004 and 1322/2004: Republic of Korea 23/01/2007, CCPR/C/88/D/1321-1322/2004 (jurisprudence) Views of the Human Rights Committee under article 5(4) of the Optional Protocol of the International Covenant of Civil and Political Rights, Human Rights Committee, 88th Session (16 October–3 November 2006) [9].

276 UN Doc CCPR/C/88/D/1321-1322/2004, [8.4].

277 Dissenting Opinion by Committee member Hipólito Solari-Yrigoyen and Dissenting Opinion by Committee member Ruth Wedgwood, *see* Appendix of UN Doc CCPR/C/88/D/1321–1322/2004.

278 Dissenting Opinion by Committee member Hipólito Solari-Yrigoyen, *see* Appendix of UN Doc CCPR/C/88/D/1321–1322/2004) [8.2].

279 Dissenting Opinion by Committee member Hipólito Solari-Yrigoyen, *see* Appendix of UN Doc CCPR/C/88/D/1321–1322/2004) [8.3].

280 Dissenting Opinion by Committee member Hipólito Solari-Yrigoyen, *see* Appendix of UN Doc CCPR/C/88/D/1321–1322/2004) [8.4].

may be summarised as follows. Firstly, the claim of conscientious objection to military service as a protected form of manifestation of religious belief may be assessed under article 18 of paragraph 1 as the authors assert (see Note 280). Secondly, the limitation on the right to manifest one's religion or belief shall be consistent with and justified by article 18, paragraph 3 (see Note 280). Finally, the Committee considers that the State party has failed to show in the meaning of article 18, paragraph 3, what special disadvantage would be involved for it if the rights of the authors under article 18, paragraph 1, were fully respected (see Note 280). In so doing, the Committee notes in relation to relevant State practice that: 'an increasing number of those States parties to the Covenant which have retained compulsory military service have introduced alternatives to compulsory service' (see Note 280). There is no statement of recognition of violation of article 18, paragraph 1, for failing to provide a procedure for conscientious objection to military service.

The reasoning shown by the dissenting opinion of Solari-Yrigoyen should be evaluated as clearer with respect to logic. Solari-Yrigoyen first of all admits that the prosecution, conviction and prison term imposed on the authors directly violated the authors' right to religious beliefs, established in article 18, paragraph 1 (see Note 280). The recognition of the human right to conscientious objection may have been first of all dealt with by consulting article 18, paragraph 1. Instead of doing this, the majority embarked upon examination of the restriction of this right by referring to article 18, paragraph 3. The majority opinion may for some reflect a leap in logic. Nonetheless, both the majority opinion and the dissenting opinion by Solari-Yrigoyen admitted the violation of article 18, paragraph 1 as the authors originally claimed.

The other dissenting opinion, written by Professor Ruth Wedgwood, takes the very formalistic approach which had been taken by the Committee itself a decade ago. The opinion concludes that: 'the right to refrain from mandatory military service is strictly required by the terms of the Covenant, as a matter of law'.[281] It further interprets article 18 as not suggesting that: 'a person motivated by religious belief has a protected right to withdraw from the otherwise legitimate requirements of a shared society' (see Note 281). Without referring to any resource, the dissenting opinion holds that a number of parties to the Covenant still rely upon military conscription without providing *de jure* for a right to conscientious objection. Additionally, this opinion criticises that the majority opinion fails to provide evidence of *travaux préparatoires* and state practices establishing that article 18 may be interpreted to differentiate military service from other state obligations. Further, Professor Wedgwood notes that in the interval of more than a decade since the Committee adopted General Comment No. 22, the Committee has never suggested in its jurisprudence under the Optional Protocol that such a 'derivation' is in fact required by the Covenant. In addition to that, for this member, the language of article 8, paragraph 3(c) is an obstacle to the conclusion of the majority opinion.

---

[281] Dissenting Opinion by Committee Member Ms Ruth Wedgwood, *see* Appendix of UN Doc CCPR/C/88/D/1321–1322/2004.

2.2.3 Consideration of Reports Submitted by States Parties Under Article 40 of the Covenant

The Committee recently raised appropriate national legislation on the right to conscientious objection in its observations on reports submitted by State parties. For instance, the Committee recommends that: 'a law exempting conscientious objectors from compulsory military service and providing for alternative civil service of equivalent length be passed at an early date in compliance with article 18 of the Covenant and the Committee's General Comment No. 22 (48)' as the observations on a national report by Belarus in November 1997.[282] In April 2001, the Committee takes 'note of the fact that the law makes no provision for the status of conscientious objector to military service, which may legitimately be claimed under article 18 of the Covenant' in the concluding observations on the report submitted by the Dominican Republic.[283] Furthermore, the Committee requires a national law which recognises conscientious objection to military service 'without restrictions (article 18)'.[284] The Committee also requests Israel to 'review the law, criteria and practice governing the determination of conscientious objection, in order to ensure compliance with article 18 of the Covenant'.[285] According to the interpretation of article 18 by the Committee, establishing the conscientious objection system itself does not appear to be enough; instead, what is required are the equal application and non-discriminatory nature of the conscientious objector assessment procedure.

References to the issue of conscientious objection in concluding observations by the Committee are becoming more precise each year. In the 1990s, the concluding observations of the Committee merely made cursory remarks where the absence of the right to conscientious objection is listed among other absences of the rights protected by the Covenant.[286] In recent years the Committee in its observations has unequivocally urged State parties that do not recognise the right to conscientious objection to compulsory military service to take all necessary measures to recognise it, as well as to introduce alternative service without discrimination.[287] For example, the concluding observations of the Human Rights Committee on the fifth report

282 Concluding observations of the Human Rights Committee on the fourth periodic report of Belarus, CCPR/C/79/Add.86 (19 November 1997).

283 Concluding observations of the Human Rights Committee on the fourth periodic report of the Dominican Republic, CCPR/CO/71/DOM (26 April 2001) [21].

284 Concluding observations on the initial report by Serbia and Montenegro, CCPR/CO/81/SEMO (8 December 2004) [21].

285 Concluding observations of the Human Rights Committee on the second report of Israel, CCPR/CO/78/ISR (21 August 2003) [24].

286 Concluding observations of the Human Rights Committee on the initial report by Slovakia, CCPR/C/79/Add.79 (4 August 1997) [12]. *See also* Concluding observations of the Human Rights Committee on the second report of the Libyan Arab Jamahiriya, CCPR/C/79/Add.45 (23 November 1994) [13].

287 For example, *see* concluding observations on the second report by the Azerbaijan Republic, CCPR/CO/73/AZE (12 November 2001) [21]; concluding observations on the initial report of Tajikistan, CCPR/C/SR.2299 (22 July 2004) [20].

by Colombia holds that the State party should guarantee that conscientious objectors are able to opt for alternative service whose duration would not have punitive effects.[288] The concluding remarks on the third report by Venezuela put emphasis on the availability of procedures for conscientious objection and alternative service without discrimination.[289]

The Committee is also concerned with the condition of alternative service and the eligibility criteria for the application of conscientious objection.[290] For those States having compulsory military service, such as Kuwait, the Committee 'notes the existence of compulsory military service and that Kuwaiti law does not contain any provision on conscientious objection. In order to implement article 18 of the Covenant, the State party should reflect in its legislation the situation of persons who believe that the use of armed force conflicts with their convictions, and establish for these cases an alternative civilian service'.[291]

The Committee seeks for the entire populations of State parties to enjoy the right to conscientious objection. With regard to Paraguay, while the Committee welcomes the recognition in Paraguay's Constitution of conscientious objection to military service and the provisional measures passed by the Chamber of Deputies to guarantee respect for conscientious objection, given the lack of specific regulations governing this right, the Committee regrets that access to information on conscientious objection appears to be unavailable in rural areas by referring to article 18 of the Covenant.[292] The Committee also takes note of and deplores 'the instances of reprisals against... family members' of conscientious objectors.[293] In November 1998, the Committee, in the concluding observations on the initial report of

---

[288] Concluding observations of the Human Rights Committee on the fifth report by Columbia CCPR/CO/80/COL (26 May 2004) [17]. *See also* concluding observations of the Human Rights Committee on the second report of Viet Nam, CCPR/CO/75/VNM (26 July 2002) [17]; concluding observations of the Human Rights Committee on the fourth report by Mexico, CCPR/C/79/Add.109 (27 July 1999) [20].

[289] 'The State party should see to it that individuals required to perform military service can plead conscientious objection and perform alternative service without discrimination'. Concluding observations of the Human Rights Committee on the third report by Venezuela, CCPR/CO/71/VEN (26 April 2001) [26]. *See also* concluding observations of the Human Rights Committee on the initial report of Lithuania, CCPR/C.79/Add.87 (19 November 1997) [19]: 'The Committee recommends the State party clarify the grounds and eligibility for performing, without discrimination, alternative service and grounds of conscience or religious belief to ensure that the right to freedom of conscience and religion is respected'.

[290] 'The Committee recommends that the State party clarify the grounds and eligibility for performing alternative service to persons objecting to military service on grounds of conscience or religious belief, to ensure that the right to freedom of conscience and religion is respected by permitting in practice alternative service outside the defence forces, and that the duration of service is not punitive in nature (arts 18 and 26)'. Concluding observations of the Human Rights Committee on the second report of Lithuania, CCPR/CO/80/LTU (4 May 2004) [17].

[291] Concluding observations of the Human Rights Committee on the initial report by Kuwait, CCPR/CO/69/KWT;A/55/40 (27 July 2000) [43]–[44].

[292] Concluding observations of the Human Rights Committee on the second report of Paraguay, CCPR/C/PRY/CO/2 (24 April 2006) 4 [18].

[293] Concluding observations of the Human Rights Committee on the initial report of Armenia, CCPR/C/79/Add.100 (19 November 1998) [18].

Armenia, markedly stated that: '[t]he Committee regrets the lack of legal provision for alternatives to military service in case of conscientious objection. The Committee deplores the conscription of conscientious objectors by force and their punishment by military courts, and the instances of reprisals against their family members' (see Note 293).

A country might not recognise the right to conscientious objection but permit some of those who do not wish to perform such service to pay a certain sum in order not to do so. This is the case of Syria. Nonetheless, in such a case, the Committee reminded that: '[t]he State party should respect the right to conscientious objection to military service and establish, if it so wishes, an alternative civil service of a non-punitive nature'.[294]

The right to conscientious objection should be acknowledged both in wartime and peace time according to the Committee. It recommended that: '[t]he State party should fully acknowledge the right to conscientious objection and, accordingly, *guarantee it both in wartime and in peacetime*, it should also end the discrimination inherent in the duration of alternative civilian service and the categories that can benefit from it [arts 18 and 26 of the Covenant]' (emphasis added).[295]

The timing of the claim of conscientious objection should also be flexible. The Committee is concerned that: 'the application must be made in advance of the conscript's entry into military service and that the right cannot be exercised thereafter' in the context of the concluding observations for France in 1997.[296] Its concern is also described in the concluding observations for Spain: 'the Committee is greatly concerned to hear that individuals cannot claim the status of conscientious objectors once they have entered the armed forces, since that does not seem to be consistent with the requirements of article 18 of the Covenant as pointed out in general comment No. 22 (48)'.[297] To those States which do not recognise the right to conscientious objection, the Committee sends a clear message, urging them to recognise the right of conscientious objectors to be exempted from military service.[298] Along with the concerns of the availability of conscientious objection to military service, the Committee sometimes shows its concerns over 'the allegation of widespread cruelty and ill-treatment of young conscript-soldiers'.[299] Nowadays numerous States no longer have compulsory military service. However, some States seem to be in between compulsory and voluntary military service and for such a

[294] Concluding observations for the third report of the Syrian Arab Republic, CCPR/CO/84/SYR, (9 August 2005) 4 [11].

[295] Concluding observations for the fifth report of Finland, CCPR/CO/82/FIN (2 December 2004) [14].

[296] Concluding observations of the Human Rights Committee on the third report of France, CCPR/C/79/Add.80 (4 August 1997) [19].

[297] Concluding observations of the Human Rights Committee for the fourth report of Spain, CCPR/C/79/Add.16 (3 April 1996) [15].

[298] Concluding observations of the Human Rights Committee for the initial report of Tajikistan, CCPR/CO/84/TJK (18 July 2005) 4 [20].

[299] Concluding observations of the Human Rights Committee for the fourth report of the Russian Federation, CCPR/C/79/Add.54 (26 July 1995) [21].

country the Committee is inclined to advise the establishment of a conscientious objection procedure. For instance, 'compulsory military service is a fallback applicable only when not enough professional soldiers can be recruited' in Morocco.[300] Therefore the Committee finds it necessary to urge the State party to 'fully recognize the right to conscientious objection in times of compulsory military service' (see Note 300) and to 'establish an alternative form of service, the terms of which should be non-discriminatory (Covenant, arts 18 and 26)' (see Note 300).

The Human Rights Committee's concluding observations following examination of the various States parties' reports submitted especially after 2000 show that the Committee's interests are extending to the treatment of conscientious objectors and the qualities of alternative service, especially in light of article 26, demanding equality before the law, of the International Covenant on Civil and Political Rights. Concerns about the lack of an independent decision-making process[301] and disproportionately lengthy alternative service continue to be raised.[302] The Human Rights Committee has recommended that States parties recognise the right of conscientious objection without discrimination,[303] recalling that 'conscientious objectors can opt for civilian service the duration of which is not discriminatory in relation to military service, in accordance with articles 18 and 26 of the Covenant'.[304]

The Committee is anxious about the length of alternative service for conscientious objectors, which may be much longer than military service.[305] The Committee is thus of the opinion that: '[t]he State party should ensure that the length of service alternative to military service does not have a punitive character, and should consider placing the assessment of applications for conscientious objector status under the control of civilian authorities' (see Note 305). The Committee refers not only to article 18 but also to article 26 with regard to the duration of alternative service

[300] Concluding observations for the fifth report of Morocco, CCPR/CO/82/MAR (1 December 2004) [22].

[301] *See* UN Doc E/CN.4/2006/51 (27 February 2006) 6 [13]; for example, concluding observations of the Human Rights Committee on: Israel, *Official Records of the General Assembly, 58th Session, Supplement No. 40* (A/58/40), vol. I [85].

[302] E/CN.4/2006/51 (27 February 2006) 6 [13]; for example, concluding observations of the Human Rights Committee on: Israel, *Official Records of the General Assembly, 58th Session, Supplement No. 40* (A/58/40), vol. I [85]. For example, concluding observations of the Human Rights Committee on: Latvia, CCPR/CO/79/LVA (6 November 2003) [15]; Georgia, *Official Records of the General Assembly, 57th Session, Supplement No. 40* (A/57/40), vol. I [78].

[303] Georgia, *Official Records of the General Assembly, 57th Session, Supplement No. 40* (A/57/40), vol. I [78].

[304] Georgia, *Official Records of the General Assembly, 57th Session, Supplement No. 40* (A/57/40), vol. I [18].

[305] *See* Concluding observations of the Human Rights Committee on the initial report of Greece, CCPR/CO/83/GRC (25 April 2005) 4 [15].

for conscientious objectors.[326,327] Especially with respect to article 26, the Committee states in the observations for the report prepared by Finland that Jehovah's Witnesses are granted preferential treatment by domestic law compared with other groups of conscientious objectors, and recommends that Finland review the law to bring it into full conformity with article 26 of the Covenant.[328]

With respect to the alternative service, the Committee also urges States parties to eradicate lengthy imprisonment 'as a form of punishment'.[329] This represents the trend of the concluding observations by the Committee of the late 1990s and the first decade of the twenty-first century. For example, the concluding observations on the initial report of Greece recommends that: '[t]he State party should ensure that the length of service alternative to military service does not have a punitive character'.[330] In another case it notes that while Russia had introduced alternative service for military service, its enforcement Act seemed to be punitive in nature by prescribing civil service of a length 1.7 times that of normal military service.[331] For Estonia, where the duration of alternative service for conscientious objectors may be up to twice as long as the duration of regular military service, the Committee also requests it to 'ensure that conscientious objectors can opt for alternative service, the duration of which is without punitive effect'.[332] Georgia also has double-length alternative service and the Committee expresses its concern at the discrimination suffered by conscientious objectors owing to the fact that non-military alternative

---

326 'The Committee is concerned over the unfair treatment accorded to conscientious objectors in Cyprus, who are subject to an excessive period of alternative service lasting 42 months, which is not compatible with the provisions of article 18 and 26 of the Covenant, and that persons may also be subject to punishment on one or more occasion for failure to perform military service'. Concluding observations of the Human Rights Committee on the second report by Cyprus, CCPR/C/79/Add.39 (3 August 1994) 3 [10] and *see also* Concluding observations of the Human Rights Committee, CCPR/C/79/Add.39; A/49/40 [312]–[333] (21 September 1994). *See also* Concluding observations of the Human Rights Committee on the fifth report of Columbia, CCPR/CO/80/COL (26 May 2004) [17].

327 'The Committee is concerned that the duration of alternative service for conscientious objectors may be up to twice as long as the duration of regular military service. The State party is under an obligation to ensure that conscientious objectors can opt for alternative service, the duration of which is without punitive effect (articles 18 and 26 of the Covenant)'. Concluding observations of the Human Rights Committee on the second periodic report of Estonia (15 April 2003) 4 [15].

328 Concluding observations of the Human Rights Committee on the fourth report of Finland, CCPR/C/79/Add.91 (8 April 1998) [21].

329 Concluding observations of the Human Rights Committee on the third report of Cyprus, CCPR/C/79/Add.88 (6 August 1998) [17].

330 Concluding observations of the Human Rights Committee on the first report of Greece, CCPR/CO/83/GRC (25 April 2005) [15]. *See also* Concluding observations of the Human Rights Committee on the fourth report of Yemen, CCPR/CO/84/YEM (9 August 2005) 5 [19].

331 Concluding observations of the Human Rights Committee on the fifth report of the Russian Federation, CCPR/CO/79/RUS (6 November 2003) [17].

332 Concluding observations of the Human Rights Committee on the second report of Estonia, CCPR/CO/77 (15 April 2003) [15].

service lasts for 36 months compared with 18 months for military service.[333] For Belarus, the Committee recommends that: 'a law exempting conscientious objectors from compulsory military service and providing for alternative civil service of equivalent length be passed at an early date in compliance with article 18 of the Covenant and the Committee's General Comment No. 22(48)'.[334]

In the concluding observations for Greece, the Committee has its say on the assessment of applications for alternative service as well. Thus the Committee recommended that Greece should consider placing the assessment of applications for conscientious objector status under the control of civilian authorities.[335]

The grounds for conscientious objection in law also gain the attention of the Committee. Thus, for Ukraine, the Committee observes that: '[t]he State party should widen the grounds for conscientious objection in law so that they apply, without discrimination, to all religious beliefs and other convictions and that they any alternative service required for conscientious objectors be performed in a non-discriminatory character'.[336]

The Committee argues that conscientious objection should be applied without discrimination among the grounds of conscience. Hence conscientious objection should be open to non-believers as well. For Kyrgyzstan it says that:

> The Committee takes note that conscientious objection to military service is allowed only to members of a registered religious organization whose teachings prohibit the use of arms. The Committee regrets that the State party has not sought to justify why the provision on alternative service entails a period of service twice as long as that required of military conscripts, and why persons of higher education serve for a considerably lesser period in the military and in alternative service (articles 18 and 26).[337] Conscientious objection should be provided for in law, in a manner that is consistent with articles 18 and 26 of the Covenant, bearing in mind that article 18 also protects freedom of conscience of non-believers. The State party should fix the periods of military service and alternative service on a non-discriminatory basis (see Note 337).

As of September 2006, Kyrgyzstan still appeared to have such a system of alternative military service according to the United States' Report on International Religious Freedom for 2006.[338] In short, the right to conscientious objection should

---

[333] Concluding observations of the Human Rights Committee on the second report of Georgia, CCPR/CP/74/GEO (19 April 2002) [18].

[334] Concluding observations of the Human Rights Committee on the fourth report of Belarus, CCPR/C/79/Add.86 (19 November 1997) [16].

[335] Concluding observations of the Human Rights Committee on the first report of Greece, CCPR/CO/83/GRC (25 April 2005) [15].

[336] Concluding observations of the Human Rights Committee on the fifth report of Ukraine, CCPR/CO/73/UKR (12 November 2001) [20].

[337] According to the International Religious Freedom Report prepared by the Bureau of Democracy, Human Rights and Labor of the United States Department of State, as of 2005 Kyrgyzstan still has the system of alternative military service for registered religious groups and 3,000 people annually apply.

Concluding observations of the Human Rights Committee on the initial report of the Kyrgyz Republic, CCPR/CO/69/KGZ (24 July 2000) [28].

[338] *See* http://www.state.gov/g/drl/rls/irf/2006/index.htm (last visited 10 April 2007).

be provided for without discrimination by a national law in accordance with articles 18 and 26 of the Covenant.[339] 'The fair treatment' of conscientious objectors under the law must be the key.[340]

2.3 Concluding Remarks

Article 8 has constituted interpretative impediment for the Human Rights Committee even though the travaux préparatoires do not support the construction deterring the Committee from recognising the right to conscientious objection. However the situation is gradually changing. Most significantly, the Committee now does not hesitate to urge States to recognise the right to conscientious objection at domestic level.

United Nations human rights law has been the best source of the right to conscientious objection to military service as an international human right. Not only has the United Nations produced a number of resolutions on the right to conscientious objection, but its enforcement mechanism has also produced international practices supporting the existence of such a right under international law. The Human Rights Committee has changed its attitude toward and interpretation of the right to conscientious objection to military service, unlike the invariant interpretation adopted by the European Court of Human Rights as we will see in the next chapter.

It is true that at the time of drafting the International Covenant on Civil and Political Rights there was no consensus on the right to conscientious objection under international law. However, the mere fact that the drafters of the Covenant do not seem to have contemplated the Covenant as giving rise to a generalised right to assert an objection to the performance of military service does not preclude the establishment of such a right for all time.[341] Therefore, at the very least international law recognises that treaty provisions such as article 18 of the Covenant can have a norm creating function informing the development of binding rules of customary international law.[342] One can see that this development in United Nations human rights law has great importance for the future development of international law on the issue of the right to conscientious objection as an international human right.

---

339 Concluding observations of the Human Rights Committee on the fourth report of Romania, CCPR/C/79/Add.111 (28 July 1999) [17].

340 Concluding observations of the Human Rights Committee on the third report of Cyprus, CCPR/C/79/Add.88 (6 August 1998) [17].

341 New Zealand Refugee Status Appeals Authority, Refugee Appeal No. 75378/05 (19 October 2005) [3].

342 New Zealand Refugee Status Appeals Authority, Refugee Appeal No. 75378/05 (19 October 2005) [3], citing the ICJ Judgment, *North Sea Continental Shelf Case, (Federal Republic of Germany v Denmark; Federal Republic of Germany v Netherlands)* [1969] ICJ Rep 3 [70]–[71].

References

Journal Article

Engram JM (1982) Conscientious objection to military service: a report to the United Nations division of human rights. Geo J Int Comp Law 12:359–398
Epstein AD (2002) The freedom of conscience and sociological perspectives on dilemmas of collective secular disobedience: the case of Israel. J Hum Right 1:305–320
Lebranc LJ (1996) Reservations to the rights of the child: A macroscopic view of State practice. Int J Child Right 4:357–381
Lippman M (1990/1991) The recognition of conscientious objection to military service as an international human right. Calif West Int Law J 21:31–66
Mann H (1987) International law and the child soldier. Int Comp Law Q 36(1):32–57
Major M (1992) Conscientious objection and international law. Case West Reserv J Int Law 24:349–378
Schaffer P, Weissbrodt D (1972) Conscientious objection to military service as a human right. Rev Int Comm Jurists 9:33–67
Sullivan RR (1970) Saudi Arabia in international politics. Rev Polit 32(4):436–460
Weissbrodt D (1988) The United Nations commission on Human Rights confirms conscientious objection to military service as a Human Right. Neth Int Law Rev 35:53–72

Book

Alfredsson G, Eide A (1999) The universal declaration of human rights: a common standard of achievement. Martinus Nijhoff Publishers, The Hague
Angel WD (1995) The international law of youth rights: source documents and commentary. Martinus Nijhoff Publishers, Dordrecht
Brems E (2006) A commentary on the United Nations convention on the rights of the child: Article 14: the right to freedom of thought, conscience and religion. Martinus Nijhoff Publishers, The Hague
Bossuyt MJ (1987) Guide to the 'travaux préparatoires' of the international covenant on civil and political rights. Martinus Nijhoff Publishers, Dordrecht
De Jong CD (2000) The freedom of thought, conscience and religion or belief in the United Nations (1946–1992). Intersentia, Antwerpen
Detrick S (ed) (1992) The United Nations convention on the rights of the child: a guide to the 'travaux préparatoires. Martinus Nijhoff Publishers, Dordrecht
Hammer L (2001) The international human right to freedom of conscience: Some suggestions for its development and application. Ashgate, Aldershot Jørgensen NHB (2000) The responsibility of States for international crimes. Oxford University Press, Oxford
Nowak M (2005) UN covenant on civil and political rights: CCPR commentary, 2nd rev edn. Kehl am Rhein, Engel, p. 421
Ouguergouz F (2003) The African charter on human and people's rights: a comprehensive agenda for human dignity and sustainable democracy in Africa. In: Sutcliffe H (Tr.). Martinus Nijhof Publishers, The Hague
Sunga LS (1992) Individual responsibility in international law for serious human rights violations. Martinus Nijhoff Publishers, Dordrecht
United Nations Yearbook (1958) Department of Public Information, United Nations, New York, p. 205

Yearbook of the United Nations (1977) vol. 31 Department of Public Information, United Nations, New York, pp. 732–733

Yearbook of the United Nations (1979) vol. 33 Department of Public Information, United Nations, New York, p. 864 and 893

UNHCR (1979) Handbook on procedures and criteria for determining refugee status. United Nations, pp. 51–53, 156 (re-edited 1992)

Van Bueren G (1995) The international law on the rights of the child. Martinus Nijhoff Publishers, The Hague

Vandewiele T (2006) A commentary on the United Nations convention on the rights of the child: optional protocol: the involvement of children in armed conflicts. Martinus Nijhoff Publishers, Leiden

Book Chapter

Brems E (2006) Article 14: The right to freedom of thought, conscience and religion. In: Alen A, Lanotte JV, Verhellen E, Ang F, Berghmans E, Verheyde M (eds) A commentary on the United Nations convention on the rights of the child. Martinus Nijhoff Publishers, Leiden, p. 14

Boyle K (1999) Freedom of thought, freedom of conscience, freedom of religion and freedom of belief as internationally protected rights: What is agreed and what is not agreed. In: Cotran E, Sherif AO (eds) Democracy, the rule of law and Islam. Boston, Kluwer, pp 373–392

Wessells M (2002) Recruitment of children as soldiers in sub-Saharan Africa: An ecological analysis. In: Mjøset L, Van Holde S (eds) The comparative study of conscription in the armed forces, comparative social research, vol. 20. Amsterdam, JAI, pp. 237–254

Other Reference

Eide A., Mubanga-Chipoya C. (1985) Conscientious Objection to Military Service, Report prepared in pursuance of resolutions 14 (XXXIV) and 1982/30 of the Sub-Commission on Prevention of Discrimination and Protection of Minorities, pp 4–7

Chapter 3
Right to Conscientious Objection in European Human Rights Law

Abstract Compared to the United Nations Human Rights Committee, the attitude of the European Court of Human Rights has shown only subtle changes over the years. Central to the positive position of the right to conscientious objection in the European human rights regime is the fact that the Council of Europe appears to consistently promote the right through their resolutions. The European Union has followed this position by expressly protecting the right to conscientious objection under Article 10(2) of the Charter of Fundamental Rights of December 2000. Despite the hesitant attitude of the European Court of Human Rights towards the recognition of the right to conscientious objection, the applications of individuals before the Court demands that it be more and more attentive to the treatment of conscientious objectors and the alternative service assigned to them. These tendencies can also be seen in the opinions of the Commissioner for Human Rights of the Council of Europe and the jurisprudence of the European Committee of Social Rights.

> Recalls that the ECHR advised Turkey to prepare a new legal framework for conscientious objectors and reminds Turkey that the right to conscientious objection is recognised in the EU Charter of Fundamental Rights; therefore welcomes the initiative by the Ministry of Justice to legalise the right to conscientious objection and to propose the introduction of an alternative service in Turkey; is concerned that in recent judgment of the Turkish military court a conscientious objector to military service was sentenced to imprisonment and that the military court openly declined to follow a relevant ruling of the ECHR; condemns the on-going persecution of journalists and writers who have expressed their support for the right of conscientious objection to military service.
>
> European Parliament Resolution on Turkey's Progress Towards Accession (2006).[1]

[1] INI/2006/2118, AFET/6/37036, (27 September 2006) [40].

H. Takemura, *International Human Right to Conscientious Objection to Military Service and Individual Duties to Disobey Manifestly Illegal Orders.*

3.1 European Human Rights Norms

In Europe the initiative to develop a regional understanding of the right to conscientious objection was identified as early as the 1960s by means of a Resolution by the Council of Europe.[2] The Charter of Fundamental Rights of the European Union, signed by the President in office of the Council of the European Union, the President of the European Commission and the President of the European Parliament on 12 December 2007, is among the first international human rights instruments to provide for the right to conscientious objection to military service.[3] Despite these achievements and its foresight, the European Court of Human Rights has hesitated to find that the right to conscientious objection to military service is derived from article 9 of the European Convention on Human Rights.

However the recent jurisprudence of the European Court of Human Rights show that the European Court of Human Rights is more conscious of how conscientious objectors or deserters in State parties.[4] Moreover the European Union's Charter of Fundamental Rights with the explicit provision of the right to conscientious objection was officially proclaimed by the European Union institutions in December 2007 and with Lisbon treaty the Charter has same legally binding character as the treaty itself to all EU institutions, bodies and member states applying community law, except for Poland and the United Kingdom, which were granted opt-outs.

3.1.1 Drafting the European Convention on Human Rights

Following the adoption of the Universal Declaration of Human Rights in December 1948, the Statute of the Council of Europe was signed by 10 European States[5] and the Council of Europe was established.[6] At the beginning of its first session, the Consultative Assembly of the Council of Europe proposed to include in its agenda the study of measures for the maintenance and further realisation of human rights and fundamental freedoms.[7] The Committee of the Ministers of the Council of Europe approved the inclusion of the agenda and decided to appoint a committee of governmental experts to prepare a draft Convention, 'due attention being paid to the

---

[2] Resolution 337 of the Committee of Ministers of the Council of Europe (1967).

[3] *See* Article 10(2) of the Charter of Fundamental Rights of the European Union, Official Journal of the European Communities, C/364/1, 2000/C 364/01 (18 December 2000).

[4] *See Thlimmenos v Greece* (App 34369/97) ECHR (December 4, 1998), Judgment (April 6, 2000); *Ülke v Turkey* (App 39437/98) ECHR (January 24, 2006).

[5] Namely, Belgium, Denmark, France, Ireland, Italy, Luxembourg, the Netherlands, Norway, Sweden and the United Kingdom.

[6] For a concise history of the drafting history of the European Convention on Human Rights, *see for example*, AH Robertson, 'The European Convention for the Protection of Human Rights' (1950) 27 BYBIL 145–163.

[7] For a concise history of the drafting history of the European Convention on Human Rights, *see for example*, AH Robertson, 'The European Convention for the Protection of Human Rights' (1950) 27 BYBIL 146.

progress achieved in this matter by the competent organs of the United Nations'.[8] The Consultative Assembly held a general debate on human rights and a proposal was made for the establishment of an organisation within the Council of Europe to ensure the collective guarantee of human rights (Robertson 1950, p. 146). This proposal was eventually referred to the Committee on Legal and Administrative Questions, presided over by Sir David Maxwell Fyfe and Pierre-Henri Teitgen as *rapporteur* (Robertson 1950, p. 146). In approaching the general problem of the definition of rights and liberties which are to be guaranteed, the Committee considered that it was preferable to make use, as far as possible, of the definitions set out in the Universal Declaration of Human Rights recently approved by the United Nations General Assembly.[9] The Committee thus based itself, as far as possible, on this document, and referred to both articles 4 (freedom from slavery or servitude) and 9 (right to freedom of thought, conscience and religion) in drafting the Convention.[10]

Following the adoption of the Universal Declaration of Human Rights in December 1948, the Statute of the Council of Europe was signed by ten European States[11] and the Council of Europe was established. At the beginning of its first session, the Consultative Assembly of the Council of Europe proposed to include in its agenda the study of measures for the maintenance and further realisation of human rights and fundamental freedoms.[12] The Committee of the Ministers of the Council of Europe approved the inclusion of the agenda and decided to appoint a committee of governmental experts to prepare a draft Convention, 'due attention being paid to the progress achieved in this matter by the competent organs of the United Nations'.[13] The Consultative Assembly held a general debate on human rights and a proposal was made for the establishment of an organisation within the Council of Europe to ensure the collective guarantee of human rights (Robertson 1950, p. 146). This proposal was eventually referred to the Committee on Legal and Administrative Questions, presided over by Sir David Maxwell Fyfe and Pierre-Henri Teitgen as *rapporteur* (Robertson 1950, p. 146). In approaching the general problem of the definition of rights and liberties which are to be guaranteed, the Committee considered that it was preferable to make use, as far as possible, of the definitions set out in the Universal Declaration of Human Rights recently approved by the United Nations General Assembly (see Note 9). The Committee thus based itself, as far as possible, on this document, and referred to both articles 4 (freedom from slavery or

---

[8] The Council of Europe, *Collected Edition of the 'Travaux Préparatoires' Vol. I, Preparatory Commission of the Council of Europe, Committee of Ministers, Consultative Assembly, 11 May–8 September 1949* (Martinus Nijhoff Publishers, The Hague 1975) xxvi.

[9] The Council of Europe, *Collected Edition of the 'Travaux Préparatoires'* Vol. I, 194 [6].

[10] The Council of Europe, *Collected Edition of the 'Travaux Préparatoires'* Vol. I, 196 [8].

[11] Namely, Belgium, Denmark, France, Ireland, Italy, Luxembourg, the Netherlands, Norway, Sweden and the United Kingdom.

[12] The Council of Europe, *Collected Edition of the 'Travaux Préparatoires'* Vol. I, 146.

[13] The Council of Europe, *Collected Edition of the 'Travaux Préparatoires' Vol. I, Preparatory Commission of the Council of Europe, Committee of Ministers, Consultative Assembly, 11 May–8 September 1949* (Martinus Nijhoff Publishers, The Hague 1975) xxvi.

servitude) and 9 (right to freedom of thought, conscience and religion) in drafting the Convention (see Note 10).

Since the Consultative Assembly is the deliberative organ of the Council and has no powers of decision but makes recommendations to the Committee of Ministers according to the Statute of the Council of Europe, the Consultative Assembly submitted its proposal to the Committee of Ministers (Robertson 1950, pp. 147–148). In turn, the Committee of Ministers decided to appoint a committee of government experts to prepare a draft Convention (Robertson 1950, pp. 148).

Right from the beginning of the discussion of the Committee of Experts, certain members, represented by the United Kingdom, considered that the fundamental rights to be safeguarded and the limitations of these rights should be defined in the Convention in as detailed a manner as possible.[14] The United Kingdom representative felt that it would be impossible for States to undertake to respect rights which had not been defined with sufficient precision.

The text of a preliminary draft Convention was, therefore, drawn up on the basis of the Consultative Assembly's draft during the first phase of the Committee's work. On 6 March 1950, the Government of the United Kingdom sent to the governments of Member States the text of 15 articles, containing for the most part definitions of human rights.[15] These articles were intended to amend articles 1, 2, 4, 5, 6, 8 and 9 of the preliminary draft drawn up by the Committee. These recommended provisions were in line with the wording of the International Covenant of Civil and Political Rights, which was still being drafted, and the proposed articles 6 (exemption from slavery and servitude) and 11 (right to freedom of thought, conscience and religion) are also similar to the provisions of the International Covenant on Civil and Political Rights in their final form.[16]

The Committee decided, after examination of the proposal by the United Kingdom and the draft by the Assembly, that it was impossible to amalgamate the text of

---

[14] The Council of Europe, *Collected Edition of the 'Travaux Préparatoires'* Vol. IV, 8.

[15] The Council of Europe, *Collected Edition of the 'Travaux Préparatoires'* Vol. III, 280, Vol. IV, 14 and 16.

[16] Article 6

1) No one shall be held in slavery or servitude.
2) No one shall be required to perform forced or compulsory labour.
3) For the purpose of this article, the term 'forced or compulsory labour' shall not include:
    a) any work required to be done in the ordinary course of detention imposed by the lawful order of a court;
    b) any service of a military character or service in the case of conscientious objectors exacted in virtue of compulsory military service laws;
    c) any service exacted in case of emergency or calamity threatening the life or well-being of the community;
    d) any work or service which forms part of normal civic obligations.

Article 11 -

1) Everyone shall have the right to freedom of thought and to freedom of expression without governmental interference; these rights shall include freedom to hold opinions and to receive and impart information and ideas without governmental interference regardless of frontiers, either orally, in writing or in print, in the form of art or by duly licensed visual or auditory devices.

the articles defining human rights in the United Kingdom's proposals and the text of the articles listing these rights in the Assembly's draft, since the system on which these two drafts were based were essentially different.[17] No particular comments were made by the United Kingdom representative with regard to its draft article 3 (exemption from slavery and servitude). As for draft article 9 (freedom of thought, conscience and religion), the United Kingdom commentary did not relate to the issue of the right to conscientious objection.[18]

The Conference of Senior Officials met in June 1950 and prepared a draft Convention incorporating the greater part of the texts submitted by the legal experts. This draft adopted a compromise formula on the question of the enumeration or definition of human rights, and proposed the creation of a European Court with optional jurisdiction.[19]

Based on the report prepared by the Senior Officials together with the comments of the Assembly's Legal Committee, the Committee of Ministers adopted a revised text of the draft Convention on 7 August 1950 (Robertson 1950, p. 148). Although the draft was passed to the Consultative Assembly and was considered and approved there, the Committee of Ministers was unable to accept the amendments proposed by the Consultative Assembly (Robertson 1950, p. 149). The Convention was signed substantially in the form approved by the Committee of Ministers in August 1950.[20]

The European Convention on Human Rights was signed on 4 November 1950 and entered into force on 3 September 1953. This was the first regional and to some extent international legal instrument safeguarding human rights. The completed European Convention on Human Rights referred to the collective enforcement of the Universal Declaration of Human Rights adopted by the General Assembly of the United Nations on 10 December 1948 through the adoption of the European Convention of Human Rights.[21]

The provisions on the right to freedom of thought, conscience and religion in the Universal Declaration of Human Rights and the European Convention on Human Rights are almost identical. This may be due to the fact that both were drafted and made only two years apart and that many of the authors were the same people. With clear memories of the atrocities committed in the Second World War, the 15 Member

---

2) The exercise of these freedoms carries with it duties and responsibilities and may therefore be subject to such penalties, liabilities, and restrictions as are prescribed by law and are necessary in the interests of national security or public safety, for the prevention of disorder or crime, for the protection of health or morals, for the protection of the reputations or rights of other persons, for preventing the disclosure of information received in confidence, or for maintaining the authority and impartiality of the judiciary.

[17] The Council of Europe, *Collected Edition of the 'Travaux Préparatoires'* Vol. IV, 16.

[18] The Council of Europe, *Collected Edition of the 'Travaux Préparatoires'* Vol. IV, 32. According to the representative of the United Kingdom, the end of article 9(2) 'was intended to cover those reasonable restrictions on the eligibility for public office of members of certain religious faiths which are prescribed in the constitutions of certain States and which, it was recognised, could not be removed immediately'.

[19] The Council of Europe, *Collected Edition of the 'Travaux Préparatoires'* Vol. I. xxvi.

[20] The Council of Europe, *Collected Edition of the 'Travaux Préparatoires'* Vol. I. xxviii.

[21] The European Convention on Human Rights [2] [3] and [6].

States of the Council of Europe drafted the Convention expeditiously (Scheib 1997, pp. 103–104).

3.1.2 Silence of the Travaux Préparatoires of the European Convention on Human Rights with Respect to Conscientious Objection

The *travaux préparatoires* of the European Convention on Human Rights do not reveal any arguments on the issue of conscientious objection. This may be partly due to the circumstances in which the Convention was drafted. As mentioned above (Sect. 3.1.2.1.2), the Convention followed the Universal Declaration of Human Rights and the International Covenant on Civil and Political Rights which was then in the drafting stage.

While article 4(3)(b) mentions ‘conscientious objectors’ in the context of the exemption of forced labour, the more relevant provision for the topic of conscientious objection, namely article 9, does not directly touch upon conscientious objection. For article 9, too, the *travaux préparatoires* are of no help (Decker and Fresa 2001, p. 393). Article 9 originated from the proposal by the United Kingdom.

Decker and Fresa interpret this silence of the *travaux préparatoires* as follows:

> It is the authors’ belief that irrespective of the interpretation of Article 4 by the Commission, the drafters did not want to decide this question definitively either way. One must keep in mind that the drafters were seeking to develop a list of rights that were essential to ensure democracy and human dignity. They wanted the list to include only rights which were currently recognized by the countries of Europe. While none of the rights were supposed to be ‘aspirational,’ they did not want the Convention to be so narrow as to deprive rights either. Taking all these points into consideration, *conscientious objection was an issue that the drafters probably wanted left to be decided at another time* (emphasis added) (Decker and Fresa 2001, pp. 397–398).

Additionally one should note that the *travaux préparatoires* of the Convention do not even clearly state that the drafters chose to remain silent on the issue of conscientious objection. This may reveal the fact that at the time of drafting the Convention, at the end of the 1940s and in 1950, the issue of conscientious objection may not have been recognised as an international phenomenon or a matter of international human rights instead of a domestic phenomenon. Behind this perception, there was the fact that in the aftermath of the two World Wars there was less sympathy for the issue of conscientious objection than there would be later, such as at the time of the Vietnam War.

3.1.3 Resolutions by the Council of Europe

In spite of the silence on the right to conscientious objection in the European Convention on Human Rights, an attempt to establish an international right to conscientious objection started with Europe (Lippman 1990/1991, p. 46). The

Council of Europe Parliamentary Assembly adopted its first Resolution and recommendation on the right of conscientious objection in 1967, with Resolution 337[22] and Recommendation 478,[23] respectively.[24] Resolution 337 was based upon the Report on the Right of Conscientious Objection presented to the Assembly by the Legal Committee.[25] The adoption of Resolution 337, in 1967, coincides with the height of the Vietnam War.

The Resolution clearly recognises conscientious objection as a human right: 'Persons liable to conscription for military service who, for reasons of conscience or profound conviction arising from religious, ethical, moral, humanitarian, philosophical or similar motives, refuse to perform armed service shall enjoy a personal right to be released from the obligation to perform such service.'[26] Philosophical motive as a ground of conscientious objection deserves attention, since resolutions and recommendations of other European and international institutions normally enumerate only 'religious, moral, ethical and humanitarian' motives as examples of grounds of conscientious objection. The Assembly, furthermore, clearly stated in the same Resolution that the right to conscientious objection shall be regarded as deriving logically from the fundamental rights of the individual in democratic rule of law States which are guaranteed in article 9 of the European Convention on Human Rights, that is the individual's freedom of conscience and religion.[27] The Assembly was ambitious enough to suggest prescribing this right in a Convention or a recommendation to governments and modifying national legislation to be in line with the principles adopted by the Resolution of the Assembly. The Assembly thus recommended that the Committee of Ministers 'instruct the Committee of Experts on Human Rights to formulate proposals to give effect to the principles laid down by the Assembly in its Resolution 337 by means of a Convention or a recommendation to Governments so that the right of conscientious objection may be firmly implanted in all member States of the Council of Europe'.[28] All of these European efforts eventually stimulated a similar effort within the United Nations (Lippman 1990/1991, p. 46).

The Committee of Ministers declined to act pursuant to the Assembly's recommendation: first of all, because several States had already settled the problem of conscientious objection in the framework of their domestic law; secondly, other States were unable to envisage amending their law for various reasons; and thirdly,

[22] Resolution 337 (1967), on the Right of Conscientious Objection, Assembly Debate on 26th January 1967 (22nd Sitting) (*See* Doc 2170, Report of the Legal Committee), text adopted by the Assembly on 26th January 1967, 22nd Sitting.

[23] Recommendation 478 (1967), on the Right of Conscientious Objection, Assembly Debate on 26th January 1967 (22nd Sitting). *See also* Doc 2170, Report of the Legal Committee, text adopted by the Assembly on 26th January 1967, 22nd Sitting.

[24] *Cf.* Report of the High Commissioner submitted pursuant to Commission Resolution 2000/34, (14 March 2002) UN Doc E/CN.4/2002/WP.2 [19].

[25] Report of the Legal Committee, Eur. Consult. Ass., 18th Session, Doc. No. 2170 (1967). *See* Engram (1982, p. 359, 365).

[26] Resolution 337 (1967) [1].

[27] Interestingly, to date the European Court of Human Rights has not tried to deduce the right to conscientious objection from article 9. *See* arguments below.

[28] Recommendation 478 (1967) [1].

several Member States, while supporting the idea behind Recommendation 478, were sceptical about the possibility of reaching an international agreement on the subject by means of action in the Council of Europe.[29] Moreover, there were doubts among some Member States that the actions of the Council of Europe could lead to the achievement of an international agreement on conscientious objection (Lippman 1990/1991, p. 47).

Despite this inaction of the Committee of Ministers, in 1977 the Parliamentary Assembly passed a recommendation similar to the 1967 recommendation.[30] Its appendix almost literally restates the principles set out in Resolution 337. There are noteworthy differences between the 1967 recommendation and the 1977 recommendation, however. The latter especially focused on the governments of Member States which have not introduced a conscientious objection system into domestic law and urged them to bring their legislation into line with the principles adopted in the 1967 Resolution. Recommendation 816 of 1977 additionally recommended that the Committee of Ministers introduce the right of conscientious objection to military service into the European Convention on Human Rights.[31] Again, the Ministers did not take any action following the recommendation of the Parliamentary Assembly, concluding they were not in a position at the time to act on the recommendation for the same reasons as applied to Recommendation 478 of 1967.[32]

The Committee of Ministers finally took action towards recognition of the right to conscientious objection by adopting Recommendation R(87) 8 in 1987.[33] Although the recommendation did not suggest the necessity of European legislation to protect conscientious objection to military service as an international human right, it stated that '[w]ishing that conscientious objection to compulsory military service be recognized in all the member states of the Council of Europe and governed by common principles'.[34]

A few key changes exist between the principles relating to the right to conscientious objection to military service adopted by the Consultative Assembly of the Council of Europe in Resolution 337 of 1967 and the one adopted by the Committee of Ministers in Recommendation R(87) 8 of 1987, while the 1967 and the 1977 Resolutions were both adopted by the Assembly, so that the recommendations are virtually identical. The first retrograde change is that Recommendation R(87) 8 confines its recognition of a right to conscientious objection to 'compelling

[29] Nineteenth Report of the Committee of Ministers to the Consult. Ass., Eur. Consult. Ass., Doc 2359 (1967) 159–160 (regarding recommendation 478).

[30] Recommendation 816 (1977), on the Right of Conscientious Objection to Military Service, Assembly Debate on 7 October 1977 (10th Sitting) (*See* Doc 4027, report of the Legal Affairs Committee). Text adopted by the Assembly on 7 October 1977, 10th Sitting.

[31] Recommendation 816 (1977) [4(b)].

[32] Communication on the Activities of the Committee of Ministers, Eur. 4197, Parl. Ass., 30th Session. Doc 4197 (1978) 2 (regarding Recommendation 816).

[33] Committee of Ministers of the Council of Europe, Recommendation No. R(87) 8 of 9 April 1987 regarding Conscientious Objection to Compulsory Military Service.

[34] Committee of Ministers of the Council of Europe, Recommendation No. R(87) 8 of 9 April 1987 regarding Conscientious Objection to Compulsory Military Service. preambular paragraph [7].

reasons of conscience', avoiding any exemplification of the grounds of conscientious objection.[35] The second retrograde change is that Recommendation R87(8) did not explicitly recognise that the right to conscientious objection is logically derived from the fundamental human rights guaranteed in article 9 of the European Convention on Human Rights, namely the right to freedom of thought, conscience and religion, unlike both Resolution 337 of 1967 and Recommendation 816 of 1977.

Nevertheless, Recommendation R87(8) presents progressive guidelines with regard to alternative service. Firstly, the interest of alternative service 'shall be in principle civilian and in the public interest',[36] though there is a proviso which permits States to provide for unarmed military service 'in addition to civilian services' for those 'whose objections are restricted to the personal use of arms'.[37] Secondly, as for the nature of the service, '[a]lternative service shall not be of a punitive nature'.[38] The importance of the introduction of alternative civilian service for persons who refuse to perform military service is so fundamental to Recommendation R(87) 8 that the European Committee of Social Rights regarded the introduction of alternative civilian service by Greece as progress in the implementation of Recommendation R(87) 8 in the case of *The Quaker Council for European Affairs (QCEA) v Greece*.[39]

The next major step taken by the Council of Europe occurred in relation to the crisis in the former Yugoslavia in the mid-1990s. The number of men who fled the former Yugoslavia because they refused to take part in the fighting is estimated to be at least 100,000.[40] While some of them were arrested, prosecuted, sentenced and imprisoned as a result of conscientious objection to military service, others fled to another country or became internally displaced for fear of severe penalties. After receiving the report by the *Rapporteur* to the Council of Europe Parliamentary Assembly in June 1994,[41] the Parliamentary Assembly adopted Resolution 1042(1994)1 on deserters and draft resisters from the former Yugoslavia.[42] The Assembly, in this Resolution, recalls its Recommendation 816 of 1977 on the right

[35] Committee of Ministers of the Council of Europe, Recommendation No. R(87) 8 of 9 April 1987 regarding Conscientious Objection to Compulsory Military Service. preambular paragraph [1].

[36] Committee of Ministers of the Council of Europe, Recommendation No. R(87) 8 of 9 April 1987 regarding Conscientious Objection to Compulsory Military Service. preambular paragraph [9].

[37] Committee of Ministers of the Council of Europe, Recommendation No. R(87) 8 of 9 April 1987 regarding Conscientious Objection to Compulsory Military Service. preambular paragraph [7].

[38] Committee of Ministers of the Council of Europe, Recommendation No. R(87) 8 of 9 April 1987 regarding Conscientious Objection to Compulsory Military Service. preambular paragraph [1].

[39] Complaint No. 8/2000, *The Quaker Council for European Affairs (QCEA) v Greece*, the European Commission of Social Rights (ECSR), committee of independent experts established under article 25 of the European Social Charter, during its 177th Session [19] (13 February, 13 March, 14 March and 25 April 2001).

[40] Resolution 1042 (1994) 1 on deserters and draft resisters from the republics of the former Yugoslavia, 1 July 1994 (23rd Sitting) [5].

[41] CE Doc 7102, 10 June 1994.

[42] Resolution 1042 (1994) 1 on deserters and draft resisters from the republics of the former Yugoslavia, 1 July 1994 (23rd Sitting).

of conscientious objection to military service, which it regards as a human right.[43] The Assembly deplores the fact that neither Croatia nor the Federal Republic of Yugoslavia recognise this right in practice and both severely punish men refusing to take part in military operations which have been condemned by the international community as serious violations of humanitarian law, particularly 'ethnic cleansing'.[44] The report by the *Rapporteur*, the precursor to Resolution 1042 (1994) 1, reached the conclusion with regard to deserters and draft resisters from the former Yugoslavia at an earlier stage of the conflicts in the region that 'refusal to take part in a fratricidal war condemned by the international community because of serious violations of international humanitarian law in the former Yugoslavia should be considered as grounds for granting asylum'.[45] The Assembly considered establishing a conscientious objector status and granting amnesties for deserters and draft resisters from Croatia as a condition for Croatia's application for membership of the Council of Europe.[46]

Such strong words and positive action by the countries of Europe may have been either atonement or strange irony for what the Western countries did in the process of encouraging many conscientious objectors in the former Yugoslavia, since most countries belonging to the Council of Europe also belong to the North Atlantic Treaty Organisation. Millions of leaflets dropped by NATO aircraft over various parts of the Federal Republic of Yugoslavia must have had some causal influence on the great number of conscientious objectors arising out of the Kosovo conflict. The NATO countries have been blamed for their indifference to the uncertain future of conscientious objectors and their families.[47]

The shortcomings of Recommendation R87(8) were more or less overcome by Recommendation 1518 of 2001, which the Standing Committee, acting on behalf of the Parliamentary Assembly of the Council of Europe, issued on 23 May 2001.[48] First of all, the Assembly noted that: 'the exercise of the right of conscientious objection to military service has been an on-going concern of the Council of Europe for over 30 years'. Secondly, the Assembly regarded the right to freedom of thought, conscience and religion enshrined in the Universal Declaration of Human Rights and the European Convention on Human Rights as 'a fundamental aspect' of conscientious objection.[49] These improvements can be referred from State practices described in paragraph 3: '[m]ost Council of Europe member states have introduced

---

[43] Resolution 1042 (1994) 1 on deserters and draft resisters from the republics of the former Yugoslavia, 1 July 1994 (23rd Sitting) [7].

[44] Resolution 1042 (1994) 1 on deserters and draft resisters from the republics of the former Yugoslavia, 1 July 1994 (23rd Sitting) [8].

[45] CE Doc 7102, 10 June 1994.

[46] Resolution 1042 (1994)1 on deserters and draft resisters from the republics of the former Yugoslavia, 1 July 1994 (23rd Sitting) [14(i)] and [14(ii)].

[47] Amnesty International, Report, 'Federal Republic of Yugoslavia: the Forgotten Resisters: the Plight of Conscientious Objectors to Military Service after the Conflict in Kosovo' (October 1999).

[48] Recommendation 1518 (2001), adopted by the Standing Committee, acting on behalf of the Council of Europe, 23 May 2001 (*see* Doc 8809).

[49] Recommendation 1518 (2001), adopted by the Standing Committee, acting on behalf of the Council of Europe, 23 May 2001 (*see* Doc 8809) [2].

the right of conscientious objection into their constitutions or legislation. There are only five member states where this right is not recognised' (see Note 49). The Recommendation urged that the situation of conscientious objector is 'wholly unsatisfactory' even in Member States having recognised the right of conscientious objection, since the position of conscientious objectors still differs considerably from one country to another.[50] For ensuring the right to conscientious objection in the framework of the European Convention on Human Rights, the Committee on Legal Affairs and Human Rights of the Council of Europe recommended the incorporation of the right of conscientious objection to military service into the European Convention on Human Rights 'by means of a protocol amending arts. 4.3(b) and 9'.[51]

The five Member States which did not recognise the right of conscientious objection at the time of Recommendation 1518 were enumerated in the report prepared by the *Rapporteur* of the Committee on Legal Affairs and Human Rights presented on 4 May 2001. Those member states are Albania, Armenia, Azerbaijan, the Former Yugoslav Republic of Macedonia and Turkey.[52] The report further noted that Russia and Cyprus were also not free from problems on the right to conscientious objection to military service. Although the Russian Constitution of April 1992 recognised the right of conscientious objection, there was no legitimate alternative civilian service available in Russia.[53] Cyprus was blamed by the United Nations Commission on Human Rights for having convicted and imprisoned objectors who persistently refuse to perform any service, and for severe penalties and long periods of alternative service.[54]

In June 2002, the Directorate General of Human Rights of the Council of Europe published a booklet titled 'Conscientious objection to compulsory military service'.[55] This booklet is to 'make the authorities and the public at large aware of the problems currently raised in Europe by conscientious objection to compulsory military service and of the solution needed at international and national level'.[56] This must be a useful tool not only for European citizens who would like to invoke

---

50 Recommendation 1518 (2001), adopted by the Standing Committee, acting on behalf of the Council of Europe, 23 May 2001 (*see* Doc 8809) [4].

51 Recommendation 1518 (2001), adopted by the Standing Committee, acting on behalf of the Council of Europe, 23 May 2001 (*see* Doc 8809) [6].

52 Doc 8809 revised, 'Exercise of the right of conscientious objection to military service in Council of Europe member states', *Rapporteur*: Dick Marty, Committee on Legal Affairs and Human Rights (4 May 2001) II, B [5].

53 Doc 8809 revised, 'Exercise of the right of conscientious objection to military service in Council of Europe member states', *Rapporteur*: Dick Marty, Committee on Legal Affairs and Human Rights (4 May 2001) II, B [11]. This is also suggested in the Concluding Observations of the Human Rights Committee of the United Nations, UN Doc CCPR/C/79/Add.54 (26 July 1995) [21].

54 Doc 8809 revised, II, B [11].

55 Director General of Human Rights, 'Conscientious objection to compulsory military service' (Council of Europe, June 2002) available at <http://www.coe.int/T/E/Human_rights/objcone.pdf> accessed 8 February 2006.

56 'Conscientious objection to compulsory military service', 3.

the right to conscientious objection to military service but for conscientious objectors all over the world, even though its contents in eight pages are relatively brief and mainly focus on the development of this right in documents of the Council of Europe. The efforts of the Council of Europe on the issue of the right to conscientious objection as a human right have now become steady, almost 50 years since the first effort was made.

3.1.4 Charter of Fundamental Rights of European Union

The efforts of the European Union to recognise the right to conscientious objection came to a climax with the Charter of Fundamental Rights of the European Union. The Charter is the first regional, and therefore to some extent international, human rights instrument explicitly recognising the right to conscientious objection as part of the right to freedom of conscience.[57] The Charter was proclaimed on 7 December 2000 during the Nice Council by the European Commission, the European Parliament and the Council of the European Union. The Charter was incorporated in the draft EU Constitution. It is an authoritative statement of general principle of European human rights law, although it has been without any binding effect due to the prolonged and uncertain ratification procedures of some Member States of the European Union. Accordingly, it remains without any binding effect. Both the European Court of Justice[58] and the European Parliament[59] have nevertheless made reference to the Charter.

On 23 June 2007, the European Council decided to break the stalemate concerning the fate of the EU Constitution and basically abandoned the idea of a constitution.[60] Accordingly, the new treaty was planned by an intergovernmental

[57] *See* article 10 (freedom of thought, conscience and religion), paragraph 2, 'The right to conscientious objection is recognised, in accordance with the national laws governing the exercise of this right'. Official Journal of the European Communities, C/364/1, 2000/C 364/01 (18 December 2000).

[58] For example, *Parliament v Council*, Case No. C-540/03, Judgment (27 June 2006) [38]: 'The Charter was solemnly proclaimed by the Parliament, the Council and the Commission in Nice on 7 December 2000. While the Charter is not a legally binding instrument, the Community legislature did, however, acknowledge its importance by stating, in the second recital in the preamble to the Directive, that the Directive observes the principles recognised not only by Article 8 of the European Convention on Human Rights but also in the Charter. Furthermore, the principal aim of the Charter, as is apparent from its preamble, is to reaffirm "rights as they result, in particular, from the constitutional traditions and international obligations common to the Member States, the Treaty on European Union, the Community Treaties, the [ECHR], the Social Charters adopted by the Community and by the Council of Europe and the case-law of the Court... and of the European Court of Human Rights"'.

[59] For example, Freedom of Expression and Information, European Parliament Resolution on the Risk of Violation, in the EU and especially in Italy, of Freedom of Expression and Information (Article 11(2) of the Charter of Fundamental Rights) (2003/2237 (INI)) adopted on 30 March 2004.

[60] *See* Council of the European Union, Presidency Conclusion, 1177/07 (23 June 2007). <http://www.consilium.europa.eu/ueDocs/cms_Data/docs/pressData/en/ec/94932.pdf> accessed 4 July 2007) 15 [1].

conference. The Charter of Fundamental Rights of the European Union was signed by the leaders of the European Parliament, the Council of the European Union and the European Commission. The Treaty of Lisbon which was signed by the Heads of State and Government on 13 December 2007 confers on the Charter the same legally binding character as the Treaties themselves. However the United Kingdom and Poland opted out the Charter by the Protocol annexed to the Lisbon Treaty.

The Charter is clearly a welcome development along with the recent development of the right to conscientious objection in international law. The Commentary written by the EU Network of Independent Experts on Fundamental Rights, set up by the European Commission, wrote that: 'The right to conscientious objection to military service, which is recognised in article 10(2) of the EU Charter, has no equivalent in the European Convention for the Protection of Human Rights and Fundamental Freedoms (the European Convention on Human Rights) but it is increasingly accepted in international human rights law. According to the official explanations of the Charter, article 10(2) reflects national constitutional traditions and developments in domestic law'.[61] The draft Charter of Fundamental Rights of the European Union is also in the same vein. It states that: 'the right to conscientious objection guaranteed in paragraph 2 corresponds to national constitutional traditions and to the developments of national legislation on this issue'.[62]

The attitude of the European Union on the issue of the right to conscientious objection became very clear when the European Union 'urge[d] all countries concerned to recognise the rights of conscientious objectors' at the OSCE Human Dimension Implementation Meeting 2006.[63] The European Union noted the importance of the relevant resolutions of the United Nations and considers that: 'there ought to be arrangements for conscientious objectors to fulfil alternative, non-military service, which should not be of a punitive nature'.[64] The European Union also noted the punitive treatments of conscientious objectors by several countries, such as Azerbaijan and Turkmenistan (see Note 64).

3.2 The European Commission of Human Rights and the European Court of Human Rights

Whereas the enforcement mechanism of the European Convention on Human Rights comes into play only after an exhaustion of domestic remedies, the enforcement bodies, namely the European Commission of Human Rights and the European

---

[61] The EU Network of Independent Experts on Fundamental Rights, Commentary of the Charter of the European Union (June 2006) 106.

[62] Draft Charter of Fundamental Rights of the European Union, (Brussels, 11 October 2000) Charter 4473/00 (18.10) Convent 49, 13.

[63] EU Statement for Working Session 13: Fundamental Freedoms II, OSCE Human Dimension Implementation Meeting 2006 (10 October 2006, Warsaw) HDIM.DEL/412/06 (10 October 2006) 2.

[64] HDIM.DEL/412/06 (10 October 2006), 2.

Court of Human Rights, have taken an important part in the normative development of international human rights law. This holds true especially because the Court is the longest standing international human rights court (Steiner and Alston 2000, p. 808). The Commission and the Court have received a number of petitions regarding conscientious objection to military service. Neither the European Commission of Human Rights nor the European Court of Human Rights have directly upheld military conscientious objection as a right. Moreover, both have declined to find a violation of article 9 of the European Convention on Human Rights, even though article 9, stipulating freedom of thought, conscience and religion, seems to be 'the most obvious article' to deal with the right to conscientious objection (Decker and Fresa 2001, p. 381).

3.2.1 Earlier Individual Petitions

Although there has been an emerging trend in Strasbourg to recognise conscientious objection as a legitimate exemption to military conscription or military draft (Decker and Fresa 2001, pp. 380–381), it may be too early to be optimistic about the attitude of Strasbourg on the issue of conscientious objection. It is also said that: 'Historically, in some European States, military service was expected of all able-bodied young men and no exemptions on the basis of conscience were permitted' (Evans 2001, p. 170). This may be the historical and cultural background that accounts for the hesitance of recognition of this right by the European Court of Human Rights. The European Court of Human Rights has taken a more conservative attitude than the Human Rights Committee. Unlike the Human Rights Committee, the European Court of Human Rights does not have the system of 'general comments' which enabled the Human Rights Committee to shift its attitude. The attitude of the European Court of Human Rights followed the practices of the European Commission on Human Rights, and did not show any progressive attitude on the right to conscientious objection. Nonetheless, future progress may be expected since the Charter of Fundamental Rights of the European Union upholds the right to conscientious objection in article 10(2) 'in accordance with the national laws governing the exercise of this right'.[65]

While the Council of Europe and the European Union are two different international organs, both prioritise respect for human rights of individuals in their Member States. Thus synergistic efforts of protection of human rights in Europe are expected, though the fear of the diverging interpretations of human rights in Europe is real.[66] The Venice Commission, studying the implications of the incorporation of the EU Charter of Fundamental Rights in regard to the European Convention on Human Rights by the Parliamentary Assembly of the Council of Europe, opines that certain

[65] Charter of Fundamental Rights of the EU 2000/C 364/01 (18 December 2000).

[66] See for example, Opinion No. 256/2003 of the European Commission for Democracy through law (Venice Commission) *on "The Implications of a legally-binding EU Charter of Fundamental Rights on Human Rights Protection in Europe"*.

rights guaranteed by the Charter are not listed in the European Convention on Human Rights, but have been recognised by the case-law of the European Court as being encompassed by it.[67] Judges of the European Court of Human Rights have already held in their joint concurring opinion in the judgment of Grand Chamber in *Bosphorus Hava Yollari Turizm Ve Ticaret Anonim Sirketi v. Ireland* that in order to avoid any danger of double standards between the Court and the European Union law, the Court is necessary to remain vigilant.[68]

The European Commission on Human Rights, which was functioning until 31 October 1999, had hesitated to find a violation of article 9, which deals with freedom of thought, conscience and religion, with regard to conscientious objection (Decker and Fresa 2001, p. 381). Instead, the European Commission on Human Rights had addressed conscientious objection through article 4. Article 4(3)(b) is similar to article 8(3)(c)(ii) of the International Covenant on Civil and Political Rights. The European Commission on Human Rights and the European Court of Human Rights, in numerous admissibility decisions, have both found it unnecessary to examine a right to conscientious objection under article 9 on account of the wording of article 4(3)(b), 'in countries where they are recognized'.[69] Eventually the Commission and the Court 'have adopted an approach concerning conscientious objection cases by interpreting article 4, in effect, to supersede article 9 (Decker and Fresa 2001, p. 381).' Thus the European Court of Human Rights has qualified article 9 by the terms of article 4 (Hammer 2001, p. 193).

The *Grandrath* case interpreted article 4(3)(b) of the European Convention on Human Rights as providing that 'objections of conscience do not, under the Convention, entitle a person to exemption from such service'.[70] The *Grandrath* case is the first Commission case to state that the Convention did not call for the interpretation of article 9 when the issue of conscientious objection within the system of compulsory military service is addressed (Harris, O'Boyle and Warbrick 1995, p. 369). The Commission observed that article 4 of the Convention contains a provision which expressly deals with the question of compulsory service exacted in place of military service in the case of conscientious objectors.[71] Consequently, the Commission found it necessary to examine the allegation 'primarily on the basis of article 4 of the Convention' (see Note 71). Therefore, even though the applicant alleged a violation of article 9, the Commission considered the issue under article 4.

---

[67] Opinion No. 256/2003 of the European Commission for Democracy through law (Venice Commission) *on "The Implications of a legally-binding EU Charter of Fundamental Rights on Human Rights Protection in Europe"* [27].

[68] *Bosphorus Hava Yollari Turizm Ve Ticaret Anonim Sirketi v. Ireland*, App. No. 45036/98 (30 June 2005) [4].

[69] Grandrath v FRG (App. 2294/64) (1966) 10 [32]; X v FRG (App. 7705/76) (1977) 9 DR 196, 203; X. v Austria (App. 5591/72) (1973) 43 CD 161 (Dec. 1973); Johansen v Norway (10600/83) (1985) 44 DR 155 (Dec. 1985); A v Switzerland (App. 10640/83) (1984) 38 DR 219 (Dec. 1984); Autio v Finland (App. 17086/90) (1991) 72 DR 245; X v Belgium (App. 24631/94) (Dec.1995).

[70] Com., 2299/64, Grandrath Case [32], reprinted in *Digest of Case-Law Relating to the European Convention on Human Rights (1955–1967), Edition administratives* (U.G.A., Heule, Belgium, 1970) 188.

[71] *Grandrath v FRG* [32].

As a result, the Commission found that article 4(3)(b) expressly recognised that civilian service may be imposed on conscientious objectors as a substitute for military service, and it must be concluded that objections of conscience do not, under the Convention, entitle a person to exemption from civilian service (see Note 71). The later case followed the literal interpretation of article 4(3)(b) of the Convention that according to the Convention conscientious objection does not imply a right to be exempted from substitute civilian service.[72] In *Johansen v Norway*, the legality of compulsory alternative service was at issue, and the Commission seemed to uphold its legality by holding that: 'The Convention does not oblige the Contracting States to make available for conscientious objectors to military service any substitute civilian service'.[73] Moreover, the Convention was interpreted as not preventing a State from imposing sanctions on those who refuse such service, *mutatis mutandis*.[74]

The Commission limited the wording of article 4(3)(b) so that it does not guarantee a right to be exempted from civilian service, since the article expressly recognises that conscientious objectors may be required to perform civilian service.[75] Relying on such a literal interpretation, the Commission did not consider the compatibility of article 9 and compulsory alternative service. It follows that where conscientious objectors are permitted to perform alternative service in lieu of military service, they cannot claim, under article 9, exemption from alternative service (Ovey and White 2006, p. 314). Hence no one is entitled under article 9 to exemption on grounds of conscience either from military service or from alternative service.[76]

Not only the right to alternative service was found not to be guaranteed in the European Convention on Human Rights, but the right to conscientious objection to military service itself was found not to be included in the European Convention on Human Rights. The European Commission on Human Rights found that the Convention does not give conscientious objectors the right to exemption from military service, but left each contracting state to decide whether or not to grant such a right in *A v Switzerland* in 1984.[77] The wording of article 4(3)(b), 'in countries where they are recognised', was invoked as justification for this interpretation (see Note 77).

For the European Commission on Human Rights, the application of a general law to someone who has reasons of conscience for not complying with it does not violate article 9(1).[78] It is evaluated that the Commission had invariably found that refusals to comply with the general law are not a direct exercise of religious or conscience-driven practices (Harris, O'Boyle and Warbrick 1995, p. 368).

---

[72] *X v FRG*, 203; *X. v Austria; Johansen v Norway*, 155.

[73] *Johansen v Norway* (App 10600/83) (1985) 44 DR 155, 162.

[74] *X v FRG* 204; *X v Austria*, 161.

[75] *Johansen v Norway* (App 10600/83) (1985) 44 DR 155, 165.

[76] *Autio v Finland*, (App 17086/90) (1991) 72 DR 245.

[77] A v Switzerland, 222–223.

[78] *Seven Individuals v Sweden* (App 8811/79) (1982) 29 DR 104. *See* Harris, O'Boyle Warbrick (1995, p. 368).

As a result of avoiding touching upon article 9 in connection with conscientious objection to military service, the European Commission of Human Rights has interpreted freedom of conscience and religion as not including the right to be exempted from military service in countries of conscription.[79] In *X v Austria* of 2 April 1973, the Commission made it clear that by including the words 'in countries where they are recognised' in article 4(3)(b), a choice is left to the High Contracting parties to the Convention whether or not to recognise conscientious objectors and, if so recognised, to provide some substitute service for them.[80] Later, in the admissibility decision of *Autio v Finland*, the Commission summarised its own case law: 'a right to conscientious objection is not as such guaranteed by article 9 of the Convention or any other provision of the Convention or its Protocols' by referring to a number of its cases, putting *X v Austria* at its head.[81] According to the interpretation by the Commission, in sum, States parties are not obliged under article 9 of the Convention to recognise an applicant as a conscientious objector (see Note 81).

> The Commission, for this reason, finds that article 9, as qualified by article 4(3)(b) of the Convention, does not impose on a state the obligation to recognise conscientious objectors and, consequently, not to make specific agreements for the exercise of their right to freedom of conscience and religion as far as it affects their compulsory military service.[82]

The Commission recognised in *Autio v Finland* that the applicant's complaints nevertheless fall within the ambit of article 9 where the applicant complains that the discriminatory length of substitute civilian service for conscientious objectors related to the enjoyment of his right to freedom of thought, conscience and religion.[83] The standpoint of the European Commission of Human Rights is seemingly inconsistent with the view of the Parliamentary Assembly which calls for the recognition of a right to conscientious objection from time to time.

Apart from the right to conscientious objection, the European Commission of Human Rights, in its earlier decision, noted that the philosophy of pacifism may be considered as a belief protected by article 9, freedom of thought, conscience and religion, of the European Convention on Human Rights.[84] The right to freedom of thought, conscience and religion was adopted into the Convention from article 18 of the Universal Declaration of Human Rights.[85] Although article 9 of the European Convention of Human Rights is not non-derogable under article 15(2), unlike the International Covenant on Civil and Political Rights, article 9 contains less justifiable interference than articles 8, 10 and 11 (Decker and Fresa 2001, p. 395).

---

[79] *E.g.* Applications 2299/94, 5591/72, 7548/76 and 7705/76; Alfredsson and Eide (389).

[80] *X v Austria*, 161.

[81] *Autio v Finland*, 245.

[82] *X v Austria*, 161.

[83] *Autio v Finland*.

[84] *Arrowsmith v UK*, Report of the European Commission of Human Rights, (App 7050/75), 12/10/78 [69].

[85] Adopted and proclaimed by General Assembly Resolution 217 A (III) of 10 December 1948, UN Doc A/810 (1948) 71.

3.2.2 Individual Petitions Arguing Violation of Prohibition of Discrimination

Several questions emerge as to the prolonged length of alternative service provided for conscientious objectors. If a State provides for an alternative service to compulsory military service for a period longer than for military service, does this constitute a violation of either article 9 or article 14 of the European Convention on Human Rights, on prohibition of discrimination? The European Commission held that it does not violate article 9, alone or in conjunction with article 14.[86] For the Commission, it falls within the margin of appreciation to make the length of civilian service greater than the length of military service as a form of disincentive to ensure that only those with a genuine conviction seek alternative service.[87] However, such an extension of time is subject to the principle of proportionality (Evans 2001, p. 171). While a State may extend the time, to discourage all but genuine conscientious objectors from taking the easier option of substitute service, a State cannot use this extension in a manner that is unduly oppressive or punitive.[88]

Another question relating to discrimination is the discriminatory treatment of conscientious objectors themselves as against other law-abiding citizens performing compulsory military service. The Commission held that an exemption from even substitute service for those who object to it on religious grounds does not violate article 14 with regard to the rights of others who are obliged to complete the civilian activities.[89]

As for the periphery of violation of article 14, the Commission valued 'a high degree of probability that exemption is not granted to persons who simply wish to escape service' (see Note 89). Yet the Commission has not defined the point at which an extension would become disproportionate and it has never found a State in breach of the Convention for its system of substitute service (Evans 2001, pp. 171–172).

The quite recent case of *Thlimmenos v Greece* (April 2000) before the European Court of Human Rights concerned article 14 on the prohibition of discrimination and article 9 on freedom of thought, conscience and religion, along with article 6 on the right to a hearing within a reasonable time. The applicant experienced discriminatory treatment when he was refused the status of chartered accountant by reason of having a criminal conviction for disobeying military enlistment due to his religious convictions. The applicant, Iakovos Thlimmenos, a Greek national, was a Jehovah's Witness. He was found guilty by a Permanent Army Tribunal in Greece of insubordination for having refused to wear the military uniform at a time of general mobilisation.[90] After his release from imprisonment, the applicant took a

86 *Autio v Finland,* (App. 17086/90) (1991) 72 DR 245.

87 *E.g. Johansen v Norway,* No. 10600/83, 44 DR 155, 165 (1985); *Autio v Finland.* App. No. 17086/90, 72 DR 245, 249 (1990).

88 *Autio v Finland,* (App. 17086/90) 72 DR 245, 250 (1990).

89 *N v Sweden,* (App. 10410/83) (1984) 40 DR 203, 208

90 *Thlimmenos v Greece* (App. 34369/97) ECHR (December 4, 1998), Judgment (April 6, 2000) [7].

public examination for the appointment of 12 chartered accountants.[91] Although he came second among 60 candidates, on 8 February 1989 the Executive Board of the Greek Institute of Chartered Accountants refused to accept him on the ground that he had been convicted of a serious crime (see Note 91).

In December 1996, his application was lodged with the European Commission of Human Rights. The Commission found the application partly admissible. In its report, dated 4 December 1998, the Commission opined that there had been a violation of article 9 in conjunction with article 14. The Commission referred the case to the European Court of Human Rights on 22 March 1999. The Court unanimously held that there had been a violation of article 14 in connection with article 9 and a violation of article 6, paragraph 1 of the European Convention on Human Rights.

The point in dispute before the European Court of Human Rights had shifted from the recognition of the right to conscientious objection to military service *per se* to the discriminatory treatment of objectors. Yet the former question will not cease to be raised before the European Court of Human Rights unless article 9 of the European Convention on Human Rights is found to imply the right to conscientious objection to military service by the European Court of Human Rights.

3.2.3 *Individual Petitions Arguing Violation of Prohibition of Degrading Treatment*

Applicants have argued that even if the European Convention on Human Rights does not provide immunity for conscientious objectors, it does, where relevant, provide a right of substitute service for the oppressive obligation (Harris 1995, p. 368). However, the European Commission of Human Rights has also relied on a literal reading of article 4(3)(b) and denied such claims (Harris 1995, p. 368).

The right to be excused from alternative service in States where alternative service is permitted is also not recognised by the Commission. The Commission held that States are free to imprison those who refuse to undertake alternative service and, if necessary, to continue to do so to attempt to pressure recruits into complying with their obligations.[92]

Whereas the exemption from alternative service on the basis of freedom of thought, conscience and religion may be recognised with difficulty by the European Court of Human Rights, lengthy alternative service may be a violation of article 3 of the European Convention on Human Rights, which prohibits torture and inhuman or degrading treatment. The European Court of Human Rights recently found a violation of article 3 of the European Convention on Human Rights in the case of *Ülke v Turkey* (application no. 39437/98). A Turkish national, Ülke was prosecuted nine

[91] *Thlimmenos v Greece* (App 34369/97) ECHR (December 4, 1998), Judgment (April 6, 2000) [8].

[92] *Raninen v Finland* (App 20972/92) (1996) 84-A DR 17, where the applicant was subject to a pattern of arrest, detention, release and re-arrest for continuing to refuse to undertake military or substitute service. His application was held to be manifestly ill-founded.

times, imprisoned eight times and served 701 days in military prison because of his refusal to perform military service.[93] On 24 January 2006, the European Court of Human Rights held unanimously that there had been a violation of article 3 of the European Convention on Human Rights as a consequence of the *cumulative* nature of the penalties without paying much attention to simultaneous issue of discrete length of the penalties. Acting under article 41, the Court awarded the applicant 10,000 Euros for pecuniary damage and 1,000 Euros for costs and expenses.

The facts of the case, in more detail, were that the applicant, Osman Murant Ülke, was first called up for military service in his native Turkey in August 1995, but refused to do his military service on the ground that he had firm pacifist convictions. On 28 January 1997 the Court of Ankara sentenced him to six months' imprisonment. On 22 November 1996 the applicant was transferred to the 9th Regiment, attached to the Bilecik *gendarmerie* command. He refused to wear a uniform. As a result, between March 1997 and November 1998 he was convicted on eight occasions of persistent disobedience. In addition to the convictions resulting from refusal to wear a uniform, he was convicted on two occasions of desertion, because of his failure to rejoin his regiment. He subsequently served 701 days of imprisonment. The applicant complained that he had been prosecuted on account of his convictions as a pacifist and conscientious objector. He relied on article 3 (prohibition of inhuman or degrading treatment), article 5 (right to liberty and security), article 8 (right to respect for private and family life) and article 9 (right to freedom of thought, conscience and religion) of the Convention.

Whereas the Court made a legal finding on article 3, it noted that the facts which the applicant complained of were practically the same as those which underlay the complaints examined under the other articles. The Court accordingly held that it was not necessary to give a separate ruling on the complaints under articles 5, 8 and 9. Although the Court did not find compulsory military service contrary to the European Convention on Human Rights, it decided that the numerous criminal prosecutions against the applicant, the cumulative effects of the criminal convictions which resulted from them and the constant alternation between prosecutions and terms of imprisonment, together with the possibility that he would be liable to prosecution for the rest of his life, had been disproportionate to the aim of ensuring that he did his military service.[94] Therefore, the problem here is not a system of compulsory military service but of potential prison sentences which might deter persons from using conscientious objection as an excuse to avoid military service.[95] On 17 October 2007, the Committee of Ministers of the Council of Europe adopted an exceptional Interim Resolution in the case of Ülke against Turkey in order to urge the Turkish authorities to execute the judgment of the Court.[96]

---

[93] *Ülke v Turkey* (App 39437/98) (January 24, 2006).

[94] *Ülke v Turkey* (App 39437/98) (January 24, 2006) [62].

[95] 'Mehmet Ali Birand New Regulations Needed for Conscientious Objection', *Turkish Daily News* (28 January 2006).

[96] 'Execution of the judgment of the European Court of Human Rights Ülke against Turkey' Resolution CM/ResDH(2007) 109, adopted by the Committee of Ministers on 17 October 2007 at the 1007th meeting of the Ministers' Deputies.

The recent attitudes of the European Court of Human Rights show its agitation at the almost unfettered discretion of a State to deal with conscientious objectors under the European Convention on Human Rights. The Inter-American Commission on Human Rights evaluates the recent European case of *Thlimmenos v Greece*[97] as casting doubt on the European Court of Human Rights' jurisprudence that a sentence passed for refusal to perform military service was not considered in itself to constitute a breach of article 9 of the European Convention on Human Rights.[98]

3.2.4 European Committee of Social Rights

The Council of Europe adopted the European Social Charter, which guarantees social and economic human rights, in 1961. It was revised in 1996. The European Committee of Social Rights is the body responsible for monitoring compliance of the States party to the Charter. Rules of the European Committee of Social Rights set out the role of the Committee.[99] According to rule 2, first of all the Committee is to make a legal assessment of the conformity of national situations with the European Social Charter, the 1988 Additional Protocol and the Revised European Social Charter.[100] Secondly, the Committee is to adopt conclusions in the framework of the reporting procedure and decisions under the collective complaints procedure.[101]

The claim of conscientious objectors was brought before the European Committee of Social Rights as a form of collective complaint. The Committee decided that the length of alternative service for conscientious objectors was disproportionate to that of military service and accordingly the situation in Greece was contrary to article 1(2).[102] The reasoning was based on the fact that during the additional period those concerned are deprived of their right to earn a living in an occupation freely entered upon (see Note 102). Article 1(2) of the European Social Charter does not deal specifically with either the conscientious objection or the alternative service for conscientious objectors, rather it deals with 'the effective exercise of the right to work' and with especially the duty of the Contracting parties to 'protect effectively the right of the worker to earn his living in an occupation freely entered upon'.

The jurisprudence of the European Committee of Social Rights is of great significance since neither the Human Rights Committee nor the European Court of Human Rights have jurisdiction to consider the issue of alternative service for conscientious

---

97 *Thlimmenos v Greece*. (App 34369/97) Comm. Rep. (December 4, 1998), Judgment (April 6, 2000).

98 Report No. 43/05, Case 12.219, Merits, *Christián Daniel Sahli Vera et al. v Chile*, March 10, 2005 [71].

99 Rules of the European Committee of Social Rights adopted during the 201st Session on 29 March 2004 and revised during the 207th Session on 12 May 2005.

100 Rule 2(1) of the Rules of the European Committee of Social Rights.

101 Rule 2(2) of the Rules of the European Committee of Social Rights.

102 *Quaker Council for European Affairs v Greece*, Complaint No. 8/2000, Decision on the merits (5 December 2000) [25].

objectors from the perspective of the right to work. The Committee dealt with the issue of the length of alternative service for conscientious objectors through article 1(2) and thus extended its interpretation of the Charter provision to include areas that fall outside the traditional sphere of economic and employment rights (Brillat 2005, p. 31, 38). Such jurisprudence broadens the legal issues surrounding the right to conscientious objection.

This decision on a collective complaint influenced later examination of national reports. The Committee's practice in this regard is systematic and progressive. Once the Committee has reached a decision on a collective complaint, it then systematically examines the issues raised by the complaint in all the States parties to the Charter when it next considers their reports on the relevant provision (Brillat 2005, pp. 36–37). After deciding that the situation in Greece was contrary to article 1(2) because the period of alternative service was disproportionate to that of military service, the Committee raised the matter with every country and concluded that the situation in Greece was not in conformity with that in other States.[103]

3.3 Commissioner for Human Rights of the Council of Europe

Since the right to conscientious objection in international law has been gradually recognised at international level, the question becomes more that of the appropriate treatment of conscientious objectors than the existence of the right to conscientious objection or its nature. The opinions of the Commissioner for Human Rights of the Council of Europe have shown the same tendency as the Human Rights Committee and the European Court of Human Rights, in that the concerns of the Commissioner have shifted to the treatment of conscientious objectors and the nature of alternative service. The Commissioner for Human Rights is an independent institution within the Council of Europe, mandated to promote the awareness of and respect for human rights in the 46 Council of Europe Member States.[104] The idea of setting up this institution was initiated by the Council of Europe's Heads of State and Government at their Second Summit in Strasbourg on 10–11 October 1997. On 7 May 1999, the Committee of Ministers adopted a Resolution which instituted the Office of the Commissioner and elaborated the Commissioner's mandate. It is a non-judicial organ.[105] Therefore the Commissioner's Office cannot act upon individual complaints, but the Commissioner can draw conclusions and take wider initiatives on the basis of reliable information regarding human rights violations suffered by individuals. In this sense, his or her report may serve as somewhere between the

[103] *Conclusions 2004* (Cyprus), at 91–92, (Romania), at 450–451; *Conclusions XVII-1* (Finland) 165–166.

[104] *See* http://www.coe.int/t/commissioner/Activities/mandate_en.asp (last visited, 19 January 2007).

[105] Resolution (99) 50 of the Council of Europe, Commissioner for Human Rights (Adopted by the Committee of Ministers on 7 May 1999, at its 104th Session, Budapest) article 1.

Human Rights Committee's practices of concluding observations on State reports and decisions on individual complaints.

3.3.1 Greek Practice

The Commissioner has touched on the issue of conscientious objection on several occasions, in particular concerning Greece. The Commissioner had much welcomed the fact that the revised Greek Constitution of 2002 now guarantees a right to conscientious objection.[106] However, he deemed an extra term of 18 months for such objectors a disproportionate measure in practice at that time.[107] He advised the Greek government to reduce the duration of alternative service to an equitable term in comparison with military service and to work along the lines of recommendations from the Greek Ombudsman in order to rectify the disproportionate character of the present legislation (see Note 107). The Commissioner also recommended the transfer of responsibilities for granting conscientious objector status from the Ministry of Defence to an independent civilian department.[108]

Following this recommendation from the Commissioner in 2002, the Greek National Commission for Human Rights proposed to the Government in 2004 that the duration of the alternative social service be longer than that of the regular military service by 50%; that the duration of the unarmed military service be longer than the regular military service by 30%; that the instigation of continuous and repeated prosecutions for refusing to perform military service be abolished; that, as far as the competence of the Supervisory Body for Conscientious Objectors is concerned, it should be initially the responsibility of the Ministry of National Defence, on the condition that, when conscientious objectors are removed from the Enlistment Register, there would be a joint responsibility of the Ministry of the Interior and the Ministry of Health on the matter; that rejections by the Committee for the Examination of Objections of Conscience be justified in detail; that the composition of the aforementioned Committee be strengthened with two more State representatives, one from the Ministry of the Interior and one from the Ministry of Health; that a special list of public benefit NGOs in which conscientious objectors may serve be drafted by a joint ministerial committee; that the geographical criterion for the completion of the alternative unarmed military or social service be brought to conform to the same rules that apply to regular armed military service, and that the Council

[106] Report by Mr. Alvaro Gil-Robles, Commissioner for Human Rights, on his visit to the Hellenic Republic (2–5 June 2002), for the attention of the Committee of Ministers and the Parliamentary Assembly, 17 July 2002, CommDH(2002) 5, original version in French, 7 [17]. *See also* Follow-up report on the Hellenic Republic (2002–2005), Assessment of the Progress in implementing the recommendations of the Council of Europe Commissioner for Human Rights, for the attention of the Committee of Ministers and the Parliamentary Assembly, CommDH (2006) 13, (Strasbourg, 29 March 2006) [34].

[107] CommDH (2002) 5, 7 [17].

[108] CommDH (2002) 5, 7 [18].

of Europe Resolution providing for long-term and elderly conscientious objectors to meet their military obligations be implemented.[109]

The report of the Commissioner of 2006 noted the progress made by the Greek government after 2002. As of March 2006, regular military service was 12 months.[110] It can be served in all parts of the country and is indeed quite demanding, especially when served in remote border regions (see Note 111). For conscientious objectors there are two regimes (see Note 111). The 'unarmed military service' lasts 6 months longer than the armed service and is served within military compounds (see Note 111). Objectors prefer the other option of 'alternative service'. This lasts 11 months longer than the regular military service whereas, at the time of the Commissioner's visit, it was still 18 months longer (see Note 111). Some 1,000 conscripts were doing alternative service, out of 40,000 conscripts annually, at the time of the 2006 report (see Note 111). Under the law, they are barred from serving in the six biggest urban areas (see Note 111). This rule, in addition to the additional time of service, is considered to compensate for the fact that the alternative service is generally much less uncomfortable than the military service and that conscripts do not spend the nights confined in their workplace (see Note 111). As to the body which makes the recommendation on whether or not to accept granting the status of conscientious objector to an applicant, it is composed of a majority of civilians (one assistant judge of the Legal Council of the State, two university professors, two members of the military) and 98% of its advisory opinions are accepted by the Ministry of Defence, the conscript having the possibility to appeal before the administrative courts (see Note 111). Naturalised immigrants who have completed military service in another country cannot be granted the status of conscientious objector and have to serve a three-month military service in Greece as long as they are aged under 35; if they are older, they are exempted.[111] The Commissioner recommends that the Greek authorities grant conscientious objector status to persons who have already performed a military service in another country if they had no realistic possibility to refuse it or when their experience has been traumatic.[112]

3.3.2 *Finnish Practice*

In the report of the Council of Europe Commissioner for Human Rights regarding his visit to Finland during 4–7 June 2001, he referred to the issue of conscientious objectors. The main focus, as was the case of the report on the Greek situation, was on the excessive duration of alternative civilian service as well as the term of

---

[109] Follow-up report on the Hellenic Republic (2002–2005), Assessment of the Progress in implementing the recommendations of the Council of Europe Commissioner for Human Rights, for the Attention of the Committee of Ministers and the Parliamentary Assembly, CommDH (2006) 13, (Strasbourg, 29 March 2006) [35].

[110] CommDH (2006) 13, (Strasbourg, 29 March 2006) [37].

[111] CommDH (2006) 13, (Strasbourg, 29 March 2006) [38].

[112] CommDH (2006) 13, (Strasbourg, 29 March 2006) [39].

imprisonment for those refusing to perform it.[113] There was also alleged discrimination in the conditions of execution of sentences for conscientious objectors, owing to the different treatment which they received (see Note 113). For example, according to the statistics issued on 1 June 2001, 18 conscientious objectors were serving their sentence under semi-custodial conditions while another was confined to a closed prison.[114] The Commissioner held that:

> In my opinion, regarding civilian service and its duration, the Government of Finland should take into consideration the Macciocchi Resolution approved on 7 February 1983 by the European Parliament, according to which the duration of alternative civilian service ought not to exceed that of military service, and especially the recommendation of the Committee of Ministers of the Council of Europe of 9 April 1987 and Resolution 1998/77 of the United Nations Commission on Human Rights of 22 April 1998 as it relates to civilian service. According to these texts, the duration of civilian service, in order to be deemed 'reasonable', should not be 'punitive' by comparison with that of military service.
>
> Otherwise, 'absolute' objectors receive a 197 day prison sentence, amounting to half the duration of the alternative civilian service (395 days). I consider it important to seek other methods than the strict application of the Penal Code to 'absolute' objectors, which in my opinion is not the appropriate way to deal with this question (see Note 114).

A follow-up visit to assess any progress made was carried out by members of the Commissioner's Office from 29 to 31 August 2005.[115] The issue of conscientious objection was reviewed in its follow-up report. This revealed that there had been no change in the duration of the civilian service in Finland since the Commissioner's visit: it stands at 395 days, which is significantly longer than average military service.[116] Under current Finnish law, the minimum length of regular military service is 180 days, and the maximum 363 days.[117] Most conscripts serve the minimum length of service (see Note 117). Non-governmental organisations have called for the shortening of the duration of the civilian service to 240 days, which is the estimated average length of military service (see Note 117). Furthermore, the penalty for total refusal continues to be imprisonment for the duration of half of the time remaining from the mandatory service period, i.e., a maximum of 197 days (see Note 117). Although the prison sentence is usually served in open prisons with the

---

[113] Report by Mr. Alvaro Gil-Robles, Commissioner for Human Rights on his visit to Finland (4–7 June 2001) for the Committee of Ministers and the Parliamentary Assembly, Strasbourg, 19 September 2001, CommDH (2001) 7, Original Version in French, Chap. 3.

[114] Report by Mr. Alvaro Gil-Robles, Commissioner for Human Rights on his visit to Finland (4–7 June 2001) for the Committee of Ministers and the Parliamentary Assembly, Strasbourg, 19 September 2001, CommDH (2001) 7, Original Version in French, Chap. 3. Following a 1997 reform, the periods of armed national service are respectively 180, 270 or 362 days, compared to 330 days for non-combatant national service. The duration of alternative civilian service, however, is 395 days. According to the statistics, the term of national service actually performed averages 8.5 months.

[115] Follow-up Report on Finland (2001–2005), Assessment of the Progress made in Implementing the Recommendations of the Council of Europe Commissioner for Human Rights, Strasbourg, 29 March 2006, CommDH (2006) 9 [1].

[116] CommDH (2006) 9 [42].

[117] CommDH (2006) 9 [42], fn. 11.

possibility to work or study outside, according to the law, the prison sentence cannot be conditional, and the prisoner can only be released on probation if he wishes and can serve the remaining time of his civilian service (see Note 117). In 2004, 71 persons were sentenced to prison terms due to their refusal to take up military or civilian service (see Note 117).

The Commissioner referred to both the Human Rights Committee and the European Committee of Social Rights which have recently found that the length of civilian service in Finland was punitive and discriminatory.[118] The Commissioner also pointed out the fact that the Human Rights Committee has concerns that the preferential treatment accorded to Jehovah's Witnesses in exempting them from military and civilian service has not been extended to other groups of conscientious objectors.[119]

The Commissioner referred to problems caused by accommodation costs during the civilian service, and the insufficient number of places to perform civilian service, which had been pointed out by NGOs.[120] Whereas the public authority or service where civilian service takes place is required by law to provide accommodation to civilian servicemen, this obligation does not always appear to be respected in practice (see Note 119). A number of conscientious objectors do not consider civilian service as an appropriate alternative, since it exempts persons from military service only during peace time (see Note 119).

The only progress made regarding the Civilian Service Decree was the amendment in 2002 when a new provision regarding safety at work is provided for.[121] However, no substantial improvements have taken place in the situation of conscientious objectors in recent years (see Note 121). Government proposals to shorten the length of civilian service have not yet met with Parliamentary approval (see Note 121). While the working group for improving the situation of civilian service was set up under the auspices of the Ministry of Labour, the issue of the length of civilian service is reported to have been ruled as beyond its mandate (see Note 121).

In the conclusion of the follow-up report, the Commissioner regretted the lack of progress and therefore reiterated his recommendations made in the 2001 report.[122] The Commissioner concluded:

> It is clear that the current length of civilian alternative service provided by Finland is punitive and discriminatory in comparison with the length of military service while it is detrimental to equal opportunities for work and study among civilian and military service men. The social and financial rights of civilian service men should be protected in a comparable way with those of conscripts. Although the Commissioner notes the exemption of Jehovah's Witnesses from military and civilian service, he considers that a similar provision should also be applied to other persons objecting to military and civilian service on the

---

[118] CommDH (2006) 9 [43].

[119] CommDH (2006) 9 [43]. *See also* Concluding Observations of the Human Rights Committee: Finland. 2 December 2004. UN Doc CCPR/CO/82/FIN; European Social Charter – European Committee of Social Rights, Conclusions XVII-1 (Finland).

[120] CommDH (2006) 9 [44].

[121] CommDH (2006) 9 [45].

[122] CommDH (2006) 9 [46].

ground of belief. The Commissioner urges the Finnish Government to draw inspiration from its Anti-Discrimination Act and Protocol 12 to the European Convention on Human Rights in speedily addressing the situation of conscientious objectors while actively persuading the Parliament to back a long-waited reform in this field (see Note 122).

3.4 Concluding Remarks

The right to conscientious objection in international law should be regarded as being in the process of clarification and crystallisation as a right, since no international law currently in force explicitly provides for such a right. This development should be seen as an interesting phenomenon for evolving international human rights law. Human rights should be enjoyed by human beings just because they are human beings and each should be respectfully treated by others. Each human being's conscience should be respected on the sole basis that man is a 'thinking reed', in Pascal's words. Thus, today it may be safe to say that there is no doubt that the right to conscientious objection to military service may be deduced from the freedom of thought, conscience and religion. Additionally, several other human rights, such as the right to life and the right to self-determination, may be legal bases for this right.

Even though the right to conscientious objection may be normally exercised after recognition of a counterpart legal obligation to perform alternative civilian service, the treatment of conscientious objectors has become of great concern to the international community. The lengthy civilian service alternative to military service has been judged not acceptable from the European and international legal standard, though it may still be controversial as to what length of term of alternative service may be seen as appropriate.

References

Journal Article

Decker DC, Fresa L (2001) The status of conscientious objection under article 4 of the European convention on human rights. New York Univ J Int Law Politics 33:379–418

Engram JM (1982) Conscientious objection to military service: A report to the United Nations division of human rights. Geo J Int Comp Law 12:359–398

Lippman M (1990/1991) The recognition of conscientious objection to military service as an international human right. Cal West Int Law J 21:31–66

Robertson AH (1950) The European convention for the protection of human rights. Br Yearbk Int Law 27:145–163

Scheib JM (1997) Enforcing Judgments of the European Court of Human Rights: the Conduit Theory. New York Int Law Rev 101–130

Book

European Commission of Human Rights (1970) Digest of case-law relating to the European convention on human rights (1955–1967), edition administratives. U.G.A., Heule, Belgium

Evans C (2001) Freedom of Religion under the European Convention on Human Rights. Oxford University Press, New York

Hammer L (2001) The international human right to freedom of conscience: Some suggestions for its development and application. Ashgate, Aldershot

Harris DJ, O'Boyle M, Warbrick C (1995) Law of the European convention on human rights. Butterworths, London

Steiner HJ & Alston P (2000) International human rights in context: law, politics, morals: text and materials, 2nd edn. Oxford University Press, New York

The Council of Europe (1975) Collected edition of the 'travaux préparatoires' vol. I, preparatory commission of the council of Europe, committee of ministers, consultative assembly, 11 May–8 September 1949. Martinus Nijhoff Publishers, The Hague

Book Chapter

Brillat R (2005) The supervisory machinery of the European social charter: recent developments and their impact. In: de Búrca G, de Witte B (eds) Social rights in Europe. Oxford University Press, New York, pp. 31–44

Chapter 4
Inter-American Human Rights Law

Abstract The Inter-American human rights system appears to be inconsistent in its recognition of the right to conscientious objection. The first conscientious objector case decided under the Inter-American system occurred in March 2005. The Inter-American Commission on Human Rights stated that international human rights jurisprudence recognises the status of conscientious objectors only in countries recognising such status in their national laws. This statement exactly contradicts the statement of the Inter-American Commission on Human Rights of 1997 which invited the Member States not recognising the system of conscientious objection and alternative service to review their legal systems. The Commission's attitude towards narrower interpretations of the right to conscientious objection is not in line with the recent development of this right before the United Nations and the European human rights institutions. It is hoped that the Inter-American human rights system will recognise the right to conscientious objection to military service in accordance with the development of the other international human rights institutions.

American Officer's Wife:

Do you mean if Bertie here was on the opposite side, you would shoot him?

Kuribayashi:

I would have to follow my convictions.

American Officer:

Do you mean you would have to follow your convictions? Or your country's convictions?

Kuribayashi:

Are they not the same?

From the Script of 'Letters from Iwo Jima' (2006)

H. Takemura, *International Human Right to Conscientious Objection to Military Service and Individual Duties to Disobey Manifestly Illegal Orders*.

4.1 Inter-American Human Rights Institutions – an Unsettled Position

The first attempt to bring about a regional human rights instrument in the Americas took place at the Inter-American Conference on Problems of War and Peace, held in Mexico City in 1945.[1] The Conference, in Resolution XI, assigned to the Inter-American Juridical Committee the drafting of this latter 'Declaration,' to be submitted through the Pan-American Union (see Note 1). The draft prepared by the Judicial Committee was submitted to the Ninth International Conference of American States at Bogotá, where Resolution XXX known as the American Declaration of the Rights and Duties of Man was adopted and it was decided that: 'the Inter-American Juridical Committee prepare a draft statute for an Inter-American Court to Protect the Rights of Man' (see Note 1). Thus at the Bogotá Conference, the American Declaration of the Rights and Duties of Man was adopted on 2 May 1948, 7 months prior to the Universal Declaration of Human Rights of the United Nations. It contains 28 rights and 10 duties. The declaration constituted a basis for the preparation of an Inter-American Convention.

The lack of positive substantive law on the subject hampered the drafting work by the Juridical Committee. Although sporadic efforts were made by the Organization of American States to establish institutional mechanisms, no tangible results were produced until 1959 (Buergenthal, Norris and Shelton 1990, p. 4). As late as August 1959, the 5th Meeting of Consultation of Ministries of Foreign Affairs entrusted the Inter-American Council of Jurists with the preparation of a draft Convention on Human Rights.[2] The Inter-American Council of Jurists prepared a draft Convention on Human Rights, which consisted of 88 articles, during its 4th Meeting in Chile (see Note 2). The examination of this draft as well as two drafts submitted by Chile and Uruguay, respectively, took place before the Inter-American Conference held in November 1965 (see Note 2). According to Resolution XXIV of the Conference, the draft prepared by the Inter-American Council of Jurists was based on the European Convention on Human Rights (Rome, 1950) and on the draft covenants, prepared by the United Nations Commission on Human Rights in 1952–1953, which up to 1959 had only been studied by the Third Committee of the General Assembly.[3]

The Inter-American Conference of 1965 decided to send the three proposed drafts to the Council of the Organization of American States.[4] In the following year, May 1966, the Council of the Organization of American States sent its draft to the Inter-American Commission on Human Rights.[5] The Inter-American Commission

[1] *Inter-American Yearbook on Human Rights* (1968) General Secretariat of the Organization of American States (Washington, DC 1973) 65.

[2] *Inter-American Yearbook on Human Rights* (1968) 67.

[3] *Inter-American Yearbook on Human Rights* (1968) 71.

[4] *Inter-American Yearbook on Human Rights* (1968) 71. *See also* Svensson-McCarthy (1998, p. 248).

[5] *Inter-American Yearbook on Human Rights* (1968) 71 and 73.

on Human Rights sent its opinion on the draft in 1967.[6] In reply, the Council of the Organisation resolved:

[t]o ask the Inter-American Commission on Human Rights to draw up a revised and complete text of a preliminary draft convention, containing the amendments and changes set forth in its Opinion [...] and that that text be in harmony with the International Covenants of the United Nations, in accordance with the Opinion dated 11 April 1968, so that the Council, after having made the amendments to the text it deems necessary, may convey it to the governments in order for them to make the observations and amendments they deem pertinent, within 3 months.[7]

In order to respond to this request from the Council, a special session of the Inter-American Commission on Human Rights was held at the permanent headquarters in Washington DC in July 1968 (see Note 7). The Commission prepared the Preliminary Draft. Later the Secretariat of the Inter-American Commission on Human Rights prepared a document to facilitate a comparative examination of the Covenants, the Optional Protocol, the Inter-American Council of Jurists' Draft and the Amendments suggested by the Inter-American Commission on Human Rights.[8] According to this research, there is no difference except in choice of words in relation to the draft of the Council of Jurists and the amendments of the Inter-American Commission on Human Rights.[9] As for the provision of freedom of thought, conscience and religion, there is no distinguishable difference between the draft, the amendment and the International Covenant on Civil and Political Rights, except the freedom of parents to educate their children in accordance with their own convictions.[10] Such a provision is located in article 18(4) of the Covenant (see Note 10). Chile noted, during the Inter-American Specialized Conference on Human Rights, that:

> In regard to freedom of conscience and religion (article 11 of the Parliamentary Draft), it is worth noting that the provision, included in the United Nations Covenant, on the liberty of parents to educate their children according to their own convictions is not included. It appears desirable that this right, already accepted on the world level, be set forth on the regional level.[11]

There seems to have been almost no argument over the issue of conscientious objection during the drafting of the American Convention on Human Rights. However, a slightly relevant discussion is found in relation to article 6 of the freedom from slavery. The International Labour Organisation remarked on the draft prepared for the Inter-American Specialized Conference on Human Rights, convoked by the

---

[6] *Inter-American Yearbook on Human Rights* (1968) 77.

[7] *Inter-American Yearbook on Human Rights* (1968) 93.

[8] *Inter-American Yearbook on Human Rights* (1968) 191.

[9] *Inter-American Yearbook on Human Rights* (1968) 195.

[10] *Inter-American Yearbook on Human Rights* (1968) 197.

[11] Doc. 7 (English) 26 September 1969, Original: Spanish, 'Observations of the Governments of the Member States Regarding the Draft Inter-American Convention on Protection of Human Rights: 3. Chile', in Norris and Buergenthal (1982, pp. 99–107, 102[6]).

Council of the Organization of American States to be held in San José, Costa Rica, from 1 to 13 September in 1969:

> The Spanish text refers to '*el servicio de carácter militar*', and the English text, to 'Any military service'. The corresponding exception, provided for in article 2(2) of Convention No. 29 [concerning Forced or Compulsory Labour] refers to any work or service extracted in virtue of compulsory military service laws for work of purely military character', but the English text might be interpreted as applying to all service required by virtue of compulsory military service laws, including service utilized for purposes that are not of a military nature (footnote omitted).[12]

To obtain a better wording of this article, the Chairman of the Draft Committee appointed a working group consisting of the delegations of Argentina, Guatemala, Honduras and Costa Rica, which submitted its report in due course, presenting a text that contained the additions mentioned by the International Labour Organisation (see Note 12).

In terms of the right to freedom of conscience and religion, with which article 12 deals, there was no major discussion of substance. The debate was concentrated, almost in its entirety, on the incorporation of a fourth paragraph. It would have covered the right of parents or guardians, as the case may be, to see that their children or wards receive a religious and moral education that is in accord with their own convictions.[13]

Therefore the survey of the *travaux préparatoires* of the Convention reveals no discussion of the issue of conscientious objection *per se* at the time of drafting the Convention. The completed article 12 is entitled 'freedom of conscience and religion' while freedom of thought is located separately in article 13 with the heading 'freedom of thought and expression'.

In the case of *Cristián Daniel Sahli Vera et al. v Chile*, the violation of human rights of conscientious objectors was at issue for the first time before the Inter-American Commission on Human Rights.[14] The legal issue there was whether articles 11 and/or 12 of the American Convention on Human Rights create(s) a right to object, for reasons of conscience, to compliance with the domestic law as regards compulsory military service when the domestic law does not provide for such exemptions.[15] Chilean law provides for compulsory military service but does not provide for conscientious objector status.[16]

---

[12] Doc. 14 (English), 17 October 1969, Original: English, 'Comments of the International Labour Office on the Draft Inter-American Convention on Human Rights', in Buergenthal, *Human Rights*, 209 [6].

[13] Doc. 14 (English), 17 October 1969, Original: English, 'Comments of the International Labour Office on the Draft Inter-American Convention on Human Rights', in Buergenthal, *Human Rights*, 165 [6].

[14] Report No. 43/05, Case 12.219, Merits, *Christián Daniel Sahli Vera et al. v Chile*, March 10, 2005.

[15] Report No. 43/05, Case 12.219, Merits, *Christián Daniel Sahli Vera et al. v Chile*, March 10, 2005 [32].

[16] Report No. 43/05, Case 12.219, Merits, *Christián Daniel Sahli Vera et al. v Chile*, March 10, 2005 [33].

Surprisingly, there had been no cases decided under the Inter-American system before the *Christián Daniel Sahli Vera et al. v Chile* case.[17] Even though article 6(3)(b) of the freedom from slavery is equivalent to article 8(3)(c)(ii) of the International Covenant on Civil and Political Rights and article 4(3)(b) of the European Convention on Human Rights, the Inter-American Commission on Human Rights was of the opinion that the American Convention neither expressly creates nor mentions a right to 'conscientious objection'.[18] In the opinion of the Inter-American Commission on Human Rights, international human rights jurisprudence recognises the status of conscientious objectors only in countries that provide for such status in their national laws, whereas in countries that do not provide for conscientious objector status, the international human rights bodies find that there has been no violation of the right to freedom of thought, conscience or religion.[19] In other words, the Commission read article 12 in conjunction with article 6(3)(b) of the American Convention as expressly recognising the right to conscientious objector status in those countries in which the status is recognised in domestic law.[20]

This conclusion seems to contradict an earlier statement by the Inter-American Commission on Human Rights, in its annual report of 1997:

> The Commission takes note of the suggestions made by other international bodies to the effect that States must effectively implement the right to freedom of conscience and religion, through legislative amendments providing for exemptions from military service in cases of conscientious objection. [...] *The Commission also invites the member States whose legislation still does not exempt conscientious objectors from military service or alternative service, to review their legal regimes and make modifications consistent with the spirit of the international law of human rights* (emphasis added).[21]

This statement 'clearly interprets the international law of human rights in such a way that it imposes a duty to provide exemption from military service for conscientious objections and, it seems, even exemptions from alternative service' (Brems 2006, p. 17). Therefore it seems that the Commission had regarded there being a positive duty of States to implement the right to freedom of conscience and religion in order to avail exemptions from military service in cases of conscientious objection. The Commission's conservative position is regrettable. The reason for its change in attitude may be the international community's lack of support for the more progressive position taken by the Commission in 1997.

In its decision of 13 October 2004 in *Alfredo Bustos v Bolivia*, the Inter-American Commission on Human Rights concludes that it is competent to examine the case

[17] Report No. 43/05, Case 12.219, Merits, *Christián Daniel Sahli Vera et al. v Chile*, March 10, 2005 [36].

[18] Report No. 43/05, Case 12.219, Merits, *Christián Daniel Sahli Vera et al. v Chile*, March 10, 2005 [37].

[19] Report No. 43/05, Case 12.219, Merits, *Christián Daniel Sahli Vera et al. v Chile*, March 10, 2005 [38].

[20] Report No. 43/05, Case 12.219, Merits, *Christián Daniel Sahli Vera et al. v Chile*, March 10, 2005 [97].

[21] Annual Report of the Inter-American Commission on Human Rights 1997, OEA/Ser.L/V/II.98, doc. 6 rev, original Spanish (13 April 1998) Chapter VII [10].

presented by the petitioner, the Ombudsman of the Republic of Bolivia, concerning the Bolivian State's alleged violation of the rights claimed by the petitioner.[22] In June 2005 the Bolivian government inquired if the petitioner would be willing to resolve the case with a friendly settlement. Accordingly the parties came to an agreement. This interpretation is in line with the jurisprudence of the European Court of Human Rights which has refused to recognise a right to conscientious objector status within the larger context of the right to freedom of thought, conscience and religion, due to the explicit reference to 'conscientious objectors' in the article exempting military service or alternative service from the definition of forced or compulsory labour in article 4(3) of the European Convention on Human Rights.[23]

The agreement of the friendly settlement contains especially the following matter although the Commission missed an opportunity to reveal its opinion on the issue of conscientious objection. The Bolivian State, represented by the Ministry of Defence, agrees 'in accordance with international human rights law, to include the right to conscientious objection to military service in the preliminary draft of the amended regulations for military law currently under consideration by the Ministry of Defence and the armed forces'.[24] Moreover, both the Ministry of Defence and the Deputy Ministry of Justice of the Bolivian State encourage congressional approval of military legislation that would include the right to conscientious objection to military service.[25]

The Commission greatly appreciated the efforts put forth by both parties to achieve this settlement, which was compatible with the procedure prescribed by articles 48(1)(f) and 49 of the American Convention.[26] Whereas the Commission was not required to make a legal assessment of the original claims by the petitioner, the Commission had an opportunity to make a reference to the status of the right to conscientious objection. The Commission considered that: 'this friendly settlement is fully consonant with the evolving nature of international human rights law, which protects the status of conscientious objector in those countries in which that status has been established by law'.[27] Then the Inter-American Commission on Human Rights quoted a paragraph from the General Comment No. 22 of the Human Rights Committee of the United Nations.[28] This reference may be seen to indicate that the Inter-American Commission adheres fundamentally to the position of the Human

[22] *Alfredo Bustos v Bolivia*, Case 14/04, Report No. 52/04, Inter-Am. C.H.R., OEA/Ser.L/V/II.122 Doc. 5 rev. 1 (2004) 147.

[23] Report No. 43/05, Case 12.219, Merits, *Christián Daniel Sahli Vera et al. v Chile* [96].

[24] *Alfredo Bustos v Bolivia*, Case 14/04, Report No. 97/05, Petition 14/04, Friendly Settlement (27 October 2005) [16] Agreement I (d).

[25] *Alfredo Bustos v Bolivia*, Case 14/04, Report No. 97/05, Petition 14/04, Friendly Settlement (27 October 2005) [16]. Agreement I (e).

[26] *Alfredo Bustos v Bolivia*, Case 14/04, Report No. 97/05, Petition 14/04, Friendly Settlement (27 October 2005) [22] Agreement I (e).

[27] *Alfredo Bustos v Bolivia*, Case 14/04, Report No. 97/05, Petition 14/04, Friendly Settlement (27 October 2005) [19] Agreement I (e).

[28] *Alfredo Bustos v Bolivia*, Case 14/04, Report No. 97/05, Petition 14/04, Friendly Settlement (27 October 2005) [20] Agreement I (e).

Rights Committee of the United Nations, although the Inter-American Commission merely held that '[the General Comment No. 22] is a significant reference in this regard' (see Note 28).

The condition set out in the above remark of the Commission, that is, 'in those countries in which that status has been established by law', in the case of *Alfredo Bustos v Bolivia* follows the line of argument in its own decision in the *Cristián Daniel Sahli Vera et al. v Chile case on 10 March 2005.*[29] *In Cristián Daniel Sahli Vera et al. v Chile, the Commission* found that: 'the American Convention, in Article 12, read in conjunction with Article 6(3)(b), expressly recognises the right to conscientious objector status in those countries in which conscientious objectors are recognized'.[30]

The most recent evidence of the practice of the Inter-American Commission on Human Rights is the admissibility decision in *Xavier Alejandro León Vega v Ecuador*.[31] The petitioner alleges violation by the State of Ecuador (hereinafter 'the State' or 'Ecuador') of articles 12 (freedom of conscience and religion), 13 (freedom of thought and expression), and 22(2) (freedom of movement and residence) of the American Convention on Human Rights, and of article 6 (right to work), and article 13(1)(2)(3) (right to education) of the Additional Protocol to the American Convention on Human Rights in the area of economic, social and cultural rights (hereinafter 'Protocol of San Salvador') to the detriment of his person. Having studied the positions of the parties, the Commission concluded that it had competence to examine the petition lodged by the petitioner and that the case was admissible in the light of articles 46 and 47 of the American Convention on Human Rights.[32]

Although the decision of 2 March 2006 in *Xavier Alejandro León Vega v Ecuador* is an admissibility decision, the Commission made a *prima facie* examination to determine whether the petition substantiates the apparent or potential violation of a right protected by the American Convention and not to determine the existence of a violation.[33] The Commission seemingly reaffirmed the position held in *Cristián Daniel Sahli Vera et al. v Chile*. The Commission held, with a reference to the precedent case, that: 'the Commission considers that the right to refuse to comply with military service or conscientious objection is a right that could derive from articles 11 and 12, read together with article 6(3)(b) of the American Convention on Human Rights where conscientious objectors are expressly recognised in the legislation of the State under consideration'.[34] This leads to the conclusion that the Inter-American Commission on Human Rights deems the right to privacy

---

[29] *Cristián Daniel Sahli Vera et al. v Chile, Report No. 43/05, Case 12/219, Merits.*

[30] *Cristián Daniel Sahli Vera et al. v Chile, Report No. 43/05, Case 12/219, Merits* [86].

[31] Report No. 22/06, Petition 278-02, Admissibility *Xavier Alejandro León Vega v Ecuador* (2 March 2006).

[32] Report No. 22/06, Petition 278-02, Admissibility *Xavier Alejandro León Vega v Ecuador* (2 March 2006) [4] and [33].

[33] Report No. 22/06, Petition 278-02, Admissibility *Xavier Alejandro León Vega v Ecuador* (2 March 2006) [30].

[34] Report No. 22/06, Petition 278-02, Admissibility *Xavier Alejandro León Vega v Ecuador* [31], citing IACHR, Report 43/05, Case 12.219, *Cristián Daniel Sahlí Vera et al.* (Chile) [86].

(article 11) and the freedom of conscience and religion (article 12) as legal bases of the right to conscientious objection with the possibility of limitations set forth under the provision of the freedom from slavery (article 6(3)(b)).

4.2 Concluding Remarks

The practice of the Inter-American Commission on Human Rights seems inconsistent. This may be due to the fact that the Inter-American Commission on Human Rights' members are not permanent and are elected for terms of 4 years and may be reelected only once.[35] The Commission's attitude towards narrower interpretation of the right to conscientious objection is not in line with the recent development of this right before the United Nations and the European human rights institutions. Since the Commission's attitude varies greatly, the development and progress towards promotion of the recognition of the right to conscientious objection should be promoted among its Member States.

References

Book

Brems E (2006) A commentary on the United Nations convention on the rights of the child: Article 14: The right to freedom of thought, Conscience and religion. Martinus Nijhoff Publishers, The Hague

Buergenthal T, Norris R, Shelton D (1990) Protecting human rights in the Americas: selected problems, 3rd edn. NP Engel, Kehl

Inter-American Commission on Human Rights (1968) Inter-American yearbook of human rights. General Secretariat of the Organization of American States, Washington D.C.

Norris RE, Buergenthal T (1982) Human rights: The inter-American system, part 2, The legislative history of the American convention on human rights. Oceana Publications, New York

Svensson-McCarthy A (1998) The international law of human rights and States of exception: With special reference to the travaux préparatoires and case-law of the international monitoring organs. Martinus Nijhoff Publishers, The Hague

[35] *See* Article 6 of the Statute of the Inter-American Commission on Human Rights, O.A.S. Res. 447 (IX-0/79), O.A.S. Off. Rec. OEA/Ser.P/IX.0.2/80, Vol. 1 at 88, Annual Report of the Inter-American Commission on Human Rights, OEA/Ser.L/V/11.50 doc.13 rev. 1 at 10 (1980), reprinted in Basic Documents Pertaining to Human Rights in the Inter-American System, OEA/Ser.L.V/II.82 doc.6 rev.1 at 93 (1992).

Chapter 5
International Refugee Law and Conscientious Objection

Abstract This chapter deals with conscientious objectors as asylum seekers. The question discussed here includes under what conditions conscientious objectors may claim refugee status. The United Nations High Commissioner for Refugees regards punishment for desertion or draft evasion as persecution – one of the refugee status requirements – where military actions are condemned by the international community contrary to basic rules of human conduct. The corollary of this interpretation is that Member States of the United Nations or parties to the Refugee Convention have a duty, both legal and moral, to offer asylum to individuals who refuse to be associated with actions that are contrary to the basic rules of human conduct. However it is not clear whether both *jus ad bellum* and *jus in bello* violations may be regarded as grounds of asylum in this context. Whereas the applicant, a conscientious objector as an asylum seeker, needs to establish the possibility of involvement with a *jus in bello* violation, the personal conviction of a *jus ad bellum* violation would have been the likely trigger of his or her conscientious objection to military service. In this circumstance, the grounds of asylum seekers that are based upon violation of international law by their States should not be limited to *jus in bello* violations

> I believe we can restore and extend the rule of law throughout the world. But ultimately, that will depend on the hold that the law has on our consciences.

Address by the Secretary General Kofi Annan at the general debate of the 59 session of the General Assembly, 21 September 2004.

5.1 Conscientious Objector as Asylum Seeker

It is debatable whether deserters and draft evaders are seen as eligible for refugee status on the ground of recognised or unrecognised conscientious objector status. It may be argued that the treatment they fear from the authorities on account of their actions is considered punishment for their failure to obey a law of universal

H. Takemura, *International Human Right to Conscientious Objection to Military Service and Individual Duties to Disobey Manifestly Illegal Orders*.

application, rather than persecution (Goodwin-Gill 1983, p. 33 and Happold 2005, p. 161). Difficulties exist in such a claim. 'Asylum seekers are required to show that the conscription they sought to avoid was conducted in a discriminatory manner so as to amount to persecution; or that their desertion or evasion was to avoid participating in an illegitimate conflict or (possibly) as the result of a conscientious objection to military service' (Happold 2005, p. 161). However, it cannot be said that there is no practice of recognising the treatment of conscientious objectors as persecution. In 1976, the United Kingdom's Immigration Appeal Tribunal found that punishment of conscientious objectors amounted to persecution on the basis of the law and practice then applying in Greece.[1] Although the Tribunal admitted the possibility of persecution, the Tribunal considered that the immediate cause of the persecution is a refusal to obey the law of the land, and the fact that such refusal may be due to religious beliefs or political opinion is only the secondary cause. Since refusal to bear arms is a political act for States, focusing on the cause of refusal to bear arms and deeming it as 'the law of universal application' enables States to single out those holding certain political views (Goodwin-Gill 2005, p. 34). Yet the existence of this kind of law and its application may infringe one's belief or conscience. The Tribunal's attitude ignored the importance of the infringement of beliefs and conscience and merely switched the subject.

The reluctance of the recognition of 'persecution' in the meaning of the Refugee Convention is distilled to the conundrum of how to distinguish between those opponents of States authority who do and those who do not require international protection (Goodwin-Gill 2005, p. 34).

> States are free to recognize conscientious objection in itself as a sufficient ground upon which to base recognition of refugee status. In this sense, they are free to attribute such value to the fundamental right to freedom of conscience that any measures having as their object to compel the individual to act contrary to sincerely held belief, or any punishment, such as deprivation of liberty, imposed to that end, amounts to persecution within the meaning of the 1951 Convention, regardless of its duration (Goodwin-Gill 2005, p. 59).

In the current practice of the United States, an alien must establish that punishment for the failure to serve is on account of the alien's beliefs, not just the failure to perform a legal duty.[2] While it is still difficult for conscientious objectors to seek asylum because of resistance to recognising the right to conscientious objection as an international human right, there are some positive developments for conscientious objectors (Musalo 2007, p. 69, 72).

---

[1] *Doonetas v Secretary of State for the Home Department*, TH/12339/75 (820) (unreported), approved and applied in *Atibo v Immigration Officer, London (Heathrow) Airport* [1978] ImmAR 93.

[2] *Ilchuk v Attorney General,* 434 F.3d 618, 626 (3d Cir.2006).

5.2 Thresholds for Conscientious Objector as Asylum Seeker

Conscientious objectors may claim refugee status under certain conditions under international refugee law.[3] The United Nations 'Handbook on Procedures and Criteria for Determining Refugee Status' under the 1951 Convention and the 1967 Protocol relating to the Status of Refugees prepared by the Office of the United Nations High Commissioner for Refugees of January 1992 is designed for the guidance of refugee status in the various States and the help of all those concerned with refugee problems.[4] In Part One, the criteria for the determination of refugee status is provided. Among those special cases, deserters and persons avoiding military service are enumerated.[5]

The rationale behind the general rule that prosecution and punishment of conscientious objectors can constitute persecution is that to punish an individual for adhering to a religion or belief is tantamount to prosecuting him or her for these beliefs (Musalo 2007, p. 69, 72).[6] While fear of prosecution and punishment for desertion or draft-evasion does not in itself constitute well-founded fear of persecution under the definition, desertion or draft-evasion does not exclude a person from being a refugee, and a person may be a refugee in addition to being a deserter or draft-evader.[7]

According to the United Nations High Commissioner for Refugees, persons who are deserters or draft evaders solely due to dislike of military service or fear of combat may not be considered as refugees. Therefore, 'other relevant motives for leaving or remaining outside his country [...] within the meaning of the definition' is necessary for persons claiming refugee status based on the refusal of military service (see Note 7). Namely, the necessity to perform military service may be the sole ground for a claim to refugee status, where it is established that: (1) one would suffer disproportionately severe punishment for the military offence on account of one's race, religion, nationality, membership of a particular social group or political opinion;[8] (2) one has well-founded fear of persecution on account of one's race, religion, nationality, membership of a particular social group or political opinion

[3] The Department of International Protection, Office of International Protection, Office of the United Nations High Commissioner for Refugees, *Refugee Status Determination: Identifying Who is a Refugee*, Self-study module 2 (1 September 2005) 43.

[4] UNHCR, 'Handbook on Procedures and Criteria for Determining Refugee Status under the 1951 Convention and the 1967 Protocol relating to the Status of Refugees' (United Nations, 1979, Reedited Geneva, January 1992) HCR/IP/4/Eng/REV.1 Foreword 7, 2.

[5] 'Handbook on Procedures and Criteria for Determining Refugee Status under the 1951 Convention and the 1967 Protocol relating to the Status of Refugees' [167]ff.

[6] K Musalo, 'Legal and Protection Policy Research Series: Claims for Protection Based on Religion or Belief: Analysis and Proposed Conclusions', Protection Policy and Legal Advice Section (PPLA) Department of International Protection, United Nations High Commissioner for Refugees, PPLA/2002/01 (December 2002) 39.

[7] 'Handbook on Procedures and Criteria for Determining Refugee Status under the 1951 Convention and the 1967 Protocol relating to the Status of Refugees' [168].

[8] 'Handbook on Procedures and Criteria for Determining Refugee Status under the 1951 Convention and the 1967 Protocol relating to the Status of Refugees' [169].

(see Note 8); (3) the performance of military service would have required one's participation in military action contrary to one's genuine political, religious or moral convictions, or to valid reasons of conscience.[9] As for the type of military action in the third criterion, it is not sufficient for a person to be in disagreement with his government regarding the political justification for a particular military action.[10] Where the type of military action is condemned by the international community as contrary to basic rules of human conduct, punishment for desertion or draft-evasion could in itself be regarded as 'persecution' (see Note 10).

This last condition may provide a selective conscientious objector with the opportunity of claiming refugee status. This paragraph is said to have its roots in the Nuremberg Judgment (Oostvogels 1973, pp. 143–147). For instance, the defence of superior orders is proscribed, and there is a duty on the part of individuals to abstain from military action when gross violation of human rights is likely to occur (Kuzas 1991, p. 447, 461). Member States of the United Nations or parties to the Refugee Convention have a duty, both legal and moral, to offer asylum to individuals who refuse to be associated with actions that are contrary to the basic rules of human conduct (Kuzas 1991, p. 447, 461). However, it is not completely clear, especially from the paragraphs of the Handbook, whether both *jus ad bellum* and *jus in bello* violations may be regarded as grounds of asylum in this context. The next section tackles this issue through examining domestic case law.

For the establishment of the genuineness of a person's political, religious or moral convictions, a thorough investigation of one's personality and background may be necessary.[11] This requirement would lay a burden on people claiming asylum status. The timing of the applicant's views on military service and the coerciveness of joining military service also 'may be indicative of the genuineness of one's convictions according to the Handbook' (see Note 11). This statement reflects 'a narrow view that ignores the fact that professional or voluntary soldiers may have issues of conscience, and that the notion of autonomy invites a change of view or action during the course of human experience' (Bailliet 2006, p. 344).

In sum, where a refugee claim is based on conscientious objection, the decision-maker must assess: (1) whether the applicant's religious, moral or political conviction is genuine and sufficiently profound (this requires a thorough investigation of the applicant's personal, social, religious and political profile and background); (2) whether military service would require the applicant to engage in conduct contrary to this conviction; and (3) whether there is a possibility of alternative service such as community service, which is compatible with the applicant's conviction, and which is neither excessively lengthy nor punitive in nature (if there is, refugee status

---

[9] 'Handbook on Procedures and Criteria for Determining Refugee Status under the 1951 Convention and the 1967 Protocol relating to the Status of Refugees' [170].

[10] 'Handbook on Procedures and Criteria for Determining Refugee Status under the 1951 Convention and the 1967 Protocol relating to the Status of Refugees' [171].

[11] 'Handbook on Procedures and Criteria for Determining Refugee Status under the 1951 Convention and the 1967 Protocol relating to the Status of Refugees' [174].

will not normally be granted).[12] Goodwin-Gill claims that whether prosecution and punishment amount to persecution in the sense of the Convention will depend on the 'object and purpose of the law, the precise motivation of the individual who breaches such law, the interest which such individual asserts and the nature and extent of the punishment' (Goodwin-Gill 1983, p. 59). In all cases eligibility for refugee status requires a link between the feared persecution and a Convention ground. Most of the well-founded conscientious objection cases generally show the appropriate ground under the Convention, such as political opinion and/or religion.[13]

There is an emerging State practice of recognising conscientious objectors as asylum seekers if they are forced to object due to the internationally condemned armed conflict or military service of States. It is also pointed out by the Handbook prepared by the UNHCR that: '[a]n increasing number of States have introduced legislation or administrative regulations whereby persons who can invoke genuine reasons of conscience are exempted from military service, either entirely or subject to their performing alternative (i.e. civil) service'.[14] Hence where alternatives to military service, such as community service, are imposed there would not usually be a basis for claim.[15]

Although those criteria and conditions seem to be not harmless at first sight and highly dependent on the interpretation of State parties, the website of the Office of the United Nations High Commissioner for Refugees gives a clear message to conscientious objectors who would like to claim refugee status later on. The website poses a question, among 'frequently asked questions': 'Can a draft evader be a refugee?' The answer given is: 'Every country has the right to ask its citizens to bear arms in periods of national emergency. However, citizens should have an equal right to conscientious objection. In cases where the option of conscientious objection is not observed, or where a conflict violates international norms, draft evaders who fear prosecution on political or other grounds may be eligible for refugee status'.[16] Therefore the Office of the United Nations High Commissioner for Refugees clearly recognises the right to conscientious objection under international law. The Director of the Department of International Protection of the Office of the United Nations High Commissioner for Refugees acknowledged that:

> UNHCR supports the original Commission proposal which recognised that the risk of punishment for the refusal to perform compulsory military service in the form of draft evasion or desertion may, in itself, provide grounds for a refugee claim if the reasons for the refusal

---

[12] The Department of International Protection, Office of International Protection, Office of the United Nations High Commissioner for Refugees, *Refugee Status Determination: Identifying Who is a Refugee*, Self-study module 2 (1 September 2005) 43.

[13] United Nations High Commissioner for Refugees, *Refugee Status Determination: Identifying Who is a Refugee*, 43–44.

[14] 'Handbook on Procedures and Criteria for Determining Refugee Status under the 1951 Convention and the 1967 Protocol relating to the Status of Refugees' [173].

[15] UNHCR, Guidelines on International Protection, Religion-Based Refugee Claims under article 1A(2) of the 1951 Convention and/or the 1967 Protocol relating to the Status of Refugees (28 April 2004) UN Doc HCR/GIP/04/06, 9 [26].

[16] *See* UNHCR, Protecting Refugees – Questions & Answers (2005) on the website of UNHCR.

> to perform the required military service are based on specific individual circumstances relating to deeply held moral, religious or political convictions. This interpretation is consistent with the United Nations High Commissioner for Refugee's Handbook and evolving human rights law. The Human Rights Committee in General Comment 22 (48) on Article 18 ICCPR (right to freedom of thought, conscience and religion) states that a right to conscientious objection can be derived from Article 18.[17]

The recognition of conscientious status by the home country does not seem to affect a subsequent evaluation of refugee status. To sum up, the asylum claim is likely to be granted when unrecognised conscientious objectors are opposed to any armed conflict, in other words, to those who are absolute conscientious objectors, or opposed to an armed conflict which amounts to widespread human rights violation and/or which is condemned by the international community (Kuzas 1991, p. 447, 478). It is undesirable for individuals acting out of deeply rooted conscience to have their asylum status evaluated on the basis of a number of criteria, especially those which are not relevant to the usual examination standard of a refugee.

5.3 State Practice

Looking into State practices regarding conscientious objectors as asylum seekers, military services against which people might object on the grounds of conscience, and become asylum seekers, may be divided into military activities constituting either *jus ad bellum* violation or *jus in bello* violation. However, most people tend to feel an objection to military service as soon as they realise a *jus ad bellum* violation might be involved in the initiation of an armed conflict. Soldiers might be inclined to avoid becoming involved in an unauthorised armed conflict before they commit any *jus in bello* violations. Not a few people would like to flee from situations where they are likely to be involved with doubtful military conduct before they actually have significant evidence of the fear of committing *jus in bello* violations. The *jus ad bellum*-based refugee status claim is unsuccessful, as are selective conscientious objection claims in domestic society, since there are always political considerations and sensibilities when the domestic court must decide on the legality of an armed conflict. In this sense, a careful balance should be struck between at least moral State responsibilities of protecting foreigners in its territory who are under serious human rights violations, and diplomatic considerations, though the latter must not be exaggerated, especially because normally not the executive but the judiciary has the final say on refugee status in the domestic legal system. Kuzas suggested this must be achieved by means of limiting construction of the operative phrase in paragraph 171 of the Handbook of the United Nations High Commissioner for Refugees (Kuzas 1991, p. 461). To examine to what extent the asylum applicant's perception of himself as a defender of *jus ad bellum* or *jus in bello* is taken into consideration in asylum determinations is very important (Bailliet 2006, p. 338).

---

[17] Statement by Ms. Erika Feller, Director, Department of International Protection, UNHCR, SCIFA (Brussels, 6 November 2002).

5.3.1 The Krotov Case

A British court in May 2004 granted political asylum to Andrel Krotov, a Russian conscript who fled hostilities in Chechnya and came to the United Kingdom in February 2000 and requested asylum.[18] Krotov may be characterised as a selective conscientious objector since 'he objected to the war as politically motivated and although he had no in principle objection to war in circumstances such as those of the Second World War' (see Note 18). He objected to a war in which he would be required to kill innocent civilians and destroy property in a reprehensible manner (see Note 18). Krotov also had a fear of the poor conditions of service and the treatment which he would receive as a deserter who was likely to be imprisoned for a disproportionately long time in bad conditions (see Note 18).

In the decisions of his motion and appeals, the debate was fought over the selective nature of his conscientious objection and the onus of proof that the war in Chechnya had been condemned by the international community as contrary to the basic rules of human conduct.[19] Thus the original adjudicator, Mr. D. J. Boyd QC, dismissed his appeal, finding that while he did not qualify as a conscientious objector in general, he might nevertheless qualify if the Chechnya conflict had been condemned by the international community, but there was no evidence of this.[20] The Immigration Appeal Tribunal dismissed an appeal on 2 May 2002, where the Tribunal again found evidence well short of the international condemnation which in their view is required for the applicant to succeed on this point.[21] However, the Court of Appeal granted the appeal and remitted the matter to a differently constituted Immigration Appeal Tribunal on 11 February 2004. While granting the appeal, Lord Justice Potter stressed the importance of the judicial review over the situation of a controversial armed conflict:

> It is (or certainly should be) the function of the Home Department to keep under review the conditions prevailing in 'hot spots' such as Chechnya in order to inform its decision in respect of an applicant relying upon those conditions as justifying his refusal to serve. So far as adjudicators are concerned, it will be appropriate for the Immigration Appeal Tribunal by 'starred' decisions from time to time, triggered by the appeal of an applicant who relies upon up-to-date reports and other authoritative materials available as to the nature of the conflict concerned, to review such conditions and material for the purpose of providing guidance to adjudicators in subsequent cases.[22]

Hence, for the Tribunal there is 'the necessity for the courts, in seeking to define and apply the working test in cases of this kind, to have regard to the realities of

[18] AK (Russia-Chechnya Deserter) Russia [2004] UKIAT 00294, 29 October 2004 [1].

[19] AK (Russia-Chechnya Deserter) Russia [2004] UKIAT 00294, 29 October 2004 [2]–[3].

[20] Decision of Mr. DJ Boyd QC [25], quoted in the Supreme Court of Judicature Court of Appeal (Civil Division) on Appeal from the Immigration Appeal Tribunal, [2004] EWCA Civ 69, Case No. C1/2002/1537/IATRF (11 February 2004) [2].

[21] Decision on AK (Article 3 – Military Service – Chechen War) Russia CG, [2002] UKIAT 01325, Appeal no. HX 42619–01 (2 May 2002) [4].

[22] The Supreme Court of Judicature Court of Appeal (Civil Division) on Appeal from the Immigration Appeal Tribunal, [2004] EWCA Civ 69, Case No. C1/2002/1537/IATRF, 11 February 2004 [52].

the particular conflict in which an applicant has refused to participate rather than to the specific question whether or not that conflict has yet been internationally condemned'.[23] The Convention ground in the meaning of paragraph 171 of the Handbook has been established:

> [i]f a court or tribunal is satisfied (a) that the level and nature of the conflict, and the attitude of the relevant governmental authority towards it, has reached a position where combatants are or may be required on a sufficiently widespread basis to act in breach of the basic rules of human conduct generally recognised by the international community, (b) that they will be punished for refusing to do so; and (c) that disapproval of such methods and fear of such punishment is the genuine reason motivating the refusal of an asylum seeker to serve in the relevant conflict (see Note 23).

The Immigration Appeal Tribunal, Britain's highest judicial authority on asylum applications, decided to grant asylum to Andrei Krotov on 29 October 2004.[24] In order to assess the evidence of the conduct of the war in Chechnya at the time Krotov served, the Tribunal looked at the 2001 US State Department Report on Russia for 2000, the CIPU (Country Information and Policy Unit) report of 2000 and 2001, reports by Non-Governmental Organisations such as Amnesty International and Human Rights Watch, and the United Nations Commission on Human Rights Resolution of April 2000, as well as the Resolution of the Parliamentary Assembly of the Council of Europe of January 2001. The Tribunal observed that the evidence of the breaches of the basic rules of human conduct by the Russian operation in Chechnya showed that they are widespread enough to have occurred in the frontline involving ordinary frontline soldiers.[25] The Tribunal thus concluded that: 'at least during this period of large scale conflict the evidence shows that breaches of those basic rules were widespread'.[26]

The Appeals Tribunal then considered the question whether Krotov was required or may have been required to participate in the actions containing violations of the rules of human conduct. Since a counsel for Krotov essentially relied on the asserted widespread nature of inhuman conduct as demonstrating the reality of the requirement to participate, Krotov's evidence was silent as to any personal evidence or knowledge.[27] The Appeals Tribunal eventually inferred the possibility of participation from the evidence of widespread breaches.[28] The Tribunal allowed the appeal and concluded that:

> The evidence shows that breaches of the basic rules of human conduct are sufficiently widespread that it should be inferred that the Appellant was at a real risk of being required to participate in such acts in the broad sense described, that he would have been formally

---

[23] The Supreme Court of Judicature Court of Appeal (Civil Division) on Appeal from the Immigration Appeal Tribunal, [2004] EWCA Civ 69, Case No. C1/2002/1537/IATRF, 11 February 2004 [51].

[24] A Modesty, 'Britain Grants Russian Soldier Asylum', *Moscow Times* (22 November 2004).

[25] AK (Russia-Chechnya Deserter) Russia [2004] UKIAT 00294, 29 October 2004 [25].

[26] AK (Russia-Chechnya Deserter) Russia [2004] UKIAT 00294, 29 October 2004 [26].

[27] AK (Russia-Chechnya Deserter) Russia [2004] UKIAT 00294, 29 October 2004 [28].

[28] AK (Russia-Chechnya Deserter) Russia [2004] UKIAT 00294, 29 October 2004 [30].

> or informally punished for any refusal to do so and that fear of the consequences was a significant part of his claim for asylum.[29]

This clear recognition of judicial review of the contested armed conflict's human rights violations claimed by an asylum seeker is definitely progress in both recognising the necessity of judicial review and opening the way to inference of the possibility of participation in a *jus in bello* violation. One may compare this decision with the precedent case, *Sepet v Secretary of State*, which was upheld by the House of Lords.[30] In the *Sepet* case of 2001, Justice Laws noted that:

> The balance here between legal duty and private conscience touches the question, what may the State demand of its citizens; and it does so in a context where the State's very function of protecting its people from internal or external threats – sometimes thought to be the first duty of governments – is or may be immediately involved. It might reasonably be thought that the striking of such a balance, at least in a democracy, is for the legislative and executive arms of government, and not for the judiciary'.[31]

The practices of the Norwegian Immigration Appeals Board are more conservative than the *Krotov* decisions. They evinced some refusals of granting asylum for selective conscientious objectors from Israel on account of the lack of evidence of 'real risk' of participation in military actions condemned by the international community (Bailliet 2006, p. 374).

5.3.2 Hinzman Case

Jeremy Hinzman was an American soldier who deserted the United States Army after his unit was deployed to fight in the Iraq armed conflict that began in 2003.[32] Hinzman claimed that in mid-January 2004, he received notification that his battalion was to be deployed to Iraq.[33] Hinzman deserted because of his strong moral objections to the war in Iraq, and his belief that the American-led military action in that country is illegal.[34] After deserting the military, Hinzman went to Canada and claimed refugee status for himself as well as for his wife and his son. The family's claims were rejected by the Refugee Protection Division of the Immigration and Refugee Board of Canada.[35] Hinzman then sought a judicial review of the Board's decision.

---

[29] AK (Russia-Chechnya Deserter) Russia [2004] UKIAT 00294, 29 October 2004 [31].

[30] *Sepet v Secretary of the State for the Home Dep't* [2003] HL 15, [2003] 1 WLR 856 (20 March 2003).

[31] *Basin Sepet, Redeem Bulbul v Secretary of State for the Home Department*, in the Supreme Court of Judicature Court of Appeal (Civil Division) on Appeal from the Immigration Appeal Tribunal, [2001] EWCA Civ. 681, Case No: C/2777 & C/2000/2794 (11 May 2001) [72].

[32] *Hinzman v Canada (Minister of Citizenship & Immigration)* 31 March 2006 [1].

[33] Jeremy Hinzman and Liam Lime Nguyen Hinzman, Immigration and Refugee Board Decision (16 March 2005) 2 [4]. <http://www.cisr-irb.gc.ca/en/decisions/public/hinzman/hinzman_e.pdf> accessed 3 July 2007.

[34] *Hinzman v Canada (Minister of Citizenship & Immigration)* 31 March 2006 [1].

[35] *Hinzman v Canada (Minister of Citizenship & Immigration)* 31 March 2006 [2].

The issue seemingly centred on granting refugee status on the ground of conscientious objection due to the *jus ad bellum* violation. One of the grounds of appeal by Hinzman was that the Immigration and Refugee Board was wrong to conclude that the 'type of military action' mentioned in paragraph 171 refers to 'on the ground' violations of international humanitarian law governing the conduct of actions during an armed conflict (*jus in bello*), and not to violations of international law governing the use of force or the prevention of war itself (*jus ad bellum*).[36] After examining the case law, Justice Anna MacTavish found that:

> These cases clearly establish that direct participation or complicity in military actions that are in violation of international humanitarian law will bring a refugee claimant within the exception contemplated by paragraph 171 of the Handbook. What is less clear is whether the mere participation of a foot soldier in an illegal war of aggression will also allow a claimant to derive the benefit of the provision.[37]

In the course of a closer look at case law, the level of participation of the claimant showed great significance.[38]

The unwillingness of the Judge of the Federal Court of Appeal, Justice MacTavish, to decide upon the illegality of the Iraqi war was evident when she noted that: 'the question of whether the American-led military intervention in Iraq is in fact illegal is not before the Court, and no finding has been made in this regard'.[39] Referring to the documents of the Preparatory Commission for the International Criminal Court, the Court found that the jurisprudence of the international military tribunals and other international practice establish that an individual must be involved at the policy-making level to be culpable of crime against peace.[40] Conversely, the Court clarified that an individual cannot be held criminally responsible merely for fighting in support of an illegal war, assuming that his or her own personal wartime conduct is otherwise proper.[41] The reasoning is significant in that it associates international criminal law and international refugee law, which is more broadly characterised as

[36] *Hinzman v Canada (Minister of Citizenship & Immigration)* 31 March 2006 [95].

[37] *Hinzman v Canada (Minister of Citizenship & Immigration)* 31 March 2006 [130].

[38] *For example,* in *Zolfagharkhani v Canada (Minister of Employment & Immigration)* [1993] 3 FC 540 (Fed CA), the Federal Court of Appeal found that the level of participation of the claimant as a paramedic would have been of material assistance in advancing the goals of the Iranian forces by helping the violators of international humanitarian law with the side-effects of the unlawful weapon. In *Diab v Canada (Minister of Employment & Immigration)* [1994] FCJ No. 1277 (Fed CA), the Court also allowed the appeal of a refugee claimant who refused to be involved in military activities which amounted to crimes against humanity. In the case of *Randosevic v Canada (Minister of Citizenship & Immigration)* [1995] FCJ No. 74 (Fed TD), the Court dismissed an application for judicial review since it found that it was unlikely that the claimant would personally have been called upon to commit atrocities. See the *Hinzman* decision, [125]–[129].

[39] *Hinzman v Canada (Minister of Citizenship & Immigration)* 31 March 2006 [5].

[40] *Hinzman v Canada (Minister of Citizenship & Immigration)* 31 March 2006 [157], the Papers for the Preparatory Commission for the International Criminal Court, PCNICC/2002/WGCA/L.1, and PCNICC/2002/WGCA/L.1/Add.1.

[41] *Hinzman v Canada (Minister of Citizenship & Immigration)* 31 March 2006 [158], the Papers for the Preparatory Commission for the International Criminal Court, PCNICC/2002/WGCA/L.1, and PCNICC/2002/WGCA/L.1/Add.1.

international human rights law. Yet the *Hinzman* decision also introduced the interpretations of elements of international crimes for decisions on asylum in the context of international refugee law.

On the one hand this decision is criticised as 'discriminatory' since this decision means Canadian authority only permits higher level commanders to raise conscientious objection grounded in *jus ad bellum*, but not lower rank soldiers (Bailliet 2006, p. 373).

> A soldier may hold himself morally responsible for his participation in a war of aggression, irrespective of whether or not he may be held *liable under international law*.... This is an inappropriate amalgamation of international criminal law upon refugee law which infringes upon the right to conscience....(Bailliet 2006, p. 373) [Therefore], [the] identification of a low standard of proof relating to the applicant's belief (as understood within refugee law), leaving room for the adoption of human rights law standards that call for accepting conscientious objection claims to be accepted without further examination rather than examination of whether the military action may be prosecuted under international criminal law' (emphasis added) (Bailliet 2006, p. 383).

On the other hand, the systematic approach to the crime of aggression may be desirable for normative consistency of public international law. Even though a consistent and systematic interpretation of the crime of aggression within public international law is preferred, it is dubious whether an interpretation of paragraph 171 of the Handbook of the United Nations High Commissioner for Refugees itself provides any implication on the crime of aggression. Thus this case certainly raises the question of the emergence of either unintended amalgamation or dissonance between international criminal law and international refugee law.

5.3.3 Position of Refugee Status Appeals Authority of New Zealand

Once the authority in New Zealand tended to deny asylum claims from conscientious objectors, since they understood that military service is imposed by way of a law of universal application and no convention ground exists in the service itself and in punishment for refusal (Musalo 2007, p. 75). In 2005 the case of a Kurdish conscientious objector, the Refugee Status Appeals Authority concluded that an intent to persecute was not required and what was required was only a showing that the 'Convention-protected ground' was 'a contributing cause' to a risk of being persecuted.[42] Moreover, the Refugee Status Appeals Authority reiterated its preference for determining refugee status issues via a human rights approach.[43] This human rights approach 'requires the decision-maker to determine first, the nature and extent of the right in question and second, the permissible limitations which may be imposed by the state'.[44] The structure for the analysis under the human rights

[42] Musalo (2007, p. 75); Refugee Status Appeals Authority, Refugee Appeal No. 75378/05 (19 October 2005) [112].

[43] Refugee Appeal No. 75378/05 (19 October 2005) [43].

[44] Refugee Appeal No. 74665/03 (7 July 2004) [115].

approach is 'principled, flexible, politically sanctioned and genuinely international' (see Note 44). Under this approach, the critical question is whether an objection by a refugee claimant to the performance of military service can be considered to be within the ambit of a right contained in any of the international human rights instruments such as the Universal Declaration of Human Rights and the International Covenant on Civil and Political Rights.[45]

The Kurdish conscientious objector from Turkey was granted asylum status under this approach. The Refugee Status Appeals Authority referred to the British cases of Krotov and Sepet and held that no one can be compelled to undertake military service where a real chance exists that this will require the refugee claimant to commit human rights abuses.[46]

> Given the history of the conflict, attendant breaches of the laws of war on a widespread scale in the past and a continuing climate of impunity for those who commit the breaches, the chance of the appellant being personally involved by being required to commit acts in breach of the laws of war now that open conflict has resumed, cannot be dismissed as mere surmise or conjecture.[47]

Here it is unique that a climate of impunity for perpetrators of gross human rights abuses is considered to be one of the factors of the likelihood of being compelled to commit humanitarian law violations. The New Zealand authority thus regarded the likelihood of being forced to commit humanitarian law violations as his or her potential imprisonment for resisting service and translated it into persecution for a Convention reason (Musalo 2007, p. 75).

5.3.4 Iranian Selective Conscientious Objector in Time of Peace

A United Kingdom case concerning an Iranian deserter who refused to plant landmines in a civilian area in Iranian Kurdistan invokes several issues including an issue of the status of selective conscientious objector as a ground of asylum and the applicability of international humanitarian law (*jus in bello*) in peace time. The Iranian deserter claimed to be a refugee under the 1951 UN Convention relating to the Status of Refugees and the Protocol of 1967 on the basis that, if returned, he will be punished (or killed) by the Iranian military authorities for having deserted from the Iranian army on being ordered to plant landmines in a civilian area in Iranian Kurdistan.[48]

The Asylum and Immigration Tribunal drew three alternative conditions from *Sepet* that punishment of disobeying military orders would amount to persecution under the meaning of the Refugee Convention: (i) refusal to obey the order on the ground that obedience would or might amount to commission of 'atrocities

[45] Refugee Appeal No. 75378/05 (19 October 2005) [45]–[46].

[46] Refugee Appeal No. 75378/05 (19 October 2005) [88].

[47] Refugee Appeal No. 75378/05 (19 October 2005) [142].

[48] BE (Disobedience to orders – landmines) Iran [2007] UKAIT 00035 (12 March 2007) [1].

or gross human rights abuses'; (ii) refusal to obey on the ground that obedience would mean participation in 'a conflict condemned by the international community'; and (iii) refusal to obey where the refusal itself would 'earn grossly excessive or disproportionate punishment'.[49]

First of all, the Tribunal rejected the possibility of the applicability of the condition (ii) on the ground that military order in question was not given in the situation of armed conflict.[50] The Tribunal also rejected the condition (iii) since the international law of armed conflict is more extensive and detailed than international law as it applies to situations other than armed conflict, and it cannot be assumed that an act prohibited in armed conflict is also prohibited in peace.[51] Condition (iii) seems to be not to have been dealt with seriously by either the defence or the judgment.

As for international criminal obligation to disobey illegal orders which would constitute crimes against humanity or war crimes, under the terms of article 1F(a) of the Refugee Convention, the Tribunal required the circumstantial evidence drawn from article 6 of the Charter of the International Military Tribunal (Nuremberg Charter) and said that: "[there is] in our view no doubt both from the wording of these clauses and their context that they refer only to acts committed in a conflict or (in the case of (c)) before a conflict that actually takes place".[52] Article 1F(c) of the Refugee Convention was further interpreted as follows: "[it is] inconceivable that an ordinary soldier carrying out orders could be seen as having such individual responsibility for the maintenance of international peace that he could be penalised under this head".[53]

This judgment by the Asylum and Immigration Tribunal is problematic in that it narrowed the interpretation of individual criminal responsibility for international crimes and unnecessarily associated the issue of recognition of refugee status with this narrowed interpretation of international criminal law.

5.3.5 European Union Qualification Directive

A Directive adopted by the European Union is a noteworthy document for conscientious objectors as asylum seekers. The Council of the European Union adopted the European Union Qualification Directive on 29 April 2004.[54] The Directive entered into force on 20 October 2004. It is to ensure that Member States of the European Union apply common criteria for the identification of asylum seekers and that a

---

[49] BE (Disobedience to orders – landmines) Iran [2007] UKAIT 00035 (12 March 2007) [13].

[50] BE (Disobedience to orders – landmines) Iran [2007] UKAIT 00035 (12 March 2007) [14].

[51] BE (Disobedience to orders – landmines) Iran [2007] UKAIT 00035 (12 March 2007) [16]–[13].

[52] BE (Disobedience to orders – landmines) Iran [2007] UKAIT 00035 (12 March 2007) [43].

[53] BE (Disobedience to orders – landmines) Iran [2007] UKAIT 00035 (12 March 2007) [49].

[54] Council Directive 2004/83/EC of 29 April 2004 on Minimum Standards for the Qualification and Status of Third Country Nationals or Stateless Person as Refugees or as Persons Who Otherwise Need International Protection and the Content of the Protection Granted [2004] OJ L304/12.

minimum level of benefit is available for asylum seekers in all Member States.[55] In article 9, the acts of 'persecution' include 'prosecution or punishment for refusal to perform military service in a conflict, where performing military service would include crimes or acts falling under the exclusion clauses'.[56] This clause may be significant in that the Directive grants refugee status in the case of someone performing military service that has the possibility of including crime against peace, war crime, crime against humanity, serious non-political crime or acts contrary to the purposes and principles of the United Nations as set out in the Preamble and Articles 1 and 2 of the Charter of the United Nations.[57] The Directive recognises the possibility of a *jus in bello* violation as a ground of persecution.

However, the definition of persecution in relation to military service in the Directive appears to be narrower than the definition taken by the United Nations High Commissioner for Refugees. For the United Nations High Commissioner for Refugees recommends refugee status whenever the military service is contrary to genuine political, religious or moral convictions, or to valid reasons of conscience.[58] The wider interpretation of article 9 enables military service to be considered as persecution in other two cases (Lambert 2006, p. 161, 168): where the punishment is found to be disproportionately harsh or severe,[59] and where the conditions of military service are themselves so harsh as to amount to persecution on the facts.[60]

Yet the fact remains that the draft of the Directive allowed for the reasons for the refusal to perform military service to be based on specific individual circumstances relating to deeply held moral, religious or political convictions.[61] This wording was not retained.

---

[55] Council Directive 2004/83/EC of 29 April 2004 on Minimum Standards for the Qualification and Status of Third Country Nationals or Stateless Person as Refugees or as Persons Who Otherwise Need International Protection and the Content of the Protection Granted [2004] OJ L304/12, Preamble (6).

[56] Council Directive 2004/83/EC of 29 April 2004 on Minimum Standards for the Qualification and Status of Third Country Nationals or Stateless Person as Refugees or as Persons Who Otherwise Need International Protection and the Content of the Protection Granted [2004] OJ L304/12, Preamble (6), Article 9(2).

[57] Council Directive 2004/83/EC of 29 April 2004 on Minimum Standards for the Qualification and Status of Third Country Nationals or Stateless Person as Refugees or as Persons Who Otherwise Need International Protection and the Content of the Protection Granted [2004] OJ L304/12, Preamble (6), Article 9(2), Article 12(2)(a)–(c).

[58] United Nations High Commissioner for Refugees, UNHCR Refugee Policy and Practice, Information Note on Article 1 of the 1951 Convention (March 1995).

[59] The European Union Qualification Directive, Article 9(2)(c).

[60] The European Union Qualification Directive, Article 9(2)(a).

[61] European Council on Refugees and Exiles, Information Note on the Council Directive 2004/83/EC of 29 April 2004 on Minimum Standards for the Qualification of Third Country Nationals and Stateless persons as refugees or as Persons Who Otherwise Need International Protection and the Content of the Protection Granted, IN1/10/2004/ext/CN, 9.

5.4 Conscientious Objection to Military Service Itself as Ground for Asylum

A survey of the case laws concerning the validity of conscientious objections against military service as ground for asylum shows that national practices are split on this issue. While Austrian and German courts do not acknowledge the validity of such claims, the United States' courts do (Davy 1995, p. 53, 103).

As far as the deserters from the conflict in former Yugoslavia are concerned, the United States courts admitted that applicants rejecting military service for political or religious reasons might be eligible for asylum from time to time.[62] The US Ninth Circuit Court ruled that the enforcement of 'facially neutral' conscription laws might nonetheless result in different punishment when applied to conscientious objectors.[63] It should be noted that: 'United States courts also found that forced conscription amounted to persecution if the applicant was compelled to participate in activities contrary to international humanitarian law'.[64] Likewise the United States also granted asylum status to a Serbian soldier, Radisav Vujisic, who fled Yugoslavia and entered the United States by falsely claiming American citizenship. The conflict in former Yugoslavia was so widely and publicly condemned by the international community that it was not difficult for the American judiciary to conclude that there had been continued international condemnation of Yugoslavia's campaign in Kosovo and Bosnia since 1991.[65] Still, this conclusion must be seen as positive when one compares this American judicial attitude with that of Austria at the same time (Davy 1995, pp. 66–74). For the Austrian Asylum Office, since the military obligation is derived from an indigenous and sovereign right of the state, enforcement of this obligation would not constitute persecution, even if the alleged sanctions seemed very harsh.[66]

5.5 Concluding Remarks

Case law in various jurisdictions shows a range of difficulties arising from asylum claims of conscientious objectors to military service. One of the biggest difficulties may be the unwillingness of many national and international institutions to issue

---

[62] Abedni v INS, 971 F.2d 188, 191 (9th Cir. 1992); Castillo v INS, 951 F.2d 1117, 1122 (9th Cir. 1991); Alonzo v INS, 915 F.2d 546, 548 (9th Cir. 1990); M.A. A26851062 v INS, 858 F.2d 210, 215 (4th Cir. 1988). *See* Davy (1995, p. 96).

[63] Canas-Segovia v INS, 902 F.2d 717 (9th Cir. 1990). *S*ee Davy (1995, pp. 96–97).

[64] Davy (1995, pp. 98–99). In *Barraza Rivera v INS*, the Ninth Circuit recognized that the applicant did not object to military service in general, but to performing inhuman acts under military orders, the court found the concept of conscience broad enough to cover the applicant's dilemma. *Barraza Rivera v INS*, 913 F2d 1443, 1450 (9th Cir. 1990).

[65] *Vujisic v INS*. 224 F. 3d 578 (7th Cir. 2000), decided 7 August 2000.

[66] Decision of 9 August 1993, Asylum Office, Branch Office Innsbruck, No. 93.02.804, at 4, cited by Davy (1995, p. 68).

condemnations in order to preserve their own diplomatic and economic considerations (Bailliet 2007, p. 354). However, the British *Krotov* case may be suggestive and promising in recognising that judicial review is necessary for checking human rights abuses in the conflict at issue. This kind of judicial review tends to be over a *jus in bello* violation rather than *jus ad bellum* violation, though both may be seen as connected somehow by the authorities of States. If one takes into account the international criminal norm, the recognition of a *jus ad bellum* violation is likely to be found unnecessary by domestic courts, as in the Hinzman case, since a *jus ad bellum* violation in international criminal law is often only attributed to leaders having made general policy concerning the violation in question, not to lower rank soldiers.

Hence a claim based on a *jus in bello* violation appeals to an immigration authority in the domestic sphere because such a claim tends to be more concrete than one based upon a *jus ad bellum* violation. States are more likely to point their fingers at another State if they have concrete evidence of a *jus in bello* violation.

Whereas the applicant, a conscientious objector as an asylum seeker, needs to establish the possibility of involvement with a *jus in bello* violation, the personal conviction of a *jus ad bellum* violation would have been the likely trigger of his or her conscientious objection to military service from the outset. At least the wordings of paragraph 171 of the United Nations High Commissioner for Refugees 'Handbook on Procedures and Criteria for Determining Refugee Status' appear to require the judgment of the *jus ad bellum* violation. Although 'military action' being condemned seems to suggest the *jus in bello* violation, normally the international community condemns military action in the sense of the *jus ad bellum* violation rather than only the *jus in bello* violation.

> Where, however, the type of military action, with which an individual does not wish to be associated, is condemned by the international community as contrary to basic rules of human conduct, punishment for desertion or draft-evasion could, in the light of all other requirements of the definition, in itself be regarded as persecution.[67]

The position of the United Nations High Commissioner for Refugees, which demands from authorities consideration on the basis of *jus ad bellum*, is more obvious on its website, as stated above. Its question and answer shows that 'where *a conflict* violates international norms, draft evaders who fear persecution on political or other grounds may be eligible for refugee status' (emphasis added). This implies that even draft evaders who were not eligible for or who did not qualify as conscientious objectors may be regarded as refugees on the sole basis of a *jus ad bellum* violation of their State.

The grounds of asylum seekers that are based upon violation of international law by their States should not be limited to *jus in bello* violation. This is partly because there is a practical difficulty in proving a likelihood of participating in a *jus in bello* violation. Another reason is that lower rank soldiers and reservists may not be familiar with the distinction between *jus ad bellum* and *jus in bello*. They are

[67] 'Handbook on Procedures and Criteria for Determining Refugee Status under the 1951 Convention and the 1967 Protocol relating to the Status of Refugees' [171].

possibly influenced more by *jus ad bellum* and world opinion against a conflict in which their State is involved than by a *jus in bello* violation. Moreover, of course, the cumulative violations of *jus in bello* may affect a domestic judicial review over *jus ad bellum*, and the relationship between them seems never to be clarified, even in the international dimension. The issue of the relationship between *jus ad bellum* and *jus in bello* is considered in Chap. 7, after Chap. 6 explores the question of how international criminal law develops the duty of individuals to disobey manifestly illegal orders under international criminal law as a corollary of limiting the defence of superior orders.

References

Journal Article

Bailliet C (2006) Assessing jus ad bellum and jus in bello within the refugee status determination process. Georget Immgr Law J 20(3):337–384

Davy U (1995) Refugees from Bosnia and Herzegovina: Are they genuine? Suffolk Transnatl Law Rev 18:53–131

Kuzas KJ (1991) Asylum for unrecognized conscientious objectors to military service: 'Is there a right not to fight?' Va J Int Law 31:447–478

Lambert H (2006) The EU asylum qualification directive, its Impact on the jurisprudence of the United Kingdom and international law. Int Comp Law Q 55:161–192

Musalo K (2007) Conscientious objection as a basis for refugee status: Protection for the fundamental right of freedom of thought, conscience and religion. Refug Surv Q 26:69–78

Oostvogels SAM (1973) Foreign deserters and asylum in the Netherlands: The case of Ralph J. Waver. Neth Yearbk Int Law 4:143–192

Book

Goodwin-Gill GS (1983) The refugee in international law. Clarendon Press, Oxford

Happold M (2005) Child soldiers in international law. Manchester University Press, Manchester

Chapter 6
Defence of Superior Orders: Duties of Individuals to Disobey Manifestly Illegal Orders under International Law

Abstract This chapter looks at the history and the obstinate problem of the defence of superior orders. It is an indisputable fact that international criminal law has sought to narrow the scope of the defence of superior orders. Even domestic practices show that manifestly illegal orders should not be obeyed. Although it is safe to state that soldiers have duties to disobey manifestly illegal orders under international criminal law, the scope of duties is not crystal-clear especially in relation to *jus ad bellum* violations. Therefore this chapter considers the criminality and illegality of particular types of acts under international criminal law, genocide, apartheid and aggression in light of manifest illegality in international law. Such an examination will contribute to our knowledge of what the boundaries of individual criminal responsibility for these acts are and ultimately of the extent of the individual's duty to disobey orders to commit these acts.

> 26. Obedience to superior orders shall be no defence if law enforcement officials knew that an order to use force and firearms resulting in the death or serious injury of a person was manifestly unlawful and had a reasonable opportunity to refuse to follow it. In any case, responsibility also rests on the superiors who gave the unlawful orders.

Basic Principles on the Use of Force and Firearms by Law Enforcement Officials (1990).[1]

6.1 Defence of Superior Orders and Duties of Individuals

The defence of superior orders is a defence which is claimed by a subordinate who commits a violation of international humanitarian law by following an order of his or her superior. The problem of the defence of superior orders concerns whether

[1] Adopted by the Eighth United Nations Congress on the Prevention of Crime and the Treatment of Offenders, Havana, Cuba, 27 August to 7 September 1990, U.N. Doc. A/CONF.144/28/Rev.1 at 112 (1990).

H. Takemura, *International Human Right to Conscientious Objection to Military Service and Individual Duties to Disobey Manifestly Illegal Orders.*

superior orders can excuse the illegal conduct of one who is ordered to commit an illegal act. The answer to this question has been pursued and has evolved over the centuries with both domestic and international dimensions. Therefore the problem concerning the plea of superior orders has been generally conceived as one of the great complexities in international and in domestic law (Lauterpacht 1944, p. 58, 70).

There are duties of States and individuals in relation to the defence of superior orders under public international law. A court confronted with the plea of superior orders adduced in justification of a war crime is bound to take into consideration the fact that obedience to military orders, not manifestly illegal, is the duty of every member of the armed forces.[2] Individuals cannot be expected to weigh scrupulously the legal merits of an order received under conditions of war (see Note 2). Hence there exists a major principle that: 'Members of the armed forces, in particular, are bound to obey lawful orders only and that they cannot therefore escape liability, if, in obedience to a command, they commit acts which both violate unchallenged rules of warfare and outrage the general sentiment of humanity'.[3]

However, the problem of the 'soldier's dilemma' often appears in the face of both strict military discipline and humanitarian considerations, required by international norms. The rules of warfare are often controversial. As seen above, there is also an unresolved issue of the relationship between *jus ad bellum* and *jus in bello*. For instance, '[a]n act otherwise amounting to a war crime may have been executed in obedience to orders conceived as a measure of reprisal' (see Note 2). The vagueness of *jus ad bellum* and the periphery of uncertainty surrounding *jus in bello*, especially war crimes, in the twenty-first century may have great influence on soldiers, volunteers and conscripts facing manifestly illegal orders. The application of the prohibition of the use of force is even more controversial. Neither *jus ad bellum* nor *jus in bello* may be crystal-clear in practice to foot-level soldiers, though it is desirable to make them fully aware of these international norms.

The next section will provide a short history of the defence of superior orders. The defence of superior orders reveals a broad picture of the duties of individuals, especially those of lower ranks, under public international law. This section will contribute to provide general ideas: What may be legal grounds for conscientious objections?

[2] Daes Report, 57 [268].

[3] Daes Report, 57 [269].

6.2 History of Defence of Superior Orders Under International Law

The history of the defence of superior orders is as old as the history of the international criminal trial. A medieval attempt at international criminal justice took place in 1474.[4] This was the trial of the Governor of Breisach, Peter von Hagenbach, who raised the plea of obedience to orders of his superior, the Duke of Burgundy, at his trial for murder, arson and rape (Schwarzenberger 1968, pp. 462–466). The Duke of Burgundy had let Peter von Hagenbach take the helm of the government of the fortified city of Breisach, located on the Upper Rhine (Greppi 1999, p. 533). It is said that Hagenbach merely carried out his master's instruction to reduce the citizens of Breisach to a state of submission (Schwarzenberger 1968, p. 462). The outcome of the brutality committed by him affected the inhabitants of neighbouring territories as well as Swiss merchants on their way to and from the Frankfurt fairs (Schwarzenberger 1968, pp. 462–463). The outrageous acts of Hagenbach led to alliances against Burgundy by all her neighbours: Austria, Berne, France and the towns and knights of the Upper Rhine (Schwarzenberger 1968, p. 463). Finally, a revolt by Hagenbach's German mercenaries in Breisach and the citizens of that town enabled his enemies to seize Hagenbach and put him on trial even before the end of their war with the Duke of Burgundy (Schwarzenberger 1968, p. 463).

The archduke of Austria, who had petitioned the Duke of Burgundy to take Breisach, ordered Hagenbach's trial. The ad hoc tribunal was composed of 28 judges from the allied towns, though a local court was selected for the forum (Schwarzenberger 1968, p. 463). It appears more like a regional effort to make an ad hoc criminal court applying international law.[5] Regardless of his plea of superior orders, Hagenbach was convicted and deprived of his knighthood for crimes he had owed a duty to prevent (Parks 1973, p. 1, 5). Even though he was in compliance with the orders of his superior, he had 'trampled under foot the laws of God and of man' (Schwarzenberger 2003, p. 309, 311).

Having acknowledged this experimental medieval trans-regional criminal justice, the issue of superior orders has been recognised as an issue of public international law since the twentieth century, especially since World War I, as the history of individual criminal responsibility under international law itself. In 1906, one of the most prominent international law scholars at the time, Lassa Oppenheim, published the first edition of his treatise on international law, which recognised the absolute effect of the defence of superior orders (Oppenheim 1906, p. 264). Hence Oppenheim did not regard members of armed forces committing violations of the rules

[4] Control Council Law No. 10 Case, *Trial of Wilhelm von Leeb & 13 Others ('German High Command')*, 28 October 1948, 'We also refer to an article from *The Manchester Guardian* of 28 September 1946, containing a description of the trial of Sir Peter of Hagenbach held at Breisach in 1474. The charges against him were analogous to the modern concept 'crimes against humanity'. He was convicted.'

[5] Schwarzenberger (1968, p. 463). 'It is debatable whether, in form, the tribunal can be described as an international tribunal. The question turns on the date when the Swiss Confederation had effectively seceded from the Holy Roman Empire'.

of warfare following orders of their Government as war criminals. This position was not changed until the fifth edition of the treatise (Oppenheim 1906, pp. 264–265; 1912, p. 310; 1921, p. 342–343; 1926, pp. 410–411; 1935, pp. 453–454 and Dinstein 1965, p. 38). Moreover, the then British Manual of Military Law, in its paragraph 443 of Chapter XIV, took the same approach as the first edition of the Oppenheim's textbook.[6] The United States Rules of Land Warfare adopted the same principle in its paragraph 347 (see Note 6).

Prior to World War I, the problem of superior orders did not play a large role, since the so-called 'Act of State' doctrine had reigned until that time (Eser 1996, p. 251, 254). Under this doctrine, only States could be held liable in international law, while the responsibility of individuals was basically irrelevant. Nevertheless, some jurisprudence exists from after World War I. The Treaty of Versailles, signed at Versailles on 28 June 1919, called for the trials of William II of Hohenzollern and persons accused of having committed acts in violation of the laws and customs of war.[7] Before reaching the agreement that led to the Versailles Treaty, there was much discussion on the issue of the superior order defence (Lauterpacht 1944, p. 69). A Commission on the Responsibility of Authors of the War and on Enforcement of War was created to inquire into individual criminal responsibilities during the war. In the report presented to the Preliminary Peace Conference at Paris in 1919, the Commission on Responsibility stated that:

> We desire to say that civil and military authorities cannot be relieved from responsibility by the mere fact that a higher authority might have been convicted of the same offence. It will be for the court to decide whether a plea of superior orders is sufficient to acquit the person charged with responsibility.[8]

Therefore the issue of the defence of superior orders was decided to be left untouched in the Versailles Treaty.

Against the terms of the Versailles Treaty,[9] Germany refused to extradite nationals charged with war crimes. A compromise was reached between the Allies and Germany, with the Allies agreeing to allow Germany to prosecute a selected number of individuals before the Criminal Senate of the Imperial Court of Justice of Germany, which was located at Leipzig (Solis 2000, p. 481, 498). In 1921, the Supreme Court of Leipzig held that obedience to a superior order was a defence. According to German Law, section 47(1) of the Military Penal Code, the subordinate must obey the orders of his superior, but he will be liable as an accomplice if he knows that the order involved the commission of an act regarded as criminal in either civil or military law. Therefore in both the *Robert Neumann* case[10] and

---

[6] The United Nations War Crimes Commission, *History of the United Nations War Crimes Commission and the Developments of the Laws of War* (His Majesty's Stationery Office, London 1948) 281.

[7] *See* articles 227–228 of the Versailles Treaty.

[8] Commission on the Responsibility of the Authors of the War and on Enforcement of Penalties, 'Report Presented to the Preliminary Peace Conference' (1920) 14 AJIL 95, 117.

[9] *See* articles 227–230 of the Versailles Treaty.

[10] *Judgment in the Case of Robert Neumann: June 2, 1921*, (1922)16 AJIL 696, at 696–704.

the *Dover Castle* case,[11] the subordinates who committed offences in obedience to superior orders were found not to incur criminal responsibility, while in the *Llandovery Castle* case[12] the defence was rejected, since the superior order in question was universally known without any doubt to be against the law. While one may argue that this was the inevitable result of the Germans judging their own alleged offenders, the British interpretation of the law until the mid 20th century followed even more lenient lines in fact (Blackett 1994, p. 12, 13). The failure to carry out the penalty clauses in the Treaty of Versailles was not only attributed to the judges in Leipzig but also to the leading writers on international law of those days and the military manuals issued by the British and American Governments. The rule concerning the defence of superior orders that appeared in those documents could have been good authority for defending the positions of alleged perpetrators before the Leipzig trial (see Finch 1921, p. 440, 441).

During World War II, opinion developed strongly against the position taken by the British Manual and the American Rules of Land Warfare which recognised the absolute effect of the defence of superior orders.[13] The position espoused by the first to the fifth edition of Oppenheim is known as the doctrine of *respondeat superior* which makes the fact of obedience to superior orders a complete and absolute defence against a criminal prosecution (Dinstein 1965, p. 38). As clarified by Lauterpacht himself, who reversed the position of the defence of superior orders in the sixth edition of Oppenheim's treatise, even at the time before the end of World War II, this doctrine was almost universally rejected by writers on international law (Lauterpacht 1944, p. 58, 73). For instance, as early as in 1919, Bartlett wrote that, as a general rule, a soldier acting under the lawful orders of his military superior cannot be held personally liable for his acts, but this general rule applies only to lawful orders, therefore a soldier who executes an illegal order remains personally liable for his or her act (Bartlett 1919, p. 177, 189). Subsequent to this change of Oppenheim's treatise, the British Manual and the American Rules were amended and redrafted in line with the new statement of the law.[14]

Eventually, Lauterpacht's position discarding the idea of complete defence of superior orders was submitted to a Committee established by the International Commission for Penal Reconstruction and Development. Lauterpacht's position, which had been to try and find a compromise over the fact of obedience to superior orders, gained general approval from the Commission and various Governments of the

[11] *Judgment in the Case of Command Karl Neumann: Hospital Ship 'Dover Castle', June 4, 1921*, (1922) 16 AJIL 704, 704–708.

[12] *Judgment in the Case of Lieutenants Dithmar and Boldt: Hospital Ship 'Llandovery Castle': Rendered July 16, 1921*, (1922) 16 AJIL 708, 708–724.

[13] The United Nations War Crimes Commission, 281.

[14] The United Nations War Crimes Commission, *History of the United Nations War Crimes Commission and the Developments of the Laws of War* (His Majesty's Stationery Office, London 1948) 282. Dinstein (1965, p. 47).

United Nations.[15] Lauterpacht brought up an approach, derived from state practice, that the fact of obedience to superior orders should be assessed on the basis of the general principles of criminal law (Lauterpacht 1944, p. 58, 73). He argued that the subject of superior orders would be an element in ascertaining the existence of *mens rea* as a condition of accountability (Lauterpacht 1944, p. 58, 73). The amendments of the British Manual and American Rules of Land Warfare were indeed in line with this understanding of the issue of obedience to superior orders. These two rules emphasised that the subordinate's responsibility is incurred when accepted or unchallenged rules of warfare were violated and stressed the subordinate's *mens rea*.[16] However, the American Rules of Land Warfare did not explicitly deny that the plea of superior orders can be taken into consideration even as a defence (see Note 16). While the American provision expressly defines the consequences of the defence of superior orders by declaring that it can lead to acquittal or to mitigation of punishment, a careful reading of the British Manual led to the conclusion that the same consequences are implied in the British Manual (see Note 16).

Prior to the establishment of the International Military Tribunal, the so-called Nuremberg Tribunal, several international bodies were established to discuss how to punish alleged offenders for crimes committed during Wold War II. In 1941 the London International Assembly was created under the auspices of the League of Nations.[17] The London International Assembly took a position similar to that taken by the 1919 Commission on Responsibilities, though it was more detailed. In 1943 the Assembly adopted a Resolution containing the opinion that an order issued by a superior to a subordinate to commit an act violating international law was not in itself a defence, but a state of compulsion may be considered as one of the exculpating or extenuating circumstances.[18] It is remarkable that the Resolution clarified that such exculpating or extenuating circumstances should in all cases be disregarded if the act was so obviously heinous that it could not be committed without revolting the conscience of an average human being (see Note 18). The Resolution not only denied the defence of superior orders itself, but also appeared to deny the defence of duress or compulsion where the order in question was manifestly unlawful.

Hence by the time the United Nations War Crimes Commission was created on 20 October 1943, the debate on the issue of obedience of superior orders converged on the subjective criteria for considering the obedience of superior orders that is a general principle of criminal law, *mens rea*, and the objective criteria for considering

[15] The United Nations War Crimes Commission, *History of the United Nations War Crimes Commission and the Developments of the Laws of War* (His Majesty's Stationery Office, London 1948) 277. Dinstein (1965, p. 104).

[16] The United Nations War Crimes Commission, *History of the United Nations War Crimes Commission and the Developments of the Laws of War* (His Majesty's Stationery Office, London 1948) 282.

[17] The United Nations War Crimes Commission, *History of the United Nations War Crimes Commission and the Developments of the Laws of War* (His Majesty's Stationery Office, London 1948) 266.

[18] The United Nations War Crimes Commission, *History of the United Nations War Crimes Commission and the Developments of the Laws of War* (His Majesty's Stationery Office, London 1948) 275.

the obedience of superior orders that is manifest illegality of conduct. Therefore it may not be surprising that a Draft Convention on the Trial and Punishment of War Criminals containing a proposal on the defence of superior orders proposed by the United States as article 30 was as follows:

> 1. The plea of superior orders shall not constitute a defence [...] if the order was so manifestly contrary to the laws of war that a person of ordinary sense and understanding would know or should know, given his rank or position and the circumstances of the case, that such an order was illegal.[19]

Although the report prepared by the Chinese representative suggested that it would be futile to attempt to formulate an agreement on the defence of superior orders, the Sub-Committee to deal with the problem of superior orders adopted the recommendation containing the proposed paragraph by the United States.[20] However, the recommendation was not unanimous and much debate took place afterwards (see Note 20). In the next memorandum to the Draft Convention for the Establishment of a United Nations War Crimes Court, the Commission decided to leave out any provision on this subject.[21] Later the discussion was re-opened and the Commission adopted a formal report to the Governments dated 29 March 1945. In this report the Commission confirmed that it unanimously maintained the view, which it expressed in connection with the United Nations War Crimes Court, that the mere fact of having acted in obedience to the orders of a superior does not of itself relieve a person who has committed a war crime from responsibility, while the Commission did not consider it could usefully propound any principle or rule on the treatment of the fact of obedience to the superior orders (see Note 21). The Commission left the future tribunal no discretion in deciding what to do with a plea of superior orders, though it can be interpreted that the fact of obedience to superior orders may be considered a defence in conjunction with other factors (Sliedregt 2003, p. 319).

The second international body which contributed to the discussion of the defence of superior orders for alleged perpetrators of the atrocities during World War II was the Cambridge International Commission for Penal Reconstruction and Development.[22] It began its work on 14 November 1941. The findings of this body were summed up by the aforementioned position taken by Lauterpacht who recommended that every case be solved on the basis of general principles of penal

---

[19] The United Nations War Crimes Commission, *History of the United Nations War Crimes Commission and the Developments of the Laws of War* (His Majesty's Stationery Office, London 1948) 278.

[20] The United Nations War Crimes Commission, *History of the United Nations War Crimes Commission and the Developments of the Laws of War* (His Majesty's Stationery Office, London 1948) 279.

[21] The United Nations War Crimes Commission, *History of the United Nations War Crimes Commission and the Developments of the Laws of War* (His Majesty's Stationery Office, London 1948) 280.

[22] The United Nations War Crimes Commission, *History of the United Nations War Crimes Commission and the Developments of the Laws of War (His Majesty's* Stationery Office, London 1948) 266.

law, and that individual responsibility be determined in ascertaining the existence of *mens rea* of the accused.[23]

After the London Conference, the more severe position was adopted for the provision of the defence of superior orders in the Charter of the International Military Tribunal since the Soviet delegate wanted the absolute denial of the defence of superior orders (Dinstein 1965, pp. 113–115 and Sliedregt 2005, p. 319). The provision appears to be stricter than the documents that appeared in the drafting history suggest in that acquittal is not mentioned, but only mitigation of punishment as a possibility.[24] Accordingly article 8 of the Nuremberg Charter provides as follows:

> The fact that the defendant acted pursuant to order of his Government or of a superior shall not free him from responsibility, but may be considered in mitigation of punishment if the tribunal determines that justice so requires.[25]

Article 6 of the Tokyo Charter, the Charter of the International Military Tribunal for the Far East, is more in line with the conclusion drawn by the United Nations War Crimes Commission, since the provision stipulates as follows:

> Neither the official position, at any time, of an accused, nor the fact that an accused acted pursuant to order of his government or of a superior shall, of itself, be sufficient to free such accused from responsibility for any crime with which he is charged, but such circumstances may be considered in mitigation of punishment if the Tribunal determines that justice so requires.[26]

Accordingly it might have left the judges of the Tokyo Tribunal some leeway to take into account the fact of obedience to superior orders in the context of other defences, such as duress or a mistake of law (Dinstein 1965, p. 157 and Sliedregt 2003, p. 320). Nonetheless, the Judges before the Tokyo Tribunal may have felt obliged to operate under the same law as that of the Nuremberg Tribunal (Sliedregt 2003, p. 320).

Similar lines to those of the Nuremberg Charter were adopted for Control Council Law No. 10 of 1945 which was to provide a unified legal basis in Germany to try war criminals other than those dealt with by the Nuremberg Tribunal.[27] Its article II(b) reads:

> The fact that the person acted pursuant to the order of his Government or of a superior does not free him from responsibility for a crime, but may be considered in mitigation.

---

[23] The United Nations War Crimes Commission, *History of the United Nations War Crimes Commission and the Developments of the Laws of War (His Majesty's* Stationery Office, London 1948) 277.

[24] The United Nations War Crimes Commission, *History of the United Nations War Crimes Commission and the Developments of the Laws of War* (*His Majesty's* Stationery Office, London 1948) 283.

[25] Charter of the International Military Tribunal (1945) 82 UNTS 279.

[26] Charter of the International Military Tribunal for the Far East (1946); Special Proclamation by the Supreme Commander for the Allied Powers, as amended 26 April 1946, T.I.A.S. No. 1589.

[27] Control Council Law No. 10: Punishment of Persons Guilty of War Crimes, Crimes Against Humanity (1945) 3 Official Gazette of the Control Council for Germany (Berlin, 31 January 1946).

No reference to acquittal but only reference to mitigation of punishment can be found here as is the case with article 8 of the Nuremberg Charter. Similar provisions, without mentioning the possibility of extenuating circumstance but with the reference to mitigating circumstance, were found in the American Regulations for the Trial of War Crimes of 1945, the Canadian War Crimes Regulation of 1945 and the Polish Decree concerning the Punishment of Traitors to the Polish Nation.[28] However, it is doubtful whether these provisions led to the construction by the judges that the fact of obedience to superior orders could not be taken into consideration as an exonerating factor in the context of a defence other than the defence of superior orders itself. Since the Control Council Law No. 10 proscribed the plea of superior orders, in some cases of national tribunals the defence of superior orders was dealt with as an issue of duress, such as in the *Einsatzgruppen* case.[29] In terms of duress, since the defence of superior orders is surely distinct from duress,[30] the defence of duress could be available even if the defence of superior orders was not.

Some other national laws to prosecute war criminals following the atrocities during World War II made clear that the plea of superior orders may have the effect of acquitting the accused.[31] Those rules are the French Ordinance of 28 August, 1944, concerning the Suppression of War Crimes and the Norwegian Law on the Punishment of Foreign War Criminals of 12 December 1946.[32]

The defence of superior orders was the most common defence raised before international and national military tribunals after World War II,[33] as well as one of the most controversial defences under international criminal law (Jescheck 1952, p. 255). Although most of the accused before the Nuremberg Trial pleaded not guilty on the grounds of superior orders emanating from Hitler himself, the Tribunal

---

[28] The United Nations War Crimes Commission, *History of the United Nations War Crimes Commission and the Developments of the Laws of War* (His Majesty's Stationery Office, London 1948) 283–284.

[29] *United States of America v Ohlendorf et al.* ("Einsatzgruppen trial"), 9 April 1948 (1948) Law Reports of the Trials of War Criminals, vol. IV (His Majesty's Stationery Office, London 1948) 411.

[30] *See Prosecutor v Dražen Erdemović*, Sentencing Judgment, Case No. IT-96–22-T, Ap. Ch., 7 October 1997, Joint Separate Opinion of Judge McDonald and Judge Vohrah, para.34 *See also* Rowe (1998, p. 210, 216).

[31] The United Nations War Crimes Commission, *History of the United Nations War Crimes Commission and the Developments of the Laws of War* (His Majesty's Stationery Office, London 1948) 285.

[32] The United Nations War Crimes Commission, *History of the United Nations War Crimes Commission and the Developments of the Laws of War* (His Majesty's Stationery Office, London 1948) 284–285.

[33] *Prosecutor v Erdemović* (Sentencing Judgment) IT-96–22T, T.Ch.I (29 November 1996) [49] (hereinafter, *Erdemović TC* case). See also *United States v Sawada et al., Trial of Lieutenant-General Shigeru Sawada and Three Others*, United States Military Commission, Shanghai, Case No. 25, 27. February 1946 –15 April 1946 in *Law Reports of Trials of War Criminals: Selected and Prepared by the United Nations War Crimes Commission* (H. M. Stationers Office, London 1948) vol. V, 13.

dismissed the plea by holding that:

> The provisions of this Article are in conformity with the law of all nations. That a soldier was ordered to kill or torture in violation of the international law of war has never been recognised as a defence to such acts of brutality, though, as the Charter here provides, the order may be urged in mitigation of the punishment. The true test, which is found in varying degrees in the criminal law of most nations, is not the existence of the order, but whether moral choice was in fact possible.[34]

In reality, in the subsequent tribunals after Nuremberg, the question of the defence of superior orders remained unsettled. For example, the *Hostage* case could be regarded as sympathetic to the *mens rea* principle,[35] and the *High Command* case might be deemed sympathetic to the manifest illegality principle.[36]

The development of the defence of superior orders experienced hard times after World War II. Basically there have been two developments of rules regarding the defence of superior orders in the post-war period. One is the endeavour of the international community to codify the Nuremberg Principles. The other is the jurisprudence of the various national courts. In the international arena, the International Law Commission (ILC) in 1950 proposed a draft that contained seven basic principles which allegedly were recognised by both the Nuremberg Judgment and the Nuremberg Charter.[37] The draft recognised and comprehensively followed the Nuremberg Charter, and added the words 'provided a moral choice was in fact possible to him' in the fourth principle. This 'moral choice test' was derived from the notable paragraph of the Nuremberg Judgment, where the Tribunal stated regarding Article 8 of the Nuremberg Charter that: 'The true test, which is found in varying degrees in the criminal law of most nations, is not the existence of the order, but whether moral choice was in fact possible.'[38] Although the principle relating to the superior order defence in the Nuremberg Principles is said to be unacceptable as an articulation of principles of international law,[39] this moral choice test was also taken into consideration in one of the earliest cases of the International Criminal Tribunal for the Former Yugoslavia, in the context of duress.[40]

---

[34] Judgment, Part 25, The Law of the Charter: Conclusion, in *Trial of the Major War Criminals before the International Military Tribunal*, vol. I (Nuremberg, 1947) 224.

[35] *United States v List et al., The Hostage Trial of Wilhelm List and Others*, United States Military Tribunal, Nuremberg, Case No. 47, 8 July 1947–19 February 1948, Law Reports of the Trials of War, vol. VIII, Criminals (H.M. Stationers Office, London 1949) 34–92, *see* especially 90–92.

[36] 'Military commanders in the field with far reaching military responsibilities cannot be charged under international law with criminal participation in issuing orders which are not obviously criminal or which they are not shown to have known to be criminal under international law.' *United States v von Leeb et al., Trial of Wilhelm von Leeb and Thirteen Others*, United States Military Tribunal, Nuremberg, Case No.72, 30 December 1947–28 October 1948, vol. XII, 73–74.

[37] *See* Report of the International Law Commission, UNGAOR, V, Supp. 12 (A/1316) (1950).

[38] Judgment of October 1, 1946, International Military Tribunal, Judgment and Sentences, (1947) 41 AJIL 172, 221.

[39] Due to its status of resolutions, recommendations and drafts of the General Assembly or the ILC. *See* Vogler (1973, pp. 619–622)and *see also* (Grayson 1995, p. 243, 247)

[40] *See* Erdemović TC case [18].

The International Law Commission amended the wording of the 'moral choice' clause in the 1954 Draft Code of Offences against the Peace and Security of Mankind into the wording 'in the circumstances at the time it was possible for him not to comply with that order'.[41] This clause was also retained in the 1991 Draft Code of Offences against the Peace and Security of Mankind. These formulas are basically in line with the Nuremberg Charter where the defence of superior orders cannot be accepted by itself.

Not many international conventions have been able to agree on an inclusion of the provision of the defence of superior orders. For example, although the draft Convention for the Prevention and Punishment of Genocide prepared by the Secretariat of the United Nations actually contained the provision of the defence of superior orders in article 5,[42] the provision was eventually decided not to be included in the Genocide Convention. No provision on the defence of superior order was agreed upon in the drafting processes for the 1949 Geneva Conventions and the 1977 Additional Protocol I to the Geneva Conventions (Dinstein 1965, pp. 223–225). However, the International Committee of the Red Cross had included a special article dealing with the effect on the guilt of the author of a criminal act having acted in obedience to the orders of a superior or in pursuance of a general law or regulation to which he was subject in the proposals to the Diplomatic Conference to include it in each of the four Geneva Conventions:

> The fact that the accused acted in obedience to the orders of a superior or in pursuance of a law or regulation shall not constitute a valid defence, if the prosecution can show that in view of the circumstances the accused had reasonable grounds to assume that he was committing a breach of this Convention. In such a case the punishment may nevertheless be mitigated or remitted, if the circumstance justify. Full responsibility shall attach to the person giving the order, even if in giving it he was acting in his official capacity as a servant of the State (Pictet 1952, p. 359, fn. 1).

In terms of the presumption of innocence, this draft seems very favourable to lower rank soldiers. Nevertheless, the Diplomatic Conference for the Establishment of the International Conventions for the Protection of Victims of War at Geneva decided not to include the proposed provision in the Conventions.[43] The Diplomatic Conference preferred to leave the solution of the problem to national legislation (see Note 43). The result was the same for the Sixth Committee of the General Assembly which drafted the Genocide Convention of December 1948 (Dinstein 1965, p. 225). When the drafters reached the core of this issue, they preferred to do so without debating it rather than spend time and energy on this discussion (Dinstein 1965, p. 225). Yet the Commentary on the Geneva Conventions at least identifies the view of the International Red Cross Committee with the draft article on the defence of superior orders prepared by the International Law Commission for the Draft Code of Offences against the Peace and Security of Mankind of 1954 (see Note 43). The commentary indicates the view of the International Committee of the Red

---

[41] Article 4, UNGAOR, Supp. No. 9, UN Doc. A/2693, 12.

[42] UN Doc. E/447 (1947).

[43] Red Cross Commentary, vol. I, 365.

Cross on the issue of the defence of superior orders in connection with the Geneva Conventions as follows:

> Whatever view is taken in the matter, it is to be hoped that the responsibility of the author of an offence committed in obedience to orders or in pursuance of a general law or regulation will be treated in the same way in the case of a national as in the case of an enemy.

The defence of superior orders was also provided in article 77 of the final draft text of the Protocol. It resembles the Nuremberg Charter and the relevant national laws for the prosecution of war criminals following World War II in content, with a trace of the absolute responsibility principle.

> The mere fact of having acted pursuant to an order of an authority or a superior does not absolve an accused person from penal responsibility if it be established that, in the circumstances of the time, he should have reasonably known that he was committing a grave breach of the Conventions or of the present Protocol and that he had the possibility of refusing to obey the order.[44]

Later the Syrian Arab Republic submitted an amendment to add the possibility of disobeying an order as requirement with the wording as follows:

> The fact of having acted pursuant to an order does not absolve and accused person from penal responsibility if it be established that, in the circumstances at the time, he should have reasonably known that he was committing a grave breach of the Conventions or of the present Protocol and that he had the possibility of not carrying out the order.[45]

Later the delegate from Australia suggested the deletion of the words 'and that he had the possibility of refusing to obey the order' from the proposed draft article (see Note 45). Then the Swiss delegate suggested the deletion of the entire proposed article 77 (see Note 42). The final version of draft article 77 was proposed by the United States who basically restored the original draft article of 1973.[46] Ultimately draft article 77 was rejected by the Diplomatic Conference in May 1977 since it had not obtained the necessary two-thirds majority.[47] The result of the vote reflects the divided views on this issue at that time; 36 in favour, 25 against and 25 abstentions.[48] Mexico abstained from the vote because it considered that article 77 should

[44] International Committee of the Red Cross 'Draft Additional. Protocols to the Geneva Conventions of August 12, 1949' of June 1973, in *Official Records of the Diplomatic Conference on the Ratification and Development of International Humanitarian Law Applicable in Armed Conflicts: Geneva (1974–1977)*, vol. I (Federal Political Department, Bern 1978).

[45] CDDH/I/74, original: French (20 March 1974) in *Official Records of the Diplomatic Conference on the Ratification and Development of International Humanitarian Law Applicable in Armed Conflicts: Geneva (1974–1977)*, vol. III (Federal Political Department, Bern 1978) 331.

[46] CDDH/I/74, original: French (20 March 1974) in *Official Records of the Diplomatic Conference on the Ratification and Development of International Humanitarian Law Applicable in Armed Conflicts: Geneva (1974–1977)*, vol. III (Federal Political Department, Bern 1978) 332.

[47] *Official Records of the Diplomatic Conference on the Ratification and Development of International Humanitarian Law Applicable in Armed Conflicts: Geneva (1974–1977)*, vol. III (Federal Political Department, Bern 1978) 331.

[48] CDDH/SR.45 (30 May 1977), in *Official Records of the Diplomatic Conference on the Ratification and Development of International Humanitarian Law Applicable in Armed Conflicts: Geneva (1974–1977)*, vol. VI (Federal Political Department, Bern 1978) 308.

apply not merely to grave breaches, but to all breaches (see Note 48). Both Iran and the United Kingdom voted against draft article 77, though Iran did not specify any reason for its vote.[49] The United Kingdom referred to the wording 'or should have known' in the draft article and said that:

> If those words were to be taken as meaning that a soldier was to be expected to carry out his own detailed investigation of the facts of a situation before complying with an order, the result would not merely be impracticable but totally impossible in a combat situation.[50]

Therefore the United Kingdom was of the view that the best course would be the omission of the article, leaving the situation to be regulated by the existing rules of international law concerning the defence of superior orders.[51] These international instruments did thus neither proscribe nor endorse the defence of superior orders – they just could not reach an agreement and thus left the problem for domestic courts.

The Conventions that succeeded in encompassing the provision relating to the defence of superior orders are the Convention against Torture and Other Cruel, Inhuman or Degrading Treatment or Punishment adopted by General Assembly Resolution 39/46 of 10 December 1984[52] and the Inter-American Convention to Prevent and Punish Torture of 1986.[53] The provisions that appeared in both Conventions are simpler than the Nuremberg Charter and the Nuremberg Principles. Article 2(3) of the Torture Convention of 1984 provides as follows:

> An order from a superior officer or a public authority may not be invoked as a justification of torture.

Article 4 of the Inter-American Convention to Prevent and Punish Torture is similar to this provision and reads as follows:

> The fact of having acted under orders of a superior shall not provide exemption from the corresponding criminal liability.

In line with these developments after Nuremberg and the adherence to the Nuremberg Charter and the Nuremberg Judgment, the Statutes of the International Criminal Tribunal for the Former Yugoslavia and the International Criminal Tribunal for Rwanda were adopted. The Commission of Experts, which was set up by

---

[49] CDDH/SR.45 (30 May 1977), in *Official Records of the Diplomatic Conference on the Ratification and Development of International Humanitarian Law Applicable in Armed Conflicts: Geneva (1974–1977)*, vol. VI (Federal Political Department, Bern 1978) 307.

[50] CDDH/SR.45 (30 May 1977), in *Official Records of the Diplomatic Conference on the Ratification and Development of International Humanitarian Law Applicable in Armed Conflicts: Geneva (1974–1977)*, vol. VI (Federal Political Department, Bern 1978) 308 [5].

[51] CDDH/SR.45 (30 May 1977), in *Official Records of the Diplomatic Conference on the Ratification and Development of International Humanitarian Law Applicable in Armed Conflicts: Geneva (1974–1977)*, vol. VI (Federal Political Department, Bern 1978) 308 [6].

[52] Convention Against Torture and Other Cruel, Inhuman or Degrading Treatment of Punishment, adopted on 10 December 1984, entered into force 26 June 1987, G.A. Res. 39/46, 39 UN GAOR, Supp. (No. 51), UN Doc. A/39/51 (1984) 197, reprinted in 23 ILM 1027 (1984).

[53] Inter-American Convention to Prevent and Punish Torture, signed 9 December 1985, entered into force 28 February 1987, OASTS 67, GA Doc. OEA/Ser.P, AG/doc.2023/85 rev.1 (1986) 46–54, reprinted in 25 ILM 519 (1986).

Security Council Resolution 780 to examine and analyse information with a view to providing the Secretary-General with its conclusions on the evidence of grave breaches of the Geneva Conventions and other violations of international humanitarian law committed in the territory of the former Yugoslavia,[54] recognised the position of the jurisprudence of the International Military Tribunal (alternatively, the Nuremberg Tribunal), as customary international law.[55] There is divergence of views among publicists.[56] The wording appeared in Article 7(4) of the Statute of the International Criminal Tribunal for the Former Yugoslavia, which is essentially identical to article 6(4) of the Statute of the International Criminal Tribunal for Rwanda, and reads as follows:

> The fact that an accused person acted pursuant to an order of a Government or of a superior shall not relieve him of criminal responsibility, but may be considered in mitigation of punishment if the International Tribunal determines that justice so requires.

After adopting the Nuremberg Principle of the mitigation factor, in the Statutes of the International Criminal Tribunal for the Former Yugoslavia and the International Criminal Tribunal for Rwanda, the ILC Draft Code of Crimes Against Peace and Security of Mankind changed the provision of the defence of superior orders with the wording of the Nuremberg Charter.[57] The Nuremberg Principles have been hailed in these statutes of international or quasi-international tribunals since the end of the Cold War.

In national jurisdictions, the principle of manifest illegality before national tribunals has become main stream after the Cold War. While the treatment of superior orders as a defence to military crimes is not universal and has changed across various national legal systems over time (Grayson 1995, p. 248), the defence of superior orders in the national dimension is a complete defence if the superior's order is not manifestly unlawful and the defendant did not know of the order's illegality .[58]

There are two famous Israeli cases which refined the manifest illegality principle. The Israeli Military Court of Appeal referred to the standard of reasonableness on

---

[54] United Nations Security Council Resolution 780 (Establishing a Commission of Experts to Examine and Analyze Information Submitted Pursuant to Resolution 771) SC Res. 780, 47 UN SCOR 36, UN Doc. S/RES/780 (1992).

[55] Annex: Final Report of the Commission of Experts Established Pursuant to Security Council Resolution 780 (1992); UN Doc S/1994/674, 16 (1994) [61]–[62].

[56] It is often said that since Nuremberg, under international law the mere fact that a subordinate followed the orders of a superior is not a defence to an international crime. *See* Ratner and Abrams (2001, p. 136) Nonetheless, there are some who are willing to recognise the superior order as an available defence. For example, Insco proposes, in the context of the United States Military Tribunal which is supposed to punish individuals accused of criminal terrorist actions, that the United States should take the lead in enunciating the defence of superior orders under international law by providing it to defendants before military commissions. *See*, Insco (2003, pp. 389–418)

[57] *See* 1996 ILC Draft Code, Commentary on Article 5.

[58] *See* Gaeta (1999, p. 172, 176, fn. 7) Gaeta enumerated national/military laws, such as in Denmark, Germany, Israel, the Netherlands, Spain, Swiss, Norway. Even in countries like Greece and Italy, which have legislation of the absolute liability principle, the conditional liability approach has been affirmed by case law.

the issue of manifest illegality in the *Kafr Qassem* case.[59] The Israeli District Court in the *Eichmann* case found the orders calling for the physical extermination of the Jews were manifestly illegal, and quoted the precedent case.[60]

As for the cases of war criminals before national tribunals, the *Finta* case in Canada[61] and the *Priebke* case[62] in Italy are of significance in modern times, because both of these cases referred to the manifest illegality principle. Prior to these cases, for instance, *R v Smith*,[63] *United States v Kinder*,[64] and *United States v Calley*[65] are all famous for adopting the test of manifest illegality before national tribunals.

The history of the defence of superior order at a domestic level tells us that after World War I most States adopted the conditional liability approach in their national criminal laws and military manuals (Sliedregt 2003, p. 329). At an international level, the absolute liability approach toward the defence of superior order has been preferred. Arguably, these two developments are consistent with two major models or schemes of international criminal law, as will be seen below in their histories. An international court was entrusted with the task of dealing with the major crimes, whereas national courts were called upon to handle the minor crimes (Cassese 2003, p. 353).

In its Resolution 47/33 of 25 November 1992, the General Assembly made a priority request to the International Law Commission to draft a statute establishing an international criminal court.[66] In 1994, the International Law Commission

---

[59] *Chief Military Prosecutor v Malinki*, Israel Court of Appeal 279–283/58, (1958), English translation in (1985) 2 Palestine Yearbook of International Law 69, 69–119.

[60] *Attorney General of the Government of Israel v A. Eichmann* (1968) 36 ILR 18 (29 May 1962).

[61] *R v Finta* was the first and most significant case of a prosecution of war crimes and crimes against humanity in Canada. The majority judgment in the Supreme Court of Canada adopted the manifest illegality principle, *R. v Finta*, [1994] 1 SCR 701, Supreme Court of Canada, March 24, 1994.

[62] In the *Priebke* case, an Italian military tribunal employed the manifest illegality doctrine. Erich Priebke, a former Nazi S.S. captain, was prosecuted for shooting Italian partisans and irregulars in 1944. He was first found guilty of the alleged acts, but the Italian Military Tribunal ordered his release because of the expiration of the statutory limitations. The second trial applied the Italian military code in force at the time of the facts, where the relevant provision had adopted the manifest illegality principle. In the tribunal's opinion, the defence of superior orders could not be invoked, since Priebke was indifferent to the criminal character of the order and thus superior orders could not be considered as a defence but as a mitigating circumstance. This finding was confirmed on appeal. Finally, Priebke brought a case before the European Court of Human Rights. However, the Court also found the application inadmissible. *See* the decision of the Rome Military Court of Appeal of 7 March 1998, in L'Indice Penale (1999), 959 et seq.; *Priebke v Italy* (App 48799/99) ECHR, 5 April 2001. *See generally*, F. Martines (1998, pp. 354–361) *see also* Cornelius (1997, pp. 3–10).

[63] *R v Smith* (1900) 17 SC 561. This case relates to the treatment of internees during the Boer War.

[64] *United States v Kinder* (1968) 14 CMR 133.

[65] *United States v Calley* (1973) 22 USCMA 534. This case is famous for adopting an objective standard based on the intelligence of the reasonable person.

[66] Report of the International Law Commission on the 44th Session, G.A. Res. 47/33, 47 UNGAOR Supp. (No. 49) 287, UN Doc. A/47/49 (1992).

submitted its draft statute for an international criminal court to the General Assembly (Bassiouni 1998, p. 17). Although a conference to establish an international criminal court was recommended by the International Law Commission, the General Assembly instead established an Ad Hoc Committee for the International Criminal Court.[67] The work of the Ad Hoc Committee led to a decision by the General Assembly to create the Preparatory Committee.[68] The Committee held six sessions between 1996 and 1998 (Butler 1999, p. 121, 123). An intersessional meeting at Zutphen, in the Netherlands, produced a consolidated text.[69] This includes a rather long provision of the defence of superior orders and it may be of interest here to cite the entire provision for it resembles the completed article on the defence of superior orders of the Rome Statute of the International Criminal Court:

> 1. The fact that a person's conduct was pursuant to an order of a government or of a superior [whether military or civilian] shall [not] relieve the person of criminal responsibility [[if] [unless] the order [was known to be unlawful or] appeared to be manifestly unlawful].
>
> [The perpetrator of or an accomplice in a crime of genocide [or a crime against humanity] [or a...] shall not be exempted from criminal responsibility government or a superior, or pursuant to national legislation or regulations.]
>
> [2. Persons who have carried out acts ordered by the Security Council or in accordance with a mandate issued by it shall not be criminally responsible before the Court.][70]

Paragraph 2 led to widespread doubts about its contents and placement and it was deleted in the final Draft Statute issued by the Preparatory Committee at its final session in April 1998.[71] Nonetheless, one may see that a consensus appeared to emerge at the stage of the work by the Preparatory Committee not to accept the defence of the obedience to superior orders in case of genocide and crimes against humanity (Zimmerman 2002, p. 966).

Later at the Rome Conference there was still friction between the two schools of thought (Zimmerman 2002, p. 967). The more severe approach taken by a number of international instruments since the Nuremberg Charter and the manifest illegality-based conditional approach were the two main approaches which divided the negotiation table over the provision of the defence of superior orders of the Statute of the International Criminal Court (Gaeta 1999, pp. 172–188, Zimmerman 2002, p. 967 and Sliedregt 2003, p. 322). The former, the absolute liability approach, was strongly pushed by the German delegation (Gaeta 1999, pp. 172–188, Zimmerman 2002, p. 967 and Sliedregt 2003, p. 322). The latter, conditional approach, was strongly adhered to by the United States delegation

[67] UN Doc. A/RES/49/53, adopted at the 84th Plenary Meeting on 9 December 1994 (17 February 1995).

[68] UN Doc. A/RES/50/46, adopted at the 87th Plenary Meeting on 11 December 1995 (18 December 1995).

[69] *Report of the Inter-Sessional Meeting From 19 to 30 January 1998 in Zutphen, The Netherlands*, UN Doc. A/AC.249/1998/L.13 (1998).

[70] UN Doc. A/AC.249/1997/L.9/Rev.1 (18 December 1997) 18–19.

[71] UN Doc. A/CONF.183/2/Add.1 (14 April 1998) 59. *See also* UN Doc. A/AC.249/1997/L.9/Rev.1 (18 December 1997) 19, fn. 17.

(Gaeta 1999, pp. 172–188, Zimmerman 2002, p. 967 and Sliedregt 2003, p. 322). Thus the proposal by the United States reads as follows:

> [...] a person is not criminally responsible if at the time of that person's conduct:
>
> [...] (c) The person was a member of forces acting pursuant to the order of a Government or of a military commander, unless the person knew the order to be unlawful or that the order was manifestly unlawful.[72]

The two opposing positions were merged into one provision after tough discussions (Gaeta 1999, p. 189). The provision in the Rome Statute of the International Criminal Court eventually took a middle position between the histories of international and national legislations and jurisprudences. Thus the foundation of current article 33 emerged as Option B of the working paper by the working group on general principles of criminal law which reads as follows:

> The fact that a crime referred to in article 5 has been committed pursuant to an order of a Government or of a superior, whether military or civilian, shall not relieve the perpetrator of criminal responsibility unless:
>
> (a) The person was under a legal obligation to obey orders of the Government or the superior in question; and
> (b) The person did not know that the order was unlawful; and
> (c) The order was not manifestly unlawful.
>
> 2. For the purpose of this article, orders to commit genocide or crimes against humanity are manifestly unlawful.[73]

This compromised provision relieved the anxiety of the United States that American servicemen abroad would face international criminal responsibility in the event that they obeyed orders whose legality they are not in a position to appraise (Gaeta 1999, p. 189). In the end, the contents of the completed article 33 came to bear a resemblance to the draft article of the Preparatory Committee.[74]

Since the Rome Statute, there may have been emerging uniformity between national and international case law and legislation on the issue of the defence of superior orders. Recent scholarship tends to see that the manifest illegality principle has gained ground in the national dimension.[75] Therefore there is hardly any doubt that the defence of superior orders in matters of apparent gross violations of human rights has no autonomous efficacy even before national courts. While the defence of superior orders itself is completely ruled out in some international criminal law instruments as is the provision in the Nuremberg Charter,

[72] UN Doc. A/CONF.183/C.1/WGGP/L.2 (16 June 1998).

[73] UN Doc. A/CONF.183/C.1/WGGP/L.9/Rev.1 (25 June 1998).

[74] UN Doc. A/CONF.183/2/Add.1 (14 April 1998) 59.

[75] Many scholars find difficulty ascertaining the customary rule on this matter. However, the scholars mentioned below are willing to find the minimum international rule in the manifest illegality principle. *See* Zimmerman (2002, p. 957, 965), *see* McCoubrey (2001, pp. 386–394); Cornelius (1997, p. 10) Green (1993, pp. 320–333) 'The majority approach in the industrialized democratic West appears to be the manifest illegality rule', Osiel (1998, p. 939, 950).

including the East Timor Special Panel for Serious Crimes,[76] the Special Court for Sierra Leone[77] and the Iraqi Special Tribunal,[78] the article of the ICC Statute appears to have adopted conditional liability, more precisely the manifest illegality principle, for war crimes and possibly for the crime of aggression (Gaeta 1999, p. 189). As regards the Statute for the International Criminal Tribunal for the Former Yugoslavia, the United States Permanent Representative, Madeline Albright, alluded to the existence of the defence of superior orders under the circumstances when the subordinate did not know the orders were unlawful and the orders were objectively not manifestly unlawful.[79] The International Criminal Tribunal for the Former Yugoslavia Trial Chamber, in the *Mrda* case, also seemed to have adopted the manifest illegality test for considering whether obeying superior orders could be a mitigating factor.[80]

Therefore it seems right to claim that the judgments of national and international tribunals have mainly displayed a commendable uniformity in the matter of superior orders and the standards of reasonableness and manifest illegality have received widespread acceptance (Lippman 1996, p. 1, 54). Yet it should be noted that the authority on this issue, Dinstein, actually evaluates article 33 of the Rome Statute as denying the obedience to superior orders itself as a defence in the way the Nuremberg Charter did (Dinstein 2001, p. 130). For Dinstein, article 33 only recognises the obedience to superior orders as an element in the defence of mistake of law defined in article 32(2) (Dinstein 2001, p. 130). This interpretation may cast doubt on the existence of two separate articles in the Rome Statute for the defence of mistake of law. The conclusion may be drawn that under the Rome Statute the fact of obedience to superior orders cannot be served as a defence as a general principle (Zimmerman 2002, p. 973). In the following section, various international instruments' provisions of the defence of superior orders will be examined by way of introducing main scholarly theories of the defence of superior orders.

---

[76] United Nations Transitional Administration in East Timor, Regulation 2000/15, UN Doc UNTAET/REG/2000/15 (6 June 2000). Section 21 of the Regulation is substantially identical to article 7(4) of the Statute of the International Criminal Tribunal for the Former Yugoslavia.

[77] "Article 6(4) of the Statute of the Special Court for Sierra Leone is worded in terms identical to that of Statutes of the ICTY and the ICTR", Staker (2005, p. 431, 440).

[78] The ICTY Statute, Article 7(4); The ICTR Statute, Article 6(4); Code of Crimes against the Peace and Security of Mankind, Article 5; The Statute of the Special Court for Sierra Leone, Report of the Secretary-General on the Establishment of a Special Court for Sierra Leone, UN Doc S/2000/915, Enclosure, 4 October 2000, Article 6(4); Regulation on the East Timor Panels with Exclusive Jurisdiction over Serious Criminal Offences, UN Doc UNTAET/REG/2000/15, 6 June 2000, Section 21; Coalition Provisional Authority, The Statute of the Iraqi Special Tribunal, 10 December 2003, in (2004) 43 ILM 231, 242, Article 15(e) 'The fact that an accused person acted pursuant to an order of a Government or of a superior shall not relieve him of criminal responsibility, but may be considered in mitigation of punishment if the Tribunal determines that justice so requires'.

[79] UN Doc S/PV.3217, 25 May 1993, at 15 (1993).

[80] *Prosecutor v Mrda* (Sentencing Judgment) IT-02–59-S, T. Ch. I, 31 (March 2004) [67].

6.3 Main Theories of the Defence of Superior Orders

Looking back on the history of the defence of superior orders, five schools of thought concerning this problem are discernable. The following sections will introduce these theories and focus on problems arising from each school of thought.

6.3.1 Doctrine of Respondeat Superior

The first, and the theory most in decline, is the doctrine of *respondeat superior*.[81] According to that doctrine, obedience to superior orders is automatically and *a priori* an absolute defence to a criminal prosecution. The person who bears the responsibility must be the superior and not the subordinate. However, this doctrine has not gained ground since the Nuremberg Charter's restriction on the defence of superior orders.

Despite the fact that this doctrine has its roots in ancient Rome, where the duty to obey was integral to both civilian and military society, this doctrine seems to have the fewest advocates with not many grounds in contemporary international law. The most authoritative supporter of this doctrine is Oppenheim's treatise *International Law*, volume 2, first published in 1906, and maintaining this position until the fifth edition, published in 1935 (Oppenheim 1906, p. 264–265; 1912, p. 310; 1921, p. 342–343; 1926, pp. 410–411; 1935, pp. 453–454). Allowing obedience to superior orders as an absolute defence does not eliminate criminal responsibility; instead, it shifts the locus upward to the person who issued the illegal orders (Bakker 1989, pp. 55–57).

Although Oppenheim failed to give any compelling grounds for this doctrine, four rationales are given. First of all, this doctrine finds its reason in the binding effect of an order as national law. The second rationale is the subjective impossibility of refusing an order. According to Renault, to whom Oppenheim referred as an advocate of this doctrine, firstly, it is not acceptable that subordinates make objections to orders which are given to them, since they cannot always understand the illegality of these orders (Renault 1915, p. 313, 341). Thirdly, even if somehow a subordinate is convinced of the illegality of a given order, one should take account of the subordinate's situation under imminent coercion (Renault 1915, p. 313, 342). The fourth rationale is that a deterrent effect is expected through placing responsibility for issuing an illegal order onto superiors.

This doctrine is hardly acceptable to modern publicists and those who pursue the rule of law in the international sphere. Under this doctrine, the requirement that military subordinates be safe to execute the orders of their superiors is given priority over the maintenance of the law (Keijzer 1978, p. 78, 79).

The rise and fall of the doctrine of the *respondeat superior* can be accounted for by glancing at the historical development of military organisational structure.

---

[81] This doctrine is sometimes also termed as 'the doctrine of passive obedience' or '*Befehl ist Befehl*'.

The rigid organisation of the Roman army, which had dissolved during the Middle Ages, was reintroduced in the sixteenth century. This rigid structure and the introduction of new weapons were followed by detailed training and military drill with severe penal sanctions against disobedience, in order to make each individual soldier a reliable cog in a complex military machine (Keijzer 1978, p. 82). From the eighteenth century, the commander- subordinate relationship became the mirror of a stratified, aristocratic society. Eventually, the nineteenth century saw the attainment of total submission of subordinates in military structures. In the twentieth century, at least since World War II, the structure of military organisation has become less rigid and the doctrine of *respondeat superior* consequently has lost power.

6.3.2 Doctrine of Absolute Liability

Secondly, as an antithesis to *respondeat superior*, the doctrine of absolute liability has come into being. Once there was a time when the doctrine of absolute liability took the position that superior orders cannot be a defence and cannot be taken into considerations in any other defences. This doctrine claims that the fact of obedience to orders does not create a defence *per se*, in other words, superior orders do not justify an unlawful act, but can be considered in mitigation. The rationale behind this approach is that a soldier is a reasoning agent, and is supposed to be capable of appraising the legality of the orders he or she receives, whereas in the *respondeat superior* approach the subordinate is regarded as an automaton or instrument in the hands of the superior. This position is partly based on the argument that soldiers from the very outset are only duty-bound to execute orders that are lawful.

Although this approach has been regarded as gaining ground in the international dimension, it also is not without problems. First, it is said to be unable to appraise the subjective element of crimes, the *mens rea* of the defendant. Second, it is said to not take into account the special position of a subordinate in a hierarchic organisation. Third, in numerous cases in which subordinates are required to execute orders, the legality or illegality of the order, for ordinary soldiers, is doubtful and not clear. There even exists a danger of infringement of due process in that the fact of obedience to superior orders may never be used for defence purposes and a person without criminal intent may be liable for the act in compliance with his or her superior's order(s).

Generally speaking, the absolute liability doctrine is said to be supported by international legislation and jurisprudence prior to the Statute of the International Criminal Court, while the conditional liability doctrine is generally adopted by national legal systems (Gaeta 1999, pp. 174–175; Sliedregt 2003, p. 329, 322). The absolute liability doctrine is used, though not by many States, on several national levels as well,[82] whereas the conditional liability doctrine is now appearing in the

[82] According to Gaeta, the absolute liability approach has been taken in Argentina, Austria, Iran, Romania and the United Kingdom, Gaeta, 'The Defence of Superior Orders: The Statute of the International Criminal Court versus Customary International Law', 179, fn.21.

Statute of the International Criminal Court. Normally States are unwilling to adopt the extreme; on the one hand, none of the legal systems recognised the unconditional impunity of the subordinate performing the command of a superior, on the other hand, none of the national systems completely ignored, as a defence, the fact that the deed was done pursuant to an order (Vogler 1973, p. 619, 634).

The absolute liability doctrine may have been a suitable instrument specifically for trying the major war criminals whose acts were by nature manifestly unlawful (Cornelius 1997, p. 10). The general tendency of treatment of the defence of superior orders is that illegality of orders is subject to the manifest illegality test. This approach is called the manifest illegality principle and the contents of this doctrine will be clarified next.

6.3.3 Conditional Liability Approach: Manifest Illegality Principle

Thirdly, there is a middle of the road approach, which exists in various forms. The position is that a soldier who obeyed an order issued by a superior to perform an act which later proved to have been unlawful would have a defence in any consequent legal proceedings, if, and only if, the order was one which could credibly have appeared lawful at the time when it was received (McCoubrey 2001, p. 386). This approach is also known as the 'manifest illegality principle', which is to preclude reliance on a superior order as a defence, at least in cases where the unlawfulness of the order is obvious (Eser 1996, p. 259). In the United States, the meaning of manifest illegal orders has been tried to be clarified since the early twentieth century (Solis 2004, p. 988, 992).

This approach was taken by the Rome Statute of the International Criminal Court. To be sure, it is widely recognised that the Rome Statute adopts the absolute liability approach for the crime of genocide and crimes against humanity. During the negotiation phase of the Rome Statute, the Rome Conference, the delegate from Botswana noted that: 'The plea of acting under superior orders could no longer be accepted'.[83] However, this position was only taken as a result of having already applied the manifest illegality test to the crime of genocide and crimes against humanity by the drafters of the Rome Statute.

Although this approach is mainly an objective test for the soldiers obeying illegal orders, many advocates think that the ultimate object of this test is to ascertain the subjective knowledge of the defendant regarding the illegality of the order (Dinstein 1965, p. 30). Apparently, there is another test that the subordinate can be acquitted if he believed 'honestly' or in 'good faith (*bona fide*)' that he had to obey the order. This 'good faith' test is a rather subjective one, taking the actual mental state of the defendant into consideration (Sliedregt 2003, p. 329). This subjective

[83] United Nations Diplomatic Conference of Plenipotentiaries on the Establishment of an International Criminal Court (Rome, 15 June–17 June 1998) Official Records, vol. II, Summary Records of the Plenary Meetings and of the Meetings of the Committee of the Whole, UN Doc A/CONF.183/13, 118 [65].

approach is called the '*mens rea* principle', meaning that obedience to orders could be regarded as a factual detail germane to the offence, just like the time when, and the place where, the offence was committed (Dinstein 1965, p. 88). Even though obedience to superior orders may not be a 'defence *per se*', it may be acknowledged in conjunction with the other circumstances of a given case, within the ambit of a defence based on lack of *mens rea* such as 'compulsion' or 'mistake' (Dinstein 1965, p. 88 and Dinstein 1985, p. 206, 237). Lauterpacht has pointed out that: '[I]t is necessary to approach the subject of superior orders on the basis of general principles of criminal law, namely, as an element in ascertaining the existence of *mens rea* as a condition of accountability (Lauterpacht 1944, 73).'

In sum, the general conception of the manifest illegality principle seems to be that obedience to superior orders is allowed as a defence only where orders are not so manifestly illegal that subordinates did not know or could not have known them to be unlawful.[84] Strictly speaking, there is a difference between the manifest illegality principle and the *mens rea* principle. While according to the manifest illegality principle, the execution of an order, which was not obviously illegal, may constitute an in dependent defence, the *mens rea* principle seems to regard the moment of the order, if it considers it at all, only as a component of another defence, such as compulsion (Eser 1996, pp. 259–260). The *mens rea* principle was referred to in a case of the International Criminal Tribunal for the Former Yugoslavia prior to the adoption of the Statute of the International Criminal Court and is now better understood as the doctrine of mitigation factor.[85]

6.3.4 Doctrine of Mitigation Factor

Fourthly, there is a preference in drafting instruments of international tribunals to follow 'the doctrine of Ground of Mitigation'. This position holds that obedience to a superior order is not *per se* a defence and should be regarded as a factual detail, or at least as a ground for mitigation. This approach is derived from the absolute liability principle.

This position was recognised by the Charter of the Military Tribunal at Nuremberg[86] and subsequently affirmed by the Statutes of two *ad hoc* international criminal tribunals, the International Criminal Tribunal for the Former Yugoslavia

[84] Dinstein called this principle 'the personal knowledge principle', and under this principle if the order was manifest illegal, the defendant is presumed to have been aware of this illegality, and perhaps will not be allowed to present proof in rebuttal of the presumption. *See* Dinstein (1965, p. 30). *See also* Greenspan (1959, p. 495) and *see also* Bakker (1989, p. 66)

[85] *Prosecutor v Dražen Erdemović*, Sentencing Judgment, Case No. IT-96–22-T, Ap. Ch., 7 October 1997, Separate and Dissenting Opinion of Judge Stephen [59]–[60]; and *see also* Joint Separate Opinion of Judge McDonald and Judge Vohrah [34]. Here Judge Mc Donald and Judge Vohrah subscribe to the *mens rea* principle.

[86] 1945 Charter of the International Military Tribunal, in Agreement for the Prosecution and Punishment of the Major War Criminals of the European Axis Powers, 8 August, 1945, 82 UNTS 279.

and the International Criminal Tribunal for Rwanda.[87] Recently, in the sentencing judgment for the AFRC case of July 2007, the Trial Chamber of the Special Court for Sierra Leone did not accept the plea of obedience to superior orders as a mitigating factor in the defence of Santigie Borbor Kanu, who was a sergeant in the SLA. The Kanu Defence recalls the Trial Chamber's findings that on several occasions Kanu followed or reiterated the orders of Brima and submits that this lesser culpability is relevant to sentencing.[88] The Trial Chamber said there was no duress circumstance and found that the fact that Kanu had voluntarily reiterated criminal orders previously issued by Brima cannot, in the Chamber's opinion, be considered as mitigation in sentencing.[89] Here the Trial Chamber might not have distinguished between the defence of superior orders itself and duress and may have taken the absolute liability test by way of taking only moral choice, in the words of the Nuremberg Charter, into consideration.

In the case of the Statute of the International Criminal Court, this proposition has not been adopted. Whereas the Statute of the International Criminal Court has a provision on mistake of law, it also has a provision of the defence of superior orders. Under Article 33 of the Statute of the International Criminal Court, the defence of superior orders can be a defence *per se*, while, as Dinstein urged, the superior order is closely linked to mistake of law. If the low-level subordinates do not know, either due to complexity or circumstances, that a particular order is unlawful, then they would have recourse to excuse them from liability under Article 32 on mistake of law (Sadat, p. 220). With regard to mitigation of punishment and the defence of superior orders under article 33 of the Rome Statute, even though article 33 is silent on mitigation of punishment, article 78(1) of the Rome Statute would permit mitigation on a case by case basis (see Note 89).

6.3.5 Doctrine of Justification and Excuse

Fifthly, some claim that notwithstanding a clear rejection of obedience to superior orders as an absolute *justificatory* defence for an accused acting under military authority in armed conflict, this substantive defence to war crimes by virtue of a legal *excuse* ought to be maintained (Kremnitzer 1992, p. 337, 345 and Knoops 2001, p. 170). This school of thought could be termed 'the doctrine of Justification and Excuse'.

[87] The Statute of the International Tribunal for the Prosecution of Persons Responsible for Serious Violations of International Humanitarian Law Committed in the Territory of the Former Yugoslavia since 1991, United Nations, S.C.Res.827 (hereinafter, the ICTY Statute), 25 May 1993, Article 7(4); The Statute of the International Tribunal for the Prosecution of Persons Responsible for Genocide and Other Serious Violations of International Humanitarian Law Committed in the Territory of Neighbouring States, between 1 January 1994 and 31 December 1994, United Nations, S.C.Res.955 (hereinafter, the ICTR Statute), 8 November 1994, Article 6(4).

[88] *Prosecutor v Alex Tamba Brima, Brima Bazzy Kamara, Santigie Borbor Kanu*, Case No. SCSL-2004–16-T, Trial Chamber II, Sentencing (19 July 2007) 37 [6]–[9].

[89] *Prosecutor v Alex Tamba Brima, Brima Bazzy Kamara, Santigie Borbor Kanu*, Case No. SCSL-2004–16-T, Trial Chamber II, Sentencing (19 July 2007) 37 [10]–[14].

In the case of justification an action that would *per se* be considered contrary to law is regarded as lawful and does not amount to a crime, but in the case of excuse, the action contrary to a norm remains unlawful; nonetheless, the wrongdoer is not punished, because of either or both of lack of *mens rea* and special circumstances approved by law and society.

Not a few contemporary international criminal lawyers support this view and the distinction between justification and excuse.[90] This distinction has also been recognised by the ILC *Special Rapporteur* with regard to self-defence and coercion in articles of the Draft Code of Crimes against Peace and Security of Mankind of 1996.[91] Moreover, this proposition to explain the characteristics of the defence of superior order is not wholly an outgrowth of contemporary international criminal law. Fifty years ago, Glaser wrote:

> On peut donc considerer aujourd'hui comme un principe bien établi du droit international que l'ordre reçu ne constitute pas, en soi-même, une cause *justificative*, mais qu'il peut néanmoins *exonérer* l'agent de la pénalité et même de la responsibilité si, eu égard aux circonstances concrètes, il se vérifie comme une des causes auxquelles le droit attribute une telle importance. (emphasis added) (Glaser 1954, p. 131)

Jescheck also wrote over fifty years ago that both article 8 of the Nuremberg Charter and article 2(4)(b) of the Control Council Law No. 10[92] were total nonsense, because neither admits superior order as a ground of excuse (Jescheck 1952, p. 262).

In the present day context, this line of thought seems to be still valid because of the chaotic situation of the defence of superior orders, totally dead (under the Statutes of the *ad hoc* international criminal tribunals) and partly alive (under the Statute of the International Criminal Court). Triffterer concludes his commentary on article 33 of the Statute of the International Criminal Court, stating:

> *In conclusion* it should be kept in mind that whatever conceptual framework is selected in the future, orders to commit a crime can never *justify* the crime committed in executing the order. However, the possibility remains of using this defence *not by itself*, but when the conditions come close to other defences like duress or coercion, as an *excuse*. (emphasis added) (Triffterer 1999, pp. 580–581)

There are four reasons why it is wise to distinguish between justification and excuse: (1) to optimise justice; (2) to allow sanctioning of non-culpable but wrongful acts;[93] (3) to grant an excuse without approving conduct as lawful; (4) to differentiate the treatment of complicity (Eser 1987, pp. 26–34). In the case of the

[90] *See* Cassese (951–956). Sadat suggests that the International Criminal Court distinguish between grounds excusing responsibility and those justifying the accused's actions. *See* Sadat (214–215).

[91] *See* Ambos (2002, p. 1003, 1037). *See* 1996 ILC Draft Code, Report of the International Law Commission on the Work of its 48th Session, 6 May–26 July 1996, Draft Code of Crimes against the Peace and Security of Mankind, UN Doc A/51/10, Commentary on Article 14(2).

[92] Control Council Law No. 10, 'Punishment of Persons Guilty of War Crimes, Crimes Against Peace and Against Humanity, Official Gazette of the Control Council for Germany', No. 3, Berlin, 31 January 1946.

[93] For example, even though a defendant who caused a traffic accident while driving a car in a state of intoxication and who accordingly cannot be punished for manslaughter due to *lack of culpability* may have his driver's licence revoked because of his *wrongful act*.

defence of superior orders, the third rationale is of importance. The distinction between justification and excuse correlates with unlawfulness of the act and culpability (Eser 1987, pp. 28). Due to the anxiety that conceding a defence would be interpreted as endorsement of an unlawful order, many authors seem to feel forced to refuse reliance on an order even in cases where the subordinate performed it in good faith (Eser 1996, p. 260). In some good faith cases, the alleged criminal act committed pursuant to a superior order remains unlawful and the culpability of the subordinate is negated or mitigated.

For the International Criminal Court especially, allowing the defence of superior orders under certain circumstances becomes important when thinking about the distinction between justification and excuse along with their underlying policy reasons as it shapes its jurisprudence in the context of international prosecutions for the most serious crimes (Sadat 215).

6.3.6 Observation on Theories of Defence of Superior Orders

There seem to be common policy considerations between the Charter of the International Military Tribunal and the Statutes of the International Criminal Tribunal for the Former Yugoslavia and the International Criminal Tribunal for Rwanda adopting absolute liability. Since there are common policy considerations, the provisions of the International Military Tribunal Charter and Nuremberg Principles might be repeatedly incorporated into some of the Statutes of international or quasi-international criminal tribunals. These common policy considerations may be well inferred from the following utterance of a statesman and comments by a scholar.

On drafting the International Military Tribunal Charter, General Nikitchenko representing the USSR, commented: 'Would it be proper really in speaking of major war criminals to speak of them as carrying out some order of a superior?... I wonder if that is necessary when speaking of major war criminals (Jackson 1971, p. 367).'

In the same vein, one scholar wrote on the subject of the International Criminal Tribunal for the Former Yugoslavia that:

> The tribunal should aim at higher officials who have guided or at least benefited from the atrocities that anger the world. It is not clear how useful Articles 7(1) and 4 will be in this regard. In the former Yugoslavia, the military situation appears (on the basis of information available at the time of writing) to be chaotic, with front-line forces operating under opaque (and perhaps nonexistent) lines of authority, spotty communications and rare direct orders (O'Brien 1993, p. 639, 651).

These comments and the strategies of these tribunals' prosecutions should be thought about together. Where politicians of cabinet rank and officers at the most senior levels of command are on trial, it is difficult to see how, upon the face of this doctrine, the defence of superior orders could have been available to them (McCoubrey 2001, pp. 389–390). The Charters of Nuremberg and Tokyo[94] and

[94] Special Proclamation by the Supreme Commander for the Allied Powers, Charter of the International Military Tribunal for the Far East, 19 January 1946, as amended 26 April 1946, TIAS No. 1589.

the International Criminal Tribunal for the Former Yugoslavia and the International Criminal Tribunal for Rwanda Statutes simply stated the natural application of the established manifest illegality doctrine in the very particular context of the cases with which they were called upon to deal (see McCoubrey 2001, pp. 389–390). Thus there was no practical possibility of the defendants before the International Military Tribunal or the International Military Tribunal for the Far East successfully advancing a plea of superior orders in either defence or mitigation, and the same is argued to be true of the 1990s *ad hoc* tribunals as well.

The provision of the international criminal tribunals for 'big fish' has thus excluded the possibility of the defence of superior orders because in those cases the manifest illegality test was thought to be clearly fulfilled in advance, though there remains the fact that a provision which is the same as the Nuremberg Charter was subsequently inserted in Allied Control Council Law No. 10, which was provided for the trials in Germany of lesser war criminals, that is, applicable law for 'small fish' tribunals.

In the end, the provisions which could be regarded as adopting absolute liability or the mitigation factor principle are specifically motivated by an attempt to prevent major war criminals from placing all the blame on Hitler or Milosević.[95] The provisions adopting absolute liability or the mitigation factor principle were always adopted when parties did not apply these provisions to themselves. This explanation is also confirmed by the fact that provisions of recent quasi-international special tribunals, such as those for Sierra Leone or East Timor, have adopted the Nuremberg Principle.

However, there has been some debate about the practice of the *ad hoc* international criminal tribunals in prosecuting some of the small fish. The debate can be traced back to the Nikolić indictment, and the Tadić and Erdemović trials. These three defendants are all regarded as small fish. Even the Prosecutor of the International Criminal Tribunal for the Former Yugoslavia, Justice Goldstone himself, does not hesitate to admit the fact. Nikolić was a Bosnian Serb and a commander of a detention camp. The first International Criminal Tribunal for the Former Yugoslavia indictment resulted in a sentence of 20 years' imprisonment. Goldstone reflected elsewhere that Nikolić was hardly an appropriate defendant for the International Criminal Tribunal for the Former Yugoslavia.[96] Tadić is a Bosnian Serb and was a President of the Local Board of the Serb Democratic party. He was also sentenced to 20 years' imprisonment. Erdemović was a member of the Bosnian Serb army and sentenced to 5 years' imprisonment. There was also an argument for the International Criminal Tribunal for Rwanda such that Akayesu was only a mayor of a region, just a small fish.[97] Therefore the practice of international criminal prosecution is not as straightforward as expected by the drafters of the provisions of the *ad hoc* international criminal tribunals.

---

[95] In the same vein, *see* Grayson (1995, p. 248).

[96] R Goldstone (2006, p. 106). *See also* Justice Richard Goldstone 'Crimes Against Humanity – Forgetting Victims' The 2001 Ernest Jones Lecture <http://www.psychoanalysis.org.uk/goldstone.htm> (31 January 2007).

[97] Jean Paul Akayesu – Prosecution Closing Arguments, ICTR/UPD/008 (Arusha, 19 March 1998).

Although the manifest illegality principle remains valid, the threshold of manifest illegality becomes higher and higher today, especially before international criminal tribunals/courts. Many war crimes, especially those against persons protected by the Geneva Conventions, cannot be justified by a superior order (O'Brien 1993, p. 654). It may well be difficult to imagine that the Serbs, Croats or other aggressors in the Former Yugoslavia believe that some of the atrocities they are alleged to have committed are just and lawful (Blackett 1994, p. 12, 16). It is also true that nobody has attempted to argue that the provisions of the defence of superior orders in the Statutes of the *ad hoc* international criminal tribunals for the Former Yugoslavia and Rwanda, adopting absolute liability, are contrary to customary international law. Yet the practice of the International Criminal Court on the issue of the defence of superior orders remains to be seen. Theoretically an alleged perpetrator of a war crime may be able to invoke the defence of superior orders in front of the International Criminal Court since article 33 of the Rome Statute adopts the manifest illegality approach for war crimes.

Virtually everywhere the law requires soldiers to presume the lawfulness of their orders (Osiel 1999, pp. 54–55).

> The manifest illegality rule embodies this approach. Only the most transparent form of illegality can effectively rebut the law's presumption that the soldier was ignorant of the illegality of orders of his superior. But once the presumption of soldier's ignorance is overcome, an opposing presumption arises. It is then conclusively presumed that the soldier could not have been ignorant of the order's illegality or of his corresponding duty to disobey it (Osiel 1999, p. 55).

6.4 Criminality and Illegality of International Wrongful Act

The following sections will consider the criminality and illegality of particular types of acts under international criminal law, genocide, *apartheid* and aggression, as case studies for the application of the principles discussed above. Such an examination will contribute our knowledge of what the boundaries of individual criminal responsibility for these acts are and ultimately of the extent of the individual's duty to disobey orders to commit these acts.

6.4.1 Genocide

Genocide constitutes the 'crime of crimes'.[98] It is well-known that the term of 'genocide' was coined by Raphael Lemkin, and some defendants before the International Military Tribunal, the Nuremberg Tribunal, were indicted and convicted of war crimes and crimes against humanity some parts of which were later labelled 'genocide'. General Assembly Resolution 96(I) dated 11 December 1946 later

[98] *Prosecutor v Jean Kamhanda*, Judgment and Sentence (Trial Chamber I, 4 September 1998)[16].

affirmed that genocide is a crime under international law, contrary to the spirit and the aims of the United Nations and the civilised world, for which individuals are criminally responsible.[99] Therefore genocide was recognised as an international crime in this Resolution,[100] which was also drafted by Lemkin (Kunz 1949, p. 738, 739). The United Nations Economic and Social Council appointed the drafting committee, which produced a draft during April–May 1948 (Kunz 1949, p. 739). The Genocide Convention was adopted unanimously by 55 member States with no abstentions before the General Assembly.[101]

The Genocide Convention of 1948 does not contain any provision concerning the defence of superior orders (Keijzer 1978, p. 213). An amendment excluding the defence of superior orders with regard to genocide was rejected by 28 votes to 15 with 6 abstentions.[102] The cause of rejection was a lack of consensus among States on the defence of superior orders, and this issue especially divided the countries in favour of the absolute liability approach such as the Soviet Union and the countries in favour of retaining the defence of superior orders as a defence such as the United States.

The Secretariat of the United Nations supported the former position and the Soviet Union's draft article 5 of the Genocide Convention was in line with the Secretariat's draft (Schabas 2000, p. 36). The Soviet's draft provision reads: 'Command of the law of superior orders shall not justify genocide'.[103] Nonetheless, the Soviet Union and France remarked on the difference in scope of the Nuremberg Charter and the Genocide Convention. While the former had been set up at a special moment in order to judge the question of acts committed by the 'major war criminals of the European Axis', the latter mainly legislated against crimes committed in time of peace.[104]

The Belgian delegate raised the issue of the difficulty of harmonising various pieces of national legislation on this matter and pointed out that there were

---

[99] UNGA Res 96(I), UN GAOR (1946) UN Doc A/64 Add. 1.

[100] *See* Case concerning the Application of the Convention on the Prevention and Punishment of the Crime of Genocide, *Bosnia and Herzegovina v Serbia and Montenegro*, International Court of Justice (26 February 2007) 60 [161].

[101] United Nations. Convention for the Prevention and Punishment of the Crime of Genocide, GA Res. 260 (III)(A), UN GAOR, 3rd Sess., 179th Plenary Meeting, 1948, UN Doc A/810, 174.

[102] UN Doc. A/C.6/SR.92, 313. The vote was taken by roll-call as the Soviet Union wished. Bolivia, having been drawn by lot to be Chairman, voted first. In favour (15): Byelorussian Soviet Socialist Republic, Czechoslovakia, Egypt, Ethiopia, France, Guatemala, Mexico, Norway, Panama, Poland, Syria, Ukranian Soviet Socialist Republic, Union of Soviet Socialist Republics, Yemen, Yugoslavia. Against (28): Brazil, Canada, Chile, China, Cuba, Denmark, Dominican Republic, Ecuador, El Salvador, Greece, India, Iran, Liberia, Luxemburg, Netherlands, New Zealand, Nicaragua, Siam, Sweden, Turkey, United Kingdom, United States of America, Uruguay, Venezuela, Afghanistan, Argentina, Australia, Belgium. Abstentions (6): Columbia, Pakistan, Peru, Philippines, Saudi Arabia, Union of South Africa.

[103] A/C.6/215/Rev.1 (9 October 1948) 3 [5].

[104] UN Doc. A/C.6/SR.92 (1948) 306.

serious obstacles to the insertion of the draft paragraph of the Soviet Union.[105] The Venezuelan delegate raised the issue of incompatibility between the special intent of genocide required by the definition of genocide in the Convention and the absolute liability proposed by the Soviet Union's draft.[106] Greece also observed that an individual might well commit an act of genocide by complying with an order, but the element of intent, which was an essential element of genocide, would be lacking (see Note 106). Moreover, the Venezuela delegation had warned the Sixth Committee of the General Assembly against the danger of including in the convention such provision which might form an obstacle to its ratification (see Note 106). Denmark and the Philippines were also of the view that the Convention should be acceptable to a very large number of States; despite this they had no problem with the draft so that they would not vote in favour of the Soviet Union draft.[107] The provisions of the Constitutions of Venezuela and the Dominican Republic were incompatible with the draft of the Soviet Union (see Note 106). Iran also pointed out that the legislation and the jurisprudence of Iran did not generally recognise that obedience to an order constituted justification in civil life.[108] The United States opposed the adoption of the draft of the Soviet Union because it thought that it would be more satisfactory to leave the judge free to pronounce judgment in each individual case, taking special circumstances into account.[109] Chile sided with the United States.[110] The Swedish delegation sympathised with the representatives of Belgium, Venezuela, Greece and the United States, whereas Egypt supported the Soviet Union draft due to the primacy of the Convention over national legislation (see Note 119).

The Czechoslovak delegation held that national legislation should not be allowed to infringe international law and supported the Soviet Union draft since it would make an important contribution to the struggle to prevent the crime of genocide.[111] Yugoslavia was also in favour of the Soviet Union draft in anticipation of the deterrent effect (see Note 118).

After voting, the delegations of the Netherlands, the United States and Brazil noted that the scope of the principle of the defence of superior orders should be defined by the International Law Commission.[112] Even though the majority delegates may not have had any difficulties with adopting the absolute liability approach, the matter was left for the International Law Commission to secure enough States to implement the Convention effectively. The reason for the negative attitudes of

---

[105] Ninety-Second Meeting Held at Palais de Chaillot, Paris, on Friday, 5 November 1948, 6th Committee, General Assembly, 3rd Session, UN Doc. A/C.6/SR.92 (1948) 302.

[106] UN Doc. A/C.6/SR.92 (1948) 306.

[107] UN Doc. A/C.6/SR.92 (1948) 311–312.

[108] UN Doc. A/C.6/SR.92 (1948) 310.

[109] UN Doc. A/C.6/SR.92 (1948) 307.

[110] UN Doc. A/C.6/SR.92 (1948) 308.

[111] UN Doc. A/C.6/SR.92 (1948) 308–309.

[112] UN Doc. A/C.6/SR.92 (1948) 314.

many States instead of supporting the extreme of the absolute liability approach is explained by the fact that the time was not ripe for the adoption of the amendment and the whole Convention (Dinstein 1965, p. 223).

Since the Genocide Convention keeps silent on the defence of superior orders, the relationship between the specific intent of the crime of genocide and the defence of superior orders remains unclear. The *travaux préparatoires* imply that the drafters chose to leave this matter to judges of national or international courts. The District Court of Jerusalem convicted Adolf Eichmann under an Israeli version of the prohibition against genocide, and it rejected the defence of superior orders by stating that the accused well knew that the order for the physical extermination of the Jews was manifestly unlawful and that in carrying out this order he engaged in criminal acts on a colossal scale.[113]

The contents of the Genocide Convention were recognised as reflective of principles recognised by civilised nations as binding on States by the International Court of Justice as early as 1951 in its Advisory Opinion.[114] Judge Weeramantry went one step further and wrote in his Separate Opinion that the human rights and humanitarian principles contained in the Genocide Convention are principles of customary international law.[115] The International Court of Justice affirmed that the norm prohibiting genocide was assuredly a peremptory norm in international law,[116] namely that the prohibition of genocide is widely recognised as one of the peremptory norms that is *jus cogens*. The two different responsibilities of individual criminal responsibility and State responsibility for the crime of genocide have been long recognised by the General Assembly of the United Nations and affirmed later by the International Court of Justice.[117]

Today the manifest illegality of the crime of genocide is firmly established by international practices. The Statutes of the International Criminal Tribunal for the Former Yugoslavia and the International Criminal Tribunal for Rwanda both include the crime of genocide, adopted from article II of the Genocide Convention word for

---

[113] Attorney General of the Government of Israel v Adolf Eichmann, 36 I.L.R. 228 (D. C. Jm. 1961) 257. *See* Lippman (1996, p. 199, 214); Greenawalt (1999, p. 2259, 2281); Schabas (2000, p. 328).

[114] *Reservations to the Convention on the Prevention and Punishment of the Crime of Genocide* Case (1951) ICJR. 23. See also *Case concerning the Application of the Convention on the Prevention and Punishment of the Crime of Genocide, Bosnia and Herzegovina v Serbia and Montenegro*, International Court of Justice (26 February 2007) 60 [161].

[115] Separate Opinion of Judge Weeramantry, *Case Concerning Application of the Convention on the Prevention and Punishment of the Crime of Genocide (Bosnia and Herzegovina v Yugoslavia) (Preliminary Objections)* [1996] ICJ Rep. 595, 648.

[116] *Armed Activities on the Territory of the Congo (New Application 2002) (Democratic Republic of the Congo v Rwanda)* [64].

[117] *Case concerning the Application of the Convention on the Prevention and Punishment of the Crime of Genocide, Bosnia and Herzegovina v Serbia and Montenegro*, International Court of Justice (26 February 2007) 61–62, 65 [163] and [173], referring to A/RES/180 (II) (1947), the Nuremberg Principles and A/RES/177 and A/RES/178(II).

word.[118] The crime of genocide, exactly as it appeared in the Genocide Convention, was also incorporated into the Rome Statute of the International Criminal Court in 1998. Later, out of fear of prosecuting individual 'lone *genocidaires*', an additional requirement was included at the stage of drafting the elements of crimes for genocide, namely that the conduct either took place in the context of a manifest pattern of similar conduct directed against a group, or was conduct that could itself effect such destruction.[119]

The prohibition of the crime of genocide was developed as a consequence of the emerging international efforts to protect human rights after World War II. The United Nations decided to adopt the Genocide Convention as the first human rights convention. The Convention on the Prevention and Punishment of the Crime of Genocide, which was adopted by the General Assembly of the United Nations in 1948, prohibits acts committed with intent to destroy, in whole or in part, a national, ethnical, racial or religious group.[120] Genocide may be committed both in war time and peace time so that the element of the existence of armed conflict is not necessary for this crime. This crime has been incorporated into the Statutes of the International Criminal Tribunal for the Former Yugoslavia and the International Criminal Tribunal for Rwanda.[121] The material jurisdiction of the International Criminal Court also embraces the crime of genocide.[122] It seems that individual criminal responsibility is incurred upon a violation of the prohibition of the crime of genocide under international criminal law. Such a prohibition and evident individual criminal responsibility has the high potential of providing a ground of conscientious objection.

Article 33(2) of the Rome Statute of the International Criminal Court stipulates that: 'For the purpose of this article, orders to commit genocide or crimes against humanity are manifestly unlawful'. Therefore no defendant, even the lowest-ranking soldier, may claim the defence of superior orders if he or she is alleged to have committed a crime of genocide. This legal provision under international law may contribute to advocate the right to conscientious objection to military service which relates to the crime of genocide.

The report of Eide and Mubanga of 1985 enumerated the obligation to abstain from participating in the crime of genocide as a relevant international standard of conscientious objection (Eide and Mubanga-Chipoya 1985, pp. 50–51). The report of 1985 advocates both the right and duty to refuse to participate in genocide: 'the individual is not only entitled, for reasons of conscience, to refuse to participate in genocide; he is even obliged to abstain from such participation, since he is criminally liable under article IV of the Genocide Convention, whether he is a constitutionally

[118] The Statute of the International Criminal Tribunal for the Former Yugoslavia, article 4; the Statute of the International Criminal Tribunal for Rwanda, article 2.

[119] Elements of Crimes, Assembly of State parties ICC/ASP/1/3 (part II-B) (9 September 2002) Common Element 4; Cryer (2005, p. 247).

[120] Article 2 of Convention on the Prevention and Punishment of the Crime of Genocide (9 December 1948) General Assembly Resolution 260 A(III).

[121] The ICTY Statute, article 4; the ICTR Statute, article 2.

[122] The ICC Statute, article 6.

responsible ruler, public official, or private individual (Eide and Mubanga-Chipoya 1985, p. 50).'

6.4.2 Apartheid

'Apartheid' means apartness or separation in Afrikaans, the language of the Afrikaaners, South Africans of Dutch origin (Sunga 1992, p. 74). Most people associate the term '*apartheid*' with an infamous period in South Africa. In fact, the South African case has been the only obvious case of *apartheid* officially blamed by the international community, though the 'Report of the *Special Rapporteur* on the situation of human rights in the Palestinian territories occupied since 1967' of 29 January 2007 claimed that: 'the 1973 International Convention on the Suppression and Punishment of the Crime of Apartheid appears to be violated by many practices, particularly those denying freedom of movement to Palestinians'.[123]

As early as the very first session of the General Assembly, a complaint was lodged by India against South Africa's increasing discrimination against people of Indian origin.[124] The involvement of the General Assembly began on 8 December 1946 when it first challenged the then Union of South Africa by a vote of 32 to 15 with 7 abstentions. The Resolution, titled 'Treatment of Indians in the Union of South Africa',[125] resulted from the failure of negotiation over the South African government's enactment in 1946 of the Asiatic Land Tenure and Indian Representation Act, which prohibited people of Indian origin from acquiring land.[126] After the Resolution, the South African government continued to maintain that the matter was within its domestic jurisdiction.[127]

Racial tension escalated when the National party came to power in South Africa in 1948 and promoted the policy of *apartheid* (see Note 127). India in 1948 made the first formal reference to *apartheid* at the United Nations in a letter requesting consideration of the matter.[128] The international attention of the General Assembly soon went beyond the realm of the question of discrimination against people of Indian origin (see Note 127). The General Assembly declared for the first time, on 2 December 1950, that 'a policy of "racial segregation" (*apartheid*) is necessarily

---

[123] Human Rights Council, Report of the Special Rapporteur on the situation of human rights in the Palestinian territories occupied since 1967, John Dugard, UN Doc A/HRC/4/17 (29 January 2007) 2.

[124] *The United Nations and Apartheid 1948–1994*, The United Nations Blue Book Series, volume I, Department of Public Information, United Nations, New York, (United Nations, 1994) 8.

[125] UNGA, General Assembly Resolution: Treatment of Indians in the Union of South Africa, 8 December 1946, UN Doc A/RES/44 (I).

[126] *The United Nations and Apartheid 1948–1994*, 9.

[127] *The United Nations and Apartheid 1948–1994*, 10.

[128] Letter dated 12 July 1948 from the representative of India to the Secretary-General concerning the treatment of Indians in South Africa, 16 July 1948, UN Doc A/577.

based on doctrines of racial discrimination'.[129] Although the earliest matter of concern before the United Nations was specifically related to the question of discrimination against people of Indian origin, consideration of the matter by the General Assembly attracted broader international attention to the racial situation in South Africa (see Note 127).

The General Assembly rejected the South African contention of non-interference in internal affairs, and on 5 December 1952 adopted a Resolution establishing a three-member United Nations Commission on the Racial Situation in the United South Africa (UNCORS) to study the problem in the light of both the purposes and principles of the Charter and the United Nations Resolutions on racial persecution and discrimination.[130] The Commission submitted annual reports to the General Assembly in 1953, 1954 and 1955.[131]

The South African Government objected strongly to the inclusion of the issue of *apartheid* on the agenda of the General Assembly.[132] It refused to cooperate with the UNCORS and ignored the invitation of the General Assembly (in its Resolution 820 (IX) of 14 December 1954) to consider the suggestions of the Commission for a peaceful settlement of the racial problem (see Note 132). South Africa withdrew its delegation from the General Assembly in 1955 and 1956 and withdrew from the United Nations Educational, Scientific and Cultural Organization (UNESCO) in 1955 to protest against both the General Assembly and the UNESCO's activities against racial discrimination (see Note 132). In 1964 South Africa withdrew from the International Labour Organisation.

With these unobliging attitudes, the situation in South Africa continued to deteriorate, while the General Assembly annually adopted Resolutions appealing to the South African government to revise its racial policies (see Note 132). The Sharpeville massacre of 21 March 1960, when the police fired at a peaceful demonstration against the pass laws, killing 68 Africans and wounding more than 200, was a turning point in the international community's consideration of *apartheid* (see Note 132). The place of discussion moved to the Security Council. Following the urgent request of 29 African and Asian Member States,[133] the Security Council

---

[129] General Assembly Resolution: Treatment of people of Indian origin in the Union of South Africa, A/RES/395 (V), 2 December 1950.

[130] UNGA, The question of race conflict in South Africa resulting from the policies of apartheid of the Government of the Union of South Africa, 5 December 1952, UN Doc A/RES/616A(VII) [1]; *See The United Nations and Apartheid 1948–1994*, 11.

[131] Report of the United Nations Commission on the Racial Situation in the Union of South Africa, UN Doc A/2505 and Add.1 (1953); Second Report of the United Nations Commission on the Racial Situation in the Union of South Africa, UN Doc A/2719 (1954); Third Report of the United Nations Commission on the Racial Situation in the Union of South Africa, UN Doc A/2953 (1955).

[132] *The United Nations and Apartheid 1948–1994*, 13.

[133] Letter dated 25 March 1960 from the representatives of Afghanistan, Burma, Cambodia, Ceylon, Ethiopia, the Federation of Malaysia, Ghana, Guinea, India, Indonesia, Iran, Iraq, Japan, Jordan, Laos, Lebanon, Liberia, Libya, Morocco, Nepal, Pakistan the Philippines, Saudi Arabia, Sudan, Thailand, Tunisia, Turkey, the United Arab Republic and Yemen to the President of the Security Council requesting consideration of the situation in South Africa (25 March 1960) UN Doc S/4279 and Add. 1.

considered the matter and with none against (but with 2 abstentions, by France and the United Kingdom), the Security Council recognised that the situation in South Africa had led to international friction and, if continued, might endanger international peace and security.[134] In 1966, the General Assembly condemned *apartheid* as 'a crime against humanity'[135] and in 1973 it adopted the Apartheid Convention. In spite of the apparent illegality of *apartheid*, the international Convention proscribing this crime has not been satisfactorily ratified. The Apartheid Convention has been in existence for more than three decades. Slightly more than one hundred countries have ratified it, though a number of European countries have not ratified yet, such as Austria, Belgium, France, Germany, Italy, Japan, the Netherlands and Spain, and neither has the United States of America.

Due to the poor ratification status, a few questions arise as to the legal status of *apartheid*, such as whether *apartheid* can be applied to other situations beyond South Africa, and whether individual criminal responsibility for acts prohibited by the Apartheid Convention is customary law or not. Although it is apparent that the United Nations developed the Apartheid Convention as part of its campaign to eliminate racial discrimination in South Africa, the Convention is drafted in general terms (Ratner and Abrams 2001, p. 120 and Sunga 1992, p. 76). Thus the prohibition imposed by the Convention is not limited to one particular country. It is applicable to situations other than *apartheid* which fall within the scope of the Convention (Sunga 1992, p. 76). This general application of the crime of *apartheid* other than to South Africa is also obvious from the fact that the crime is listed in article 7(1)(j) of the Rome Statute.

The crime of *apartheid* is proscribed under article 7(1)(j) of the Rome Statute of the International Criminal Court. As is the case with the crime of genocide, the manifest illegality of crimes against humanity was clearly recognised and declared in the Rome Statute under article 33(2). Therefore a soldier following an order to commit the crime of *apartheid* as a crime against humanity under the Statute shall not be entitled to the defence of superior orders. The *a priori* judgment of manifest illegality of the crime of *apartheid* in the Rome Statute is in favour of the right to conscientious objection to military service related to the policy of *apartheid*. This should be *a fortiori* true when one expects the deterrent effect of the provision of the defence of superior orders under article 33 of the Rome Statute.

The personal scope of the Apartheid Convention has been better clarified. The Apartheid Convention, like the Nuremberg Charter, imposes individual responsibility in too broad a manner (Sunga 1992, p. 77). The States parties to the present Convention declare criminal those organisations, institutions and individuals committing the crime of *apartheid* (article I(2)). International criminal responsibility shall apply, irrespective of the motive involved, to individuals, members of organisations and institutions and representatives of the State, whether residing in the territory of the State in which the acts are perpetrated or in some other State,

[134] Question relating to the situation in the Union of South Africa (1 April 1960) UN Doc S/RES/134.

[135] Resolution 2202 (XXI) 1496th Plenary Meeting, 16 December 1966, UN Doc. A/RES/2202 A (XXI) (16 December 1966).

whenever they: (a) Commit, participate in, directly incite or conspire in the commission of the acts mentioned in article II of the present Convention; (b) directly abet, encourage or co-operate in the commission of the crime of *apartheid* (article III). Thus it does not limit individual criminal responsibility to either senior leaders of apartheid regimes or to those who commit serious violations of the Convention. Thus the intrinsic systematic nature of *apartheid* poses the question of the huge number of people involved in *apartheid*.

While no legal requirements exist to prosecute only senior level officials, there may be practical demands to focus on 'big fish' when an authority tries to prosecute those who are responsible for *apartheid*. The *apartheid* regime penetrated South African society in many ways, such as its economic, legal and political structures. It became difficult to distinguish between those who supported and those who resisted it. The Apartheid Convention does not give any guidance to prosecutorial discretion. Nonetheless, Sunga suggested that: 'In practice, however, prosecutions would probably be confined to policy-makers and members of government responsible for the perpetration and enforcement of particular inhuman acts, similar to the approach taken in the Nuremberg Trials' (Sunga 1992, p. 78). In practice, no one ever has been prosecuted for the crime against humanity of *apartheid*.

Despite the practical unlikelihood of prosecuting lower rank soldiers for the crime of *apartheid*, the norm of prohibition of *apartheid* is regarded as providing conscientious objectors with reasonable grounds. This may be supported by the General Assembly Resolution which is mentioned earlier in this study. In its Resolution 33/165, the General Assembly recognised: 'the right of all persons to refuse service in military or police forces which are used to enforce *apartheid*'.[136] According to the *Special Rapporteurs* on the issue of conscientious objection, Eide and Mubanga-Chipoya, the norm of prohibition of *apartheid* provides not only a duty but also a right under international law to object to participation in the crime of *apartheid* which is denied in the International Convention on the Suppression and Punishment of the Crime of *Apartheid* (Eide and Mubanga-Chipoya 1985, p. 54). The report named the 'Declaration on the Preparation of Societies for Life in Peace', contained in Resolution 33/73 of 15 December 1978, as a significant document in this respect (Eide and Mubanga-Chipoya 1985, p. 55).

While no one would disagree with a contention that *apartheid* constitutes a part of crimes against humanity, there could be argument about acts prohibited by the Apartheid Convention, '[t]he criminality of apartheid as an independent crime under customary international law is a matter of some conjecture' (Ratner and Abrams 2001, p. 122). The customary status of the contents of the Convention is contentious mainly because so many of the influential States of Western Europe and North America did not become State parties of the Convention. A South African, the former Prosecutor of the International Criminal Tribunal for the Former Yugoslavia, Richard Goldstone wrote reminiscently that: '*Apartheid* might well have ended ten years earlier had that Convention been taken seriously by the trading partner countries of South Africa' (Goldstone 2005, p. 554, 558). Further

[136] UNGA Res. 33/165 (20 December 1978) 33 UN GAOR Supp. (No. 45) at 154, UN Doc A/33/45 [1].

weakness of the practical outcome of the Convention is the fact that there have been no documented cases of prosecution on the basis of the Apartheid Convention (Goldstone 2005, p. 558 fn. 32) though the Apartheid Convention seems to confer universal jurisdiction for the acts of apartheid under article V.[137] In fact, there has been no international case law on the crime of *apartheid*.

Yet there are a range of international instruments describing *apartheid* as an international crime, more specifically a crime against humanity. Article 3 of the 1966 International Convention on the Elimination of All Forms of Racial Discrimination emphasises that: 'States parties particularly condemn racial segregation and apartheid and undertake to prevent, prohibit and eradicate all practices of this nature in territories under their jurisdiction'. On 16 December 1966, the General Assembly condemned as a crime against humanity the policies of *apartheid* as a whole.[138] The same formulation had also appeared in Resolutions concerning the South-West African and Southern Rhodesian questions.[139] In the 1968 Convention on the Non-Applicability of Statutory Limitations to War Crimes and Crimes against Humanity, inhuman acts resulting from the policy of *apartheid* are once again described as crimes against humanity. Criminal responsibility for the commission of *apartheid* under international law is expressed under article 19(3)(c) of the International Law Commission Draft Articles on State Responsibility of 1996, though this relates to States and not to individuals (Sunga 1992, p. 72).

The problem of the criminality of acts of *apartheid* is described as follows: 'It is not specified in any of these international instruments which of its elements makes apartheid a crime against humanity. It seems to have evolved in tune with considerations of public policy and as a reflection of public outrage' (Jørgensen 2000, p. 45). The list of international crimes prepared by Cassese does not include *apartheid* (Cassese 2003, p. 25).

> It would seem that this offence has not yet reached the status of a customary law crime, probably because it was held that it was limited in time and space. Moreover, the 101 States parties to the Convention do not include any Western country: only two major segments of the international community (developing and Eastern European countries) have agreed to label apartheid as an international crime, whereas another grouping, that of Western States, has refused to take the same view. There is therefore a case for maintaining that under customary international law apartheid, although probably prohibited as a State delinquency, is not however regarded as a crime entailing the criminal liability of individuals. Nevertheless, the fact that Article 7(l)(j) of the Statute of the ICC grants the Court jurisdiction over apartheid and article 7(2)(h) provides a definition of this crime, might gradually facilitate the formation of a customary rule (Cassese 2003, p. 25).

Hence the Statute of the International Criminal Court may provide a piece of evidence of customary international law with regard to individual criminal responsibility for *apartheid* in international criminal law. The International Court of Justice

---

137 *Cf.* Sunga (1992, p. 77): 'Whereas Article I of the Genocide Convention obliges parties to prosecute the offender if the act was committed on its territory, or by an international tribunal as may exist, the Apartheid Convention foresees a universal jurisdiction over criminal suspects on the basis of custody over the offender'.

138 UNGA Res 2202A(XXI), 16 December 1966.

139 UNGA Res 2074(XX), 17 December 1965.

also has played a major role in the development of proscribing *apartheid* though it deals with State responsibility. For example, the Court found that *apartheid* was objectively illegal and that 'to enforce distinctions, exclusions, restrictions and limitations exclusively based on grounds of race, colour, descent or national or ethnic origin [constitutes] a denial of fundamental human rights [and] is a flagrant violation of the purposes and principles of the Charter'.[140] Even though the customary nature of the crime of *apartheid* as a crime against humanity may be controversial, the manifest illegality of *apartheid* would not be denied by anybody in today's international community.

6.4.3 Aggression

As is the case with the crime of genocide, it may be safe to hold that the dual responsibilities exist in the case of the crime of aggression, though the definition of aggression does not mention such dual responsibilities in article 5(2) of the General Assembly Resolution 3314 (XXIX) of 14 December 1974. As far as States are concerned, the conduct of aggression by a State against another State was prohibited before World War II by bilateral or multilateral treaties of alliance, or the Covenant of the League of Nations, or the Paris Pact of 1928 (Cassese 2003, p. 111) . However, international law dealing with both State responsibility and individual criminal responsibility had been in abeyance for a while (Cassese 2003, p. 112). To define clearly the crime of aggression or the conduct of aggression was regarded as restricting the discretions of States to have recourse to the use of force under international law.

Individual criminal responsibility for the crime of aggression first appeared in the London Agreement of 8 August 1945, establishing the International Military Tribunal, in article 6(a) of the International Military Tribunal Charter, annexed to the Agreement. The following Charter of the International Military Tribunal for the Far East adopted basically the same provision in article 5(a) (Cryer 2005, p. 241). There had been a significant controversy surrounding the crime against peace, i.e. the crime of aggression, mainly due to the lack of precedent practices of punishment of this crime after the Nuremberg Judgment. Nonetheless, the General Assembly of the United Nations unanimously adopted Resolution 95(I), which affirms the principles of international law recognised by the Charter of the Nuremberg Tribunal and the Judgment of the Tribunal.[141] All the then member States of the United Nations 'eventually approved both the definition of crimes against peace and its application' (Cassese 2003, p. 111) by the International Military Tribunal. However, there was a long delay over the codification procedure of the crime of aggression, 'whilst other crimes were spelled out in various conventions' (Cassese 2003, p. 111).

To the degree that the judgments of the International Military Tribunal and the International Military Tribunal for the Far East were deemed to be of international

---

[140] [1971] ICJR 57.

[141] UNGA Res 95(I), UN Doc A/64/Add.1.

customary law, the crime of aggression may also be deemed to be customary in nature. There is now even an argument that the criminalisation of planning and preparing, distinguished from the complete collective act of aggression has a sound basis under customary international law and has so far been largely uncontroversial.[142]

The Chinese government tried war criminals under a law of 24 October 1946. The only trial by Chinese authorities which concerned crimes against peace that is reported is that of Takashi Sakai. The accused served as a military commander in China from 1939 to 1945 and during the hostilities which followed the Mukden incident of 1931 (Brownlie 1963, p. 181). 'With regard to his demand in 1934 for withdrawal of Chinese forces he pleaded government orders and the terms of the International Protocol of 1901. He also pleaded superior orders as a defence to the general charge of participation in a war of aggression' (Brownlie 1963, p. 182). The Tribunal rejected these pleas by holding that: 'Aggressive war is an act against world peace. Granted that the defendant participated in the war on the orders of his Government, a superior order cannot be held to absolve the defendant from liability for the crime'.[143]

The customary nature of the crime of aggression may be supported by the General Assembly Resolution 3314, affirming individual criminal responsibility for initiating wars of aggression, though the definition was evasive and not exhaustive according to article 4.[144] While neither the Statutes of the International Criminal Tribunal for the Former Yugoslavia nor the International Criminal Tribunal for Rwanda contains the crime of aggression, the Rome Statute of the permanent International Criminal Court incorporated this offence under article 5(1)(d). However, the unsettled definition of the crime of aggression led the Rome Statute to suspend the Court's jurisdiction over the crime until a definition is included by amendment to the Statute under article 5(2) of the Rome Statute. According to article 121(3) of the Rome Statute, the adoption of the definition of the crime of aggression shall be either by consensus or a two-thirds majority of State parties. The requirement of seven years' *status quo* from the date of entry into force, i.e., 1 July 2002, under article 121(1) has only two more years before it is met.

The crime of aggression is a most ambiguous and controversial international crime. This may be because, as seen below, it touches upon *jus ad bellum* whose contents are also contentious. Therefore even though its manifest illegality and customary nature have recently became more and more clear, no one may be sure whether their own State has committed this crime or not, apart from several cases clearly recognised by the international community. This fact makes it more difficult for those who want to claim conscientious objector status basing their status upon the crime of aggression committed by their own State.

---

142 ICC-ASP/4/32, Annex II.B, Discussion paper 1, 'The Crime of Aggression and Article 25(3) of the Statute'.

143 War Crimes Military Tribunal of the Ministry of National Defence; judgment on 29 August 1946. Reports; Law Reports, UNW.C.C. xiv. I; Ann. Digest, 1946, no. 93 (brief summary) pp. 197 *seq.*

144 UNGA Res 3314, UN Doc A/9631, article 5(2).

Unlike genocide or crimes against humanity, aggression was not enumerated as manifestly unlawful under article 33(2) of the Rome Statute of the International Criminal Court. Therefore the controversy over the treatment of the defence of superior orders has not abated, like its pending definition itself. Indeed, the definition of the crime of aggression and the applicability of the defence of superior orders before the International Criminal Court may be to some extent intertwined. Unless the definition of the crime of aggression is settled, no one can say that it is manifestly unlawful for anybody.

There are two opposite views, namely the one supporting the defence of superior orders and the other denying this defence in relation to this crime of aggression. The view against this defence to aggression argues that superiors were also simultaneously subordinate to other individuals.[145] The interrelating effect between the definition of aggression and the applicability of the defence is also pointed out. '[S]hould a prior determination of an act of aggression by a third party such as the Security Council or the International Court of Justice be deemed necessary, it would not be feasible to foresee such a determination and consequently an act of aggression could not be ordered' (see Note 146). The argument was also made that the applicability of the defence of superior orders to a charge of aggression could dilute the fundamental responsibility of the political leadership.[146] According to this view, military commanders could not be placed in a situation of casting doubt on the orders received from the political leadership since this could undermine the chain of command (see Note 147). The argument for the retention of article 33 was also made in order to emphasise the individual responsibility of persons in leadership roles.[147]

There was a proposal made during the meetings of the Preparatory Commission that the crime of aggression as a leadership crime be incorporated into the definition of the crime of aggression.[148] This position now seems to have gained a consensus among the participants of the Working Group on the Crime of Aggression, despite the criticism over the uncertainty of the term 'leadership'.

During the resumed fifth Session of the Assembly of States Parties of the International Criminal Court, from 29 January to 1 February 2007, the non-applicability of article 33 included in the 2002 Discussion Paper[149] was deleted.[150] Even if the defence of superior orders is made available in relation to the crime of aggression,

---

[145] ICC-ASP/3/SWGCA/INF.1 (13 August 2004) Note by the Secretariat, 3rd Session, Special Working Group on the Crime of Aggression, The Hague, 6–10 September 2004, 12 [58].

[146] ICC-ASP/3/SWGCA/INF.1 (13 August 2004) Note by the Secretariat, 3rd Session, Special Working Group on the Crime of Aggression, The Hague, 6–10 September 2004, 12 [59].

[147] ICC-ASP/3/SWGCA/INF.1 (13 August 2004) Note by the Secretariat, 3rd Session, Special Working Group on the Crime of Aggression, The Hague, 6–10 September 2004, 12 [60].

[148] Incorporating the Crime of Aggression as a Leadership Crime into the Definition (8 July 2002) UN Doc PCNICC/2002/WGCA/DP.5.

[149] Originally issued as PCNICC/2002/2/Add.2, 24 July 2002, and reissued as Annex II to the Official.

Record of the 2nd Session of the ASP (ICC-ASP/2/10, p. 234).

[150] CICC Background paper on the crime of aggression (2007) [17] 3.

the personal scope of the crime of aggression would be limited to leaders in accordance with the definition of the crime of aggression and they would not be likely to succeed in pleading this defence. Moreover, subordinates are beyond the personal scope of this crime and international criminal law must release subordinates from the issue of the defence of superior orders in relation to the crime of aggression. In other words, it may be seen that the international community which develops international criminal law essentially grants a full defence of superior orders to subordinates.

6.4.4 Crimes Against Humanity and War Crimes

As indicated above, article 33(2) of the Rome Statute of the International Criminal Court Statute stipulates that orders to commit crimes against humanity are manifestly unlawful for the purposes of the article of the defence of superior orders. Coupled with article 25(3) (b), the order to commit an act enumerated in article 7(1) of the Rome Statute of the International Criminal Court would constitute a crime if the crime is committed. Obeying and carrying out such an order is also deemed to contribute to the commission of a crime against humanity.

The rationale of the *a priori* judgment of manifest illegality for crimes against humanity may reflect the customary status of crimes against humanity in the Rome Statute. Seemingly no commentators criticise the provision in the Rome Statute that declares crimes against humanity as manifest illegal. Yet the *travaux préparatoires* show that there are some delegates willing to accept the inclusion of crimes against humanity in the paragraph on excluding the defence of superior orders, subject to the understanding that the definition of crimes against humanity will be sufficiently precise and will identify an appropriately high level of *mens rea* including knowledge of the gravity and scale of the offence.[151] Soldiers at all levels are under an obligation not to follow orders to commit any acts consisting crimes against humanity enumerated in article 7 of the Rome Statute. This may mean support for conscientious objectors who face the possibility of being ordered to commit an act constituting a crime against humanity, or actually facing this sort of order.

The manifest illegality of war crimes may be more controversial, since article 33(2) of the Rome Statute of the International Criminal Court does not provide for the given manifest illegality of war crimes. Not a few criticisms are found in relation to the introduction of this defence (Gaeta 1999, pp. 172–191 and Cassese 1999, pp. 144–171).

The argument against the non-applicability of article 33(2) for war crimes regards the Rome Statute contrary to *lex lata* as far as the defence of superior orders is concerned (Cassese 1999, p. 157). This view claims that under current public international law, any order to commit an international crime is illegal and therefore a

[151] United Nations Diplomatic Conference of Plenipotentiaries on the Establishment of an International Criminal Court (Rome, 15 June–17 July 1998) Official Records, vol. III, Document A/CONF.183/C.1/WGGP/L.9/Rev.1 (25 June 1998) UN Doc A/CONF.183/13 N. 51, 253.

superior order may not be urged in defence by the subordinate who obeys the order (Cassese 1999, p. 157). In addition, the text of the Rome Statute was drafted to publicise the criminality of those acts and may contribute to the *ipso facto* manifest illegality of a conduct enumerated as a war crime under article 8 of the Rome Statute (Cassese 1999, p. 157). Yet the first reasoning does not seem to be so logical since ordering a manifestly illegal act and obeying orders to commit manifestly illegal orders are not necessarily logically connected. It is one thing to call leaders to account for having ordered an international crime and it is another thing to call subordinates to account for having complied with illegal orders, while the second reasoning appears to be more convincing. Thus under current international law it must be judged that the possibility of defence may not be automatically denied even if the obeyed order constitutes an international crime.

Despite controversial arguments over the possibility of the applicability of the defence of superior orders to war crimes enumerated in article 8 of the Rome Statute, the Statute is supposed to be accessible by anybody, anywhere in the modern world. Soldiers may raise this defence before the International Criminal Court, while the burden of proof to show the manifest illegality of the war crime in question shall be on the Prosecutor under article 66 and article 67(1)(i) of the Rome Statute of the International Criminal Court.

The argument for application of the defence of superior orders to war crimes stresses the possibility of mistake as to the unlawfulness in the case of war crimes. Jescheck puts it: '[T]he multitude of possible scenarios which might fall within Article 8 would seem to leave ample room for mistakes, particularly in cases of offences committed during armed combat. Thus, inferiors should be protected from unjust criminalization' (Jescheck 2004, p. 38, 46).

The wording of 'manifestly unlawful' or 'unlawful' in the sense of article 33 of the Rome Statute of the International Criminal Court is interpreted as 'an order in conflict with the rules of international law applicable in armed conflict' in the *travaux préparatoires* of the Rome Statute.[152] However, if this should be so interpreted, almost no defence may be objectively justifiable. In other words, persons claiming that they did not know that the conduct in question constituted a war crime will increasingly find their credibility being challenged (Van der Vyver 2004, p. 57, 145).

For concrete examples of specific acts that officers are prohibited from ordering any circumstances, the United States Army Manual contains a list of such acts considered grave breaches of the Geneva Conventions of 1949 (Osiel 1999, 78). Under the United States Army Manual officers are prohibited from ordering acts that are given as grave breaches in the Geneva Conventions of 1949, that is, wilful killing, torture or inhuman treatment, including biological experiments, wilfully causing great suffering or serious injury to body or health, and extensive destruction

[152] Report of the Preparatory Committee on the Establishment of an International Criminal Court, Draft Statute for the International Criminal Court, UN Doc. A/CONF.183/2/Add.1, 59, fn. 36 (14 April 1998).

or appropriation of property, not justified by military necessity and carried out unlawfully and wantonly.[153]

6.5 Concluding Observation

While international law has not witnessed many international practices concerning the defence of superior orders since the Nuremberg jurisprudence after World War II, it seems that there exist scarce consistent state practices on the defence of superior orders (Insco 2003, p. 389, 410). There is some case law to suggest what is manifest illegality. Sixty years after the Nuremberg Judgment it is still contentious as to whether the defence of superior orders *per se* may be pleaded as a defence independent from the defence of duress or the defence of mistake of law. At least case law and state practice are clear in that manifest illegal orders are not to be obeyed (Sollis 2004, p. 988, 992).

Despite a lack of recent successful cases of the pleading of the defence of superior orders in the United States, the United States in principle seems to have adopted the manifest illegality principle. The Working Group Report on Detainee Interrogations in the Global War on Terrorism: Assessment of Legal, Historical, Policy, and Operational Considerations of April 2003, prepared by the United States Department of Defence, recognises that: 'the defence of superior orders will generally be available for U.S. Armed Forces personnel engaged in exceptional interrogations except where the conduct goes so far as to be patently unlawful'.[154]

It is an indisputable fact that international criminal law has curtailed the scope of the defence of superior orders since before and after Nuremberg trials. Even domestic practices show that manifestly illegal orders should not be obeyed. Although it is safe to state that soldiers have duties to disobey manifestly illegal orders under international criminal law, the scope of duties is not crystal-clear especially in relation to *jus ad bellum* violation. While the Rome Statute clearly rejects the possibility of the defence of superior orders for some *jus in bello* violations, no answer is given as for *jus ad bellum* violation under international criminal law.

What are, if any, the legal implications of the distinction between *jus ad bellum* and *jus in bello* in relation to the right to conscientious objection in international law? A soldier basing his or her right to conscientious objection to military service on manifest illegality of the military service in international law often pay less attention to the distinction between *jus ad bellum* and *jus in bello*. Both international humanitarian law and international criminal law appear to dissociate the *jus*

---

[153] The United States Army Field Manual, FM 27–10, the Law of Land Warfare, Chapter 8, sec. I, para. 502 (1976).

[154] Working Group Report on Detainee Interrogation in the Global War on Terrorism: Assessment of Legal, Historical, Policy, and Operational Considerations (4 April 2003) 33; quoted in SD Murphy, 'Contemporary Practice of the United States Relating to International Law: General International and U.S. Foreign Relations Law: Executive Memoranda on Status and Permissible Treatment of Detainees' (2004) 98 AJIL 820, 828.

ad bellum duties from the *jus in bello* duties. There also exist moral, ethical, religious and legal views which tend to advocate the relationship between *jus ad bellum* and*jus in bello*. If public international law fails to clarify the relationship and the interaction between *jus ad bellum* and *jus in bello*, the clear separation between two classifications would be not in the interests of lower rank soldiers.

Considerations of international humanitarian law clearly support the separation of both issues, yet there must be still room for consideration of the impact emanated from *jus ad bellum* on ordinary soldiers from the perspective of the superior orders defence in international criminal law. Next chapter would like to consider the issue of the impact and significance of the distinction of *jus ad bellum* and *jus in bello* on the fate of conscientious objectors.

References

Journal Article

Bakker JL (1989) The defense of obedience to superior orders: the mens rea requirement. Am J Crim Law 17:55–75
Bartlett CAH (1919) Liability for official war crimes. Law Q Rev 35:177–192
Blackett J (1994) Superior orders – the military dilemma. RUSI (Royal United Services Institute for Defence and Security Studies) Journal 139:12–17
Butler AH (1999) A selective and annotated bibliography of the international criminal court. Crim Law Forum 10:121–145
Cassese A (1999) The Statute of the international criminal court: some preliminary reflections. Eur J Int Law 10(1):144–171
Commission on the Responsibility of the Authors of the War and on Enforcement of Penalties (1920) Report presented to the preliminary peace conference. Am J Int Law 14:95–154
Cornelius S (1997) The defence of superior orders and Erich Priebke. Patterns Prejudice 31:3–19
Dinstein Y (1985) International criminal law. Isr Law Rev 20:206–242
Gaeta P (1999) The defence of superior orders: the statute of the international criminal court versus customary international law. Eur J Int Law 10:172–191
Grayson JW (1995) The defence of superior orders in the international criminal court. Nord J Int Law 64:243–260
Green LC (1993) The defence of superior orders in the modern law of armed conflict. Alta Law Rev 31:320–333
Green LC (2003) Fifteenth waldemar a solf lecture in international law. Mili Law Rev 175:309–384
Greenawalt AKA (1999). Rethinking genocidal intent: the case for a knowledge-based interpretation. Columbia Law Rev 99:2259–2294
Greppi E (1999) The evolution of individual criminal responsibility under international law. Int Rev Red Cross 81(835):531–553
Finch GA (1921) Superior orders and war crimes. Am J Int Law 15:440–445
Hinek S (2005) The superior orders defence embraced at last? N Z Postgrad Law E-J 2:1–50
Insco JB (2003) Defense of superior orders before military commissions. Duke J Comp Int Law 13:389–418
Jescheck H (2004) The general principles of international criminal law set out in Nuremberg, as mirrored in the ICC Statute. J Int Crim Justice 2:38–55
Keijzer N (1978) A plea for the defence of superior order. Isr Yearbk Int Law 8:78–103
Kunz J (1949) The United Nations convention on genocide. Am J Int Law 43:738–746

Lauterpacht H (1944) The law of Nations and the punishment of war crimes. Br YearBk Int Law 21:58–95
Lippman M (1996) Conundrums of armed conflict: criminal defenses to violations of the humanitarian law of war. Dickinson J Int Law 15:1–111
Lippman M (1996) Fifty years after Auschwitz: prosecutions of Nazi death camp defendants. Conn J Int Law 11:199–278
Martines F (1998) The defences of reprisals, superior orders and duress in the Priebke case before the Italian military tribunal. Yearbk Int Humanitarian Law 1:354–361
McCoubrey H (2001) From Nuremberg to Rome: restoring the defence of superior orders. Int Comp Law Q 50(2):386–393
Murphy SD Contemporary practice of the United States relating to international law: general international and U.S. foreign relations law: executive memoranda on status and permissible treatment of detainees. Am J Int Law 98:820–854
O'Brien JC (1993) The International Tribunal for Violation of International Humanitarian Law in the Former Yugoslavia. Am J Int Law 87:639–709
Osiel MJ (1998) Obeying orders: atrocity, military discipline, and the law of war. Calif Law Rev 86(5) 939–1129
Parks WH (1973) Command responsibility for war crimes. Mil Law Rev 62:1–104
Renault L (1915) De l'application du droit pénal aux faits de guerre (I). J du Droit Int 42:313–344
Solis G (2000) Obedience of orders and the law of war: judicial application in American forums. Am Univ Int Law Rev 15:481–526
Solis GD (2004) Obedience to orders: History and abuses at Abu Ghraib prison. J Int Crim Justice 2:988–998
Staker C (2005) Defence of superior orders revisited. Aust Law J 79(7):431–447
Van der Vyver JD (2004) The International criminal court and the concept of Mens Rea in International criminal law. Univ Miami Int Comp Law Rev 12:57–149

Book

Bassiouni, M.C. (1998). The statute of the international criminal court: a documentary history. Transnational Publishers, Ardsley
Brownlie I (1963) International law and the use of force by States. Oxford University Press, Oxford
Cassese A (2003) International criminal law. Oxford University Press, Oxford
Cryer R (2005) Prosecuting international crimes: selectivity and the international law regime. Cambridge University Press, Cambridge
Dinstein Y (1965) The defence of 'obedience to superior orders' in international law. A W Sijthoff, Leyden
Goldstone R (2000) For humanity: Reflections of a war crimes investigator. Yale University Press, New Heaven
Glaser S (1954) Introduction à l'etude du droit international pénal. Bruylant, Bruxelles
Jackson RH (1971) Report of Robert H Jackson, United Nations representative to the international conference on military trials. AMS Press, New York
Jescheck HH (1952) Die Verantwortlichkeit der Staatsorgane nach Völkerstrafrecht. Ludwig Röhrscheid, Bonn
Jørgensen N (2000) The responsibility of States for international crimes. Oxford University Press, Oxford
Knoops GGJ (2001) Defenses in contemporary international criminal law. Transnational Publishers, Ardsley
Oppenheim L (1912) International law, 2nd edn. London, Longmans
Oppenheim L (1921) International law. In: Roxburgh RF (ed) 3rd edn. Longmans, London
Oppenheim L (1926) International law. In: McNair AD (ed) 4th edn. Longmans, London

Oppenheim L (1935) International law. In: Lauterpacht (ed) 5th edn. Longmans, London
Osiel M (1999) Obeying orders: Atrocity, military discipline & the law of war. Transaction Publishers, New Brunswick
Pictet JS (Ed) (1952) Commentary I Geneva Convention for the amelioration of the condition of the wounded and sick in armed forces in the field, vol. I. International Committee of the Red Cross, Geneva
Ratner SR, Abrams JS (2001) Accountability for human rights atrocities in international law: beyond the Nuremberg legacy, 2nd edn. Oxford University Press, Oxford
Schabas WA (2000) Genocide in international law. Cambridge University Press, Cambridge
Schwarzenberger G (1968) International law as applied by international courts and tribunals, vol. II. In: The law of armed conflict. Stevens & Sons, London
Sliedregt EV (2003) The criminal responsibility of individuals of international humanitarian law. TMC Asser Press, The Hague
Sunga LS (1992) Individual responsibility in international law for serious human rights violations. Martinus Nijhoff Publishers, Dordrecht
The United Nations War Crimes Commission (1948) History of the United Nations war crimes commission and the developments of the laws of war. His Majesty's Stationery Office, London

Book Chapter

Ambos K (2002) Other grounds for excluding criminal responsibility. In: Cassese A, Gaeta P, Jones JRWD (eds) The Rome Statute of the international criminal court: a commentary. Oxford University Press, New York, pp 1003–1048
Eser A (1987) Justification and excuse: a key issue in the concept of crime. In Eser A, Fletcher GP (eds) Rechtvertigung und Entschuldigung: Rechtsvergleichende Perspektiven [Justification: Justification and excuse], vol. 1. Eigenverlag Max-Planck-Institut für Ausländisches und Internationales Strafrecht, Freiburg, pp 16–65
Eser A (1996) Defences in war crime trials. In: Dinstein Y, Tabory M (eds) War Crimes in International Law. Martinus Nijhoff Publishers, London, pp 251–273
Kremnitzer M (1992) The world community as an international legislator in competition with national legislators. In: Eser A, Lagodny O (eds) Principles and procedures for a new transnational criminal law. Max-Planck-Institut für Ausländisches und Internationales Strafrecht, Freiburg im Breisgau, pp 337–350
Triffterer O (1999) Article 33 superior orders and prescription of law. In: Triffterer O (ed) Commentary on the Rome Statute of the international criminal court: Observer's notes, article by article. Nomos Verlagsgesellschaft, Baden-Baden, pp 573–588
Vogler T (1973) The defence of "superior orders" in international criminal law. In: Bassiouni MC, Nanda VP (eds) A Treatise on International Criminal Law, vol. 1 Thomas, Springfield, pp 619–634
Zimmerman A (2002) Superior orders. In Cassese A et al (eds) The Rome statute of the international criminal court: a commentary. Oxford University Press, New York, pp 957–974

Chapter 7
Impacts of *Jus Ad Bellum* and *Jus In Bello* on Rights and Duties of Individuals to Disobey Manifestly Illegal Orders

Abstract This chapter deals with the issue of the distinction between *jus ad bellum* and *jus in bello*. What is the rationale for this distinction in international humanitarian law? How does this distinction concern individual responsibilities and duties under international law? In practice, there often exists a concurrence of *jus ad bellum* and *jus in bello* violations. One of the biggest problems is the issue of *jus ad bellum* duties under international humanitarian law, international human rights law and international refugee law. Is there a clear-cut answer for this? The expected response to the issue would not be an automatic one. For a claim of conscientious objection to military service, the principle of *in dubio pro* reo would maximise the benefits for human rights.

An unjust peace is preferable to a just war.

Desiderius Erasmus Roterodamus

7.1 On the Distinction between *Jus Ad Bellum* and *Jus In Bello*

International humanitarian law does not provide any useful guideline for the treatment of deserters acting out of conscience (Bailliet 2006, p. 344). Nonetheless, the classical division between *jus ad bellum* and *jus in bello* under international humanitarian law has affected the fate of the soldiers who have doubts on legality of their (expecting) military conducts or an armed conflict. The distinction seemingly has great impact on the fates of conscientious objectors to military service. Conscientious objectors who are normally lower rank soldiers often miss the distinction between these two classifications and judge illegality of military service often by way of claiming violation of both classifications. International humanitarian law and international criminal law, however, seem to provide a definitive distinction between the two classifications and a soldier whose conscientious objection claim involves a *jus ad bellum* violation would encounter difficulties in basing his or her claim on the manifest illegality of military service.

H. Takemura, *International Human Right to Conscientious Objection to Military Service and Individual Duties to Disobey Manifestly Illegal Orders*.

For example, Israeli reservists invoked the duty to disobey illegal orders under international law and Israeli law.[1] The Israeli soldiers claimed that they could not take tasks they were assigned to in the Occupied Territories since those acts were illegal as well as the illegality of the Israel occupation of the territory. Here the distinction between *jus ad bellum* and *jus in bello* may not be clear cut as seen in the advisory opinion of the International Court of Justice.

The question of whether *jus ad bellum* and *jus in bello* are separated or, in other words, whether a *jus ad bellum* violation has an impact on belligerent equalities before *jus in bello* appears to be not so intriguing as previously, at least from the viewpoint of international humanitarian law. The main reason is that the concept of *bellum legale* has replaced the concept of 'just war', *bellum justum*, since the development of restrictions on the use of force by the League of Nations, the Kellogg-Briand Pact (Pact of Paris) and the United Nations (Kunz 1951, p. 532). Today the illegality of use of force implies a breach of formal, procedural requirements.

During the medieval period, there was 'a much closer link [...] than today between *jus ad bellum* and *jus in bello*' (Meron 1992, pp. 1–44-5, 10). For example, 'medieval legal doctrine taught that the lawfulness of the title to the spoils of war turned on the justness of its cause' (Meron 1992, pp. 1–44-5, 10). In this sense, just cause concerned not only *jus ad bellum*, but also *jus in bello* (Meron 1992, pp. 1–44-5, 10).

The purpose of contemporary international humanitarian law is to ensure that an armed conflict is as humane as possible. Hence the application of *jus in bello* to all the parties of an armed conflict should be ensured throughout the armed conflict, irrespective of a violation of *jus ad bellum* on the part of one or more parties. Nonetheless, it is also true that international humanitarian law is silent on soldiers facing a *jus ad bellum* violation by their own country and army. Davidson summed up the position in international law as follows: 'At least with respect to aggressive wars, international law appears to permit individual participation, extending its punitive arm to those who plan such wars, but not to the lower rank soldier ordered by the State to participate in it (Davidson 2005, p. 123).'

From the policy considerations of international criminal prosecutors, whose institutions have limited resources compared to their domestic counterparts, the target of the application of laws in the sphere of international fora may necessarily be limited to military or civilian leaders and may not be extended to lower rank soldiers as suggested. Yet international humanitarian law should be observed not only by leaders but also by soldiers. In other words, international humanitarian law is preferably applied to anybody even if it is not practical to expect international legal enforcement in this way.

[1] HC/7622/02, Zonhein v. Judge Advocate General (30 December 2002). *See e.g.*, Friedman (2005, p. 109, Theoria 79).

7.2 History of *Jus Ad Bellum* and *Jus In Bello*

The justification of the use of force is an old issue. 'The wars, tortures, forced migrations, and other calculated brutalities which make up so much of recent history have for the most part been carried out by men who earnestly believed that their actions were justified and, indeed, demanded by the application of certain basic principles' (Douzinas 2006, pp. 355–375).

In classical antiquity, Christianity was linked to the secular power of the Roman Empire (Brownlie 1963, p. 5). *Jus in bello* principles do not appear in St Augustine's theories, unlike his ideas concerning *jus ad bellum* (Karoubi 2004, p. 54). The late Romans and medieval scholars analysed wars from the viewpoint of *jus ad bellum* rather than *jus in bello,* which mainly involved the 'just war' theory, the concept of *bellum justum* (McCoubrey 1998, p. 11). The 'just war' theory had matured in the works of twelfth- and thirteenth-century scholastic theorists, such as Gratian, Laurentius, St Raymond of Peñaforte and St Thomas Aquinas, who were greatly influenced by St Augustine (McCoubrey 1998, p. 11). The purport of the 'just war' theory was to limit resort to armed force to the gravest possible cases of actual or threatened injury to the State (McCoubrey 1998, p. 11). Although the intent and purpose of the just war were arguably humanitarian in nature, it soon became 'little more than a pretext for aggression' (McCoubrey 1998, p. 11).

The 'just war' theory became the dominating doctrine of the Middle Ages (Kelsen 1952, p. 35). However, the end of the Middle Ages witnessed the emergence of the Nation-States and eventually modern international law (Dinstein 2004, p. 61). Later the 'just war' theory, along with well-established religious doctrines, was absorbed by natural law theorists and the fathers of international law of the sixteenth, seventeenth and eighteenth centuries (Dinstein 2004, p. 35). Hugo Grotius is seen as taking over the 'just war' doctrine in his writing: 'No other just cause for undertaking war can there be excepting injury received' (Grotius 1925, Bk. Ii, Chap. I, sec. 1, par. 4 and Kelsen 1952, p. 35). The idea that every war must have a just cause, and the idea that this just cause can only be a wrong suffered, remained predominant until the end of the eighteenth century (Kelsen 1952, p. 35).

Positive international law during the nineteenth century took over the 'just war' theory, which 'disappeared almost entirely from positive international law' (Kelsen 1952, p. 35). The International Military Tribunal and the International Military Tribunal for the Far East, the so-called Nuremberg and Tokyo Tribunals, produced and promoted the notion of aggression in the context of individual criminal responsibility. The Charter of the United Nations was adopted to provide for a limited system of use of force under the authorisation of the United Nations Security Council. As is well known, '[t]he Security Council shall determine the existence of any threat to the peace, breach of the peace, or act of aggression and shall make recommendations, or decide what measures shall be taken in accordance with Articles 41 and 42, to maintain or restore international peace and security' under article 39 of the United Nations Charter.

It was rare for advanced societies to leave war completely unregulated (Brownlie 1963, p. 3). The rules concerning constraints of conduct of war (the *jus in bello* equivalent) seem to precede the history of the concept of *bellum justum*. Thus, the rules prohibiting excessive cruelty of conduct in armed conflict can be found especially among non-Western cultures such as the Persian, Egyptian, Indian and Chinese civilisations (Karoubi 2004, pp. 52–53). For instance, the Laws of Manu among ancient Indian texts set numerous significant limitations on the conduct of warfare and may be regarded as 'distinctly humanitarian *jus in bello* norms' (McCoubrey 1998, p. 9).

The laws of war governing the conduct of warfare (*jus in bello*) are thus not a product of Christian scholars or Western civilisation. Yet one may argue that the modern law of armed conflict, including the idea of combatant status, is generally a Western notion (Jensen 2004, p. 209, 214). Roman Law provided formal *jus ad bellum* in the 6th century BC (McCoubrey 1998, p. 11 and Karoubi 2004, p. 53). St Ambrose was the first Christian scholar to examine the concept of *jus in bello* (Karoubi 2004, p. 53).

The development of the idea of *jus in bello* is attributed to Francisco de Vitoria and Hugo Grotius. Vitoria tried to create specific restrictions on *jus in bello* in *De Jure Belli*, where he more directly addressed the problem of war (Karoubi 2004, p. 55). He made clear that deliberate slaughter of innocents is never lawful in itself, because natural law forbids it (Karoubi 2004, p. 55). Vitoria, on the one hand, developed the most powerful case to date for granting special status to innocents, and on the other hand also provided the first statement of military necessity as a justification for setting aside this protection (Karoubi 2004, p. 56). In doing so, he made military necessity a necessary condition for his application of the doctrine of 'double effect' to war. Double effect is Vitoria's way of resolving the tension between the deontological dictum that individual rights are sacrosanct, and the teleological argument that public rights sometimes outweigh individual ones.

On the one hand, the modern notion of *jus in bello* has been developed step by step, mainly in the Western hemisphere. On the other hand, it is thought that the just war theory 'had an unlimited impact' on the development of *jus in bello* (McCoubrey 1998, p. 11). The introduction of the 'just war' concept into *jus in bello* led to 'a facile justification for gross cruelties in the conduct of warfare' (McCoubrey 1998, p. 11). The fear may not be an imaginary one. In the concurring and partially dissenting opinion to the judgment for the CDF trial of the Special Court for Sierra Leone, Hon. Justice Bankole Thompson held that the crimes committed by the accused were excusable in the context of armed hostilities where one of the fighting groups was engaged in defensive military action to restore the lawful and democratically elected government to power.[2]

As is apparent from the purpose of the original 'just war' theory, the unfortunate marriage between the just war theory and *jus in bello* was not the intention of those who formulated the doctrine of just war (McCoubrey 1998, p. 12). St Augustine and St Thomas Aquinas expressly stated that an original 'just' cause might

---

[2] Annex C – Separate Concurring and Partially Dissenting Opinion of Hon. Justice Bankole Thompson Filed Pursuant to Article 18 of the Statute, *Prosecutor v Moinina Fofana, Allieu Kondewa*, Case No. SCSL-2004–14-T, Trial Chamber I, Judgment (2 August 2007) [68], [92] [101]–[103].

be rendered unjust by excessive or cruel pursuit (McCoubrey 1998, p. 12). Yet, in spite of denying the connection between the just war theory and *jus in bello*, the statements of St Augustine and St Thomas Aquinas appear to show the connection between the just war theory and *jus in bello*, since serious violation affects the justness of war in their opinions.

7.3 Relationships between *Jus Ad Bellum* and *Jus In Bello*

Jus ad bellum is the law governing the right to go to war, while *jus in bello* governs the conduct of that war once it has started (Greenwood 1983, p. 221, 221). This definition implies the difference of spheres where each rule operates according to two separate times, that is, peace time and war time. Nonetheless, the practice of modern States has blurred the distinction between peace and war (Greenwood 1983, pp. 221–222). Therefore *jus ad bellum* is no longer confined to regulating the right of States to go to 'war' but regulates the use of force as a whole (Greenwood 1983, p. 222). *Jus in bello* also applies to armed conflicts beyond the formal state of war.

It has been a 'fundamental tenet of the *jus in bello*' that it applies equally to both sides in a conflict, without regard to the legitimacy of their recourse to the use of force (Greenwood 1983, p. 225). This principle is known as 'belligerent equality'. Two aspects can be discerned with regard to belligerent equality by ethicists: no combatants have immunity against being killed by enemy combatants, and all combatants have immunity from blame for the killing of enemy combatants (Bomann-Larsen 2004, pp. 142–160, 142). Nonetheless, this right-duty approach with respect to the rules of war, *jus in bello* must be seen as dangerous since the rules of war may not be seen as conferring rights to kill on belligerents, even though article 43(2) of the Additional Protocol I to the Geneva Conventions of 12 August 1949, relating to the protection of victims of international armed conflicts, stipulates that combatants have the right to participate directly in hostilities: 'The purpose of the laws and customs of war is not to confer subjective rights on belligerents with no corresponding obligations or *vice versa*. On the contrary it is to protect the individual by establishing objective rules which impose both rights and obligations on all belligerents (Bugnion 2002, p. 15, 16).' In this sense, the standpoint of international humanitarian law on combatant immunity should be clarified.

Apparently the principle of belligerent equality is premised on a distinction between civilians and combatants in international humanitarian law, namely the law of war. While combatants can attack enemy combatants or military objectives, causing death, injury and destruction, civilians are not allowed to participate actively in the fighting.[3] This rule and distinction has been a fundamental principle under the law of international armed conflict (Dinstein 2004, p. 27). Customary international law always recognises this distinction between combatants and the civilian population (Rogers 2004, p. 8). Therefore the rule that non-combatants should not be

---

[3] Dinstein (2004, p. 27) *See* articles 42, 43, 51 of the Additional Protocol I of Geneva Conventions.

attacked had emerged by the eighteenth century at latest (Rogers 2004, p. 8). This rule and the legitimate targets of armed conflict have later been confirmed by both the Lieber Code and the preamble of the St Petersburg Declaration (Rogers 2004, p. 8).

The definition of combatant is summarised as 'any member of the armed forces of a party to the conflict except medical personnel and chaplains pursuant to Article 43 of the Additional Protocol I, while all the other persons are considered to be civilians' (Rogers 2004, p. 8). The goal of distinction between combatants and civilians is 'to ensure in every feasible manner that international armed conflicts be waged solely among the combatants of the belligerent parties' (Dinstein 2004, p. 127).

The development of combatant status corresponds to the rise of the Nation-State and its dominance as the major player in international relations (Jensen 2004, p. 215). During the age of chivalry and knighthood, ideas of who should and should not participate in conflict began to solidify, since the warrior class was limited (Jensen 2004, pp. 214–215). Later 'combatant status' developed to describe persons operating under the authority of a sovereign State to wage war (Newton 2005, pp. 75–110, 91). Instead of conferring rights to kill, international humanitarian law brings with the notion of 'combatant status' the implication that lawful combatants enjoyed protection under the laws of war when committing acts that would otherwise be unlawful, such as killing people (Newton 2005, p. 91). 'The intellectual roots of combatant immunity are thus grounded in the soil of state sovereignty' (Newton 2005, p. 91). A combatant acts on behalf of the State. If a combatant acts on his own behalf, the combatant would have no right to kill (Bomann-Larsen 2003, p. 143).

Belligerent equality not only attracts the interest of ethicists or philosophers but also lawyers and publicists. Greenwood posed the question as: 'even if one accepts that since states frequently resort to force in violation of *jus ad bellum*, there are pragmatic reasons for retaining rules governing the manner in which force is used, should those rules apply without discrimination between the aggressor and the victim? (Greenwood 1983, p. 225)'

On the one hand, Greenwood admitted that belligerent equality 'made sense in the days when international law contained few rules governing recourse to force, but it is less easy to justify in logic now that the *jus ad bellum* has become more developed' (Greenwood 1983, p. 225). On the other hand, Greenwood concluded that their application now seems to occur simultaneously but they remain distinct branches of international law, not merely for historical reasons but because they are logically independent of each other, and operate in different ways (Greenwood 1983, p. 223). Nowadays, at least as far as international lawyers are concerned, nobody seriously questions the fact that the Geneva Conventions and other basic principles of *jus in bello* have to be respected by all belligerents, legal or illegal, wherever hostilities take place (Pastor-Ridruejo 2005, p. 3, 5).

The reasoning and justification of belligerent equality tends to be practical or intuitive, described at best as scarce, though values underpinning international humanitarian law or international human rights law may provide sufficient justification on this issue. Saying that a State's duty not to massacre hostages is correlative to the duty of another state to respect the right to life and liberty of its citizens is to concentrate on the formal structure of the rule prohibiting the killing of hostages and to ignore the real purpose of that rule and the method by which it is entitled (Greenwood 1983, pp. 227–228). From the intuitive perspective, one scholar reasons that belligerent equality: '[...] is in fact pure common sense, because it would be illogical if a favour would be granted to illegal belligerents, excusing them from the obligation to respect International Humanitarian Law' (Pastor-Ridruejo 2005, p. 5).

Lauterpacht advanced three main arguments for the continued validity of the principle of equal application of *jus in bello* (Greenwood 1983, p. 226). The first reasoning is that since the rules of *jus in bello* are mostly humanitarian in character, equal application is essential to not make warfare more savage than it already is (Lauterpacht 1953, p. 206, 212 and Greenwood 1983, p. 226). A requirement of humanity insists on respect for the victims of war in all circumstances (Bugnion 2002, p. 18). Secondly, the practical difficulty is to determine which party was an aggressor and to apply *jus in bello* in a discriminatory way (Lauterpacht 1953, p. 212 and Greenwood 1983, p. 226). It is pointed out that this situation has not been changed by the practices of the Security Council because it has tended to avoid any attempt at identifying an aggressor and instead aims to bring about a ceasing of hostilities (Greenwood 1983, p. 226). Without a centralised judicial procedure for determining aggression in each case, on the basis of clear legal criteria, the theory of the discriminatory application of *jus in bello* would lead to the non-application of this body of law on either side (Bugnion 2002, p. 15). Thirdly, Lauterpacht observed that the overwhelming majority of decisions in the aftermath of World War II supported the principle of equal application of the laws of warfare (Lauterpacht 1953, p. 212 and Greenwood 1983, p. 226). The arguments by which the principle of equal application of the laws of warfare is supported are considered to be pragmatic in character for the most part (Greenwood 1983, p. 226).

7.4 Belligerent Equality

Belligerent equality leads to the corollary of the separation between *jus ad bellum* and *jus in bello*: 'the two sets of rules operate in quite distinct spheres. Once hostilities commence, *jus ad bellum* ceases to be relevant and *jus in bello* takes control. This approach had some validity in the days when international law assumed a sharp distinction between peace and war (Greenwood 1983, p. 221).'

The significance of the distinction between *jus ad bellum* and *jus in bello* lies in the peculiarity that they apply to individuals and impose obligations upon them besides State responsibility incurred by each violation (Greenwood 1983, p. 231). Presumably the consequences of a violation of *jus ad bellum* are different from those relating to a violation of *jus in bello*. The two sets of rules differ in the scope and extent of their application (Greenwood 1983, p. 231). While *jus ad bellum* is addressed to the leaders of a State regardless of civilian or military status, the application of *jus in bello* is so wide that it encompasses not only the senior officers of a State's armed forces and the members of its government but all servicemen and the entire civilian population (Greenwood 1983, p. 231).

It is said that the concept of 'belligerent rights' means that a State may acquire rights as a result of its illegal use of force, which offends many people (Greenwood 1983, p. 227). This allows the interpretation of the rules of *jus in bello* to convey that the duty of a belligerent not to violate the humanitarian provisions of the law is correlative to the right of the other belligerents that these rules be observed and, under article 3 of the Hague Convention No. IV Respecting the Laws and Customs of War on Land of 1907, a right to compensation if they are violated (Greenwood 1983, p. 227). Such an interpretation has been rebutted by the purpose of humanitarian rules, composed of the bulk of *jus in bello*, that is, not to confer benefits upon the parties to a conflict but to protect individuals and to give expression to concepts of international public policy (Greenwood 1983, p. 231 and Lauterpacht 1953, pp. 212–213). 'The provision for compensation in article 3 of the Hague Convention No. IV is very much a product of its time, when there was more a tendency to think of *jus in bello* in terms of rights and duties of belligerents *vis-à-vis* one another' (Greenwood 1983, p. 227).

The idea of reciprocal rights and duties should have come from the idea of the equality of sovereignty; however, 'the focus of protection in the modern law of war is not the state but the individual' (Greenwood 1983, p. 145). For international humanitarian law the equal application of *jus in bello* is required to protect individuals rather than States' interests.

7.5 Moralists' Views on Belligerent Equality

The reason why belligerent equality issue attracts moral ethicists may be that it originates from the lack of a solid moral foundation for belligerent equality in their eyes, especially the equal right to kill. Among moral theorists, the most famous proposition seems to be the one by Michael Walzer: 'While it is normally or even always wrong intentionally to attack or kill the innocent, people may, because of what they do, render themselves relevantly non-innocent, thereby losing their moral immunity to intentional attack and instead becoming liable, or morally vulnerable, to attack' (Walzer 1977, p. 128 and McMahan 1994, p. 193, 193). Walzer's view generally coincides with the law of war and distinguishes between *jus in bello* and *jus ad bellum*. There are common terms used by moral theorists, such as 'just combatant' and 'unjust combatant'. Just combatants are those who engage in a just war, whereas unjust combatants engage in an unjust war. In Michael Walzer's view, unjust combatants are equally allowed to attack and kill just combatants as just combatants are permitted to attack and kill unjust combatants.

The counterargument to Michael Walzer's view is labelled the Moral View, which claims that unjust combatants are justified in killing just combatants only in self-defence and only if they are morally innocent (Walzer 1977, p. 128 and

McMahan 1994, p. 198). McMahan explained the reason why the laws of war cannot treat the use of violence by so-called 'unjust combatants', who are legal combatants fighting in a situation where there has been a *jus ad bellum* violation, differently. McMahan states that the main reason is the lack of impartial institutions competent to determine which soldiers do deserve punishment and how severe a punishment (Walzer 1977, p. 128 and McMahan 1994, p. 198). This practical reason, in the Moral View, does not necessarily imply that unjust combatants do not deserve punishment even though they fight in accordance with *jus in bello*.

The Moral View is also strongly put forward by Bomann-Larsen. The questions raised by Bomann-Larsen are: Is it possible to avoid all references to culpability in our assessment of killing in war, when situated within the framework of just war theory (Bomann-Larsen 2004, p. 147); and how we can reconcile the conflict between the intuition that no action in pursuit of an objectively unjust war can be justified with the intuition that regardless of the justness of a given war, soldiers are not criminals unless they commit war crimes (Bomann-Larsen 2004, p. 150). The first question captures the essence of the dilemma soldiers face when encountering an illegal armed conflict, while the latter question is refutable in terms of both international criminal law and international humanitarian law. War crimes are attributable to an individual when all the elements of crimes are established, and war crimes do not need any *jus ad bellum* violation as an element or prerequisite by definition of the elements of war crimes. Even for the first question, Bomann-Larsen seems to provide the valid answer that:

> most of the time at the outset of war its objective justice is uncertain. And in addition, most of the time combatants have good reasons to believe (or have been forced to accept) that their cause is just. And in those cases where the soldiers have no choice, the mere fact that they are forced to fight seems sufficient to exculpate them (Bomann-Larsen 2004, p. 155).

Bomann-Larsen argues that if just war theory allows the use of force in the case of self-defence (and aggression), a moral inequality between combatants emerges (Bomann-Larsen 2004, p. 149). For instance, troops engaged in an unjust attack cannot defend themselves against a counterattack without this defence becoming a part of their initial, unjust attack (Bomann-Larsen 2004, p. 149). Thus 'the injustice on the macro-level will then be repeated on the micro-level in every encounter between individual soldiers and fractions of armies' (Bomann-Larsen 2004, p. 149).

Three issues are identified with regard to individual moral responsibility for war according to Mapel: (1) civilians' responsibility for supporting or opposing a war; (2) civilians' responsibility for volunteering or allowing themselves to be conscripted as soldiers; (3) soldiers' responsibility for the manner in which they fight (responsibility for the violation of *jus in bello*) (Mapel 1998, p. 161). When one examines individual moral responsibility in the second sense, the two situations are and should be further distinguished:

> (a) when we consider a patriotic conscript fighting a just war of national self-defence, then possible elements of excuse for individual moral responsibility are

: the unjust attacking state

: one's own state's offices of recruitment and conscription

: various social and economic pressures

(b) when we consider the situation of a conscientious citizen trying to decide whether to serve in a war one knows is unjust, then the possible elements of excuse for individual moral responsibility are

: his own government and society (Mapel 1998, p. 177).

From an ethical point of view it seems clear that if a good officer finds his or her leader or commander is wrong, he or she 'must not remain passive or act as an agent of those lacking moral rectitude or practical wisdom' (Lee 2004, p. 62). Yet the military duties of loyalty, obedience and the concept of honour conflict with moral thoughts and produce a dilemma (Lee 2004, p. 62). Nevertheless, all these military disciplines are possibly overcome by the notion of loyal disobedience. Loyal disobedience has been supported, for example, by the ancient Chinese philosopher Wei Liao and by Napoleon (Lee 2004, p. 63). Hence the morality required of a soldier is not one of unthinking loyalty to his or her country and its army, but loyalty to himself or herself 'as a moral being guided by his [or her] own conscience' (Lee 2004, p. 63).

7.6 In Defence of Belligerent Equality

From the legalistic point of view, the first problem with moralists' and ethicists' views is that they take *jus ad bellum* as a theory of just war. In other words, ethicists seem to attack the separation between *jus ad bellum* and *jus in bello* on the premise of *bellum justum*, the just war theory. From the viewpoint of international humanitarian law, the just war theory is no more than the classic basis or predecessor of *jus ad bellum*. Now, at least in terms of public international law, *jus ad bellum* is not regulated by the dichotomy between just and unjust but by the recent development of the laws prohibiting the use of force. The concept of *bellum justum* has been replaced by that of *bellum legale* (Kunz 1951, pp. 528–534, 532 and Dinstein 2004, p. 64). As natural law began to fade in consequence of the flourishing of Nation-States, and the advent of positivism as the theoretical basis of international law, represented by the works of Bynkeshock and Vattel, the division between just and unjust war more or less disappeared from the international vocabulary and from international law (Collier 1991, pp. 121–132, 122). The first and foremost norm in this regard goes to the Charter of the United Nations (articles 2(4), 51 and 53).

The development of international law following two devastating World Wars witnessed the outlawing of 'war'. 'In modern international law, the straight answer to the question "what is the basis of the institution of war?" is: "nothing"' (Collier 1991, pp. 121–132, 121). For instance, the two Additional Protocols of the Geneva Conventions use the term 'armed conflict' instead of 'war'. The end of the First World

War is associated with the first real attempt to restrict resort to war (Collier 1991, pp. 121–132, 122), with the Covenant of the League of Nations attempting 'a blanket prohibition on the use of aggressive force' (Collier 1991, pp. 121–132, 123). The General Treaty for the Renunciation of War of 1928, also known as the Pact of Paris and the Kellogg-Briand Pact, condemned recourse to war for the solution of international controversies and renounced it as an instrument of national policy in nations' relations with one another (Collier 1991, pp. 121–132, 123). After World War II, the Nuremberg Trial recognised even individual criminal responsibility for waging an aggressive war. In 1946 the United Nations Charter prohibited the use of force.

Further, Bugnion suggested that there is confusion between the source of a right or an obligation and the fact which entails the application of the right or obligation (Bugnion 2002, p. 12).

> If a house burns down, it is not the fire but the insurance policy which is the legal basis of the claim of the insured against the insurance company; if it were otherwise, no householder would ever bother to pay the premiums. In the same way, it is not war which is the source of the rights and obligations arising from the laws and customs of war but the humanitarian conventions as regards the obligations and rights deriving from those treaties, and international custom as regards the rights and obligations deriving therefrom. The armed conflict – however it may be categorized – is nothing other than the fact which results in the application of the rules stemming from the conventions or from custom. Otherwise, the belligerents would have identical rights and obligations, whether or not they were party to the humanitarian conventions (Bugnion 2002, p. 12).

On the one hand, it should be admitted that some awkwardness exists as follows: 'if starting and continuing a war is wrongful, why does international law seek to regulate the means by which it is waged?' (Collier 1991, p. 121). In other words:

> International law prohibits the aggressive use of force yet contains detailed prescriptions, binding on both the aggressor and his victim, concerning such matters as the weapons which may be used and the targets against which they may be directed. Yet although the very existence of the modern *jus in bello* may appear illogical, does it contribute to maintaining the institution of war? (Greenwood 1991, pp. 134–137, 135)

On the other hand, the existence of two laws of *jus ad bellum* and *jus in bello* cannot be regarded as problematic, since 'the modern laws of war first came into force before making war became illegal' (Greenwood 1991, p. 122).

The legal standpoint that principles of the *jus in bello* continued to apply equally to all parties to a conflict was supported by the United States Military Tribunal which tried the German commanders in the Balkans in *United States v List*, by rejecting a prosecution argument that since the German invasion and occupation of the Balkans had been a violation of the Pact of Paris, everything done by the German occupation authorities had to be judged by the same standard as those of any other belligerent occupant, irrespective of whether the initial occupation was lawful.[4] This 'principle' was reaffirmed in 1977 when the Diplomatic Conference which adopted the Additional Protocols emphatically rejected a Vietnamese argument that the laws

---

[4] (1948) 15 Annual Digest and Report of Public International Law Cases 632; *See* Greenwood (1991, p. 143).

of war should not protect anyone who served as an aggressor (Greenwood 1991, p. 143). The preamble to the Additional Protocol I reaffirms that 'the provisions of the Geneva Conventions and the Protocol must be fully applied in all circumstances to all persons who are protected by those instruments, without any adverse distinction based on the nature or origin of the armed conflict or on the causes espoused by or attributed to the parties to the conflict'.

Practical justifications for the legal standpoint are as follows. Firstly, in most conflicts both sides will claim to be acting in self-defence and the international community will be reluctant to identify one side as the aggressor (Greenwood 1991, pp. 143–144). If the Security Council never brands either party as aggressor, suggesting that international law confers rights only upon the victim of aggression, then this is likely to create a situation in which neither side honours the provisions of the Geneva Conventions and the rest of the *jus in bello* (Greenwood 1991, p. 144). Secondly, most of the rules of the modern *jus in bello* are concerned not with reciprocal rights and duties of the States involved in a conflict but with ensuring a basic level of humanitarian treatment of individuals caught up in a conflict (Greenwood 1991, p. 144). 'In that sense, the humanitarian provisions which comprise the greater part of the modern *jus in bello* are closer to the law of human rights than traditional law of inter-state relations' (Greenwood 1991, p. 144). Thirdly, 'to say that the *jus in bello* applies equally to aggressor and victim is not to confer legitimacy upon the aggressor's actions' (Greenwood 1991, p. 143).

7.7 The Case of Concurrence of *Jus Ad Bellum* Violation and *Jus In Bello* Violation

As seen above, it may be imperative for international humanitarian law to apply *jus in bello* universally, albeit the existence of alleged *jus ad bellum* violation. From various necessities of the legal nature of international humanitarian law, '[f]or at least two centuries it has been absolute dogma that international humanitarian law applies equally to all parties to a conflict, irrespective of' (Doswald-Beck 1997, p. 35, 57) the merits of the case under *jus ad bellum* (Dinstein 2001, p. 144). However, the ambiguity surrounding the relationships between these two doctrines is revealed in the recent Advisory Opinions of the International Court of Justice.

7.7.1 Legality of the Threat or Use of Nuclear Weapons

The Advisory Opinion of the International Court of Justice on Legality of the Threat or Use of Force is controversial since the Court seemingly limited the use of nuclear weapons (*jus in bello*) in relation to the *jus ad bellum*. Thus the Advisory Opinion has reopened the issue of the equal application of *jus in bello* irrespective of the merits of the case under *jus ad bellum* (Dinstein 2001, p. 144).

On 15 December 1994, the General Assembly adopted a Resolution, 49/75K, and requested the International Court of Justice to render an Advisory Opinion on the question: 'Is the threat or use of nuclear weapons in any circumstances permitted under international law?' pursuant to article 96(1) of the Charter of the United Nations.[5] The Court handed down its Advisory Opinion on 8 July 1996.

The Advisory Opinion is notoriously inarticulate. While the Court admitted the illegality of the threat or use of nuclear weapons in general, it reserved its illegality for exceptional circumstances. On the one hand, the Court recognised that: '[i]t follows from the above requirements that the threat or use of nuclear weapons would generally be contrary to the rules of international law applicable to armed conflict, and in particular the principles and rules of humanitarian law'.[6] On the other hand, the Court held that: '[h]owever, in view of the current status of international law, and of the elements of fact at its disposal, the Court cannot conclude definitively whether the threat or use of nuclear weapons would be lawful or unlawful in an extreme circumstance of self-defence, in which the very survival of a State would be at stake' (see Note 6). The last sentence is sometimes considered as *non liquet*.[7] If international law does not prohibit a certain conduct, that conduct is considered to be lawful.[8] This leads to the following interpretation of this Advisory Opinion: 'according to the majority of the Court, the use of nuclear weapons would be lawful when undertaken by the party acting in extreme self-defence, provided that its very survival was at stake' (Dinstein 2001, p. 145). To put it the other way around, the party facing off against the party in extreme self-defence, most likely the aggressor State, may not employ nuclear weapons even if its survival is at stake (Dinstein 2001, p. 145). If this interpretation is right, the question is posed: Would other breaches of international law possibly be excused in an extreme case? (Dinstein 2001, p. 145)

This Advisory Opinion thus revealed its tangled relationship of *jus ad bellum* and *jus in bello* (Dinstein 2001, p. 146). Dinstein warns that this Opinion may set a dangerous precedent for the discriminatory application of *jus in bello* pursuant to the status of *jus ad bellum* (Dinstein 2001, p. 146).

Although a nuclear weapon is unlikely to be used by lower rank soldiers, a problem may arise if the departure from the equal application of *jus in bello* of this Advisory Opinion were to extend to weapons other than nuclear weapons.

---

[5] *Legality of the Threat or Use of Nuclear Weapons* (Advisory Opinion) 8 July 1996 ICJ Rep 226–228.

[6] *Legality of the Threat or Use of Nuclear Weapons* (Advisory Opinion) 8 July 1996 ICJ Rep 266 [105].

[7] The Dissenting Opinion of Vice-President Schwebel, Legality of the Threat or Use of Nuclear Weapons, Advisory Opinion, 322–323. Dinstein, *War, Aggression and Self-Defence*, 145.

[8] The Dissenting Opinion of Judge Shahabuddeen, Legality of the Threat or Use of Nuclear Weapons, Advisory Opinion, 389–390; Dinstein, *War, Aggression and Self-Defence*, 145.

7.7.2 Legal Consequences of the Construction of a Wall in the Occupied Palestinian Territory

The case of the construction of a wall in the occupied Palestine territory might be an appropriate example of the concurrence of *jus ad bellum* and *jus in bello* violation. One may recall that the International Court of Justice delivered its Advisory Opinion, at the request of the General Assembly, stating that the construction of the wall in the occupied territory is illegal.[9]

The Court mentioned the fact that the General Assembly and the Security Council have referred to the customary rule of 'the inadmissibility of the acquisition of territory by war'.[10] The International Court of Justice itself, in its advisory opinion, seems to recognise the *jus ad bellum* violation when it states that: '[t]he Court considers that the construction of the wall and its associated régime create a "fait accompli" on the ground that could well become permanent, in which case, and notwithstanding the formal characterization of the wall by Israel, it would be tantamount to *de facto* annexation'.[11]

The 'Wall' advisory opinion is remarkable in that it also recognises a *jus in bello* violation. With regard to the settlements of Israeli people in the Occupied Palestinian Territory, the Court held that: 'The information provided to the Court shows that, since 1977, Israel has conducted a policy and developed practices involving the establishment of settlements in the Occupied Palestinian Territory, contrary to the terms of Article 49, paragraph 6 [of the Fourth Geneva Convention]' (see Note 9).

Thus the principal judicial organ of the United Nations recognised '*de facto* annexation' and the violation of the provision of the Fourth Geneva Convention in respect of the construction of the wall. This must be seen as positive basis or ground for Israelis to become conscientious objectors to service in the Occupied Territory, at least in relation to the wall.

7.8 Duties of Individuals Derived from *Jus Ad Bellum*

After examining the justifications of belligerent equality, and despite the ambiguity of the possible impacts of *jus in bello* violations on *jus ad bellum* violation, the real and sole question surrounding this issue should be distilled into the individual's duty and responsibility for *jus ad bellum* violation. For it is clear under contemporary

[9] *Legal Consequence of the Construction of a Wall* (Advisory Opinion) 2004 <http://www.icj-cij.org/icjwww/jdocket/imwp/imwpframe.htm> accessed 21 July 2007 [120].

[10] *Legal Consequence of the Construction of a Wall* (Advisory Opinion) 2004 <http://www.icj-cij.org/icjwww/jdocket/imwp/imwpframe.htm> accessed 21 July 2007 [117].

[11] *Legal Consequence of the Construction of a Wall* (Advisory Opinion) 2004 <http://www.icj-cij.org/icjwww/jdocket/imwp/imwpframe.htm> accessed 21 July 2007 [121].

international law and international humanitarian law that the individual may owe responsibility for any *jus in bello* violation. Although no one may doubt that the development of the *jus ad bellum* scheme by the United Nations after World War II constrains the use of force by States, it is not clear how far *jus ad bellum* is relevant to individuals, especially those who claim the status of conscientious objector against military service. Whereas the crime of aggression is agreed to be defined as a leadership crime, the question whether soldiers and civilians belonging to the State allegedly committing the crime of aggression are entirely free from moral culpability remains unclear.

In the Altstötter case ('the Justice trial'), the United States Military Tribunal at Nuremberg, in a Judgment given in 1947, declined to treat as relevant the fact of aggressive war in deciding whether the draconian laws enacted in Germany, for which the accused were responsible, constituted crimes against humanity:

> If we should adopt the view that by reason of the fact that the war is a criminal war of aggression every act which would have been legal in a defensive war was illegal in this one, we would be forced to the conclusion that every soldier who marched under orders into occupied territory or who fought in the homeland was a criminal and a murderer. The rules of land warfare upon which the prosecution has relied would not be the measure of conduct and the pronouncement of guilty in any case would become a mere formality.[12]

Only the people who held positions having influence on the government's policy were accused of *jus ad bellum* violations after World War II. 'The position which the Tribunal assumed may be summarized by saying that only those holding positions in which they could influence the policy of the German state were held responsible under Counts One and Two' (Brownlie 1963, p. 196).

> There is no clear indication of the degree of participation and knowledge required for the imposition of responsibility under Counts One or Two. Nevertheless the Tribunal had some guidance. There was no intention on the part of the prosecuting states to impose a collective punishment consequent on an interpretation of 'waging' which would include the soldier in the field and the civilian supporting the war effort: the Charter was expressed to be for the trial of major war criminals (Brownlie 1963, p. 195).

Even though the legal position of accountability for *jus ad bellum* violations may be confined to influential civil or military personnel, the problem has remained: What should a good man, who is an officer, do if he is engaged in a war that he cannot believe is justified? (De Lee 2004, pp. 61–67) While most soldiers do not object to war on the grounds of illegality or the unjustness of war, because they rely upon the government to make these sorts of decisions, it is suggested that this 'traditional military view' was severely qualified at Nuremberg since some of the accused were condemned for conspiring against peace (De Lee 2004, p. 61).

---

[12] 'VII: Opinion and Judgment: The Law in Action, Part 3', in Trials of War Criminals Before the Nuremberg Military Tribunals Under Control Council Law No. 10. Vol. 3: United States of America v Josef Altstoetter, et al. (Case 3: Justice Case'). District of Columbia; Law Reports of Trials of War Criminals, 6 (1948) 52.

Michael Walzer considers that a clear line exists distinguishing between the responsibilities of the leaders of States and of their followers, the soldiers:

> We draw a line between the war itself, for which soldiers are not responsible, and the conduct of the war, for which they are responsible, at least within their own sphere of activity. [...] It is conceived, both in international law and in ordinary moral judgment, as the king's business – a matter of state policy, not of individual volition, except when the individual is the king (Walzer 2000, pp. 38–39).

For Walzer, therefore, the defence of superior orders may successfully apply to the legitimacy of a war but not to a violation of the law of war (Walzer 2000, p. 39).

By the same token, from the traditional and basic international legal point of view, the legal arguments that can be raised for conscientious objectors – that the war violates the United Nations regime restricting recourse to force, the Nuremberg Principle condemning aggressive wars, and general contemporary international law – are only relevant to the high-level decision maker and perhaps to high-level military commanders (O'Brien 1968, p. 1080, 1105).

> Scruples on the legality of a war might lead to dissent within the decision making process and to resignation. Arguments concerning the legal foundation of the war are not highly relevant, however, to the plight of the ordinary draftee or even to a junior officer. The principle applied at Nuremberg, and at most of the trials of the lesser war criminals, [is] that mere service in the armed forces of a nation which is subsequently found by some authoritative international body or court to have engaged in aggression, is, in itself, not a crime under international law (O'Brien 1968, p. 1105).

McMahan challenges three tenets of the traditional theory: (1) that the principles of *jus in bello* are independent of those of *jus ad bellum*; (2) that unjust combatants can abide by the principles of *jus in bello* and do not act wrongly unless they fail to do so; and (3) that combatants are permissible targets of attack while noncombatants are not (McMahan 2004, pp. 693–773). McMahan has the following situation in mind to challenge the traditional theory: The combatants fighting in an unjust war do wrong if they attack another country's military personnel before the latter have mobilised, but they do not do wrong if they attack those same people after they have begun to mobilise in self-defence (McMahan 2004, p. 697). Thus the coercive pressures and the constraints of knowledge on the side of soldiers participating in an unjust war should be regarded as excuses at best (McMahan 2004, p. 700).

While Walzer seems to not expect moral and legal duties beyond *jus in bello* from soldiers, McMahan puts soldiers under a greater obligation:

> In the case of soldiers, it is highly important that their beliefs should be justified because of the seriousness of what they are being asked to do, namely, to kill people of whom they have no personal knowledge. Moreover, the risk that their cause is unjust is high. Because wars are rarely if ever just on both sides but are sometimes unjust on both, it is likely that most soldiers in the history of war have fought in the service of an unjust cause. Soldiers, therefore, have very strong reasons to form justified beliefs about the morality of war in which they are asked to fight (McMahan 2004, p. 701).

McMahan also points out the disproportion between the admissibility of the defence of superior orders in the case of *jus ad bellum* violation and in the case of *jus in bello* violation:

> Walzer and other defenders of the traditional view claim that combatants are accountable for obeying the rules of *jus in bello* in a way that they are not accountable for the rules of *jus ad bellum*, so it would be surprising if the same considerations that supposedly enable combatants to act with justification in violating the rules of *jus ad bellum* would also enable them to act with justification in violating the rules of *jus in bello* (McMahan 2004, p. 702).

Eide and Mubanga Chipoya noted that:

> when a person is convinced that the armed forces of his own country are being used or *may be used* in the future for purposes that are in violation of international law, and when therefore a conscience built on respect for international law reinforces the general repulsion against taking the life of others arbitrarily, should not this objection be accepted? This would form a concrete application of the extent of the right to freedom of conscience and to the freedom of action built on conscience (emphasis added) (Eide and Mubanga-Chipoya 1985, p. 6[47]).

They also highlight the fact that: 'the personal legal duty incumbent on the individual not to act contrary to international law was proclaimed in the Charter of the Nuremberg Tribunal, (Eide and Mubanga-Chipoya 1985, p. 6[47]).

Some complaints or objections regarding practical difficulties for recognising *jus ad bellum* as a ground for conscientious objectors may be expected. However, it is claimed by McMahan that the consequences for people refusing to fight in unjust wars are unlikely to be calamitous (McMahan 2004, p. 706). 'If the refusal to cooperate were successfully extensive or widespread, it could seriously degrade the ability of the aggressor' (McMahan 2004, p. 706). It also seems unlikely that allowing or even encouraging conscientious refusal would seriously impair a country's ability to fight just wars, since history confirms how easy it is to persuade people that a war in which they are ordered to fight is just (McMahan 2004, p. 707).

It is pointed out that the only case in which the right to conscientious objection is likely to be exploited by malingerers is humanitarian intervention (McMahan 2004, p. 707). Assuming that an international institution would be less likely than individual states to intervene unjustly, it is unlikely that the rights to conscientious objection would be widely exercised (McMahan 2004, p. 707).

The rationale behind denying blameworthiness of soldiers for participating in the war against *jus ad bellum* may be a practical one. Practical difficulties remain, as in the case of asylum seekers in the context of conscientious objection to military service, and the domestic courts have to decide the illegality of the war upon application, if lower rank soldiers can claim conscientious objector status or refugee status on the basis of *jus ad bellum* violation. Mapel rightly pointed out that: 'there are no impartial international institutions competent to judge and administer punishment to large numbers of ordinary soldiers' (Mapel 1998, p. 172, 186).

If not by international law, then the morality of war may govern the conscience of an individual soldier deciding whether to fight (Mapel 1998, p. 172). Such a morality of war eventually promotes the liberalisation of domestic laws concerning selective conscientious objection, which is primarily distinguished from absolute conscientious objection by the fact that the objector does not claim to be opposed to all forms of the use of armed force, and would, were the circumstances different, be willing to participate in military action (Mapel 1998, p. 172).

In practice, it should be noted that ironically many of the Israeli *refuseniks* were already concerned about the objective of the conflict (*jus ad bellum*) long before they made an issue of its conduct (*jus in bello*), since numerous *refuseniks* are dedicated soldiers with military experience (Mapel 1998, p. 173). Selective conscientious objection on the basis of personal doubts that a conflict may be a violation of *jus ad bellum* should be permissible, in order to prevent acts against both *jus ad bellum* and *jus in bello*.

7.9 State Practice of Conscientious Objector Based on *Jus Ad Bellum*

Numerous United States citizens were reported to have been prosecuted during the Vietnam War for refusing conscription on the grounds that the war was immoral and/or illegal (Osiel 1999, p. 85). This war was succeeded, to a lesser degree, by Operation Desert Storm during the Gulf War between 1990 and 1991, and more recently by the so-called Iraq War of 2003. Nonetheless, the outcomes of such claims often do not appear successful. In the United States, Captain Yoranda M Huet-Vaughn believed international law, including the Nuremberg principles, prohibited her from participating in violations both of international law and her oath as a physician and was convicted of desertion during the Gulf War.[13] The U.S. Court of Appeals for the Armed Forces rejected her argument as raising a nonjusticiable 'political question'.[14]

The Iraq War that began in 2003 also witnessed several soldiers claiming illegality or immorality of what was an unjust war in their eyes. Quite the contrary to what happened in Germany, though much predictable from Huet-Vaughn decision, the United States Military Judge Lt Col John Head told First Lieutenant Ehren Watada, the first military officer charged with public dissent since 1965,[15] that he, 1Lt Watada, could not base his defence on the war's legality (see Note 15). The defence team of Watada wished to refer to the Nuremberg Principles and the duty to disobey illegal orders, but again the 'political question' principle prevented him from pleading this defence.[16]

A European court took a more lenient approach concerning a soldier who claimed the illegality of the Iraq War. On 21 June 2005, the Federal Administrative Court of Germany (*Bundesverwaltungsgericht*) acquitted a soldier charged with disobeying an order in violation of his military duty of obedience and loyal service

[13] *Huet Vaughn v. US* 116 S.Ct. 922, 133 L.Ed.2d 851, 64 USLW 3550, 64 USLW 3557, 'On Petition for Writ of Certiorari to the United States Court of the Appeals for the Armed Forces' (22 December 1995) 4 and 23.

[14] U.S. v Huet-Vaughn, 43 M.J. 105, 107 (1995). *See* Osiel (1999), fn. 40.

[15] M. Tran, 'The Iraq War on Trial' (4 January 2007) Guardian Unlimited http://www.guardian.co.uk/Iraq/Story/0,,1982934,00.html accessed 21 June 2007.

[16] M. Barber, 'Unit Gets Ready for Iraq – Without Watada War Resister Makes Good on Promise' *The Seattle Post – Intelligencer* (23 June 2006) B1; A Massie, 'It was My Duty to Refuse to Go to Iraq, Says First American Army Officer Facing Court Martial' (23 November 2006).

(Baudisch 2006, p. 911, 911). The soldier was a major in the Federal Armed Forces (*Bundeswehr*) and in command of an information technology project aimed at improving cooperation between Germany and other North Atlantic Treaty Organisation (NATO) countries (Baudisch 2006, p. 25, 26). He refused to take part in a military software project on the basis of his belief that the military intervention in Iraq was illegal and that the software could be used in the military operation in Iraq (Baudisch 2006, p. 25, 26). As soon as the Operation Iraqi Freedom began in March 2003, he contacted an army chaplain and his unit's medical officer and told them of his legal and moral scruples about Germany's role in the conflict (Baudisch 2006, p. 911, 911). Since his superior officers could not assure him that his project would not have some impact on the military operation in Iraq, the major declared himself unable to comply with the order until the conflict had come to an end (Baudisch 2006, p. 911, 911). He invoked his right to freedom of conscience provided by article 4, paragraph 1 of Germany's Basic Law (*Grundgesetz*), Germany's constitution (Schultz 2005, p. 25, 26).

This case should be regarded as a typical case of selective conscientious objection in that the soldier did not oppose military activities in general but specific military actions which he had deemed illegal or unethical. The jurisprudence of German courts by the time of this judgment had allowed only absolute conscientious objection under the Basic Law (Baudisch 2006, p. 911, 915). According to the former jurisprudence of German courts, the Basic Law allowed an individual to refuse military service altogether, but not to refuse to participate in specific operations or situations (Baudisch 2006, p. 911, 915).

The first trial by the military court (*Truppendienstgericht*) found the defendant guilty of deliberate insubordination and demoted him from the rank of major to captain (Baudisch 2006, p. 911). Both the respondent and the attorney of the Federal Armed Forces (*Wehrdisziplinaranwalt*) appealed the decision (Schultz 2005, p. 25, 26). Whilst the former must have pursued the acquittal, the latter wanted the respondent to be expelled from the army.

On appeal, the Federal Administrative Court upheld the soldier's position that he did not act unlawfully in refusing the order (Baudisch 2006, p. 911). Recognising that the military duty, set out in section 11(1) of the Soldier's Act of 19 August 1975, was an important one, the Court decided that this duty does not demand unconditional devotion to superiors (Baudisch 2006, p. 911). According to the Court, the military is supposed to be committed to law and justice and the observance of fundamental rights (Baudisch 2006, p. 911).

While the Federal Administrative Court clarified the instances in which orders are not binding, it did not decide whether any of these instances applied to the order in this case (Baudisch 2006, p. 912). The Federal Administrative Court held that an order is not binding (i) if it violates human dignity; (ii) if it does not serve the defence of Germany but only the pursuit or achievement of political or economic aims; (iii) if obeying the order would perpetrate an offence under national or international criminal law; (iv) if it functions as part of a war of aggression that would disturb the peaceful coexistence of nations; or (v) if it contravenes fundamental rules of international law such as the United Nations prohibition on the use of force

(Baudisch 2006, p. 912). However, the Court did not decide whether the order was valid or not but held that even if assuming that the order was valid the order could be legally disobeyed (Baudisch 2006, p. 912). Thus the test for the decision of conscience within the ambit of article 4 does not include a judgment as to whether the decision is erroneous, wrong or right (Schultz 2005, p. 25, 26).

In so doing, the Court emphasised the protection of freedom of conscience under the German Basic Law. Article 4 of the German Basic Law certainly guarantees this right and the right to conscientious objection to military service involving the use of arms under article 4(1) and (3) respectively.[17] Interestingly, the Court found a right to selective conscientious objection for soldiers in active service other than the right to conscientious objection to military service provided for in article 4(1) of the Basic Law (Baudisch 2006, p. 911, 912). Accordingly, the Court held that soldiers in active service can rely on their basic right of freedom of conscience, which is distinct from the constitutional right to recognition as a conscientious objector, since the Court found that the Basic Law did not intend to limit a soldier's general right to freedom of conscience (Baudisch 2006, p. 911, 912). At the same time, the Court admitted that the freedom of conscience does not guarantee freehanded independence from the general subjugation to law (Baudisch 2006, p. 911, 912). In the opinion of the Court, the ethical implications of an order are important to balance against the soldier's freedom of conscience (Baudisch 2006, p. 911, 912). When the Court assessed the sincerity of the soldier's expression of conscience, the Court stressed the existence of objectively serious reservations surrounding the military intervention in Iraq besides the soldier's personal convictions (Baudisch 2006, p. 911, 912). Hence the Court decided that a soldier in active service needs to demonstrate that his personal belief is not only sincere but also objectively reasonable (Baudisch 2006, p. 915). Although the Court set this prerequisite of serious reservations about the legality of the individual order, it did not make decisions about either the legality of the order or the legality of the Operation Iraqi Freedom (Baudisch 2006, p. 915–916). The main question addressed by the Court was whether there was some *reasonable basis* for the individual soldier to make that judgment (Baudisch 2006, p. 916). If the Administrative Court had decided there was a military duty to obey orders from superiors unless in specific circumstances, the logical course would have been to decide whether the order at issue was binding or not, in light of the legality of war and the legal implications of the conduct the soldier would embark on (Baudisch 2006, p. 915).

The German Administrative Court denied the apparent legality of the Iraq War both by examining Security Council Resolutions 678, 687 and 1441, in light of article 2(4) of the Charter of the United Nations, and by examining justifications

[17] Article 4 (1) stipulates that: "Freedom of faith and of conscience, and freedom to profess a religious or philosophical creed, shall be inviolable". Article 4(3) stipulates that: "No person shall be compelled against his conscience to render military service involving the use of arms. Details shall be regulated by a federal law". German Bundestag, Official translation, Basic Law for the Federal Republic of Germany, (German Bundestag – Administration – Public Relations Section, Berlin 2001) available at <http://www.bundestag.de/htdocs_e/parliament/function/legal/germanbasiclaw.pdf> accessed 20 July 2007.

surrounding self-defence under article 51 of the Charter of the United Nations. At the same time the Court clearly recognised that the United Nations should remain the central forum for the maintenance and preservation of international peace and security (Baudisch 2006, p. 917). Despite this understanding of the Court, it embarked on the examination of manifest illegality of Operation Iraqi Freedom since that examination was necessary to justify the soldier's conscientious objections to the Operation. To clarify Germany's obligations as a Member State of NATO, the Court found that even the North Atlantic Treaty and its subsequent documents do not allow Member States to act in contravention of the United Nations Charter.[18]

Whereas the Court did not declare that the operation in Iraq and the commitment of the German government was unlawful, the Court recognised that the prohibition of the use of force under article 2(4) of the United Nations Charter and the corresponding *jus cogens* were *prima facie* violated (Schultz 2005, p. 25, 28 and 37). The German Administrative Court further held that the provision of article 2(4) of the Charter actually grants rights to German citizens and generates obligations by virtue of article 25 of the German Basic Law, which provides that the general rules of international law shall be an integral part of federal law (Schultz 2005, p. 27). This construction is denounced as lacking in direct enforceability of article 2(4) of the United Nations Charter (Schultz 2005, p. 28). This may be one of the core issues of the right to selective conscientious objection in international human rights law, i.e., whether article 2(4) of the United Nations Charter relating to *jus ad bellum* can be enforced by individuals before domestic courts. From this perspective, too, this judgment is important for future conscientious objectors. Such inarticulateness may be derived from the fact that partaking in an illegal war may trigger criminal liability for the members of the government and other relevant actors according to the German Constitution (Schultz 2005, p. 38).

This judgment by the German Administrative Court is suggestive and propitious with regards to conscientious objectors who might not necessarily be granted conscientious objector status under the traditional conscientious objection standard. First of all, it recognised the right to claim selective conscientious rejection in a specific military activity as a separate right from absolute conscientious objection, which is embodied in the German Basic Law. Secondly, the Court did not hesitate to begin the examination of *jus ad bellum* to some extent when it sought to look for an objective basis of conscience of the individual military personnel, even though it seems that the Court did not recognise itself as appropriate adjudicator for a *jus ad bellum* violation. Thirdly, the domestic Court decided upon an issue with highly political and diplomatic implications. Such a case law should be of significance for future selective conscientious objectors when their rights are not explicitly recognised in domestic law.

[18] Baudisch (2006, p. 917). *See* Preamble of the North Atlantic Treaty and article 1(Washington DC, 4 April 1949). *Cf* articles 5 and 7.

7.10 Religious Views

While the just war theory has been replaced by the rules governing the use of force and the rules of armed conflict, any layperson in international law can be prone to judge a war by justice and righteousness. Some Christian religions seemingly support conscientious objection to military service in the context of unjust war.

Christian doctrine generally holds that: 'Once a war is determined to be unjust, the soldier cannot fight in it' (Davidson 2005, p. 91, 128). For example, the view of the Roman Catholic Church was that acts of war could be morally justified only if they were not perpetrated against innocent civilians and if the principle of proportionality was observed between the evil to be removed and the good to be achieved.[19] However, who decides the unjustness of a war and/or modalities of war in the context of religious institutions is not clear. One author points out that the prohibition of participating in an unjust war may be triggered by an individual's subjective determination of unjustness (Davidson 2005, p. 128). Thus the United States Conference of Catholic Bishops, though in careful wordings, opined that:

> If a Catholic is utterly convinced in conscience that a war is unjust and his own role constitutes direct participation in the effort, he has the right and obligation to object and even refuse to participate, regardless of the consequences to person and career. However, prior to taking such a drastic step, I vigorously urge any Catholic in such a position to seek out the counsel of a Catholic chaplain.[20]

One of the five precepts taught by Buddhism is to refrain from harming living creatures. According to such a teaching, no distinction between just cause and unjust cause of an armed conflict may be made as to the prohibition from participation in an armed conflict involving actual combat. Therefore a country such as South Korea, where the dominant two religions are Christianity and Buddhism, generates a large number of conscientious objectors believing in Buddhism.

It may be possible to find in the teachings of the major religions support for conscientious objection, sometimes in respect of particular wars.[21] Although those religious convictions for conscientious objection to military service normally must fall under the protection of the freedom of thought, conscience and religion, religious preaching derived from just war theory rather than from pacifism may be categorised as selective conscientious objection rather than absolute conscientious objection.

---

[19] UN Doc E/CN.4/1985/SR.27, para. 29 (Mr. Zoller, Pax Christi International) (4 March 1985).

[20] The United States Conference of Catholic Bishops, Archdiocese for the Military Services, USA, <http://www.usccb.org/sdwp/peace/military2.htm> accessed 4 October 2006.

[21] UN Doc E/CN.4/1985/SR.55 (20 March 1985) [25].

7.11 Concluding Remarks

The more international criminal law matures and develops, the more vigilant individuals have to be over the legality of their conduct in the light of international law. This may be more true for civilian and military leaders who are destined to be tried in front of international fora, if indicted and apprehended by international criminal instututions. Having knowledge of abstract information regarding an armed conflict including international criminal law allows soldiers to claim their conscientious objector statuses.

The main remaining issue surrounding the right to conscientious objection is how to handle the claim of conscientious objector status based on a *jus ad bellum* violation in the contexts of both international human rights law and international refugee law for conscientious objectors to military service. In relation to the issue of *jus ad bellum* duty on individuals, as seen above in the traditional and contemporary doctrine of international humanitarian law, an examination of belligerent equality was made. The expected response to the issue would not be an automatic one. For a claim of conscientious objection to military service, the principle of *in dubio pro reo* would maximise the benefits for human rights.

References

Journal Article

Bailliet C (2006) Assessing *jus ad bellum* and *jus in bello* within the refugee status determination process. Georget Immgr Law J 20(3):337–384

Baudisch I (2006) German federal administrative court decision on a soldier's right to refuse to obey military orders for conscientious reasons. Am J Int Law 100:911–917

Bomann-Larsen L (2004) Licence to kill? The question of just vs. unjust combatants. J Mil Ethics 3(2):142–160

Bugnion F (2002) Just wars, wars of aggression and international humanitarian law. Int Rev Red Cross 84(847):3(523)–26(546)

Davidson MJ (2005) War and the doubtful soldier. Notre Dame J Law Ethics Public Policy 19:91–162

De Lee N (2004) The case of colonel Hackworth. J Mil Ethics 3:61–67

Doswald-Beck L (1997) International humanitarian law and the advisory opinion of the international court of justice on the legality of the threat or use of nuclear weapon. Int Rev Red Cross 37(316):35–55

Douzinas C (2006). Postmodern just wars and the new world order. J Hum Rights 5(3):355–375

Greenwood C (1983) The relationship between *jus ad bellum* and *jus in bello*. Rev Int Stud 9:221–234

Friedman R (2005) The challenge of selective conscientious objection in Israel. Theoria 109:79–99

Jensen ET (2004) The laws of war: Past, present and future: Combatant status: It is time for intermediate levels of recognition for partial compliance. VA J Int Law 46(1):209–249

Kunz JL (1951) Bellum justum and bellum legale. Am J Int Law 45:528–534

Lauterpacht H (1953) The limits of the operation of the law of war. Br Yearbk Int Law 206–243

Mapel DR (1998) Coerced moral agents? Individual responsibility for military service. J Polit Philos 6(2):171–189
McMahan J (1994) Innocence, self-defense and killing in war. J Polit Philos 2(2):193–221
McMahan J (2004) The ethics of killing in war. Ethics 114:693–773
Meron T (1992) Shakespeare's *Henry the fifth* and the law of war. Am J Int Law 86(1):1–45
O'Brien WV (1968) Selective conscientious objection and international law. Georget Law J 56:1080–1131
Osiel MJ (1999) Obeying orders: Atrocity, military discipline & the law of war. Transaction Publishers, New Brunswick
Schultz N (2005) Was the war on Iraq illegal? – The German federal administrative court's judgment of 21st June 2005. Ger Law J 7:25–44

Book

Brownlie I (1963) International law and the use of force. Oxford University Press, Oxford
Dinstein Y (2001) War, aggression and self-defence, 3rd edn. Cambridge University Press, Cambridge
Dinstein Y (2004) The conduct of hostilities under the law of international armed conflict. Cambridge University Press, Cambridge
Grotius H (1925) De jure belli ac pacis libri tres. Clarendon Press, Oxford
Karoubi MT (2004) Just or unjust war: international law and unilateral use of armed force by States at the turn of the 20th century. Ashgate Publishing Company, Burlington
Kelsen H (1952) Principles of international law, 1st edn. Rineheart & Company, New York
McCoubrey H (1998) International humanitarian law: modern developments in the limitation of warfare. Ashgate Publishing, Aldershot
Rogers APV (2004) Law on the battlefield, 2nd edn. Manchester University Press, Manchester
Walzer M (1997) Just and unjust wars, 1st edn. Basic Books, New York
Walzer M (2000) Just and unjust wars, 3rd edn. Basic Books, New York

Book Chapter

Collier JG (1991) Legal basis of the institution of war. In: Hinde R. A (ed) The institution of war. Macmillan, London, pp 121–132
Greenwood C (1991) In defence of the laws of war. In: Hinde RA (ed) The institution of war. Macmillan, London
Newton M (2005) Unlawful belligerency after September 11: history revisited and law revised. In: Wippman D, Evangelista M, (eds) New wars, new laws?: applying the laws of war in 21st century conflicts. Transnational Publishers, Ardsley, pp 75–110
Pastor-Ridruejo JA (2005) On the relationships between jus in bello and jus ad bellum. Can a notion of international humanitarian law influence in the determination of the legality of the use of force? In: Fernández-Sánchez PA (ed) The new challenges of humanitarian law in armed conflicts: in honour of professor Juan Antonio Carillo-Salcedo. Martinus Nijhoff Publishers, Leiden, pp 3–12

Chapter 8
Conclusion

Abstract While the duty of the individual to disobey manifestly illegal orders under international law has become clearer, the international community has not abolished completely the defence of superior orders. International criminal law still recognises the defence of superior orders at least in mitigation of punishment. This fact grants especially lower rank soldiers the possibility of resorting to the defence of superior orders at least for the mitigation of sentences. The duty to disobey manifestly unlawful orders and the right of selective conscientious objection should not be regarded as mutually exclusive. On the contrary, the individual's duty to disobey manifestly unlawful orders as well as States' duty to honour individual conscience may both be seen as the underpinning for selective conscientious objection. Although it may not make sense to use the Nuremberg principles as the grounds of selective conscientious objection when there is a duty to disobey unlawful orders, conscientious objection may be the only possible solution for soldiers facing manifestly unlawful orders. In order to improve the effectiveness of conscientious objection claims, the international community should send a clearer message that there exists the right to conscientious objection under international law.

> Mindful that during this century millions of children, women and men have been victims of unimaginable atrocities that deeply shock the conscience of humanity...
>
> 2nd Preambular Paragraph of the Rome Statute of the International Criminal Court

8.1 Towards an Approach of Complementary Rights and Duties

The duty of the individual to disobey manifestly illegal orders has become clearer especially when one looks at the history of the defence of superior orders. At the same time, the international community has not abolished completely the defence of superior orders. International criminal law still recognises the defence of superior orders at least in mitigation of punishment. This fact grants especially lower rank soldiers the possibility of resorting to the defence of superior orders at least for the mitigation of sentences.

H. Takemura, *International Human Right to Conscientious Objection to Military Service and Individual Duties to Disobey Manifestly Illegal Orders.*

The doctrine of absolute liability and the doctrine of conditional liability of the defence of superior orders under international criminal law surely have inculcated a spirit of refusal to obey a superior order to commit a manifestly illegal act into individuals. Those individuals should be especially high ranking officers who are often charged with the responsibility for training lower rank soldiers, though the rejection of manifestly illegal orders may go beyond high ranking officers.

Thus there has been a long-standing individual duty to disobey manifestly illegal orders under international law. This duty may not necessarily displace the claim of selective conscientious objection to military service in the domestic sphere. How can one claim one's own country's violation of international law before a domestic authority, and how can one legally refrain from military service following one's own finding of a manifestly illegal order? Normally a system that would allow an individual to claim having a duty under international law is not available in a domestic society. Thus it may be a natural course of action for a soldier of lower rank to associate the right to defence of superior orders under international law with a charge of having followed manifestly illegal orders under international law. The right and duty of the individual in this sense must strengthen and promote the norm of preserving international peace and security in public international law.

8.2 Status of Individuals Under International Law

Individuals enjoy rights and bear duties under public international law. Global concern for human rights has increased, in particular since World War II, promoting the status of the individual as the bearer of human rights. Coincidentally the practices of international law since the end of World War II and the Cold War have shown that individuals can bear criminal responsibility for violations of international law before international or internationalised tribunals. In this sense, individuals are today safely, at least to some degree, described as objects of international law as well as subjects of international law.[1]

Despite all these developments in relation to the status of individuals in international law, the international legal personality of individuals is quite another matter. The concept of an individual's international legal personality has been contentious. The idea that international law rules are directly binding on individuals without the intermediary of States is said to be as long as the history of international law, which arguably dates back to the sixteenth century (Korowicz 1956, p. 533, 534).

One of the authoritative sources on this issue is the International Court of Justice's Advisory Opinion in the Reparation for Injuries case in 1949.[2] The Court regarded an international legal person as 'a subject of international law and capable of possessing international rights and duties, and that it has capacity to maintain

---

[1] For the views in favour of individuals as subjects of international law, Jones (1984, pp. 61–78).

[2] *Reparation for Injuries Suffered in the Service of the United Nations* [1949] ICJ 174 (Apr. 11) (Advisory Opinion).

its rights by bringing international claims'.[3] While this assertion included the capacity to possess rights and duties under international law under the concept of international legal personality, the capacity to enforce the claim of an international legal person to such rights before an international forum is also an important matter. In the latter sense, almost every international law scholar who advocates the special status of individuals in international law along with States acknowledges that the individual cannot be a subject of the law of nations in a strict legal sense (Orakhelashvili 2001, p. 241, 245). Individuals also have limited rights and duties to participate in the legislative process in international law through States, Non-Governmental Organisations (NGOs) and individual complaints to various international and regional human rights tribunals and similar bodies. Although the mere fact that individuals have a range of rights and duties under international law cannot confer on the individual an international legal personality, the fact at least promotes the individual's status under international law.

Another issue which is often used to justify the need for the individual to have an international legal personality is the fact that under certain conditions, involving breaches of international law, persons can be held accountable and tried under international law by international judicial bodies, irrespective of the will of their national State and its domestic laws (Orakhelashvili 2001, pp. 248–249). The primary obligations of international criminal law are thus at an individual level (see Burke-White 2002, p. 1, 78). Since the Nuremberg Judgment, it has been widely accepted at the international level that individual persons are the mechanism by which a State's legal obligations are carried out (see Danner and Martinez 2005, p. 75, 169, fn. 10), even though State responsibility is not necessarily discharged upon recognition of individual responsibility.[4] It is highly significant that the Nuremberg Tribunal held that: 'Crimes against international law are committed by men, not by abstract entities, and only by punishing individuals who commit such crimes can the provisions of international law be enforced'.[5] This must be a hackneyed phrase for academics and specialists in international criminal law. However, this statement produced one of the most important principles, namely that individuals can and should be accountable for the most serious international crimes.[6] Although this fact may also contribute to the promotion of the status of individuals in international law, it cannot be connected directly to the issue of the international legal personality. An individual may be held directly accountable for violations of international law

[3] *Reparation for Injuries Suffered in the Service of the United Nations* [1949] ICJ 179 (Apr. 11).

[4] *Application of the Convention on the Prevention and Punishment of the Crime of Genocide (Bosnia-Herzegovina v Serbia and Montenegro)* (Merits) 26 February 2007 <http://www.icj-cij.org/docket/files/91/13685.pdf> accessed 25 July 2007 [167].

[5] *Trial of the Major War Criminals before the International Military Tribunal, Nürnberg*, 14 November 1945–1 October 1946, published at Nürnberg, Germany (1947) 223.

[6] Judge Philippe Kirsch, 'Applying the Principles of Nuremberg in the ICC: Keynote Address at the Conference "Judgment at Nuremberg" held on the 60th Anniversary of the Nuremberg Judgment', Washington University, St Louis, Missouri (30 September 2006), 2. Available at < http://www.icc-cpi.int/library/organs/presidency/PK_20060930_English.pdf > (last visited, 3 July 2007).

under international criminal law. Direct individual criminal responsibility appears to strengthen the position of the individual as a subject of international law.

The individual is more than merely an object or incidental beneficiary under international law, in that human rights law is specifically designed to promote individuals' rights. In other words:

> There is a strong convergence of thought that the individual should be regarded as a principal juristic entity in international law. This is certainly the case with regard to human rights and it should be no less concerning human responsibilities (Bagaric and Morss 2006, p. 157).

Whereas this study deals with the subject of individuals' rights and duties in relation to disobedience of manifestly illegal orders under international law, it does not intend to argue for the international legal personality of individuals. Beyond controversies surrounding the issue of the international legal personality of individuals, the interesting development for international law must be the existence and contents of their rights and duties under international law.

8.3 Duties of Individuals to the Community Under International Law

Whereas the rights of individuals in international law, specifically international human rights law, have become clearer and even more specific with the creation of various specialised international human rights instruments, the duties of individuals in international law are not set out in broad catalogues of individual duties equivalent to international human rights under international law. This section would like to clarify, firstly, what kinds of duties are expected of individuals under basic international human rights instruments. Secondly, even if it is agreed that individuals have duties under international law, to whom such duties of individuals are owed needs to be clarified. The question is whether it is the domestic community and/or the international community to which individuals' duties in international law are owed. The study of the duties of individuals in international law may provide a theoretical basis for individuals to act in accordance with public international law.

8.4 Article 29(1) of the Universal Declaration of Human Rights

Recognising individuals as being directly or indirectly bearers of rights and duties under international law, the meaning of the duties of individuals need to be clarified since they do not seem to be as clearly imperative as the individual's human rights in international law. References to duties are found in several human rights instruments.

Article 29 of the Universal Declaration of Human Rights[7] introduced the notion of duties of individuals in international human rights law along with a regional instrument, the American Declaration of the Rights and Duties of Man, which was adopted 6 months earlier.[8] Article 29(1) of the Universal Declaration of Human Rights provides that: 'Everyone has duties to the community in which alone the free and full development of his personality is possible'. A United Nations report prepared in 1983 on this article further clarifies the duties of individuals defined in the Universal Declaration of Human Rights.[9]

Remarkably, Daes' report contains sections on obedience to the law and the defence of superior orders as subjects of the duty of the individual to the community. The report tries to clarify the individual's duty to obey and the law to be obeyed by individuals as well as the admissibility of the defence of superior orders: 'The individual has an obligation to obey the law and other legitimate commands of the authorities of his country and those of the country in which he may be residing'.[10] It further clarifies that individuals shall obey just and good law, the law which protects every individual without discrimination of any kind and the general welfare.[11]

Article 29(1) is seen as 'of moral nature in the sense that it lays down a general rule for individual behaviour in the community to which the individual belongs'.[12] By the same token, the fifth preambular paragraph of the International Covenant on Civil and Political Rights states: 'Realizing that the individual, having duties to other individuals and to the community to which he belongs, is under a responsibility to strive for the promotion and observance of the rights recognized in the present Covenant'.[13]

It is not clear from a plain reading of article 29 of the Universal Declaration of Human Rights whether the Declaration intends to equate the duty of the individual to the international community with that owed to his or her national State. Coupled with the recognition of the status of the individual as a bearer of legal rights and duties, the duties of the individual to the international community, as perceived since World War II, have been gradually recognised on a global scale. Therefore, '[a]mong the first duties of the individual should be the duty to use his [or her] strength to maintain international peace and security'.[14] The position that the individual owes duties to the international community may be supported by the drafting histories of

[7] Universal Declaration of Human Rights, adopted on 10 December 1948, G.A. Res. 217A (III), UN Doc. A/810, at 71 (1948).

[8] American Declaration of the Rights and Duties of Man, signed 2 May 1948, OEA/Ser.L./V/11.71, at 17 (1988).

[9] UN Doc E/CN.4/Sub.2/432/Rev.2 (1983) [Daes Report] 56 [259].

[10] Daes Report, 56 [259].

[11] Daes Report, 56 [260].

[12] Daes Report, 17 [2].

[13] International Covenant on Civil and Political Rights, adopted 16 December 1966, entered into force 23 March 1976, G. A. Res. 2200A (XXI), UN Doc. A/6316 (1966), 999 UNTS 171, reprinted in 6 ILM 368 (1967).

[14] Daes Report, 53 [234].

the Universal Declaration of Human Rights and the International Covenant on Civil and Political Rights.

The *travaux préparatoires* of article 29(1) of the Universal Declaration of Human Rights show that the very first draft of article 29(1) seems to presuppose the duty of the individual to the international community. The first draft of the provision was prepared by John Humphrey, the then Director of the Human Rights Division of the United Nations Secretariat. He wrote in preambular paragraph 1(b) that:

> Every one owes a duty of loyalty to his State and *to the international community* of which he forms a part. He must accept his fair share of responsibility for the performance of social duties and also his share of any sacrifices made necessary by the exigencies of life in common (emphasis added) (Hobbins and René Cassin 1989, p. 7, 15).

This became article III of his first typed draft (Hobbins and René Cassin 1989, p. 7, 15).

René Cassin made a change to the duty of the individual to the international community which had appeared in Humphrey's original draft when he drafted article 29 (Morsink 1999, p. 251). He dropped 'duty to international society and to the United Nations' without explanation (Morsink 1999, p. 251). Later, when the draft was submitted to the Third Committee of the General Assembly (September to December 1948), two amendments to restore this provision were made (Morsink 1999, p. 251). The Egyptian delegation introduced the following as a third paragraph for the article: 'These rights can in no case be exercised contrary to the principles and purposes of the United Nations'.[15] The French delegation proposed that the second paragraph end with the phrase 'and to serve the purposes and principles of the United Nations'.[16] This may reveal the willingness of drafters to keep the idea of duty to the United Nations, which may be seen as interchangeable to some extent with 'international community'.[17]

The drafting history of the preamble of the International Covenant on Civil and Political Rights has implications for the domestic community. At the Eighth Session of the Commission on Human Rights, the Australian and Swedish delegations submitted an amendment to the draft preamble of the International Covenant on Civil and Political Rights proposed by the United States of America, taking into account article 29(1) of the Universal Declaration of Human Rights.[18] One of the drafters thought that, as States were the sum of individuals, individuals must co-operate if the Covenant was to be implemented.[19] The Chilean delegate also pointed out that

[15] UN Doc A/C.3/267, reprinted in The Official Record of the 3rd Session of the General Assembly, Part I, Third Committee Annexes to the Summary Record of Meetings, 1947, Lake Success, New York, UN Doc A/C.3/SR.74, 43.

[16] UN Doc A/C.3/345, reprinted in UN Doc A/C.3/SR.74, 44.

[17] The number of Member States of the United Nations is 192 as of 2007.

[18] UN Commission on Human Rights, Draft International Covenants in Human Rights and Measures of Implementations (22 May 1952) UN Doc E/CN.4/L.171.

[19] The Australian delegation (Weitram) stated that: 'Paragraph 1 of article 29 of the Universal Declaration of Human Rights recognised the individual's duties to the community. The draft covenant before the Committee was concerned with the obligations of States; nonetheless, States being

the individual must strive with the community for the observance of the Covenant.[20] However, the case of conflict between the duties imposed by the Covenant and duties under domestic law was not discussed.

In neither the Universal Declaration of Human Rights nor the International Covenant on Civil and Political Rights is the notion of 'the community' to which individuals belong defined, and it is not self-evident whether this includes both the domestic community and the international community. Some States think the duties of individuals in the sense of these United Nations documents embrace duties to the international community. This is revealed by studying the comments made by governments relating to the duties of the individual, in reply to the questionnaire researching the meaning of article 29 sent by the *Special Rapporteur*.[21]

A few countries made it clear that individuals have a duty towards the international community only in the sense that they are under a duty not to commit international crimes or war crimes threatening world peace.[22] For instance, Australia noted that:

> An individual is subject to duties under international law only if he can be held directly responsible in accordance with national rules of implementation, it being understood that the extent of punishment can be left to national regulation. But such direct responsibility of the individual under general international law applies exclusively to war criminals since, in accordance with traditional international practice, States have a right to punish prisoners of war who fall into their hands only if they committed acts in contravention of the law of war prior to being taken prisoner.[23]

The Federal Republic of Germany interpreted article 29, without advancing any justification, as saying that it cannot be deduced from either international instruments or general international law that the individual should resist demands and obligations *vis-à-vis* the international community which are incompatible with the United Nations Charter, the International Covenants on Human Rights and other international conventions and declarations on human rights:[24]

> The only reference in international law to direct obligation incumbent upon individuals has been that in respect of their duty to refrain from committing serious misdemeanours. There are, for example, certain situations in international customary law which also relate to individual citizens, such as the prohibition of slavery, piracy, crimes against humanity and particularly grave war crimes. It is possible that a prohibition of specific terrorist acts

---

the sum of individuals, the latter must co-operate if the covenant was to be implemented. The Australian-Swedish amendment brought that point out very clearly'. UN Doc E/CN.4/SR.308, 13.

20 UN Doc E/CN.4/SR.308, 13.

21 Daes Report, 22–31.

22 Daes Report, 28, quoting Pakistan's response: 'Individuals have a duty towards the international community not to commit any act which might destroy world peace, but this duty has not received any legal sanction in Pakistan, except that following Pakistan's accession to the Convention on the Prevention and Punishment of the Crime of Genocide, that crime is now legally recognized in Pakistan as an offence against the international community'.

23 Daes Report, 21.

24 Daes Report, 23.

> applicable to individuals is also in the process of development. On the whole, however, there have been only a few cases in international law.[25]

In general, most States seem to recognise that 'it is an individual's duty to oppose any demands of the community which are incompatible with the purposes and principles of the Charter of the United Nations' and other fundamental international human rights law, as well as the Genocide Convention.[26] However, the means to fulfil this duty are interpreted as not being unlimited. For example, Pakistan allows only the formulation of strong public opinion which may deter the community from the act.[27] The individual is not supposed to take any action to achieve this purpose which is forbidden by law (see Note 27).

Morocco interpreted the term 'community' as the whole body of citizens, the people or the State.[28] Therefore, for Morocco article 29(1) of the Universal Declaration of Human Rights does not imply any duty of the individual under international law. Only Greece clearly interpreted the term 'community' as including 'the family, other social groups, society, the State, the international community and mankind' (see Note 25).

Prior to the Universal Declaration on Human Rights, the American Declaration of the Rights and Duties of Man had already introduced the notion of duties into a regional human rights instrument. The American Declaration of the Rights and Duties of Man was adopted by the Ninth International Conference of American States of the Organization of American States in Bogotá, Columbia, on 2 May 1948.[29] Its preamble set out that:

> The fulfilment of duty by each individual is a prerequisite to the rights of all. Rights and duties are interrelated in every social and political activity of man. While rights exalt individual liberty, duties express the dignity of that liberty.

Accordingly, the preamble of the American Declaration of the Rights and Duties of Man led to the interpretation that the relationship between the rights and the duties of individuals is at least to some extent two sides of the same coin. Its Chap. 2 is specifically devoted to the duties. Ten duties are enumerated: duty to society; duties toward children and parents; duty to receive instruction; duty to vote; duty to obey the law; duty to serve the community and nation; duties with respect to social security and welfare; duty to pay taxes; duty to work; duty to refrain from political activities in a foreign country.

---

[25] Daes Report, 24.

[26] Daes Report, 28 (*see* replies from Senegal and Pakistan).

[27] Daes Report, 28.

[28] Daes Report, 27.

[29] Basic Documents Pertaining to Human Rights in the Inter-American System, OEA/Ser.L.V/II.82 doc.6 rev.1 at 17 (1992).

Chapter V of the American Convention on Human Rights, which was adopted 21 years after the American Declaration, has a chapter on personal responsibilities.[30] It was adopted by member states of the Organization of American States in San José, Costa Rica, on 22 November 1969. However, Chap. V of the Convention remains confined to a brief reference to individual responsibility with one article of two paragraphs. Article 32(1) of the Convention stipulates that: 'Every person has responsibilities to his family, his community, and mankind'. A description of the contents of such responsibilities was not incorporated in the Convention, contrary to the American Declaration.

The African Charter on Human and People's Rights, adopted 17 June 1981, is another example of a human rights instrument that imposes duties on the individual, in three of the provisions in the chapter on duties.[31] Unlike article 29 of the Universal Declaration of Human Rights, which did not define the 'community' to which individuals are said to belong, the African Charter includes the individual's duties owed to the international community. According to article 27(1): 'Every individual shall have duties towards his family and society, the State and other legally recognized communities and the international community'. The concept of duties in the African Charter reflects an original approach which tries to accommodate both the values of traditional African societies and the needs of modern African states (Kunig, Benedek and Mahalu 1985, p. 88).

Duties such as those appearing in the Universal Declaration of Human Rights and the African Charter on Human and People's Rights will form part of the basis of this study. If individuals owe duties toward the international community in addition to their own domestic communities, then this notion of duties will have an impact on the individual duty to object to participation in any military service which is in contradiction with the values of the international community.

8.5 Meanings of Duty and Community

The term 'duty' may apply to any action derived from a moral or legal imperative, apart from personal likes and dislikes.[32] Unlike in the jurisprudence of the United States of America, in the broader sense the term 'duty' is not necessarily the correlative of the term 'right' as a consequence of embracing its moral imperatives.[33] Since there is a need to inquire into moral and ethical views, this study will also tackle views on the issue of rights and duties to disobey manifestly illegal orders. This kind of broader approach to the notion of duty is supported by the counterpart to this study, namely freedom of conscience, which is also derived from moral and ethical grounds.

[30] 1144 U.N.T.S. 123, Basic Documents Pertaining to Human Rights in the Inter-American System, OEA/Ser.L.V/II.82 doc.6 rev.1 at 25 (1992).

[31] African [Banjul] Charter on Human Rights and People's Rights, adopted 27 June, 1981, OAU Doc. CAB/LEG/67/3 rev. 5, 21 I.L.M. 58 (1982, entered into force 21 October, 1986).

[32] Daes Report, 38 [96].

[33] Daes Report, 39 [99].

In order to consider the individual's rights and duties in international law, the word 'community' in article 29(1) of the United Nations Declaration of Human Rights should also be interpreted broadly and not confined to the indigenous community or State to which the individual belongs. Therefore it includes the international community in this study. The Daes Report also deems that 'the United Nations' and 'the World Community' are included in the meanings of the word 'community'.[34]

Even though the community to which individuals owe some duties encompasses the international community, the term 'international community' is rarely defined or has never been seriously subject to an attempt at definition (see Kritsiotis 2002, p. 961, 964). In the context of international law, the term international community connotes equality among States.[35] When one speaks about the international community in international law, its applicability is universal to the membership of the international community irrespective of the size or the cultural system of a State.

The former Secretary-General of the United Nations, Kofi Annan, referred to the concrete meaning of the idea of international community on 30 December 1999.[36] First of all, the shared values which make a community are, among others, faith and the defence of an idea such as democracy (see Note 36). Such values may thus be religious or political. Second, a shared vision of a better world for all people binds people into the international community (see Note 36). Annan especially emphasised the existence of the international community and its actual achievements. The notion of international community must be created by members of the international community. These commitments of States, individuals and all other relevant actors to build up the notion of international community should cast aside the doubts surrounding the term 'international community' with its possible implication of cosmopolitanism.

8.6 Conscience of Mankind

Genocide, aggression, *apartheid* and forcible denial of self-determination constitute wrongs which 'shock the conscience of mankind'.[37] Such crimes constitute the hard core of international criminal law so that they should be prohibited everywhere 'despite differences in the basic religion and morality' (Jørgensen 2000, p. 117). The concept of the conscience of mankind is, therefore, a universal one and may

---

[34] Daes Report, 39 [102]: 'The meaning of the term "community" for the purpose of this study is: ... (g) A great number of united nations [*sic*] having common purposes and noble goals, such as to save succeeding generations from the scourge of war and to promote social progress and better standards of life in larger freedom, such as the "United Nations", which will be also cited as the "World Community" in the present study.'

[35] Kritsiotis (2002, p. 967). "[T]he international community has been used to conjure the vital 'universality' of international law".

[36] Kofi Annan, *The Meaning of International Community* UNIS/SG/2478 (30 December 1999).

[37] Reservations to the Genocide Convention, I.C.J. Reports 1951, 23.

be brought into play when law and morality coincide (Jørgensen 2000, p. 117). The recognition of the conscience of mankind may eventually support the right to conscientious objection, if the term is not to remain a mere figure of speech. If atrocities universally awaken the conscience of mankind, people of the international community may have every reason to claim their conscientious objection to military service upon facing such an atrocity. This has happened once in reality, with regard to *apartheid*, and the international community should not forget how it responded by means of General Assembly Resolution 33/165 of 20 December 1978 in which the General Assembly upheld the right of all persons to refuse service in the military or in police forces which are used to enforce *apartheid*.

For the international legal standard of the test of manifest illegality, the conscience of mankind would be of great importance. Manifest illegality is a concept referring to 'a flagrant and manifest breach of the law, definite and necessary unlawfulness appearing on the face of the order itself, the clearly criminal character of the acts ordered to be done, unlawfulness piercing the eye and revolting the heart...'.[38] Here the degree of manifest illegality no doubt would cause anybody a prick of conscience. In fact, it has currently been perceived that '[m]any legal sources say that the test of illegality itself is conscience' (Minow 2006, p. 137, 144).

Nonetheless, the difficulty surrounding the concept of manifest illegality is recognised. For example, the scope of manifest illegality is by no means conclusively established. Because of this murky periphery of the test of manifest illegality, some suggest the need for an alternative approach to the issue of the defence of superior orders (Osiel 2002, p. 71).

The broad uncertainty of the scope of manifest illegality seems to be artificially maintained both in domestic and international fora. The most likely forum for prosecuting war crimes would be a national courts-martial of the defendant's nation state (Osiel 2002, p. 72). Domestic military organisations normally do not have a strong motivation to prosecute their own, men and women who have risked their lives for their own country, a mindset that may well accord with national sentiment (Osiel 2002, p. 72). In the international dimension, the *ratione materiae* and the *ratione personae* of the international military/criminal tribunals have been preconditioned so as not to raise the issue of the scope of manifest illegality. For instance, as Osiel suggested, 'the jurisdiction of the International Criminal Tribunal for the Former Yugoslavia has been restricted to the subject of offences based on rules of international humanitarian law which are beyond any doubt part of customary law'.[39]

While unfortunately the scope of manifest illegality will still be ambiguous, the act must be obviously illegal in order for the manifest illegality principle to be applied. It seems even illogical to say that the manifest illegality test is not clear.

---

[38] *A. G., Israel v Eichmann* (1962) 36 ILR 275, 277 (Supreme Court of Israel, 1962) (quoting *Kafr Kassen* case).

[39] 'Secretary-General's Report on Aspects of Establishing and International Tribunal for the Prosecution of Persons Responsible for Serious Violations of International Humanitarian Law Committed in the Territory of the Former Yugoslavia,' UN Doc S/25704, 1993 (art. 1, para. 57, para 33), 32 ILM 1159 (1993).

8.7 In Search of Pragmatic Solutions

No international instrument currently in force explicitly provides for the right to conscientious objection. However, this fact does not necessarily lead to the conclusion that international law does not recognise this right at all. On the contrary, facing the rise in the number of conscientious objectors, the international community is more vigilant than ever about this issue. The development of the right to conscientious objection in international law is dramatic when one considers the change in attitude of the Human Rights Committee of the International Covenant on Civil and Political Rights or the more recent case law from the Strasbourg. Such an extraordinary development has been driven by evolving interpretations of relevant human rights instruments.

The right to conscientious objection has been developed as the right to absolute conscientious objection to military service by those who consciously object to military service in general. Such a right may be deemed an emerging international human right which is deduced from the freedom of conscience, religion and thought found in various international and regional human rights instruments. This right should be equally available for both volunteer soldiers and conscripts. Resolutions by both the United Nations and the Council of Europe have not set a time limit for invoking conscientious objection so that an individual may apply for this status before or after he or she enrols in the military.

Even selective conscientious objection can to some extent be supported by international human rights law. The international support for conscientious objection to military service under the regime of *apartheid* is one example, and other international human rights instruments support the view that conscientious objection to military service which is universally condemned by the international community. This is also in line with international refugee law standards for recognising the refugee status of conscientious objectors seeking asylum. There are also the emerging rights of individuals to disobey military service manifestly illegal under international law. Thus the manifest illegality of international law, whether it is in *jus in bello* or *jus ad bellum*, concerns individuals.

Does a manifest illegality principle for the defence of superior orders have some normative implications? Osiel understands the gist of the manifest illegality principle as follows: 'One interpretation of the manifest illegality rule would extend liability to soldiers who voluntarily participate in unjust wars, i.e., wars of aggression (Osiel 1999, p. 83).' Is this really so? It may of course have such a normative impact on individuals if the pending issue of whether the defence of superior orders is applicable to a crime of aggression is answered positively. However, there is no apparent international legal imperative, as far as *jus ad bellum* concerned, for individuals to disassociate themselves from aggressive wars as a corollary of international criminal law. This may be partly because the crime of aggression is recognised as a leadership crime. In other words, it is due to its limited personal jurisdiction. This line of argument was prominent in the case of a conscientious objector whose claim was based on violations against *jus ad bellum* by his own State (Hinzman case). Another factor which might call into question the existence of an international legal duty to disobey manifestly illegal orders against *jus ad bellum* is the monopolisation of the regulation of the use of force by the United Nations Security Council. This factor has also stifled progress toward a definition of the crime of aggression *per se*. As seen in the recent judgment of the German Administrative Court, a domestic court may evaluate the existence of possible manifest illegality in the eyes of lower rank soldiers or any other individuals who claim conscientious objection to military service without recognising a legal duty to disobey orders apparently against *jus ad bellum*.[40] Nonetheless, it is very doubtful whether a domestic court can definitively decide whether a State takes part in an illegal use of force or even aggression. While lower rank soldiers or civilians may not bear any legal duty under international law to disobey orders to take part in an illegal armed conflict in international law, civilian and military leaders may bear a duty to not initiate or plan an illegal war as a corollary of the criminalisation of the crime of aggression.[41]

The bottom line is that there may not be an existing legal positive duty for individuals, and especially lower rank soldiers, to disobey manifestly illegal orders against *jus ad bellum*. However, there should be a legal right to selective conscientious objection as recognised in the case of the German major's claim granted by the German Administrative Court. The General Assembly's Resolution supporting conscientious objectors who had been supposed to be served in military and police service under the system of *apartheid* may be deemed an important proof of such a right as well. As for the legal duty for individuals, it may not be a matter of professional or volunteer soldiers but one of rank or responsibility by the individual in question. It may be an emerging duty of leaders and the very top level of military personnel to not wage an aggressive war though it is not clear whether one can claim that 'It might well be entirely proper for international law impose such a duty on *professional* soldiers, especially commissioned officers, who now routinely receive training in international law, including *jus ad bellum*' (Osiel 1999, p. 86). It would be unrealistic to expect international law to prohibit or criminalise the act of participation in an aggressive war in the near future, given that the nature of the crime of aggression and the crime against peace has been discussed for ages. For instance, article 5(2) of the Rome Statute of the International Criminal Court defers the exercise of jurisdiction over the crime of aggression to the future in accordance with articles 121 and 123 of the Rome Statute. This fact reflects the difficulty of reaching consensus on the definition of the crime of aggression though there is no indication to deny the concept of the crime of aggression within the international community (Dinstein 2001, p. 112). The decisions made pursuant to Control Council Law No.

[40] BVerwG, 2 WS 12.04, 21 June 2005, *available at* <http://www.bundesverwaltungsgericht.de>; http://www.bverwg.de/files/65a04cb42f2e0fffa5c82baedf43ba31/3059/2wd12-u-04.pdf> accessed 17 December 2007.

[41] Osiel (1999, p. 86). Osiel contends this duty extends to professional soldiers. "It might well be entirely proper for international law to impose such a duty on *professional* solders, especially commissioned officers, who now routinely receive training in international law including the *jus ad bellum*".

10 may support such view. In *U.S. v Ernest Von Weizsaecker*, the United States Military Tribunal concluded that:

> Obviously, no man may be condemned for fighting in what he believes is the defense of his native land, even though his belief is mistaken. Nor can he be expected to undertake an independent investigation to determine whether or not the cause for which he fights is the result of an aggressive act of his own government.[42]

Even though there exists no positive duty to disobey manifestly illegal orders against *jus ad bellum* in international law for lower rank soldiers, there is a duty for individuals to disobey manifestly illegal orders against *jus in bello* in international humanitarian law (as embodied in rule 154 of the customary rules of international humanitarian law prepared by the International Committee of the Red Cross). This should be regarded as a corollary of the restrictions relating to the defence of superior orders under international criminal law as represented in the Separate and Dissenting Opinion of the then President of the International Criminal Tribunal for the Former Yugoslavia, Judge Antonio Cassese, in the *Erdemović* case.[43] It should be recognised that there may be both a legal duty and a legal right to disobey manifestly illegal orders in *jus in bello* in international law. Such a right may be exercised through a normal procedure of the right to conscientious objection to military service on humanitarian grounds.

One should not belittle the procedure of conscientious objection in relation to the promotion of peace. As in the case of *apartheid*, the international recognition of conscientious objection may contribute to the prevention of possible future violations of international law. The co-existence of both the duty of disobeying manifestly illegal orders under international law and the right of conscientious objection to military service may sound illogical but these two should not necessarily be seen as mutually exclusive. The system of conscientious objection may sometimes be the only resort available to soldiers facing manifestly illegal orders under international law. The United Nations Commission on Human Rights encouraged 'States, as part of post-conflict peace-building, to consider granting, and effectively implementing, amnesties and restitution of rights, in law and practice, for those who have refused to undertake military service on grounds of conscientious objection' in its Resolution 2004/35 in April 2004.[44]

The Universal Declaration of Human Rights sets out that disrespect for human rights had outraged the conscience of mankind.[45] It also proclaims that all human

---

[42] *U.S. v Ernest von Weizsaecker*, in Trials of War Criminals Before the Nuremberg Military Tribunals Under Control Council Law No. 10. Vol. 14, 337: United States of America v Ernst von Weizsaecker, et al. (Case 11: 'Ministries Case'). District of Columbia: GPO, N.D. [1952].

[43] *Prosecutor v Dražen Erdemović*, Judgment, Appeals Chamber, Separate and Dissenting Opinion of Judge Cassese (7 October 1997) [15].

[44] The Human Rights Commission, 2004/35 (19 April 2004) para. 4. Adopted without a vote. See chap. XI.- E/2004/23 – E/CN.4/2004/127. *See also* <http://www.unhcr.org/home/RSDLEGAL/be85e4.pdf> (last visited, 3 April 2007).

[45] Universal Declaration of Human Rights UNGA Res 217A (III) (10 December 1948) UN Doc A/810, at 71 (1948) (adopted by 48 votes to none; 8 abstentions). Its second preambular paragraph stipulates that: 'disregard and contempt for human rights have resulted in barbarous acts which have outraged the conscience of mankind.'

beings 'are endowed with reason and conscience and should act towards one another in a spirit of brotherhood'.[46] Respect for the individual's right to conscientious objection to military service by both States and the international community may provide the cornerstone of peace and stability in situations which outrage the conscience of mankind, such as serious violations of international humanitarian law.

The right to conscientious objection in international law is still in the process of being clarified. Moreover, the recognition of selective conscientious objection in domestic societies is still relatively rare.[47] This leads to the conclusion that the international community should not hesitate to send a clearer message advocating the individual's right to conscientious objection to military service in a situation of continuing manifestly unlawful violation of international law.

Even though there seems no legal duty on individuals to take affirmative or positive action over international violations, the manifest illegality principle under international criminal law demands that individuals disobey manifestly illegal orders where possible. To this extent, individuals owe a duty to disobey manifestly unlawful orders under international law. To put it differently, individuals, especially combatants, are expected to be familiar with international humanitarian law and international human rights law in order to prevent gross violations of human rights and to observe fundamental norms of international law.

For an effective implementation of laws, international humanitarian law demands that armies and their members be well-disciplined. Traditionally, international humanitarian law, as international law, has been enforced by national law or military discipline. National military manuals can serve as a useful means of succinctly relating a large body of law that has developed over a long period to contemporary circumstances and to the obligations undertaken by a particular State. In turn, nowadays some international humanitarian law clearly obliges armed forces to be internally disciplined. Although there are still arguments surrounding the customary nature of the Additional Protocol I of Geneva Convention of 1977, Additional Protocol I is binding on all State parties. Additional Protocol I constitutes a part of international humanitarian law. Additional Protocol I, under Article 43, stipulates that:

> The armed forces of a party to a conflict consist of all organized armed forces, groups and units which are under a command responsible to that party for the conduct of its subordinates, even if that party is represented by a government or an authority not recognized by an adverse party. Such armed forces shall be subject to an internal disciplinary system, which, *inter alia,* shall enforce compliance with the rules of international law applicable in armed conflicts.

---

[46] Universal Declaration of Human Rights UNGA Res 217A (III) (10 December 1948) UN Doc A/810, at 71 (1948) (adopted by 48 votes to none; 8 abstentions) Article 1.

[47] The Office of the High Commissioner for Human Rights, Civil and Political Rights Including the Question of Conscientious Objection to Military Service – Analytical Report of the Office of the High Commissioner for Human Rights on Best Practices in relation to Conscientious Objection to Military Service, UN Doc E/CN.4/2006/51, (27 February 2006) 10 [31].

Not only armies and States have obligations to ensure their members are familiar with international humanitarian law, but individuals owe direct duties for ensuring the law of armed conflict under international humanitarian law. International humanitarian law evidently has operated on the assumption that its rules bind both States and their nationals (Meron 2006, p. 40). Today the prosecution of serious violations of international humanitarian law is of international concern. Some of the most heinous international crimes derived from international humanitarian law confer criminal jurisdiction on third-party States on the basis of universal jurisdiction, let alone genocide.[48] This contrasts with the traditional practice where soldiers who violated the laws of armed conflict could only be prosecuted by either their national State or the captor State (Meron 2006, p. 40).

These existing and expected developments must concern the increasingly important status of individuals in the sphere of public international law. Public international law, with strong backing by the development of international criminal law after the Cold War, incorporated individuals as important observants, vigilant of international law, to prevent the gross violation of human rights. In 1928, the Permanent Court of International Justice held that according to well-established international law, an international agreement cannot create direct rights and obligations for private individuals.[49] However, the Permanent Court of International Justice continued that it cannot be disputed that the very object of an international agreement, according to the intention of the contracting parties, may be the adoption by the parties of some definite rules creating individual rights and obligations and enforceable by the national courts.[50] Traditional international law has considered that some rights and duties that were conferred upon individuals by treaties would be enforced by national courts (Meron 2006, p. 40). This was the situation in the past, and today the establishment and the activities of the *ad hoc* international (and internationalised) criminal tribunals as well as the permanent International Criminal Court witness an important change in the status of individuals in international law (Meron 2006, p. 41).

The soldier's real dilemma, obeying an internationally illegal order or disobeying military discipline, is not easily solved. Even Dinstein's authoritative work on the defence of superior orders arrived at a conclusion 'with some incertitude' (Dinstein, p. 253). Instead of having found one dominant position on the issue of the defence of superior orders in international law, Dinstein expressed the hope that a pragmatic solution will overcome dogmatic barriers in the near future (Dinstein, p. 253). As shown by these remarks, laws alone may not solve the dilemma of soldiers of choosing between military solidarity and their profound convictions, in other words, solving the tension between 'conformity and independence' (Minow 2006, p. 142).

---

[48] Even though the International Court of Justice failed to decide on the admissibility of universal jurisdiction, there seems to be emerging consensus that international law permits universal jurisdiction. *Arrest Warrant of 11 April 2000 (Democratic Republic of the Congo v. Belgium)* (Merits) 14 February 2002, General List No. 121 [2002] ICJ.

[49] Advisory Opinion No. 15, Jurisdiction of the Courts of Danzig, PCIJ Rep., Ser. B. No. 15 (Advisory Opinion of March 3, 1928) 17.

[50] PCIJ Rep., Ser. B. No. 15 (Advisory Opinion of March 3, 1928) 17–18.

While conformity brings order but also risks group-thinking and even mass atrocity, independence promotes resistance to atrocity but risks disorder and inefficiency (Minow 2006, p. 142). Ideally, an international forum would hear claims from soldiers who feel compelled to disobey manifestly illegal orders under international law, but this is not practical. Especially a claim based on a *jus ad bellum* violation would often be controversial, even among the members of the UN Security Council. The United Nations Charter envisions a monopolisation of the legitimate use of force, and if there is any threat to peace, calling the police, that is, the Security Council, would be the right response. However, this response is only plausible if someone were answering the phone, and this is not a description of the world we live in. As it stands today, there are controversial examples of the use of force here and there, and even the justified use of force sometimes entails unjustified means of warfare amounting to a war crime. Considering diplomatic and political impacts, domestic fora would also be unlikely to find that a war is manifestly unlawful.[51]

There also appears a lack of systematic support for the procedure of application of disobeying manifestly illegal orders in a military. Even though military law prohibits military members from obeying any unlawful orders, soldiers have no special exemptions or privileges from military law which requires members to be obedient. An Irish military commander explains that: "the onus is on the organisation to ensure compliance with civil and military law in deciding policy and instructions and on every individual member to adhere to these laws, instructions, regulations, policies and orders that enact the aforementioned".[52] In other words, soldiers may not be expected to cast doubts on each order they are given. Yet military system still adheres that: "if an order is unlawful it is very reasonable to disobey it. The soldier receiving the order can question the order on the spot and after the fact also" (see Note 52).

In this climate, the system of conscientious objection may be the only existing solution for soldiers, *refuseniks* and draftees who find an on-going war or means of warfare contrary to their conscience. International law may provide a legal foundation for the right to conscientious objection for both those who are absolute conscientious objectors in the traditional sense and those who are selective conscientious objectors based on public international law or international criminal law.

Rather than emphasising the importance of military discipline and stability of national security, the international community should promote the broader sense of stability that is international peace and security. Does military efficiency help to promote the spirit of international humanitarian law? Is the inefficiency of an army, which acquiesces to human rights violations, worth being of concern? When one considers the *raison d'être* of international criminal tribunals and the International Criminal Court, the rule of law should be one of the main reasons.

[51] See for example, *Campaign for Nuclear Disarmament v The Prime Minister of the United Kingdom and Others* [2002] EWHC 2759.

[52] Irish Defence Forces Press Officer, Commandant Gavin Young, in reply to the author's email (17 December 2007).

Recognition of a full right to conscientious objection would promote the duty to refuse to follow manifestly unlawful orders and *vice versa*. The Nuremberg Trials and the international tribunals that followed treated an individual not as an obedient automaton, but as a reasoning agent. The duty to disobey manifestly unlawful orders and the right of selective conscientious objection should not be regarded as being mutually exclusive. On the contrary, the individual's duty to disobey manifestly unlawful orders as well as the duty of States to honour individual conscience may both be seen as the underpinning for selective conscientious objection. Although it may not make sense to use the Nuremberg Principles as the grounds of selective conscientious objection when there is a duty to disobey unlawful orders, conscientious objection may be the only possible solution for soldiers facing manifestly unlawful orders. In order to improve the effectiveness of conscientious objection claims, the international community should send a clearer message that there exists the right to conscientious objection under international law as a first priority.

References

Journal Article

Korowicz MS (1956) The problem of the international personality of individuals. Am J Int Law 50:533–562

Jones MW (1984) Individuals as subjects of international law. Cornell Int Law J 17:61–78

Hobbins AJ (1989) René Cassin and the daughter of time: The first draft of the universal declaration of human rights. Fontanus 2:7–26

Orakhelashvili A (2001) The position of the individual in international law. Calif West Int Law J 31:241–276

Burke-White W (2002) A community of courts: toward a system of international criminal law enforcement. Mich J Int Law 24:1–101

Kritsiotis D (2002) Imaging the international community. Eur J Int Law 13:961–992

Danner AM, Martinez JS (2005) Guilty associations: Joint criminal enterprise, command responsibility, and the development of international criminal law. Calif Law Rev 93:75–169

Bagaric M, Morss J (2006) In search of coherent jurisprudence for international criminal law: correlating universal human rights responsibilities with universal human rights. Suffolk Transnatl Law Rev 29:157–206

Minow M (2006) What the rule of law should mean in civics education: From the "following orders" defence to the Class Room. J Moral Educ 35(2):137–162

Book

Kunig P, Benedek W, Mahalu CR (1985) Regional protection of human rights by international law: The emerging African system. Nomos Verlagsgesellschaft, Baden-Baden

Morsink J (1999) The universal declaration of human rights: Origins, drafting, and intent. Oxford University Press, Philadelphia

Jørgensen NHB (2000) The responsibility of States for international crimes. Oxford University Press, Oxford
Dinstein Y (2001) War, aggression and self-defence, 3rd edn. Cambridge University Press, Cambridge
Osiel MJ (2002) Obeying orders: Atrocity, military discipline & the law of war. Transaction Publishers, New Brunswick
Meron T (2006) The humanization of international law. Martinus Nijhoff Publishers, Leiden

Bibliography

Books and Articles

Ajangiz R (2002) 'The European farewell to conscription?' In: Mjøset L, van Holde S (eds) The comparative study of conscription in the armed forces, comparative social research, vol 20. JAI, Amsterdam

Alfredsson G, Eide A (1999) The universal declaration of human rights: a common standard of achievement. Martinus Nijhoff Publishers, The Hague

Ambos K (2002) Other Grounds for Excluding Criminal Responsibility. In: Cassese A, Gaeta P, Jones JRWD (eds) The Rome statute of the international criminal court: a commentary. Oxford University Press, Oxford

Angel WD (1995) The international law of youth rights: source documents and commentary. Martinus Nijhoff Publishers, Dordrecht

Arendt H (1992) Eichmann in Jerusalem: a report on the banality of evil, Revised and enlarged edn. Penguin Books, New York Bagaric M, Morss J (2006) In search of coherent jurisprudence for international criminal law: correlating universal human rights responsibilities with universal human rights Suffolk Transnatl L Rev 29:157

Bailliet CM (2006) Assessing *Jus Ad Bellum* and *Jus In Bello* within the refugee status determination process: contemplations on conscientious objectors seeking asylum. Georget Immgr Law J 20:337

Bakker JL (1989) The defense of obedience to superior orders: the mens rea requirement. Am J Crim Law 17:55

Barker E (1944) The development of public services in Western Europe 1660–1930. Oxford University Press, London

Bartlett CAH (1919) Liability for official war crimes. Law Q Rev 35:177

Bassiouni MC (1998) The statute of the international criminal court: a documentary history. Transnational Publishers, Ardsley

Baudisch I (2006) German federal administrative court decision on a soldier's right to refuse to obey military orders for conscientious reasons. Am J Int Law 100:911

Bedau HA (1961) On civil disobedience J Philos 58:653

Bedau HA (1991) Civil disobedience in focus. Routledge, London

Blackett J (1994) Superior orders – the military dilemma. RUSI J 139:12

Bomann-Larsen L (2004) Licence to kill? The question of Just vs. Unjust Combatants. J Milit Ethics 3:142

Bossuyt MJ (1987) Guide to the 'travaux préparatoires' of the international covenant on civil and political rights. Martinus Nijhoff Publishers, Dordrecht

Boyle K (1999) Freedom of thought, freedom of conscience, freedom of religion and freedom of belief as internationally protected rights: what is agreed and what is not agreed. In: Cotran E, Sherif AO (eds) Democracy, the rule of law and islam. Kluwer, London

Brems E (2006) A commentary on the united nations convention on the rights of the child: article 14: the right to freedom of thought, conscience and religion. Martinus Nijhoff Publishers, The Hague

Brillat R (2005) The supervisory machinery of the european social charter: recent developments and their impact. In: de Búrca G, de Witte B (eds) Social rights in Europe. Oxford University Press, Oxford

Brownlie I (1963) International law and the use of force. Oxford University Press, Oxford

Buergenthal T, Norris R (eds) (1982) Human rights: the inter-american system. Oceana Publications, Dobbs Ferry

Buergenthal T, Norris R, Shelton D (1990) Protecting human rights in the Americas: Selected Problems, 3rd edn. N. P. Engel, Kehl am Rhein

Bugnion F (2002) Just wars, wars of aggression and international humanitarian law. Int Rev Red Cross 847:15

Burke-White W (2002) A community of courts: toward a system of international criminal law enforcement Mich J Int Law 24:1

Butler AH (1999) A selective and annotated bibliography of the international criminal court. Crim Law Forum 10:121

Cassese A (1999) The statute of the international criminal court: some preliminary reflections. Eur J Int Law 10(1):144

Cassese A (2002) 'Justifications and Excuses in International Criminal Law' in Cassese A, Gaeta P, Jones JRWD (eds) The Rome statute of the international criminal court: a commentary. Oxford University Press, Oxford

Cassese A (2003) International criminal law. Oxford University Press, Oxford

Chambers JW II (1993) Conscientious objectors and the american state from colonial times to the present. In: Moskos CC, Chambers JW II (eds) The new conscientious objection: from sacred to secular resistance. Oxford University Press, New York

Collier JG (1991) Legal basis of the institution of war. In: Hinde RA (ed) The institution of war. Macmillan, London

Commission on the Responsibility of the Authors of the War and on Enforcement of Penalties (1920) Report presented to the preliminary peace conference. Am J Int Law 14:117

Cornelius S (1997) 'The defence of superior orders and erich priebke'. Patterns Prejudice 31:3

The council of Europe, *collected edition of the 'Travaux Préparatoires'* vol I, III, IV. Preparatory Commission of the Council of Europe, Committee of Ministers, Consultative Assembly, 11 May–8 September 1949. Martinus Nijhoff Publishers, The Hague, 1975

Crook JR (2005) U.S. military justice proceedings involving alleged offenses against protected persons. Am J Int Law 99:713

Cryer R (2005) Prosecuting international crimes: selectivity and the international law regime. Cambridge University Press, Cambridge

Danner AM, Martinez JS (2005) Guilty associations: joint criminal enterprise, command responsibility, and the development of international criminal law. Cal Law Rev 93:75

Davidson MJ (2005) 'War and the doubtful soldier'. Notre Dame J Law Ethics Public Policy 91

Davy U (1995) 'Refugees from Bosnia and Herzegovina: are they Genuine?' Suffolk Transnatl Law Rev 18:53

Decker DC, Fresa L (2001) 'The status of conscientious objection under article 4 of the European convention on human rights'. N Y Univ J Int Law Pol 33:379

De Jong CD (2000) The freedom of thought, conscience and religion or belief in the United Nations (1946–1992). Intersentia, Antwerpen

De Lee N (2004) The case of Colonel Hackworth. J Milit Ethics 3:61

Detrick S (ed) (1992) The United Nations convention on the rights of the child: a guide to the 'Travaux Préparatoires'. Martinus Nijhoff Publishers, Dordrecht

(1970) Digest of case-law relating to the European convention on human rights (1955–1967), Edition administratives. U.G.A., Heule, Belgium
Dinstein Y (1965) The defence of 'obedience to superior orders' in international law. A W Sijthoff, Leyden
Dinstein Y (1985) International criminal law. Isr Law Rev 20:206
Dinstein Y (2001) War, aggression and self-defence, 3rd edn. Cambridge University Press, Cambridge
Dinstein Y (2004) The conduct of hostilities under the law of international armed conflict. Cambridge University Press, Cambridge
Douzinas C (2006) Postmodern just wars and the new world order. J Hum Rights 5:355
Doswald-Beck L (1997) International humanitarian law and the advisory opinion of the international court of justice on the legality of the threat or use of nuclear weapon. Int Rev Red Cross 37:35
Dworkin R (1977) Taking rights seriously. Duckworth, London
Engram JM (1982) Conscientious objection to military service: A report to the united nations division of Human rights. Ga J Int Comp Law 12:359
Enoch D (2002) Some arguments against conscientious objection and civil disobedience refuted. Isr Law Rev 36(2):227
Epstein AD (2002) 'The freedom of conscience and sociological perspectives on dilemmas of collective secular disobedience: the case of Israel'. J Hum Rights 305
Eser A (1987) Justification and excuse: a key issue in the concept of crime. In: Eser A, Fletcher GP (eds) Rechtfertigung und Entschuldigung: Rechtsvergleichende Perspektiven, vol 1. Eigenverlag Max-Planck-Institut für Ausländisches und Internationales Strafrecht, Freiburg
Eser A (1996) Defences in war crime trials. In: Dinstein Y, Tabory M (eds) War crimes in international law. Martinus Nijhoff Publishers, The Hague
Evans C (2001) Freedom of religion under the European convention on human rights. Oxford University Press, Oxford
Finch GA (1921) Superior orders and war crimes. Am J Int Law 15:440
Friedman R (2005) The challenge of selective conscientious objection in Israel. Theoria 109:79
Gaeta P (1999) The defence of superior orders: the statute of the international criminal court versus customary international law. Eur J Int Law 10:172
Gans C (2002) Right and left: ideological disobedience in Israel. Isr Law Rev 36:19
Gans C (1993) Procedural justice and international human rights: towards a procedural jurisprudence for human rights tribunals. Yale J Int Law 18:559
Glaser S (1954) Introduction a l'etude du droit international penal. Bruylant, Bruxelles
Goldstone R (2000) For humanity: reflections of a war crimes investigator. Yale University Press, New Heaven
Goldstone R (2005) The future of international criminal justice. Maine Law Rew 57:554
Goodwin-Gill GS (1983) The refugee in international law. Clarendon Press, Oxford
Grayson JW (1995) The defence of superior orders in the international criminal court. Nordic J Int Law 64:243
Green LC (1993) The defence of superior orders in the modern law of armed conflict. Alberta Law Rev 31:320
Green LC (2003) Fifteenth valdemar a solf lecture in international law. Mil Law Rev 175:309
Greenawalt AKA (1999) Rethinking genocidal intent: the case for a knowledge-based interpretation. Colum Law Rev 99:2259
Greenspan M (1959) The modern law of land warfare. University of California Press, Berkley
Greenwood C (1983) The relationship between *Jus Ad Bellum* and *Jus In Bello*. Rev Int Stud 9:221
Greenwood C (1991) In defence of the laws of war. In: Hinde RA (ed) The institution of war. Macmillan, London
Grene D (1994) The theban plays: oedipus the king; oedipus at colonus; antigone. David Campbell Publishers, London
Greppi E (1999) The evolution of individual criminal responsibility under international law. Int Rev Red Cross 81:531

Gulam H, O'Connor M (2006) Selective conscientious objection: the court martial of Flight Lieutenant Malcolm Kendall-Smith, raf. Adf Health J 7:68

Grotius H (1925) De jure belli ac pacis libri tres. Clarendon Press, Oxford

Hammer L (2005) The International human right to freedom of conscience: some suggestions for its development and application. Ashgate, Aldershot

Happold M (2005) Child soldiers in international law. Manchester University Press, Manchester

Harries-Jenkins G (1993) Britain: from individual conscience to social movement. In: Moskos CC, Chambers JW II (eds) The new conscientious objection: from sacred to secular resistance. Oxford University Press, New York

Harris DJ, O'Boyle M, Warbrick C (1995) Law of the european convention on human rights. Butterworths, London

Hinek S (2005) The superior orders defence embraced at last? N Z Postgrad Law E-J 2:44

Hobbins AJ (1989) René cassin and the daughter of time: the first draft of the universal declaration of human rights. Fontanus 2:7

Insco JB (2003) Defense of superior orders before military commissions. Duke J Comp Int Law 13:389

Jackson RH (1971) Report of Robert H Jackson, United Nations representative to the international conference on military trials. AMS Press, New York

Jensen ET (2004) The laws of war: past, present and future: combatant status: it is time for intermediate levels of recognition for partial compliance. VA J Int Law 46:209

Janis MW (1984) Individuals as subjects of international law. Cornell Intl J 17:61

Jescheck HH (1952) Die Verantwortlichkeit der Staatsorgane nach Völkerstrafrecht. Ludwig Röhrscheid, Bonn

Jescheck H (2004) The general principles of international criminal law set out in Nuremberg, as mirrored in the icc statute. J Int Crim Just 2:38

Jørgensen NHB (2000) The responsibility of states for international crimes. Oxford University Press, Oxford

Joseph S, Schultz J, Castan M (2000) The international covenant on civil and political rights; cases, materials, and commentary. Oxford University Press, New York

Karoubi MT (2004) Just or unjust war: international law and unilateral use of armed force by states at the turn of the 20th century. Ashgate Publishing Company, Burlington

Keijzer N (1978) Military disobedience. Sijthoff & Noordhoff, Alphen aan den Rijn

Keijzer N (1978) A plea for the defence of superior order. Isr Yearbk Int Law 8:78

Kellog WG (1919) The conscientious objector. Boni and Liveright, New York

Kelsen H (1952) Principles of international law, 1st edn. Rineheart & Company, New York

Knoops GGJ (2001) Defenses in contemporary international criminal law. Transnational Publishers, Ardsley

Kohn SM (1986) Jailed for peace. Praeger, New York

Korowicz MS (1956) The problem of the international personality of individuals Am J Int Law 50:533

Kremnitzer M (1992) The World community as an international legislator in competition with national legislators. In: Eser A, Lagodny O (eds) Principles and procedures for a new transnational criminal law. Max-Planck-Institut für Ausländisches und Internationales Strafrecht, Freiburg im Breisgau

Kritsiotis D (2002) Imaging the international community. Eur J Int Law 13:961

Kunig P, Benedek W, Mahalu CR (1985) Regional protection of human rights by international law: the emerging African system. Nomos Verlagsgesellschaft, Baden-Baden

Kunz J (1949) The United Nations convention on genocide. Am J Int Law 43:738

Kunz JL (1951) Bellum justum and bellum legale. Am J Int Law 45:528

Kuzas KJ (1991) Asylum for unrecognized conscientious objectors to military service: is there a right not to fight? VA J Int Law 31:447

Lambert H (2006) The EU asylum qualification directive, its impact on the jurisprudence of the United Kingdom and international law. Int Comp Law Q 55:161

Lauterpacht H (1944) The law of nations and the punishment of war crimes. Br Yearbk Int Law 21:58

Lauterpacht H (1953) The limits of the operation of the law of war. Br Yearbk Int Law 30:206

Lebranc LJ (1996) Reservations to the rights of the child: a macroscopic view of state practice. Int J Child Rts 4:357

Linn R (1996) Conscience at war: the israeli soldier as a moral critic. State University of New York Press, Albany

Lippman M (1990) Civil resistance: the dictates of conscience and international law versus the American judiciary Fla J Int Law 6:5

Lippman M (1990/1991) The recognition of conscientious objection to military service as an international human right. Calif West Int Law J 21:31

Lippman M (1996) Conundrums of armed conflict: criminal defenses to violations of the humanitarian law of war. Dickinson J Int Law 1 15:54

Lippman M (1996) Fifty years after Auschwitz: prosecutions of nazi death camp defendants. Conn J Int Law 11

Lubell N (2002) Selective conscientious objection in international law: refusing to participate in a specific armed conflict. Neth Q Hum Right 20(4):407

Major M (1992) Conscientious objection and international law. Case W Res J Int Law 24:349

Mann H (1987) International law and the child soldier. Int Comp Law Q 36:32

Mapel DR (1998) Coerced moral agents? Individual responsibility for military service. J Polit Philos 6:171

Martines F (1998) The defences of reprisals, superior orders and duress in the Priebke case before the italian military tribunal. Yearbk Int Human Law 1:354

McCarthy ALS (1998) The international law of human rights and states of exception: with special reference to the travaux préparatoires and case-law of the international monitoring organs. Martinus Nijhoff Publishers, The Hague

McCoubrey H (1998) International humanitarian law: modern developments in the limitation of warfare. Ashgate Publishing, Aldershot

McCoubrey H (2001) From Nuremberg to Rome: restoring the defence of superior orders. Int Comp Law Q 50:386

McMahan J (1994) Innocence, self-defense and killing in war. J Polit Philos 2:193

McMahan J (2004) The ethics of killing in war. Ethics 114:693

Meron T (1992) Shakespeare's *Henry the fifth* and the law of war. Am J Int Law 86:1

Meron T (2006) The humanization of international law. Martinus Nijhoff Publishers, Leiden

Minow M (2006) What the rule of law should mean in civics education: from the "following orders" defence to the class room J Moral Educ 35(2):137

Morsink J (1999) The Universal declaration of human rights: origins, drafting, and intent. Oxford University Press, Philadelphia

Mjøset L, Van Holde S (2002) Killing for the state, dying for the nation: an introductory essay on the life cycle of conscription into Europe's armed forces. In: Mjøset L, van Holde S (eds) The comparative study of conscription in the armed forces, comparative social research, vol 20. JAI, Amsterdam

Moskos CC, Chambers JW II (1993) The secularization of conscience. In: Moskos CC, Chambers II JW (eds) The new conscientious objection: from sacred to secular resistance. Oxford University Press, New York

Murphy SD (2004) Contemporary practice of the united states relating to international law: general international and u.s. foreign relations law: executive memoranda on status and permissible treatment of detainees. Am J Int Law 98:820

Musalo K (2002) Legal and protection policy research series: claims for protection based on religion or belief: analysis and proposed conclusions', protection policy and legal advice section (ppla) department of international protection, united nations high commissioner for refugees, PPLA/2002/01

Musalo K (2007) Conscientious objection as a basis for refugee status: protection for the fundamental right of freedom of thought, conscience and religion. Ref Surv Q 26:69

Newton M (2005) Unlawful belligerency after september 11: history revisited and law revised. In: Wippman D, Evangelista M (eds) New wars, new laws?: applying the laws of war in 21st century conflicts. Transnational Publishers, Ardsley

Nowak M (1993) UN covenant on civil and political rights: ccpr commentary, 1st edn. N.P. Engel, Kehl am Rhein

Nowak M (2005) UN covenant on civil and political rights: ccpr commentary, 2nd rev edn. N.P. Engel, Kehl am Rhein

O'Brien JC (1993) The international tribunal for violation of international humanitarian law in the former Yugoslavia. Am J Int Law 87:639

O'Brien WV (1968) Selective conscientious objection and international law. Georget Law J 56:1080

Oostvogels SAM (1973) Foreign deserters and asylum in the netherlands: the case of ralph j. waver. Neth Yearbk Int Law 4:143

Oppenheim L (1906) International law, 1st edn. Longmans, London

Oppenheim L (1912) International law, 2nd edn. Longmans, London

Oppenheim L (1921) International law, 3rd edn. In: Roxburgh RF (ed) Longmans, London

Oppenheim L (1926) International law, 4th edn. In: McNair AD (ed) Longmans, London

Oppenheim L (1935) International law, 5th edn. In: Lauterpacht (ed) Longmans, London

Orakhelashvili A (2001) The position of the individual in international law. Calf West Int Law J 31:241

Osiel MJ (1998) Obeying orders: atrocity, military discipline, and the law of war. Calf Law Rev 86:939

Osiel MJ (2002) Obeying orders: atrocity, military discipline & the law of war. Transaction Publishers, New Brunswick

Ouguergouz F (2003) The African charter on human and people's rights: a comprehensive agenda for human dignity and sustainable democracy in Africa. In: Sutcliffe H (tr.) Martinus Nijhof Publishers, The Hague

Ovey C, White R (2006) Jacobs and White: the European convention on human rights, 4th edn. Oxford University Press, Oxford

Parker P, Weissbrodt D (1991) Major developments at the un commission on human rights in 1991. Hum Rights Q 13:573

Parks WH (1973) Command responsibility for war crimes Mil Law Rev 62:1

Pastor-Ridruejo JA (2005) On the relationships between jus in bello and jus ad bellum. can a notion of international humanitarian law influence in the determination of the legality of the use of force? In: Fernández-Sánchez PA (ed) The new challenges of humanitarian law in armed conflicts: in honour of Professor Juan Antonio Carillo-Salcedo. Martinus Nijhoff Publishers, Leiden

Pictet JS (ed) (1952) Commentary I Geneva convention for the amelioration of the condition of the wounded and sick in armed forces in the field, vol I. International Committee of the Red Cross, Geneva

Ratner SR, Abrams JS (2001) Accountability for human rights atrocities in international law: beyond the nuremberg legacy, 2nd edn. Oxford University Press, Oxford

Rawls J (1999) A theory of justice, Revised edn. Oxford University Press, New York

Raz J (1979) The authority of law: essays on law and morality. Clarendon Press, Oxford

Renault L (1915) De l'application du droit penal aux faits de guerre (I). Droit Int 42:313

Robertson AH (1950) The European convention for the protection of human rights. Br Yearbk Int Law 27:145

Rogers APV (2004) Law on the battlefield, 2nd edn. Manchester University Press, Manchester

Rowe P (1998) 'Duress as a defence to war crimes after erdemović: a laboratory for a permanent court?' Yearbk Int Human Law 1:210

Rowe P (2006) The impact of human rights law on armed forces. Cambridge University Press, Cambridge

Sadat LNS (2002) *The* international criminal court and the transformation of international law: justice for the new millennium. Transnational Publishers, Ardsley

Satow MS (1992) Conscientious objectors: their status, the law and its development. Geoge Mason Univ Civ Rights Law J 3:113

Schabas WA (2000) Genocide in international law. Cambridge University Press, Cambridge

Schaffer P, Weissbrodt D (1972) Conscientious objection to military service as a human right. Rev Jurists 9:33

Scheib JM (1997) Enforcing judgments of the european court of human rights: the conduit theory. N Y Int Law Rev 10:101

Schultz N (2005) Was the war on iraq illegal? – the German federal administrative court's judgment of 21st June 2005. Ger Law J 7:25

Schwarzenberger G (1968) International law as applied by international courts and tribunals, vol II. The law of armed conflict. Stevens & Sons, London

Sibley MQ, Jacob PE (1952) Conscription of conscience: the american state and the conscientious objector, 1940–1947. Cornell University Press, Ithaca

Sliedregt EV (2003) The criminal responsibility of individuals of international humanitarian law. TMC Asser Press, The Hague

Smith III JW (2006) A few good scapegoats: the abu ghraib courts-martial and the failure of the military justice system. Whittier Law Rev 27:671

Solis G (2000) obedience of orders and the law of war: judicial application in american forums. Am Univ Int Law Rev 15:481

Solis GD (2004) Obedience to orders: history and abuses at abu ghraib prison. J Int Crim Justice 2:988

Staker C (2005) Defence of superior orders revisited. Aust Law J 79:431

Steiner HJ, Alston P (2000) International human rights in context: law, politics, morals: text and materials. Oxford University Press, New York

Sunga LS (1992) Individual responsibility in international law for serious human rights violations. Martinus Nijhoff Publishers, Dordrecht

Switzerland B (1978) Official records of the diplomatic conference on the ratification and development of international humanitarian law applicable in armed conflicts: geneva (1974–1977), vol I, III, VI. Federal Political Department, Bern

Triffterer O (1999) Article 33 superior orders and prescription of law. In: Triffterer O (ed) Commentary on the Rome statute of the international criminal court: observer's notes, article by article. Nomos Verlagsgesellschaft, Baden-Baden

Van Bueren G (1995) The international law on the rights of the child. Martinus Nijhoff Publishers, The Hague

Van Der Vyver JD (2004) 'The international criminal court and the concept of mens rea in international criminal law' 12 university of miami international and comparative law review 57

Vandewiele T (2006) A commentary on the united nations convention on the rights of the child: optional protocol: the involvement of children in armed conflicts. Martinus Nijhoff Publishers, Leiden

Vogler T (1973) The defence of "superior orders" in international criminal law. In: Bassiouni MC, Nanda VP (eds) International criminal law, vol 1. Thomas, Springfield

Walzer M (2000) Just and unjust wars, 3rd edn. Basic Books, (New York)

Weissbrodt D (2002) The United Nations commission on human rights confirms conscientious objection to military service as a human right. Neth Int Law Rev 35:53–55

Wessels M (2002) Recruitment of children as soldiers in sub-saharan africa: an ecological analysis. In: Mjøset L, van Holde S (eds) The comparative study of conscription in the armed forces, comparative social research, vol 20. JAI, Amsterdam

Zimmerman A (2002) Superior orders. In: Cassese A et al (eds) The Rome statute of the international criminal court: a commentary

United Nations Instruments

A/33/45
A/34/151
A/35/40
A/36/40
A/39/40
A/39/51
A/40/256
A/44/49
A/47/49
A/49/40
A/51/10
A/51/306
A/55/40
A/57/40
A/58/40
A/64/Add.1
A/577
A/810
A/1316
A/2505
A/2505/Add.1
A/2693
A/2719
A/2953
A/4045
A/8149
A/9631
A/AC.249/1997/L.9/Rev.1
A/AC.249/1998/L.13
A/C.3/267
A/C.3/345
A/C.3/861
A/C.3/L.682
A/C.3/L.1766
A/C.3/SR.74
A/C.3/SR.860
A/C.3/SR.861
A/CN.3/SR.1749
A/C.3/L.1766/Rev.1
A/C.3/L.1766/Rev.2
A/C.3/L.1767
A/C.3/L.1775
A/C.6/215/Rev.1
A/C.6/SR.92
A/CN.4/SER.A/1950
A/CONF. 32/41
A/CONF.144/28/Rev.1
A/CONF.183/13
A/CONF.183/2/Add.1
A/CONF.183/C.1/WGGP/L.2
A/CONF.183/C.1/WGGP/L.9/Rev.1

A/CONF.183/9
A/L.609/Rev.1
A/L.610
A/L.611
A/RES/44 (I)
A/RES/49/53
A/RES/50/46
A/RES/50/81
A/RES/54/263
A/RES/60/251
A/RES/177
A/RES/178(II)
A/RES/395 (V)
A/RES/2202 A (XXI)
CCPR/C/9/Add.39
CCPR/C/21/Rev.1/Add.4
CCPR/C/21/Rev.1/Add.6
CCPR/C/24/D/89/1981
CCPR/C/43/D/446/1991
CCPR/C/45/D/483/1991
CCPR/C/48/CRP.2
CCPR/C/48/CRP.2/Rev.1
CCPR/C/50/D/568/1993
CCPR/C/79/Add.1
CCPR/C/79/Add.16
CCPR/C/79/Add.39
CCPR/C/79/Add.79
CCPR/C/79/Add.45
CCPR/C/79/Add.54
CCPR/C/79/Add.80
CCPR/C/79/Add.86
CCPR/C.79/Add.87
CCPR/C/79/Add.88
CCPR/C/79/Add.100
CCPR/C/79/Add.109
CCPR/C/79/Add.111
CCPR/CO/69/KGZ
CCPR/CO/73/UKR
CCPR/CO/77
CCPR/CO/79/RUS
CCPR/CO/83/GRC
CCPR/CP/74/GEO
CCPR/C/88/D/1321
CCPR/C/88/D/1322/2004
CCPR/C/PRY/CO/2
CCPR/C/SR.1226
CCPR/C/SR.1237
CCPR/C/SR.1247
CCPR/C/SR.2299
CCPR/CO/69/KWT
CCPR/CO/71/DOM
CCPR/CO/71/VEN
CCPR/CO/73/AZE
CCPR/CO/75/VNM

CCPR/CO/78/ISR
CCPR/CO/79/LVA
CCPR/CO/80/COL
CCPR/CO/80/LTU
CCPR/CO/81/SEMO
CCPR/CO/82/FIN
CCPR/CO/82/MAR
CCPR/CO/83/GRC
CCPR/CO/84/SYR
CCPR/CO/84/TJK
E/447
E/800
E/1978/34
E/1980/13
E/1985/22
E/1995/23
E/1998/23
E/2002/23
E/2004/23
E/4949
E/5768
E/CN.4/149
E/CN.4/170/Add.3
E/CN.4/202
E/CN.4/353/Add.3
E/CN.4/365
E/CN.4/391
E/CN.4/1068
E/CN.4/1118
E/CN.4/1213
E/CN.4/1408
E/CN.4/1419
E/CN.4/1475
E/CN.4/1509
E/CN.4/1985/66
E/CN.4/1985/L.33
E/CN.4/1985/L.33/Rev.1
E/CN.4/1985/L.60
E/CN.4/1985/SR.27
E/CN.4/1985/SR.55
E/CN.4/1985/SR.57
E/CN.4/1987/SR.54/Add.1
E/CN.4/1988/37
E/CN.4/1989/71
E/CN.4/1989/L.19/Add.15
E/CN.4/1995/99
E/CN.4/1995/176
E/CN.4/1995/L.82/Rev.1
E/CN.4/1995/S.62
E/CN.4/1998/177
E/CN.4/1998/L.11/Add.6
E/CN.4/1998/SR.58
E/CN.4/2000/L/43
E/CN.4/2000/SR.60

E/CN.4/2002/200
E/CN.4/2002/L.62
E/CN.4/2002/WP.2
E/CN.4/2004/127
E/CN.4/2004/L.11/Add.4
E/CN.4/2004/L.54
E/CN.4/2004/SR.55
E/CN.4/2006/51
E/CN.4/L.158
E/CN.4/L.158/Rev.1
E/CN.4/L.171
E/CN.4/L.1542
E/CN.4/NGO/153
E/CN.4/RES/1998/77
E/CN.4/RES/2000/34
E/CN.4/RES/2002/45
E/CN.4/SR.94
E/CN.4/SR.104
E/CN.4/SR.119
E/CN.4/SR.142
E/CN.4/SR.154
E/CN.4/SR.308
E/CN.4/SR.313
E/CN/4/SR.1125
E/CN.4/SR.1129
E/CN.4/SR.1131
E/CN.4/SR.1132
E/CN.4/Sub.2/200/Rev.1
E/CN.4/Sub.2/1983/30
E/CN.4/Sub.2/1987/42
E/CN.4/Sub.2/1987/L.37
E/CN.4/Sub.2/1992/36
E/CN.4/Sub.2/2005/9
HCR/GIP/04/06
ICC/ASP/1/3
ICC-ASP/3/SWGCA/INF.1
ICC-ASP/4/32
PCNICC/2002/2/Add.2
PCNICC/2002/WGCA/DP.5
PCNICC/2002/WGCA/L.1
PCNICC/2002/WGCA/L.1/Add.1
S/1994/674
S/25704
S/4279
S/4279/Add.1
S/PV.3217
S/RES/134
S/RES/780
S/RES/827
S/RES/955
S/RES/1261
S/RES/1314
S/RES/1379
S/RES/1460

S/RES/1539
S/RES/1612
UNTAET/REG/2000/15

Universal Declaration of Human Rights, adopted on 10 December 1948, G.A. Res. 217A (III), UN Doc. A/810, at 71 (1948)

The United Nations War Crimes Commission, (1948) *History of the United Nations War Crimes Commission and the Developments of the Laws of War* (London: His Majesty's Stationery Office)

International Covenant on Economic, Social and Cultural Rights, G.A. res. 2200A (XXI), 21 U.N.GAOR Supp. (No. 16) at 49, U.N. Doc. A/6316 (1966), 993 U.N.T.S. 3

United Nations Yearbook (1958)

International Covenant on Civil and Political Rights, adopted 16 December 1966, entered into force 23 March 1976, G.A. Res. 2200A (XXI), UN Doc. A/6316 (1966), 999 UNTS 171, reprinted in 6 ILM 368 (1967)

Optional Protocol to the International Covenant on Civil and Political Rights, adopted 16 December 1966, entered into force 23 March 1976, 999 UNTS 171, reprinted in 6 ILM 383 (1967)

Convention Against Torture and Other Cruel, Inhuman or Degrading Treatment of Punishment, adopted on 10 December 1984, entered into force 26 June 1987, G.A. Res. 39/46, 39 UN GAOR, Supp. (No. 51), UN Doc. A/39/51 (1984) 197, reprinted in 23 ILM 1027 (1984)

Convention on the Rights of the Child (adopted 20 November 1989, entered into force 2 September 1990) UNGA Res 44/25, 44 UN GAOR, Supp. (No. 49), UN Doc A/44/49, at 166, reprinted in (1989) 28 ILM 1448

UNHCR, (1992), *Handbook on Procedures and Criteria for Determining Refugee Status* (United Nations)

The United Nations and Apartheid 1948–1994, (1994), The United Nations Blue Book Series, volume I, Department of Public Information, United Nations, New York, (United Nations)

UNHCR, (1995), *UNHCR Refugee Policy and Practice, Information Note on Article 1 of the 1951 Convention* (March 1995)

The Department of International Protection, Office of International Protection, Office of the United Nations High Commissioner for Refugees, *Refugee Status Determination: Identifying Who is a Refugee*, Self-study module 2 (1 September 2005)

United Nations Human Rights Committee

J.P. v Canada
Paavo Muhonen v Finland
Paul Westerman v The Netherlands
Yeo-Bum Yoon and Myung-Jin Choi v Republic of Korea

Organisation of African Unity Instrument

African Charter on Human and People's Rights, adopted 27 June 1981, OAU Doc CAB/LEG/67/3 rev.5, 21 I.L.M. 58 (1982) entered into force 21 October 1986

African Charter on the Rights and Welfare of the Child, adopted 11 July 1990, OAU Doc CAB/LEG/24.9/49 (1990), entered into force 29 November 1999

Organization of American States Instrument

American Convention on Human Rights, O.A.S. Treaty Series No. 36, 1144 U.N.T.S. 123, *entered into force* July 18, 1978, *reprinted in* Basic Documents Pertaining to Human Rights in the Inter-American System, OEA/Ser.L.V/II.82 doc.6 rev.1 at 25 (1992)

Inter-American Convention to Prevent and Punish Torture, signed 9 December 1985, entered into force 28 February 1987, OASTS 67, GA Doc. OEA/Ser.P, AG/doc.2023/85 rev.1 (1986) 46–54, reprinted in 25 ILM 519 (1986)

Report and Speech

Amnesty International Report, (1999), 'Federal Republic of Yugoslavia: the Forgotten Resisters: the Plight of Conscientious Objectors to Military Service after the Conflict in Kosovo'

Annual Report of the Inter-American Commission on Human Rights 1997 (1988), OEA/Ser.L/V/II.98, doc. 6 rev, original Spanish, 13 April

Annan, K.A. (2000), *Millennium Report: We the Peoples: The Role of the United Nations in the 21st Century*, United Nations, New York

Council of Europe, Director General of Human Rights, (2002) 'Conscientious objection to compulsory military service'

Eide, A. and C. Mubanga-Chipoya, (1985), *Conscientious Objection to Military Service, Report prepared in pursuance of resolutions 14 (XXXIV) and 1982/30 of the Sub-Commission on Prevention of Discrimination and Protection of Minorities*

Daes, E.A. (1983), *The Individual's Duties to the Community and the Limitations on Human Rights and Freedoms under Article 29 of the Universal Declaration of Human Rights: A Contribution to the Freedom of the Individual under Law* UN Doc E/CN.4/Sub.2/432/Rev.2

Gil-Robles, A. (2001), *Commissioner for Human Rights on his visit to Finland (4–7 June 2001) for the Committee of Ministers and the Parliamentary Assembly*, Strasbourg, CommDH (2001)7

Gil-Robles, A. (2002), *Commissioner for Human Rights, on his visit to the Hellenic Republic* (2–5 June 2002), for the attention of the Committee of Ministers and the Parliamentary Assembly, Strasbourg, CommDH (2002)5

Gil-Robles, A. (2006), *Follow-up report on the Hellenic Republic (2002–2005): Assessment of the progress made in implementing the recommendations of the Council of Europe Commissioner for Human Rights*, CommDH (2006)

Gil-Robles, A. (2006), *Assessment of the Progress in implementing the recommendations of the Council of Europe Commissioner for Human Rights, for the attention of the Committee of Ministers and the Parliamentary Assembly*, Strasbourg, CommDH (2006)

Gil-Robles, A. (2006), *Follow-up Report on Finland (2001–2005), Assessment of the Progress made in Implementing the Recommendations of the Council of Europe Commissioner for Human Rights*, Strasbourg, 29 March 2006, CommDH (2006)

Goldstone R. (2001), 'Crimes Against Humanity – Forgetting Victims' The 2001 Ernest Jones Lecture

Kirsch, P. (2006), 'Applying the Principles of Nuremberg in the ICC: Keynote Address at the Conference "Judgment at Nuremberg" held on the 60th Anniversary of the Nuremberg Judgment', Washington University, St Louis, Missouri

News

Barber, M. 2007, 'New Commander Takes Charge at Fort Lewis Jacoby Salutes Role in Iraq, Afghanistan' *The Seattle Post Intelligencer*, 12 June

Chung-a, P. 2007, 'Conscientious Military Objectors Surpass 12,000', *The Korea Times*, 21 March
Cock, A. 2004, 'Abuse Guard was "Just Having Fun" *The Daily Telegraph*, Sydney, 5 August
Heller, A. 2007, 'Israel Leaders Warn the Jewish State is Losing Touch With Its Most Admired Institution' *Associated Press*, 1 August
Joshi, J. 2007, 'Sole US Officer Charged Over Abu Ghraib to Face Trial' *Agence France Presse*, 15 May
Modesty, A. 2004, 'Britain Grants Russian Soldier Asylum', *Moscow Times*, 22 November
Rising, D. 2007, 'Army Medic Serves Sentence for Desertion' *Associated Press Online* 19 April
Peterson, T. 2007, 'US Medic in Germany guilty of desertion' *The Independent*, 7 March
Quindlen, A. 2007, 'Dissenters in Uniform' *News Week US Edition*, 25 June
Tran, M. 2007, 'The Iraq War on Trial' *Guardian Unlimited*, 4 January
2005, *Asahi Shinbun*, 28 December
2005, 'Debate Rekindled over Military Objectors', *Hankook Iibo Korea Times*, 28 December
2006, 'Defense Chief to Review Conscientious Objector Issue', *Hankook Iibo Korea Times*, 7 January
2006, 'Mehmet Ali Birand New Regulations Needed for Conscientious Objection', *Turkish Daily News*, 28 January
2007, 'US Army Medic Given Eight-Months Sentence for Refusing Iraq Duty' *Agence France Presse*, 6 March

World War I Cases

Judgment in the Case of Robert Neumann: June 2, 1921, (1922) 16 AJIL 696–704
Judgment in the Case of Command Karl Neumann: Hospital Ship 'Dover Castle', June 4, 1921, (1922) 16 AJIL 704–708
Judgment in the Case of Lieutenants Dithmar and Boldt: Hospital Ship 'Llandovery Castle': Rendered July 16, 1921, (1922) 16 AJIL 708–724

Nuremberg Case

Trial of the Major War Criminals before the International Military Tribunal, Nürnberg, 14 November 1945–1 October 1946, published at Nürnberg, Germany (1947)

CCL 10 Decisions related to crimes committed during World War II

Einsatzgruppen Case
United States v Otto Ohlendorf et al., U.S. Military Tribunal, Judgement, 8 and 9 April
1948 ("*Einsatzgruppen* Case"), in *Trials of War Criminals before the Nuernberg Military Tribunals under Control Council Law No. 10*, (1950) vol. IV
High Command Case
United States v Wilhelm von Leeb, et al., (*High Command Case*), Trials of War Criminals
before the Nuremberg Military Tribunals under Control Council Law No. 10,
Case No. 12, vol. XI (USA, Government Printing Office, Washington D. C.,
1951) 1–698; UNWCC Law Reports of Trials of War Criminals, vol. XII,
(London: His Majesty's Stationary Office, 1949) 1–127

Hostage Case
United States v Wilhelm List et al., & Others (The Hostage case), Trials of War Criminals before the Nuremberg Military Tribunals under Control Council Law No. 10, case 7, XI (USA, Government Printing Office, Washington D. C., 1951) 759–1322
Justice Case (Altstoetter et al.)
United States v Altstoetter et al., U.S. Military Tribunal, Judgement, 3–4 December 1947 ("*Justice* Case"), in *Trials of War Criminals before the Nuernberg Military Tribunals under Control Council Law No. 10* (1951), vol. III, 1–110
Ministries Trial
United States of America v. von Weizsaecker et al. (Ministries trial) 14 Trials of War Criminals Before the Nürnberg Military Tribunals Under Control Council Law No. 10, at 308 (1952)
Sawada
Trial of Lieutenant-General Shigeru Sawada and Three Others, United States Military Commission, Shanghai, 27th February–15th April, 1946, UNWCC Law Reports of Trials of War Criminals, vol. V, (London: His Majesty's Stationary Office, 1948) 1–24

National Cases

Canada

Zolfagharkhani v Canada (Minister of Employment & Immigration) [1993] 3 FC 540 (Fed CA)
R. v Finta, [1994] 1 SCR 701, Supreme Court of Canada, March 24, 1994
Diab v Canada (Minister of Employment & Immigration) [1994] FCJ No. 1277 (Fed CA)
Randosevic v Canada (Minister of Citizenship & Immigration) [1995] FCJ No. 74 (Fed TD)
Jeremy Hinzman and Liam Lime Nguyen Hinzman, Immigration and Refugee Board Decision (16 March 2005)
Hinzman v Canada (Minister of Citizenship & Immigration) 31 March 2006

Israel

Chief Military Prosecutor v Malinki, Israel Court of Appeal 279–283/58, (1958), English translated in (1985) 2 Palestine Yearbook of International Law 69–119
Attorney General of the Government of Israel v Adolf Eichmann, 36 I.L.R. 228 (D. C. Jm. 1961)
Attorney General of the Government of Israel v A. Eichmann (1968) 36 ILR 18 (29 May 1962)
Zonshein v Judge Advocate General (2002) reprinted in 'The Supreme Court Sitting as the High Court of Justice (23 November 2002)' 36 *Isr L Rev* 1

South Africa

R v Smith (1900) 17 SC 561

United Kingdom

Doonetas v. Secretary of State for the Home Department, as quoted, approved, and applied to Atibo v. Immigration Officer, London (Heathrow) Airport, (1978) Imm. AR 93
Atibo v Immigration Officer, London (Heathrow) Airport [1978] ImmAR 93
Basin Sepet, Redeem Bulbul v Secretary of State for the Home Department, in the Supreme Court of Judicature Court of Appeal (Civil Division) on Appeal from the Immigration Appeal Tribunal, [2001] EWCA Civ. 681, Case No: C/2777 & C/2000/2794 (11 May 2001)
Krotov v. Secretary of State for the Home Department, Decision on AK (Article 3 – Military Service – Chechen War) Russia CG, [2002] UKIAT 01325, Appeal no. HX 42619–01 (2 May 2002)
Campaign for Nuclear Disarmament v The Prime Minister of the United Kingdom and Others [2002] EWHC 2759 (17 December 2002)
Sepet v Secretary of the State for the Home Department [2003] HL 15, [2003] 1 WLR 856 (20 March 2003)
Krotov v. Secretary of State for the Home Department, The Supreme Court of Judicature Court of Appeal (Civil Division) on Appeal from the Immigration Appeal Tribunal, [2004] EWCA Civ 69, Case No. C1/2002/1537/IATRF (11 February 2004)
AK (Russia-Chechnya Deserter) Russia [2004] UKIAT 00294, 29 October 2004

United States

United States v Kinder (1968) 14 CMR 133
United States v Calley (1973) 22 USCMA 534
Supreme Court of the United States *Cassius Marsellus Clay, Jr. also known as Muhammad Ali v. United States*, No. 783 (28 June 1971). 403 U.S. 698, 91 S. Ct. 2068, 29 L. Ed. 2d 810
M.A. A26851062 v INS, 858 F.2d 210, 215 (4th Cir. 1988)
Alonzo v INS, 915 F.2d 546, 548 (9th Cir. 1990)
Barraza Rivera v INS, 913 F2d 1443, 1450 (9th Cir. 1990)
Canas-Segovia v INS, 902 F.2d 717 (9th Cir. 1990)
Castillo v INS, 951 F.2d 1117, 1122 (9th Cir. 1991)
Abedni v INS, 971 F.2d 188, 191 (9th Cir. 1992)
U.S. v Huet-Vaughn, 43 M.J. 105, 107 (1995)
Vujisic v INS. 224 F. 3d 578 (7th Cir. 2000)
Ilchuk v Attorney General, 434 F.3d 618, 626 (3d Cir. 2006)

The Permanent Court of International Justice Case

Advisory Opinion No. 15, Jurisdiction of the Courts of Danzig, PCIJ Rep., Ser. B. No. 15 (Advisory Opinion of March 3, 1928)

The International Court of Justice Cases

Reparation for Injuries Suffered in the Service of the United Nations [1949] ICJ 174 (Apr. 11) (Advisory Opinion)

Reservations to the Convention on the Prevention and Punishment of the Crime of Genocide Case (1951) ICJR

North Sea Continental Shelf Case, (Federal Republic of Germany v Denmark; Federal Republic of Germany v Netherlands) [1969] ICJ Rep 3

Legal Consequence for States of the Continued Presence of South Africa in Namibia (South West Africa) notwithstanding Security Council 276 (1970) Advisory Opinion [1971] ICJR 57

Legality of the Threat or Use of Nuclear Weapons (Advisory Opinion) [1996] ICJ Rep 226 (8 July 1996)

Case Concerning Application of the Convention on the Prevention and Punishment of the Crime of Genocide (Bosnia and Herzegovina v Yugoslavia) (Preliminary Objections) [1996] ICJ Rep. 595

Armed Activities on the Territory of the Congo (New Application 2002) (Democratic Republic of the Congo v Rwanda), Jurisdiction of the Court and Admissibility of the Application Judgment of 3 February 2006

Legal Consequences of the Construction of a Wall in the Occupied Palestinian Territory (Advisory Opinion) [2004] ICJ Rep, 136 (9 July 2004)

Arrest Warrant of 11 April 2000 (Democratic Republic of the Congo v. Belgium) (Merits) Judgment of 14 February 2002, General List No. 121

Application of the Convention on the Prevention and Punishment of the Crime of Genocide (Bosnia-Herzegovina v Serbia and Montenegro) (Merits) 26 February 2007

The European Court/Commission of Human Rights Cases

Grandrath v FRG (App 2294/64) (1966)

X. v Austria (App 5591/72) (1973)

X v FRG (App 7705/76) (1977)

Arrowsmith v UK (App 7050/75) (1978)

N v Sweden, (App 10410/83) (1984)

A v Switzerland (App 10640/83) (1984)

Johansen v Norway (10600/83) (1985)

Autio v Finland (App 17086/90) (1991)

X v Belgium (App 24631/94) (1995)

Raninen v Finland (App 20972/92) (1996)

Thlimmenos v Greece (App 34369/97) (1998)

Priebke v Italy (App 48799/99) (5 April 2001)

Ülke v Turkey (App 39437/98) (24 January 2006)

Parliament v Council, Case No. C-540/03, Judgment (27 June 2006)

The European Committee of Social Rights

Quaker Council for European Affairs v Greece, Complaint No. 8/2000 (2000)

The Inter-American Commission on Human Rights Cases

Alfredo Bustos v Bolivia, Case 14/04, Report No. 52/04, Inter-Am. C.H.R., OEA/Ser.L/V/II.122 Doc. 5 rev. 1, 13 October 2004

Alfredo Bustos v Bolivia, Case 14/04, Report No. 97/05, Petition 14/04, Friendly Settlement, 27 October 2005
Christián Daniel Sahli Vera et al. v Chile, March 10, 2005
Alejandro León Vega v Ecuador Report No. 22/06, Petition 278–02, Admissibility, 2 March 2006

The International Criminal Court

Le Procureur v Thomas Lubanga Dyilo, Case No. ICC-01/04–01–06, 29 janvier 2007, la Chambre Préliminaire I, Décision sur la Confirmation des Charges: Version Publique avec Annex I
The Prosecutor v Thomas Lubanga Dyilo 'Decision on the Prosecutor's Application for a Warrant of Arrest, Article 58' Pre-Trial Chamber I, Case No. ICC-01/04–01/06 (10 February 2006)

The International Criminal Tribunal for the Former Yugoslavia

Prosecutor v Erdemović (Sentencing Judgment) IT-96–22T, T.Ch.I (29 November 1996)
Prosecutor v Dražen Erdemović, Sentencing Judgment, Case No. IT-96–22-T, Ap. Ch., (7 October 1997)
Prosecutor v Mrda (Sentencing Judgment) IT-02–59-S, T. Ch. I, 31 (March 2004)

The International Criminal Tribunal for Rwanda

Jean Paul Akayesu – Prosecution Closing Arguments, ICTR/UPD/008 (Arusha, 19 March 1998)
Prosecutor v Jean Kamhanda, Judgment and Sentence (Trial Chamber I, 4 September 1998)

The Special Court for Sierra Leone

Prosecutor v Sam Hinga Norman, Decision on preliminary motion based on lack of jurisdiction (child recruitment) The Appeals Chamber, Case No. SCSL-2004–14-AR72(E) (31 May 2004)
Prosecutor v Alex Tamba Brima, Brima Bazzy Kamara, Santigie Borbor Kanu, Case No. SCSL-2004–16-T, Trial Chamber II, Sentencing (19 July 2007)
Prosecutor v Moinina Fofana, Allieu Kondewa, Case No. SCSL-2004–14-T, Trial Chamber I, Judgment (2 August 2007)

Web Resources

http://www.bundestag.de/htdocs_e/parliament/function/legal/germanbasiclaw.pdf
http://www.cisr-irb.gc.ca/en/decisions/public/hinzman/hinzman_e.pdf
http://www.coe.int/t/commissioner/Activities/mandate_en.asp
http://www.coe.int/T/E/Human_rights/objcone.pdf

http://www.consilium.europa.eu/ueDocs/cms_Data/docs/pressData/en/ec/94932.pdf
http://www.guardian.co.uk/Iraq/Story/0,1982934,00.html
http://www.humanrights.go.kr/eng/index.jsp
http://www.icj-cij.org/icjwww/jdocket/imwp/imwpframe.htm
http://www.paxchristi.org.uk/index.html
http://www.psychoanalysis.org.uk/goldstone.htm
http://www.state.gov/g/drl/rls/irf/2006/index.htm
http://www.usccb.org/sdwp/peace/military2.htm

Index

FSC
www.fsc.org
MIX
Papier | Fördert gute Waldnutzung
FSC® C083411

Kolibri 360 GmbH
Ferdinand-Jühlke-Straße 7
99095 Erfurt, Deutschland
produktsicherheit@kolibri360.de